Networks, Labour and
among Indian Muslim

C000227170

ECONOMIC EXPOSURES IN ASIA

Series Editor:
Rebecca M. Empson, Department of Anthropology, UCL

Economic change in Asia often exceeds received models and expectations, leading to unexpected outcomes and experiences of rapid growth and sudden decline. This series seeks to capture this diversity. It places an emphasis on how people engage with volatility and flux as an omnipresent characteristic of life, and not necessarily as a passing phase. Shedding light on economic and political futures in the making, it also draws attention to the diverse ethical projects and strategies that flourish in such spaces of change.

The series publishes monographs and edited volumes that engage from a theoretical perspective with this new era of economic flux, exploring how current transformations come to shape and are being shaped by people in particular ways.

Networks, Labour and Migration among Indian Muslim Artisans

Thomas Chambers

First published in 2020 by
UCL Press
University College London
Gower Street
London WC1E 6BT

Available to download free: www.uclpress.co.uk

Text © Thomas Chambers, 2020
Images © Thomas Chambers, 2020

Thomas Chambers has asserted his right under the Copyright, Designs and Patents Act 1988 to be identified as author of this work.

A CIP catalogue record for this book is available from The British Library.

This book is published under a Creative Commons 4.0 International licence (CC BY 4.0). This licence allows you to share, copy, distribute and transmit the work, to adapt the work, and to make commercial use of the work, provided attribution is made to the authors (but not in any way that suggests that they endorse you or your use of the work). Attribution should include the following information:

Chambers, T. 2020. *Networks, Labour and Migration among Indian Muslim Artisans*. London, UCL Press. https://doi.org/10.14324/111.9781787354531

Further details about Creative Commons licences are available at http://creativecommons.org/licenses/

Any third-party material in this book is published under the book's Creative Commons licence unless indicated otherwise in the credit line to the material. If you would like to re-use any third-party material not covered by the book's Creative Commons licence, you will need to obtain permission directly from the copyright holder.

ISBN: 978-1-78735-455-5 (Hbk)
ISBN: 978-1-78735-454-8 (Pbk)
ISBN: 978-1-78735-453-1 (PDF)
ISBN: 978-1-78735-456-2 (epub)
ISBN: 978-1-78735-457-9 (mobi)
DOI: https://doi.org/10.14324/111.9781787354531

Contents

List of figures   vii

List of tables   ix

Acknowledgements   x

1. Marginalisation, connectedness and Indian Muslim
   artisans: an introduction   1

2. A brief history of Indian Muslim artisans   22

3. The Indian craft supply chain: money, commodities
   and intimacy   49

4. Muslim women and craft production in India: gender,
   labour and space   78

5. Apprenticeship and labour amongst Indian Muslim artisans   107

6. Neoliberalism and Islamic reform among Indian Muslim
   artisans: affect and self-making   135

7. Friendship, urban space, labour and craftwork
   in India   160

8. Internal migration in India: imaginaries, subjectivities and
   precarity   186

9. Labour migration between India and the Gulf: regimes,
   imaginaries and continuities   215

10. Marginalisation and connectedness: a conclusion   245

Glossary of Hindi, Urdu and Arabic terms   249

References   254

Index   275

List of figures

All figures are owned and provided by the author.

Figure 1.1	An ox-cart loaded with wood enters Kamil Wali Gully	1
Figure 1.2	An example of carving	4
Figure 1.3	A carver at work	4
Figure 2.1	A woodworker demonstrating a powered *ārī* (fret)saw	22
Figure 2.2	A residential gully in the wood *mohallas*	46
Figure 2.3	A young woodcarver at work	47
Figure 3.1	The Craft Fair at Noida's Expo Mart Centre	49
Figure 3.2	Brass overlay work before buffing	76
Figure 3.3	Working in a large factory	76
Figure 4.1	Women undertaking finishing work under the supervision of a male *thēkēdār*	78
Figure 4.2	A *thēkēdār* delivering items to be finished by homeworking women	105
Figure 4.3	A gully near Ali ki Chungi	106
Figure 5.1	A young apprentice at work	107
Figure 5.2	Apprentices working on a bedhead	133
Figure 5.3	The author during apprenticeship	134
Figure 6.1	Posing with a high-end motorbike at Saharanpur's annual Gul Fair	135
Figure 6.2	Men dressed in 'Saudi style' during Eid	158
Figure 6.3	Sweets being sold during Eid	158
Figure 7.1	Young men hanging out while working	160
Figure 7.2	A craftworker displays his cards and documents issued by the state	161
Figure 7.3	'Sandeep', a Hindu resident of a village in the Garhwal Himalaya region displays his cards and documents issued by the state.	162
Figure 7.4	A carver working on a sofa back	185

Figure 8.1   Migrant workers sleeping in Hyderabad   186
Figure 8.2   Workers in Kamareddy   213
Figure 8.3   Employers socialising with their migrant labour 213
Figure 9.1   Migrant workers in Dubai   215
Figure 9.2   A dormitory in Abu Dhabi   243
Figure 9.3   Naseer looking on over a shopping mall
               in Hyderabad   243
Figure 10.1   Children peer through a rooftop rail onto the
               gully below   245
Figure 10.2   Kites flying in the evening sky over the *mohallas*   248

List of tables

Table 8.1   Length of time spent away during the most
              recent migration   198
Table 8.2   Person who had recruited the respondent to
              a factory or workshop for migrant work on
              their most recent trip   198
Table 8.3   Religion of those employing workers who
              had migrated from Saharanpur, as stated by
              respondents regarding their most recent migration   199
Table 8.4   Origin of those employing workers who had
              migrated from Saharanpur, as stated by
              respondents regarding their most recent migration   199

Acknowledgements

There are so many individuals who have contributed to this book in various ways over the years, too many to list everyone. First and foremost, however, I would like to make a heartfelt acknowledgement to my PhD supervisors, Geert De Neve and Filippo Osella, who shepherded me through the thesis which forms the underlying skeleton of much of this book. Both their voices are present in these pages at various moments and they have continued to offer me advice and mentoring since. Magnus Marsden has also provided a great deal of advice and support over the years for which I am extremely grateful. Many other colleagues at the University of Sussex have offered comments, input and broader support including Suhas Basme, Grace Carswell, Erica Consterdine, Syed Mohammed Faisal, Adam Fishwick, Diana Ibanez-Tirado, Ole Kaland, Katie McQuaid, Rebecca Prentice and Ross Wignall. My current employer, Oxford Brookes University, provided time and space for the completion of the book, Louella Matsunaga being particularly deft in helping me to balance writing time with other duties.

Beyond direct colleagues, there are many other scholars who have offered comments and support with the book, or with other publications and material, some of which is included in these chapters. Patricia Jeffery has been a wonderful guide and mentor at various stages and Shalini Grover has been an ever-present supporter of this and other projects. Alessandra Mezzadri, Madeline Reeves, Nandini Gooptu, Anita Hammer, Vegard Iversen, Nayanika Mathur and Ursula Rao have all offered support and encouragement. At UCL Press, Chris Penfold and Rebecca Empson have been patient and encouraging throughout the journey to publication, and Glynis Baguley has provided meticulous copyediting. There are, inevitably, many others but I hope I may be forgiven for not including everyone here. Critical among broader contributions has been the wonderful work of my research assistant Ayesha Ansari, who opened doors to spaces within Saharanpur where my male gender identity made access difficult. There are substantial sections of this book – chapters 3 and 4 in particular – that would have been impossible to produce without her help.

A project of this scale takes an emotional and psychological toll, one that I would not have been able to bear had it not been for various forms of personal support from friends and relatives. My mother has been relentlessly caring and, as a sociologist, has offered comments, encouragement and critical help with proofreading. My father has always been willing to listen when called upon and his encouragement to persevere through more difficult periods of the writing process has been essential. I have been very fortunate to have the love and care of my wonderful wife, Joanna Patterson, throughout, as well as gentle encouragement from the impending birth of our future son, whose nearing presence has pushed me to reach completion. Many friends from home have kept me going including Michel Dennington, Sarah Robinson, Nicholas Wride and Kate Staniforth. In India, my old and very dear friend Sandeep Arya was always on hand throughout fieldwork to offer respite and a stiff drink. Critical here were my dear friends and language teachers Mohammad Yusef and Abdul Nasir, who were central in helping me understand the context in which I would eventually work.

Finally, the deepest of all thanks must go to my many friends in Saharanpur who opened their lives, hearts and homes to me. In the interests of anonymity, I do not name them here, but they all feature in this book at various moments under pseudonyms. Many are friends for life and our ongoing relationships, both when I return to the city and via various communications media from the UK, are an endless source of warmth, pleasure and companionship.

A portion of the material presented in this book formed part of doctoral research undertaken thanks to an ESRC Studentship Grant (ES/I900934/1), held at the University of Sussex. Some additional material results from research funded by a British Academy and Leverhulme Grant (SG151257) (held by Geert De Neve and Grace Carswell at Sussex) and from the support of Early Career Funding allocated to me by Oxford Brookes University.

Map locating Saharanpur, Uttar Pradesh and neighbouring states.
Source: Martin Brown.

1
Marginalisation, connectedness and Indian Muslim artisans: an introduction

Figure 1.1   An ox-cart loaded with wood enters Kamil Wali Gully.
Source: author.

It was a late afternoon in November 2010 when I first visited Kamil Wali Gully (lane), in the small provincial city of Saharanpur, located in north-western Uttar Pradesh (India). Following one of the heavily laden buffalo carts that had started out from the wood wholesale markets on the outskirts of the city, I turned into the entrance of a narrow, roughly metalled lane. Hitting a pothole, the cart lurched heavily, its precarious load looking briefly as if it might spill, but then recovered its centre and continued on. The gully was, like so many in the city, filled with the sound of constant tapping from the chisels and hammers of carvers and carpenters. This was layered against the drone of cutting and buffing machines that threw up noise and sawdust. The woodworking mohallas (neighbourhoods) were in the Muslim areas of the city and most of the labour force was drawn from this community. Thus, the gullies were occasionally interspersed with masjids (mosques) from which the call to prayer provided the only cessation to the otherwise continuous soundscape of production.

The shop fronts of workplaces opened onto the street and a glance inside revealed the stage of woodwork in which each specialised. Movement between the shops was constant as workers, mistrīs (tradespeople) and kārīgars (artisans) joined others to socialise or grease the wheels of business. Chai (tea) boys ran up and down the gullies taking orders from craftsmen back to their employers' stalls, before returning with the sweet milky fuel that kept production ticking over. Amongst the workshops, rickshaw wallahs (drivers)[1] hauled products at various stages of manufacture as each item made its journey to completion through numerous hands. These spaces were highly public but the rickshaw wallahs also knocked on the entrances to more concealed realms, the large steel gates of mass-producing factories and the small wooden doors or curtained entrances of homes. Homeworkers were often women who, albeit in a less visible manner, provided a significant portion of the labour, passing work and arranging the means of completing orders via gendered informal networks.

Much more visible outward connections also interspersed the scene: lorries of various sizes squeezed their way through the narrow lanes, stirring up clouds of dust as they trundled towards markets near and far, carrying goods on the first leg of a journey that might finish in Mumbai or Delhi, Europe or the Gulf, America or Japan. Workers, too, were on the move as they frequently changed their work locations, utilising networks of friends, neighbours, relatives and others to negotiate their conditions of employment. Likewise, these connections fed into outward migrations. Craftworkers came and went, heading to every corner of the country, from Kashmir to Kerala and from Nagaland to Mumbai. Others travelled further afield, to the labour camps of the Arabian Gulf, bringing back stories of success and new-found wealth or failure and great loss. The largely informal arrangements of this old craft industry did not, then, project an image of peripheral decline, of slowly being usurped by globalisation and contemporary forms of capitalism. Instead, the gullies sat at the centre of a variety of complex connections and surged with manufacture enabled through variegated and interlocking modes of production.

Within this highly connected space, many individuals plied their trade in a variety of arrangements. As it cleared the entrance of the gully, the teetering buffalo cart revealed a small workshop with the proprietor's name and phone number roughly painted on an exterior wall. Mohammad Islam, a ruddy-cheeked and slightly portly man of around 30 years of age, cheerily beckoned me to approach. Married with three young children, Islam lived in a house situated in a narrow gully some ten minutes' cycle from his workshop. The house was shared with his parents and with his two brothers and their wives and children. It was his small workshop that would eventually provide a base for the majority of my fieldwork. Islam, although I did not know this at the time, would soon become a friend, confidant and ustād (teacher, master).

A few doors down, a larger cutting shop was about to receive its delivery of raw wood. Once fashioned, these slices of timber would be passed to carving shops to be transformed into bedheads and sofa backs. One such shop belonged to Rizwan Ansari, who flashed me a white-toothed smile whenever I caught his eye. Alongside Rizwan sat four of his sons: the eldest, Yousef, was seventeen and the other boys ranged from thirteen to seven. Occasionally they were joined by the youngest, four-year-old Ismail, who mimicked his siblings by tapping on spare pieces of wood. Rizwan and the boys, along with his wife Bano, one teenaged and one younger daughter, lived in two small rooms that they rented in a gully around the corner from their workshop. Immediately to the left of Rizwan's shop was a petty manufactory owned by Shahnawaz, who employed a few staff on a piece-rate basis. His most experienced woodcarver, Mohammad Naseer, had married two years previously – although he did not have children – and lived with his extended family in a nearby village. Later he would become my guide through networks of migration across the country.

As I watched the carvers work, day after day, I was struck by the ways in which the connections and niches that constituted economic life in the city echoed the relationship between carver, tools and material. Woodcarving is a tricky skill. To acquire it you must start at a young age. First, you must learn to sit, to connect to the material. Hands use the tools, but feet are also deployed to brace and steady the wood. The feet are bare, out of respect for the art that is being created, and, as a result, greater dexterity in gripping and shifting the work is achieved. Slowly, through these connections, the apprentice starts to understand the nature of the material: its feel, its texture, its problems and its constraints. As the chisel moves along the line of the grain, the wood gives easily, yielding to each impact brought upon it, allowing itself to be shaped according to the desire of the mind which guides the hand. The designs are abstract, following Islamic practice. The shapes required, however, do not always move with the grain of the wood. As a floral outline or pattern turns to take its curves across the grain, the wood begins to resist. It no longer easily gives way into smooth, satisfying surfaces. Instead, it becomes a constraint, guiding the chisel as it moves. These ingrained boundaries can be crossed with dexterity and a well-sharpened chisel point, but the design can never work beyond the limitations of the material and must eventually acquiesce to its properties. The artisan, through training and experience, knows this and does not aspire to go further than the margins that have been set.

 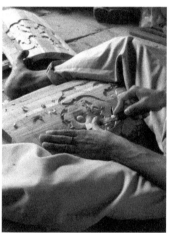

Figure 1.2 An example of carving. Source: author.

Figure 1.3 A carver at work. Source: author.

Saharanpur is a peripheral city of around 700,000 souls (Census 2011),[2] located in the north-west of Uttar Pradesh. It is a city of two halves, split by the main railway track and along communal lines. While the central area, immediately around the railway station and the city's landmark *Ganta Ghar* (clock tower), is mixed, once the tracks are crossed to the south, few markers of a Muslim presence can be found. These more affluent neighbourhoods are situated around the old colonial-era Mission Colony and the city's middle-class shopping area of Court Road. The south of the city is also the location for the symbols and offices of the state: law courts, the main government headquarters, the central police station and other sites of state bureaucracy. As one heads north across the tracks and through the city centre, the markers of an urban core and its associated infrastructure give way to more marginal spaces of small gullies, densely packed informal housing and petty commodity production.

It is in the north of the city, amongst minarets, narrow lanes and occasional hints of a lost pre-colonial splendour, that Saharanpur's sprawling woodworking *mohallas* lie. These are spaces at the margin: at the margin of the city, at the margins of the state and at the margin of circulations of capital and production in a globalising economy. The Muslim craftworkers who live and labour in the *mohallas* experience further trajectories of marginalisation that result from their minority status and from the ongoing socio-economic sidelining of India's Muslim communities (processes that have intensified extensively as this book has been going to press[3]) (Sachar 2006; Gayer & Jaffrelot 2012; A. Chatterjee 2017; Bhattacharyya & Basu 2018). These patterns of marginalisation are empirically prominent but also variegated, non-homogeneous and crosscut by intersections of class, gender, affluence and lineage (cf. Imtiaz Ahmad 1978; Irfan Ahmad 2003; Z. Hasan & Menon 2005; Punathil 2013; Susewind 2017; Williams et al. 2017; McLaughlin 2017).

Muslims comprise around 45 per cent of Saharanpur's total population (Office of the Registrar General & Census Commissioner, India 2011), a large number compared with many north Indian cities, and one that has led to Saharanpur often being called *Chota Pakistan* ('little Pakistan') by Hindus and others from neighbouring regions. This characterisation, in Hindu nationalist discourses, situates Muslim neighbourhoods in Saharanpur and similar cities as dangerous, dirty, ungoverned and uneducated – the 'danger and demonic character of the Muslim other' (Hansen 1996: 153). The marginalisation of the *mohallas* within the urban spatial setting was further constituted through Saharanpur's status as a peripheral city, one located in a tucked-away corner of the sprawling state of Uttar Pradesh, a state that – while constituting a heartland of India's body politic (Kudaisya 2006) – is often represented as backward, uneducated and riddled with criminality. Yet to reduce Saharanpur's urban Muslim *mohallas* to such a crude representation offers little in the way of potential for countering communalising forces in India and misrepresents the diversities and connections present in the lives of residents.

What, then, is this book about? Well, first and foremost it is an ethnographic account that follows the everyday lives of woodworkers, and others from Saharanpur's craft cluster, in the city, during migration to other areas of India, and when working in the Gulf. While focused on the narratives and life stories of workers, *mistrīs* (tradespeople), *kārīgars* (artisans) and others who comprise the wood craftworkers of the city,[4] the book also traces things, objects, ideas and affects. The narrative emphasises the intersection – through an anthropological lens – between space, political economy and subjectivity. To achieve this, I deploy a dialectical argument, with processes of marginalisation set against explorations of connectedness constituted within local and global contexts. This produces an analysis that aims not only to connect the local to the global but to posit the local and the global within everyday intimacies, intimacies which, I argue, are critical to understanding the woodworking *mohallas* and their connections.

The focus on connections challenges many representations of north Indian Muslims that have primarily centred on marginalisation, ghettoisation and segregation (e.g. Harman 1977; S. Khan 2007; R. Robinson 2007; Gayer & Jaffrelot 2012; Shaban 2018). Accounts of Indian Muslim artisans are likewise dominated either by romanticised images of craftwork and a lost past of Mughal rule and patronage (Waheed 2006) or by notions of marginality, marginalisation, immobility and decline (Kumar 2017; Wilkinson-Weber 1999; Mohsini 2010; Nasir 2011). While scholarly and ethnographic research has offered highly nuanced accounts (e.g. Jeffery 1979; Mehta 1997; Kumar 2017; Wilkinson-Weber 1999; Jasani 2008; Heitmeyer 2009a; Jeffrey 2010; Mohsini 2010; Williams 2012) and much has been done to de-homogenise images of Indian Muslims (e.g. M. Hasan 2008, 2018; Gottschalk 2005; Z. Hasan & Menon 2005; Gayer & Jaffrelot 2012; Susewind 2017; Williams et al. 2017; Shaban 2018), it is the narrative of marginalisation that remains prominent in both academic and public discourse.

Saharanpur's Muslim *mohallas* – like similar spaces in other Indian cities – are, however, not forged only through spatial segregation and marginalisation. Labour regimes, migration regimes, capitalist development, neoliberal reforms, state interventions and movements of corporate capital have all interplayed in shaping the *mohallas*. Saharanpur's craftworkers were highly mobile (albeit in a gendered setting), and had forged (albeit within interlocking migration regimes) complex networks of migration that stretched to every corner of India and, increasingly, to the Middle East. The movement, mobility and social or personal transformation wrapped up in travel and migration produced geographical and social imaginaries (cf. Halfacree 2004; Smith 2006; G. E. Marcus 2009; Radhakrishnan 2009; Coles & Walsh 2010; Gallo 2016; Chambers 2018) which transcended feelings of decline and nostalgia but also created new forms of flux and fluidity.

Additionally, long-duration networks of Islamic scholarship and reformist activity were a prominent part of the connections through which the *mohallas* were constituted. The nearby Darul Uloom Deoband madrassa[5] and the closely linked Jamia Mazahir Uloom, in Saharanpur itself, have long been sites of global religious exchange and discourse. The presence of various Islamic networks in Saharanpur's *mohallas* draws this book into dialogue with a wider rubric of research attending to Muslim cosmopolitanisms. Here, critical contributions have been made to challenging social evolutionary and dissemination-based conceptions of the 'west leading the rest' into an age of global connectedness (e.g. Eickelman & Piscatori 1990; Zubaida 2002; F. Osella & C. Osella 2007; Marsden 2008; Alavi 2015; Aljunied 2016). In the context of Islamic circulations, Saharanpur is not a marginal site. The two seminaries, particularly that at Deoband, have been central to Islamic thought and scholarship, the madrassa being seen as a major influence by those who subscribe to a 'Deobandi Muslim' identity, an identity that incorporates various nations, from India to the USA and Afghanistan to the UK (Metcalf 2014; Kabir 2010).

While Islamic networks and forms of cosmopolitanism interplay across this book, my primary focus is on connections forged along affective and informal lines, those constructed around conceptions of sociality, intimacy, friendship and family. The *mohallas*, I argue, are not only constituted through communalism and marginalisation but are also a realm of connection and community building, a duality Rajnarayan Chandavarkar (2003) has similarly illuminated in work on urban neighbourhoods of Mumbai. Here, I explore the role of affective and informal networks – as well as forms of urban informality – that on the one hand provide support, comfort and care and on the other act as key mediating factors in circuits of capital, labour and production (cf. Breman 2004; De Neve 2008; Elyachar 2010; Ananya Roy 2011; Lindquist 2017; Cant 2018). Increasingly emergent, across the material presented in this book, are the dualities in forms of care, affection and intimacy which intermingle with supply chains and production networks as well as labour and migration regimes. In mapping these connections the book builds on a genealogy of research (e.g. Lindell 2010; Ananya Roy 2011; Parnell & Pieterse 2014; Rizzo 2017) that has nuanced earlier literature on urban slums and informal city spaces (e.g. Davis 2006) in order to create more agentive accounts of life at the urban margin.

With much work on colonial and post-colonial spaces focusing on nodal metropolises, such as Mumbai and Kolkata, or new metro centres, such as Bangalore and Gurgaon, provincial cities and towns, such as Saharanpur, have remained peripheral in discussions of urban space in South Asia (De Neve & Donner 2007). Thus, smaller urban contexts have often been 'bypassed by the official fixation on new modernist cities, and the anthropological predisposition toward the village'. This absence of attention leads Ajay Gandhi (2011: 207) to refer to India's provincial urban centres as 'black towns'. However, growing populations and increasing, if highly unequal, affluence place peripheral urban centres at the heart of contemporary Indian development and thus they reflect not only local but also national aspirations, insecurities, patterns of consumption, style and religiosity (Gandhi 2011). Saharanpur's *mohallas* are a highly connected spatial configuration intersected not only by production networks but by circulations bound up in religiosity, affective conceptions of self-making, shifting consumption practices and large-scale migratory networks. They are characterised by gendered forms of *mohalla* sociality where the tightly packed gullies combine with degrees of urban enclosure to produce what Doreen Massey (2005) has called 'throwntogetherness'. The woodworking *mohallas*, and those who reside therein, are marginalised along a variety of trajectories, but lives, livelihoods and subjectivities are also crafted through local, national and global connections.

This is not to dismiss marginalisation; the systematic 'othering' of India's Muslims has been well documented (e.g. R. Das 2006; A. Alam 2008; I. Chatterjee 2012; Naqvi 2016), and many Muslim craft clusters have seen substantial decline in status and socio-economic position (Kumar 2017; Wilkinson-Weber 1999; Mohsini 2010, 2016). Rather, when situated dialectically within the context of connectedness, this ethnography shows how lived experiences at the margin produce marginalised subjectivities and a sense of 'enclavement' which becomes mobile and persists despite the presence of various migratory, religious and production-based networks. Marginalisation, I argue, penetrates levels from the spatial, economic and political to the personal, intimate and subjective. It is, therefore, something that is carried, tacitly felt and embodied; it is a sensation, a presence, as much as it is a quantifiable and measurable socio-economic reality.

At the material and spatial level, too, Saharanpur embodies an urban cosmology that inscribes modalities of marginalisation onto the cityscape through infrastructural and spatial cartographies (cf. Harvey et al. 2017; Low 1996) within which the *mohallas* become configured as a space of the 'marginal other'. Are the *mohallas* a ghetto? Perhaps. Certainly, many of the markers of the urban ghetto are present: communalisation along religious lines, forms of – at times violent – spatial relegation, representations of the *mohallas'* residents as undesirable citizens, limited state presence and a subjective sense of urban enclosure (Chambers 2019; Gayer & Jaffrelot 2012; Wacquant 2009). As Rajnarayan Chandavarkar (2009) argues, however, communalism and the structuring of urban space in India must be understood 'in terms of the racialization of social, especially religious, difference. It cannot be grasped as religious conflict in isolation from caste and class, language and "ethnicity"' (p. 111). Class constitutes a significant undertone to the ethnographic material detailed in this book, but communalising pressures acted to push Muslims of different classes together in the *mohallas* and, in turn, served to blur lines of class differentiation, a factor that stymied the emergence of class-based identities (see chapter 3). This blurring wove its way into circuits of production, creating ambiguous relations of labour and an intermingling of spatial factors with processes of accumulation (cf. Lefebvre 1991; Jamil 2017).

This book, then, is about the production of marginalised subjectivities and 'enclavements' which, despite the aforementioned connections, often acted to stymie the emergence of transformative processes – including class consciousness – heralded by many accounts of global connection. In this setting, the connected margin becomes an ideal site for capitalist accumulation by restraining labour resistances, producing various modalities of (self-)discipline and embedding economic activity in social and intimate relations. This is not to sideline modalities of resistance and mutuality. As the ethnographic material shows, there are moments when, for example, female homeworkers producing at the bottom of the labour hierarchy group together to assault an outsourcing factory to demand payment and when networks of sociality enable male craftworkers to negotiate haphazard and precarious conditions of work. At the same time, however, a subjective sense of enclavement is internalised and mobilised in various moments of engagement with labour markets in India and elsewhere.

At times, enclaving forces may be stark, for example the spatial segregation of construction workers in the Gulf or the violent processes of ghettoisation experienced by Muslims in some Indian cities. A subjective sense of marginalisation may, however, be subtler and become concealed in mundane everyday acts: the way someone relates to their ID card or a moment of silence in an apparently convivial everyday conversation. These scales may be very different, but empirically we are dealing with the same processes – a form of repetition that acts to create subjectivities which embody spatial and material marginalising forces within degrees of anxiety and boundedness. Here, I follow recent work on subjectivities under late capitalism which emphasises how precarity, flux and uncertainty produce anxieties. These anxieties funnel through into the consciousness, creating subjectivities that are simultaneously uneasy and unwilling (or unable) to challenge existing conditions, particularly for those further down the labour hierarchy (Ortner 2005).

In order to develop a level of engagement that attends to individual subjectivities and forms of intersubjectivity, I give particular attention to the relationship between the material and the imagined, a space that, following Tim Ingold (2013), I see as central to the production of 'ways of being' and 'ways of seeing' in the world. As Ingold contends, the formation of a dichotomy segmenting the imagination from the real renders the imagination little more than a floating 'mirage above the road we tread in our material life' (p. 735). The imagination, he suggests, is active in carving out 'paths' or 'ways'. Imagining is not an act of absentminded pondering but instead directs interactions with the material and is itself shaped via such engagements. The material world – whether it be urban spatial configurations, embodied practices of craft and labour or the lived experiences of migrant workers – acts upon the consciousness and sculpts imaginaries which in turn may open up or close down forms of potentiality.

Simultaneously, imaginaries are eternally acting upon the material, reimagining it and reconfiguring it. Just as with the carver's chisel, however, there are limits, and material constraints create resistances, diverting the hand and constraining subjectivities through material and structural pressures. An exploration of these considerations cannot be undertaken from afar. As Anasua Chatterjee (2017) points out, many empirical engagements with India's Muslim *mohallas*, *bastīs* and 'ghettos' have tended to stop at the boundary. A more subjective, affective and *felt* level of enquiry, however, demands a resolutely ethnographic approach and one that considers not only the 'marginalised Muslim' but also the sister, brother, neighbour or friend, the worker producing for global chains of supply and the labour migrant undertaking journeys to serve the needs of labour markets both near and far. Simultaneously, though, scale matters. And so, in the following section, I move away from an engagement with marginalisation in the context of Indian Muslims and turn instead to broader conceptual material that deals with the intersections between marginalisation and craftwork.

Artisans at the margin: anthropology, political economy and craftwork

It is *the imagination* – of the artisan and of imaginaries of the artisan within the minds of others – that provides a jumping-off point to situate craftwork within broader discussions emerging from intersections of anthropology, political economy and studies of marginality. In classical Marxist understandings of labour process, artisanal work is primarily envisaged as a pre-capitalist, pre-proletarian mode of production or as being part of a petite bourgeoisie based on ownership of a workplace, tools, and possibly the employment of others. In many ways, the artisan lies at the core of Karl Marx's understanding of labour process and its transformation under industrial capitalism. As Marx (1990 [1867]: 198) famously argues,

> what distinguishes the worst architect from the best of bees is this, that the architect raises his [sic] structure in imagination before he erects it in reality. At the end of every labour-process, we get a result that already existed in the imagination of the labourer at its commencement. He not only effects a change of form in the material on which he works, but he also realises a purpose of his own that gives the law to his modus operandi, and to which he must subordinate his will.

The degree of ownership – over the imagined product and the possession of tools, workshops, etc. – situates artisanal modes of production, along with land-owning peasants, as one of the primary spaces of primitive accumulation (Marx 1990 [1867]; P. Chatterjee 2011; Sanyal 2014). For Marx, it is the fragmentation of the artisanal mode under industrial capitalism that leads to labour's alienation from the product of its work. This process, Tim Ingold (2000) suggests, involves the increasing separation of art from technology, and artist from artisan (cf. Marchand 2013), although, as Ingold (2000) indicates, the process is historically recent and neither complete nor globally homogeneous.

In anthropology, sites of artisanal labour have long been of interest as spaces to examine social, cultural and economic worlds on the fringes of globalisation and capitalism, although many of these accounts also debate the extent to which artisanship persists as a mode of contemporary production (e.g. Herzfeld 2004; Nash 1993a; Wilkinson-Weber & DeNicola 2016). Marxist-influenced anthropology, more broadly, has its roots in a focus on the margins of capitalism or on those experiencing capitalist modes of production for the first time. While this has since diversified, these contributions have sought to understand how capitalist transformations, and the commodity form, money and exploitation of labour value, were enacted, as well as how capitalist regimes were experienced, interpreted, accepted or resisted by local communities (e.g. Nash 1993b; Taussig 2010 [1980]; Ong 2010; Wolf 1992). Within these and other ethnographic works, the margin is critical, as it is at the margin that capitalism's effects (and affects) are most explicit and its critiques are, potentially, most vibrant. While illustrating homogenising processes at the structural level, the descriptive material in this literature shows the diverse ways in which capitalist modes of production and accumulation intertwine and incorporate localised practices and non-capitalist sets of relations and hierarchies.

In *The Body Impolitic,* Michael Herzfeld's (2004) classic work on artisans in a small town on the Greek island of Crete, Herzfeld argues that the long duration of anthropological focus on margins offers a 'critical vantage [point] from which to challenge the generalizing claims of the global hierarchy of value' (p. 4). It is in various marginal localities, Herzfeld continues, that 'we can see how marginality itself is actively produced, and reproduced, in the lives and bodies of those who must bear its stigma' (p. 4). Importantly, Herzfeld begins the process of disrupting unidirectional representations of artisanship in Crete. On the one hand, he recognises that artisans' skills and quality products – once so highly valued – have been increasingly denigrated by factory production and that artisans have been exoticised as a curious relic of pre-modernity. On the other hand, he illustrates a duality within which the marginal artisan is simultaneously held as a central pillar of Greek/Cretan identity, a core feature in the construction – often involving reification of artisans by the state – of imaginaries around national consciousness and ideals of virtuous Greek traditions. These processes are echoed in India, where artisans are often marginalised but also constructed as central to ideals of national identity and seen as combining the 'traditional' with 'modern' aspirations (Mohsini 2010; Venkatesan 2009; Sharma 2019). Herzfeld (2004), however, tempers the reification of artisans in national discourses by arguing that this 'exalts [artisans], to be sure; but it also serves to marginalize them from some of the most desirable fruits of modernity' (p. 5).

Ambiguities regarding the position of artisans within contemporary capitalist contexts, which run through a growing body of ethnographic and other research, have illustrated the diverse trajectories of various artisanal and craft industries globally. Deskilling, fragmentation, alienation and decline are very much present in the 'craft' sectors of both the global south (e.g. Braverman 1998; Wilkinson-Weber 1999; Herzfeld 2007; Mohsini 2016; Wilkinson-Weber & DeNicola 2016) and the global north (Carrier 1992; Hadjimichalis 2006; Haakestad & Friberg 2017), but the persistence (Beinin 2001; Elyachar 2003; Ciotti 2007; Sennett 2008; Holmes 2015; Tweedie 2017) and the re-emergence (Gibson 2016) of craftwork are also part of the contemporary milieu. Running counter to teleological notions of decline, this body of research – along with other contributions – illustrates that sectors broadly classifiable as 'craft-based' are neither replaced by industrial production nor static within a reified artisanal mode, adding considerable ambiguity to the analytical constitution of craftwork both globally (e.g. Crossick 2016; Hadjimichalis 2006; Mollona 2005; White 2004) and in India (e.g. Chambers & Ansari 2018; Mezzadri 2016; Mohsini 2016; Ciotti 2007; Scrase 2003). The woodworking *mohallas* of Saharanpur are not, then, relics of the past devoid of change. Rather, Muslim-dominated craft industries that form the economic backbone of small cities and towns like Saharanpur, Meerut, Moradabad, Bareilly and Nagina – as well as areas of larger metropolises such as Delhi and Lucknow – have become thoroughly engaged with global markets and production networks (Wilkinson-Weber 1999; Chambers & Ansari 2018; Mezzadri 2016; Mohsini 2016; Ruthven 2010; cf. Rodrigues 2019).

'Bordering' the *mohalla*: from the spatial to the subjective[6]

How, then, do we connect these structural processes with the subjective and with the imagination? Achieving this requires a turn back to the spatially orientated considerations which underpin life in Saharanpur's *mohallas*. A spatial, rather than a primarily socio-economic, rendering of the margin calls for consideration of the – often unmarked – borders and boundaries that weave their way around the *mohallas* and penetrate the consciousness of their residents (cf. Demetriou 2013). Although crosscut by degrees of diversity, the *mohallas* themselves are constituted within a broader urban context that bounds and borders the area via invisible lines of demarcation. These 'imagined borders' are crossed, contested and negotiated daily (Chambers 2019; cf. Demetriou 2013), forming an ongoing background which, in degrees, shapes formations of labour, sociality and subjectivities among the *mohallas*' residents. In order to situate this narrative, the final section of this introduction works its way through literatures dealing with marginality and borders – both material and immaterial – to trace a 'border crossing' and a 'carried' or 'mobile' sense of enclavement as it feeds into everyday interactions at the levels of city, neighbourhood and street.

Partha Chatterjee (2004) defines marginalised populations as those citizens who are only tenuously rights-bearing. Significantly, he also shows that in India, as in much of the global south, they comprise the majority of the population. Marginality, then, is not a condition of exception, but rather – while it may be configured around a variety of intersections – it is the norm for many. The 'margin', as a conceptual space, can be conceived as composing areas on the fringes of the nation state (V. Das & Poole 2004), spaces and places 'situated at the margins of the political order' (Agamben 2005: 6). Margins can be seen as constituted of the 'non-privileged', with such groups often seeking salvation in 'non-state' sources or more 'traditional' or 'charismatic' forms of authority (Weber 1968). Margins may provide a place of refuge, self-governance and progressive forms of anarchic social organisation (Scott 2009). Veena Das and Deborah Poole (2004) illustrate the blurred nature of 'margins', where informal actors at times perform outside the law but also appeal to the law. To various degrees, the *mohallas* embody this 'greyness'. These neighbourhoods provide a sense of security from a potentially threatening 'other' and from a 'Hindustani'[7] state which is often seen as dubious or even hostile. Simultaneously, the state is the main target of claim-making and is regularly appealed to for interventions, welfare and security (Carswell et al. 2019).

None the less there remained a distancing from the state amongst many residents of Saharanpur's Muslim *mohallas*. At times this was explicit but it could play out in subtler ways. Inam was a neighbour of Rizwan, the woodcarver detailed in the opening vignette of this book. Like Rizwan and many others in the *mohallas* he regularly migrated to other parts of the country for work. Whenever he left, Inam was sure to take his *pehchan patra* (voting card), which was essential not just to vote but as an identity card.[8] In part, he took it to facilitate practical concerns, but for Inam and other migrants from the *mohallas* the card carried additional meaning beyond enabling modalities of migration. It was as much associated with showing 'who you were not' as it was about showing 'who you were'. A Muslim without ID in India quickly becomes suspicious, a point Islam emphasised: 'If the police catch any Muslim and he does not have all cards, then they will say "he is a terrorist". But if a Hindu is arrested, they will never say this.' Regarding *mohalla* neighbourhoods in Varanasi, Philippa Williams (2011) suggests that while an absent or inaccessible state allows us to situate 'margins' in relation to the state, we should also examine a more emotive level constituted through 'feelings of alienation and of being at the edge of the politics that mattered' (p. 277).

Similar debates have been a key part of ethnographic contributions exploring the relationship between 'borders', marginality and national identity. Hastings Donnan and Dieter Haller (2000), for example, argue that border populations, while geographically marginal to 'the centre', are, through their very locality on the fringes of nations, active in shaping and defining states themselves. Yet, here too, a feeling of 'being marginal' persists. As in the *mohallas,* spatial exclusion and socio-economic or political marginalisation are often experienced by those living close to, on or across borders. Jason Cons (2013) focuses on a border enclave, or *chhitmahal,* which is constituted as Bangladeshi territory but surrounded by land belonging to India. Those residing in the enclave found themselves in a permanent 'state of exception' (Agamben 2005), as they were simultaneously unable to access the legal and citizenship rights of Bangladesh or India, which rendered them vulnerable to exploitation and violence perpetrated by either the Indian state or local Indian citizenry.

While the assignment of a permanent 'state of exception' to the *mohallas,* in the terms defined by Giorgio Agamben (2005), would obscure forms of citizenship enacted by residents, degrees of exception are present. The notion of being apart yet within, as per Cons's *chhitmahal,* was often articulated amongst the residents. Cons's informants saw the border as a divide between nations but also 'imagined' the border as more, specifically as a divide between Hindu and Muslim. Ethnographic work has revealed how borders, including those that separate nation states, are not necessarily rigid, fixed entities but are constituted through everyday performances of power, observation (as either observer or observed), security and governance (Aggarwal 2004) which are engaged with, contested and shaped by agentive local actors in various ways (Donnan and Haller 2000).

Writing about the Line of Control (LoC) between Ladakh (India) and Pakistan, Ravina Aggarwal (2004) has described the processes that underpin and maintain borders as being constituted through the emergence of a 'border subjectivity' which is created not only by the material construct – the border – but also via everyday performances. Here, the border becomes a constant frame of reference within language, cultural practice and even religious ceremony:

the state … repeatedly asserts physical and symbolic authority over its citizens, particularly over hybrid zones and migrant bodies that contaminate dominant notions of purity and unsettle orderliness. … [B]ecause border crossings and lines of purity are carefully screened and tightly regimented, citizens of these interstitial domains can become even more disenfranchised from the mainstream or else totalitarian in their defense of it.

(Aggarwal 2004: 17)

This notion of the border beyond the border, a 'border-ness', has been discussed elsewhere. Olga Demetriou (2013) traces the Turkish–Greek border to the Muslim minority community in Greece, which she sees as a 'bordered population', a population that was confined through governmental technologies but was also involved in forms of 'counter-conduct'. Consequently, the border existed in a constant process of construction and contestation. It was made and remade, 'rendering its "border-ness" not an essence, but rather a quality. … Counter-conduct, stemming from … the state's processes of producing difference …, is what destabilizes the border so that we may see it analytically as more than just a line' (p. 10). I return to contestation and counter-conduct later on in this book (for example, chapter 7). In what follows I trace the affective sense of bordering described by Demetriou and others from the level of urban cosmology through to an everyday traverse of the city and a mundane social encounter.

Throughout my initial period of fieldwork, I lived a few doors away from a family consisting of Sabeena, her husband Mehboob and their two sons.[9] They had fallen on hard times after the closure of Mehboob's wood workshop some years before. Mehboob moved into hosiery but found only a small income. Sabeena had moved to Saharanpur from a hill town for the marriage, and her family subscribed to an ethic of social mobility through education. The move to the city, where spatial segregation and bordering were more intense than in the hills, soon became an obstacle. Sabeena's 'outsider' positionality made her particularly aware of bordering practices. She often reflected on the different 'feeling' between city and hills, describing more convivial relations among Muslims and Hindus in her previous home. The family had originated in Saharanpur, hence the ongoing connection, only moving to the hills in the 1930s. Despite Sabeena's feelings, it was Saharanpur that had provided a haven for the family during partition. Sabeena recalled her father's stories of partition, when he was taken to Saharanpur as an infant by her grandfather, hidden under clothes in a bus, in order to escape violence in their home town.

The family's story, like that of many others, was intertwined with broader histories of communal tension and violence. Sabeena's own position was also impacted by her status as a relative 'outsider'. This set Sabeena somewhat apart from other *mohalla* dwellers. It meant that navigating the complexities of Saharanpur's communal spatial context did not come easily. Shortly after their marriage, during better financial times, the family had attempted to move to a neighbourhood near Court Road, hoping that it would offer more opportunities and better schooling. They purchased a property but were confronted by the local Residents' Association, who told them that Muslims were not welcome. Eventually, they sold the property at a loss and returned to the *mohallas*. Despite this experience, Sabeena was vociferous in her defence of the need to build cross-community relations, and ensured that her children respected Hindu holy days and understood their significance. Sabeena herself honoured such days with gifts and social calls. She fostered close friendships with Hindu families in and beyond her neighbourhood and encouraged other Muslims to do likewise, actions she saw as key to being a 'modern Muslim' and in the process fulfilling many of the ideals of the convivial bridge builder (Nowicka & Vertovec 2014; Wise & Velayutham 2014).

On occasions, I accompanied Sabeena to collect her children from school. Despite the high fees and a journey across town, Sabeena had been determined to send her children to a good place of education. The institution was mainly used by Hindu families and the city's small Christian community. The playground provided a convivial space where parents would chat, share stories and discuss their aspirations for their children. On one trip, we sat chatting to Manju, another parent, at the edge of the playground. Manju turned to me and said, 'I am glad you know Sabeena; she is a good person. In that area [the *mohallas*] there are so many bad people and many criminals or people making trouble. Only some, like Sabeena, are good so you must be careful there.' Sabeena smiled, nodded convivially and, with an awkward laugh, responded, 'Yes, we try to be good hosts.' Only after our return did she express her frustration at Manju's association of Muslims with violence and criminality. She had wanted to respond but was forced to remain silent so as not to cause a scene and jeopardise her sons' education. It was a moment in a more complex picture but one that brought together various processes of marginality, bordering, othering and a particular set of power relations – factors which coalesced to insert silence into a mundane moment of convivial exchange.

For Sabeena, the moment intersected with scales beyond those of immediate spatial concern. Silence is symbolic of power, but it is also an overt form of self-governance. For Demetriou (2013), the border wound its ways into the subjectivities of Muslim communities in Greece. Like Demetriou's work on Greece, in Saharanpur 'technologies of governmentality' created a border beyond the border. Even an imagined border has its own materialities that act upon and within people in everyday life. Sabeena's dialogue in the school playground was illustrative not only of governmental technologies but also of more informal forms of bordering that play out against a background of social relations and embed themselves in everyday interactions. It was a 'border' or marginalised subjectivity, produced in Sabeena through these intersecting processes, which had rendered her 'silent'.

Conclusion

It is against this background that I develop an ethnographic narrative which crosses scales from everyday intimacy to global circulations and connections. By relating the story of Sabeena, I hope to provide the reader with a sense of the affective and spatial forces at work, as well as of the modalities through which the dialectic of marginalisation and connectedness is managed. Not all the chapters that follow explicitly orientate themselves towards this theme; rather, marginalisation and connectedness interplay in the background of the book as structuring factors in woodworkers' experiences of apprenticeship, friendship, exploitation, migration and work.

In the following chapter, I provide a detailed historical context. Chapter 3 takes a scalar approach to understanding the supply chain, from international trade shows and large-scale manufacturing units, to individual craftworkers, homeworkers and the women who are often engaged in the finishing work on wood items. This orientation towards women at the end of chapter 3 is used as a jumping-off point in the following chapter to engage with gendered dimensions of production and labour in the city, specifically by attending to women's experiences as they negotiate spaces of home, neighbourhood and factory. The narrative then shifts to male-dominated spaces. Chapter 5 focuses on apprenticeship and chapter 6 on the intersection between Islamic networks and neoliberal ideals of self and labour. Chapter 7 emphasises the importance of the male friendships produced in the dense spatial setting of the gullies. Here, the narrative falls on intersections surrounding friendship, intimacy, labour and migration. Thus it sets up the final two chapters, which deal with the migration experiences of male craftworkers in India (chapter 8) and in the Gulf (chapter 9).

The material presented in this book was collected during several periods of fieldwork, the first taking place over a year and a half from 2010 to 2012 (along with several return visits since). Field research involved the gathering of survey data, numerous interviews covering a variety of topics, and long-duration participation in labour, production, migration and sociality in the *mohallas*. My embroilment in the *mohallas* also seeped into time away from the field, mediated by technologies such as WhatsApp and Skype, which friends in Saharanpur and I regularly use to stay in touch, thus blurring the boundaries of 'field' and 'home'.

To a degree the book can be seen as a multi-sited ethnography (G. E. Marcus 1995; Gallo 2016), in that the material presented plays out across different locations in India and in the Gulf region. I prefer, however, to situate the text as an exploration of an 'ethnoscape' (Appadurai 1996), because, despite the engagement with multiple geographical locations, the emphasis is often on continuities of people, networks, sociality, intimacy and affects. This book is about women and men. However, my male positionality made ethnographic research on women's lifeworlds challenging. I hope, therefore, that I may be forgiven for the tendency to focus on men, although chapters 3 and 4 provide an ethnographic description that details the highly gendered construction of women's positions in woodcraft production within the city.

As this book focuses on one community, it is not making broader homogenising claims about Indian Muslims as a whole. The economic and social positions of Indian Muslims, along with individual experiences, life trajectories and subjectivities are diverse (M. Hasan 2018; Gayer & Jaffrelot, 2013; Mann 1992) and reducing any Muslim community to being defined through an Islamic identity alone leaves little space for empirical nuance (M. Hasan 2018; Marsden & Retsikas 2013). As Mushirul Hasan (2018) reminds us, viewing Indian Muslims as always defined by their faith is simply neo-orientalist and ignores both diversity and internal stratification. As detailed in the following chapters, even within the context of Saharanpur's Muslim *mohallas* there are a variety of intersections (class, gender, *biradari*, migrant status, age, for example) that act as structuring forces in shaping the lives and movements of craftworkers and others.

Before turning to the broader historical context, a very brief summary of the recent political history of Uttar Pradesh, the state where Saharanpur is located, is essential to aid readers who are unfamiliar with

Indian politics. India's most populous state, and traditionally a heartland for the Congress Party, Uttar Pradesh experienced a rise in nationalist politics throughout the 1980s, with traditional caste-based electioneering giving way to coalitions among the Hindu population centred on national identity and anti-Muslim rhetoric. This culminated in the demolition in 1992 of the Babri Masjid,[10] which was followed by bouts of communal violence, primarily targeted at the state's Muslims. Violence which has led to an intensifying of already exiting communal divisions. Although the emergence of Hindu nationalism as a major political force led to the successful installation of a BJP administration in 1991, the multi-caste vote base upon which it relied was not to last.

Attempts by the BJP to pander to both upper and Backward Castes (BCs) backfired. The following years saw a return of caste-based politics, particularly the emergence of the Dalit-aligned Bahujan Samaj Party (BSP). There were terms administered by the BSP and the Samajwadi Party, but in 2014 the BJP was re-elected both in Uttar Pradesh and nationally. A second resounding victory in 2017 further cemented the BJP's position and has led to a substantial increase in anti-Muslim rhetoric and activities. The following chapter brings us up to this moment via a trajectory that covers the pre-colonial, colonial and post-Independence eras and incorporates a broad history of Indian Muslim artisans, and of Indian Muslims more generally.

Notes

1. *Wallah* can refer to a person or an object (e.g. taxi wallah or 'that small wallah').
2. It is likely that the figure has increased substantially, but more recent data is not yet available.
3. The series of recent, and in the context of this book significant, events in India – the revoking of article 370, the associated lockdown in Kashmir, the introduction of the Citizenship Amendment Act (CAA), proposals for a National Register of Citizens (NRC), and the associated protests and resistances – took place during the copyediting stage. Therefore they do not feature in the text. This book, however, can most certainly be read against the background of these controversial moves by the state and their implications for marginalised groups in India, Indian Muslims in particular.
4. The industry comprises a wide range of trades, from highly skilled to low-skilled occupations. When talking in collective terms about those who glean a livelihood from the industry, I use the broader 'craftworkers'. *Kārīgar* (artisan) denotes a highly skilled occupation such as woodcarving or detailed brass work. Those engaged in trades such as carpentry or polishing work are more commonly called *mistrī* (a colloquial term in Hindi that also covers workers such as mechanics and builders). When referring to 'artisans' in more general terms, beyond Saharanpur, I default to the English usage.

5. The madrassa at Deoband is the central school of thought for what is broadly known as the Deobandi movement, which has been very influential across South and Central Asia. Its primary competitor is the Madrasa Manzar-e-Islam in Bareilly, which is seen as the seat of the Barelvi movement. While both madrassas subscribe to Sunni Islam, and were originally part of the same reformist movement, they split in the early twentieth century and developed different interpretations of what reformist Islam should embody. Although there are a variety of distinctions in the daily practice of Islam, for example a greater engagement with Sufi saints among Barelvis, the fundamental difference relates to the Prophet Muhammad. For Barelvis, the Prophet is the 'model man', and a unique man who possessed powers beyond those of mortals. For Deobandis, the Prophet is the ideal of perfection and piety but should not be venerated as superhuman. Such otherworldly power lies only with Allah (A. Alam, 2008). Tension between the two movements can be high.
6. This section is an adaptation of part of an article published in a special issue of *Modern Asian Studies* (see Chambers 2019: '"Performed conviviality": Space, bordering, and silence in the city', *Modern Asian Studies*, 53(3): 776–99). It is reproduced here in an edited form with the kind permission of the journal and the special issue editors, Magnus Marsden and Madeleine Reeves.
7. Meaning 'land of the Hindu', 'Hindustan' evokes a sense of living in a nation of and for 'the other'. It was widely used by Muhammad Ali Jinnah (founder of Pakistan) to evoke the idea of Pakistan ('land of the pure').
8. Gradually these cards were replaced by the biometric Aadhaar card.
9. Account anonymised.
10. It was claimed by the BJP, and right-wing movements such as the RSS and the VHP, that the Badri Masjid was built on the site of a Hindu temple. The riots that broke out that year saw its demolition at the hands of a mob. Since then the status of the Babri Masjid (called Ayodhya by those claiming an earlier Hindu temple) has been under the scrutiny of various courts, but in November 2019 the Supreme Court ordered that the land on which the Masjid was built should be handed over for the construction of a new Hindu temple, and that the Waqf board should be allocated a plot of land close by upon which to build a new *masjid*. In part, the ruling was based on archaeological evidence for the existence of an earlier temple, although there have been claims that this evidence was spurious.

2
A brief history of Indian Muslim artisans

Figure 2.1   A woodworker demonstrating a powered *ārī* (fret)saw.
Source: author.

On a warm afternoon in April 2010 I decided to get myself lost in the city's old neighbourhoods surrounding the mohalla of Purāni Mandi. Purāni Mandi was one of the earliest localities to emerge as a site of wood production, and the market, as well as the areas surrounding it, comprised the sections of the city most strongly associated with the Muslim community.

Much of the area consisted of small gullies and bustling markets through which rickshaws, motorbikes and pedestrians had to wind a precarious and often stalling path. The area was dominated by shop fronts adorned with wares of every sort. As I neared Purāni Mandi itself, the food sellers, eateries, hardware stores and jewellers gave way to the wood workshops. Between the workshops and the shop fronts, however, an older Saharanpur could be glimpsed. An occasional intricate archway or the façade of a once grand haveli (Mughal-era townhouse) peeked out through the maelstrom of production and commerce (cf. Verma & Gupta 2017). Some are ruinous and, as Rizwan's son Yousef indicated of one particularly decrepit structure, said to be occupied by bhuts (ghosts). As with contemporary urban cosmologies, which write the marginalisation of Saharanpur's Muslims onto the cityscape, so a lost past could be glimpsed among the jumble of more modern brickwork and reinforced concrete, providing the mohallas' residents an opportunity to declare pointedly, 'There, that is what we once were'.

This chapter fulfils two purposes. It embeds the narrative historically and begins the process of moving towards a more ethnographic engagement. I argue that, although impacted in various ways by colonialism, the loss of Muslim political and economic power, and the policies of liberalisation, craftwork in the city has also been characterised by a variety of historical and contemporary connections. To situate this within a broader context, the chapter draws on a range of historical materials dealing with craftwork in India and the position of Indian Muslims more generally across pre-colonial, colonial and post-colonial contexts. Over the duration of the chapter I orientate the narrative increasingly towards the specificities of Saharanpur's woodworking *mohallas*. I use the stories and memories of various residents, along with secondary and archival material, to detail the historical construction of the *mohallas,* the forms of spatial demarcation that have emerged, and the diversity of those who reside in the areas today.

Saharanpur and artisanship in pre-colonial India

Several narrative strands run through the literature on Indian craftworkers, including questions of identity, work, economic position, success, failure, opportunity and exploitation. While many accounts tend to begin with the colonial era (e.g. T. Roy 1999; Kumar 2017), the pre-colonial period also warrants attention. In many colonial narratives, it has been presented as, in contrast to Europe, stagnated and unchanging (e.g. Moreland [1929] 2011), a sleight of hand which sought to justify colonial projects. More recent work, however, has detailed a complex scene of movement, connection and transformation. Since medieval times Saharanpur has experienced several changes of control: from the Delhi Sultanate (1192–1526) to the Mughals (1542–1739), the Rohillas (1748–70) and the Marathas (1789–1803). Frank Perlin (1983) has argued that areas such as Saharanpur that sat at the fringes of empires and were often in flux saw the emergence of 'proto-capitalism' and vibrant forms of economic development because of limited state control. In contrast, Eugenia Vanina (2004) argues that it was politically stable urban centres which were most active, driven by the concentration of craft production in cities. Although they were dominated by feudal patronage, she contends that there was manufacture of mass-consumption items and rapid development in craft technologies. While they differ, both perspectives emphasise the forms of flux and fluidity that have long been a part of artisanal lives as well as their connection to broader economic, political and structural transformations.

Shifting political landscapes and the need to seek forms of patronage from wealthy elites have long driven patterns of migration within artisanal communities (Kerr 2006; Haynes & Roy 1999; Ramaswamy 2017). Nita Kumar (2017), for example, describes weavers in Banaras as originating from Samarkand, Kashmir and Persia. Omacanda Hāṇḍā and Madhu Jain (2000) suggest that Saharanpur's wood industry, too, was established by the migration of artisans from Kashmir after Mughal rule collapsed there in the mid-eighteenth century, a story that was also related to me by some artisans in the city. Douglas Haynes and Tirthankar Roy (1999: 36) argue that craft migration during the colonial and pre-colonial periods was not just about economic survival, suggesting that 'some sections among the weavers were always mobile, always willing to pick up from regions in decline and move to those showing signs of expansion. Mobility has always been a strategy for ensuring subsistence, surviving famine, improving economic livelihoods and, in some cases, resisting efforts to control weavers' labour.'

Likewise, Vijaya Ramaswamy (2017) shows that movement and migration were commonplace amongst artisans in pre-colonial India, although at times these movements were forced, compelled by powerful rulers demanding their services. Later, in the colonial era, this involved a shift in work regimes within which artisans operated, as they migrated not just between locations but also out of home-based manufacturing and into handicraft factories (T. Roy 2007). These factors all played a part in Saharanpur: woodcarving and associated trades were likewise connected to earlier patterns of migration, and the late colonial period saw the emergence of factory working arrangements (Hāndā & Jain 2000; Watt 1903; Nevill 1909). While large-scale handicraft manufacturing takes place in present-day Saharanpur, 'home-based' or 'cottage-style' production is still prevalent, and workers continue to use their mobility to negotiate conditions and seek employment across the country (see chapters 8 and 9).

Saharanpur's Muslim community is diverse, but Islamic identities are not exclusive of other influences. As Abdul Waheed (2006) points out, many Hindu artisans converted to Islam under the Mughals, bringing elements of caste identity and associated skills with them (cf. Batool 2018). This is not to say that caste, and the occupation-based activities of the *Jajmani* system (the system of sub-castes which connects groups to a particular type of labour), continued to be the core defining feature of those caste groups who converted. Barbara Harriss-White (2002: 13), for example, suggests that conversion to Islam enabled 'freedom from Hindus' distinctive social obligations[, which] may have encouraged innovative activity'. As shown later in this chapter, unlike in some other Muslim craft sectors in India (e.g. Kumar 2017), the workforce was not constituted along caste lines but was much more diverse. Historically, too, more recent literature on craftwork in pre-colonial India makes clear the diversity, mobility and flux of artisanal lives – a very different image from the staid picture presented in earlier representations.

Indian Muslims, craftworkers and colonialism

Abdul Waheed (2006) has described the Mughal era as a golden age of Indian craftwork, a time during which artisans were highly respected and received substantial patronage from elites. Decline started, he argues, only 'with the coming of Britishers whose economic policies ruined handicraft industries and forced artisans to become agricultural labourers' (p. 20).

Others see the deterioration of craft industries under colonial rule as part of a broader process of de-industrialisation and economic moves towards capitalism (Thorner & Thorner 1962), a development that Amiya Kumar Bagchi (1976) argues was constrained by British economic policy. Certainly, sectors such as weaving were impacted by colonial laws. The effect was that markets were flooded with cheap British cloth, which caused many weavers to relocate to urban areas (Gooptu 2001). Those who remained in weaving industries often became tied to moneylenders and merchants as a result of declining local markets and an increased reliance on export through middlemen (Gooptu 2001). While many craftworkers were displaced by the arrival of large-scale industrial production and the import of mass-produced British goods, Tirthankar Roy (2007) also suggests that the craft sector remained relatively vibrant, as craftworkers 'could gain from trade by obtaining access to imported raw materials and distant markets[…, utilizing] new opportunities of capital accumulation, which process induced changes in technology and industrial organization' (p. 963). Although craftworkers were forced to adapt, often saw a decline in status, and experienced increasing precarity and forms of marginalisation enacted during colonial rule, a large portion of India's population remained employed in the craft sector (Roy 2010).

In earlier work, too, Tirthankar Roy (1993) paints an animated scene, locating four sources of dynamic economic activity: first, the emergence of a capitalist class from amongst craftworkers; second, a shift towards an engagement with products and markets that could not be replicated in industrial manufacture; third, a movement of craftworkers to urban centres; and fourth, the adoption of new techniques, including powered manufacture, into processes of craft production. While Roy's work challenges catastrophic accounts of craft industries under colonial rule, the situation of labour and the relationship between labour and capital also changed. Douglas Haynes (2001), for example, illustrates that there were distinct similarities to 'flexible specialisation', a term applied to industrial development in peripheral areas of Europe. Under flexible specialisation Indian artisans adopted new technology to produce the larger outputs demanded by globalising markets, but the industries themselves retained their craft structure. In a few cases, this led to artisans becoming petty capitalists. For many, though, the emergence of new modalities in the labour process resulted in increased precarity, giving employers and subcontractors 'the ability to add and drop workers quickly, without fear of strong resistance organized by trade unions' (p. 172). Haynes points out that this questions the emphasis on factory production as the primary form of industrial capitalism, a point I have made in the introduction of this book.

Tirthankar Roy (1999) also discusses a shift within craft sectors in India during the late colonial era away from master–craftsman arrangements, and towards one of employee (or employer). He identifies a decline in the *ustād–shāgird* (master–apprenticeship) system, as production became deskilled and craftworkers were socialised into labour through more informal means. This and the introduction of new technology had an impact on Saharanpur during the late colonial period. The 1903 official catalogue of the Indian art exhibition in Delhi details how

Saharanpur used to enjoy a great reputation in the manufacture, in vine pattern, of [wood items], but though this still survives it has given place to the modern wholesale traffic in [items] cut by the machine fret-saw and exported to Europe and America by the thousand, and there accepted apparently as typical examples of Indian wood-carving. This new traffic has very nearly killed the ... wood-carving of Saharanpur and of one or two other neighbouring towns.

(Watt 1903: 111)

While there was decline, a loss of quality and moves towards mass production, colonialism did not lead to the collapse of the industry in Saharanpur. Instead, it pre-empted a change in the structural arrangements of production and saw the emergence of factory-style manufacturing alongside the older cottage industry. Often this meant a loss of status and increased degrees of alienation, but there was also the emergence of a small capitalist class of former craftworkers. Abdul, the owner of a large factory on the edge of town, highlighted these factors as he narrated his family history. It was his 'fourth father' (his great-great-grandfather) that began to expand from the position of craft producer, as the result of orders arriving in his workshop from British businessmen. These goods were destined for export, albeit via British intermediaries, and fed into growing demand for 'authentic' craft goods in the UK and elsewhere (cf. Venkatesan 2009).

The authentic desire for colonial possessions was, however, riddled with contradictions...., and often had ambiguous consequences for the artisans themselves. Textiles, for example, were often held up as a form of 'native' artisanship and used in the construction of discourses which subjugated and exoticised the Indian 'other' (Sharma 2019). Simultaneously, the desire for 'authentic' Indian craft goods in the UK drove a campaign in the early twentieth century to protect artisans from the ravages of industrialisation that would later influence Gandhi in his use of Indian-produced goods as symbolising the resistance struggle and his focus on village-based development (Venkatesan 2009). Nor were artisans isolated from global events elsewhere. The economic depression of the inter-war period in Europe and the USA, for example, was felt in Indian craftworking communities and resulted in increased economic insecurity (Gooptu 2001). For Muslim craftworkers, in particular, the colonial era was intersected by impactful events driven by political and economic forces. The 1857 uprising had profound effects for the Muslim population. The view of the British was that Indian Muslims were central to the resistance, and consequently many Muslims experienced a sudden loss of land and status (Waheed 2006). However, there was a revival of Islamic culture throughout the latter stages of the nineteenth century. Various ulama (scholars of Islam and Islamic law) favoured progressive policies that emphasised the creation of schools, mosques and universities. This advocacy generated several reformist movements that were concentrated not just on strengthening Islam, but also on the value of science, social welfare (Gooptu 2001) and better relations with the British (Muhammad 2002).

In his history of the Aligarh School, India's most famous Muslim university, Shan Muhammad (2002) describes the reformist activity of the school as being engaged in trying to reconcile the ideals of Islam and those of modernity. In contrast, Barbara Metcalf (1984) suggests that many other reformist organisations 'looked back, not West, and believed themselves to be in the company of the great Muslims of the past for whom precisely the end of false custom and the creation of religiously responsible individuals were central' (p. 185). The drive for reform and revival was not, then, a consolidated movement. Reformism consisted of a variety of splintered groups as leaders jostled for status as 'defenders of the faith' (Metcalf 2007). Other interventions also attempted to disrupt the more collectivising identities that were forming within some sections of the Muslim community before independence. The Muslim Mass Contact Campaign, for example, was initiated by India's future first Prime Minister, Jawaharlal Nehru, in 1937; it sought to convince poorer Muslims – artisans, peasants, workers – that their commonality lay not with a Muslim national identity (as favoured by Muhammad Ali Jinnah in his calls for a separate Muslim homeland – Pakistan) but with others – Muslim and non-Muslim – engaged in working-class occupations. The campaign would flounder and eventually collapse, Jinnah winning through in his calls for a separate Muslim homeland (M. Hasan 2018).

This is not to say, however, that class-based identities are absent. Although reformist movements were often driven by ulama and *Ashraf* elites,[1] lower classes, including craftworkers, were also involved (Metcalf 2007). Nandini Gooptu (2001) places craftworkers in the forefront of processes of Islamic reform and revival, where 'the poorer Muslims of artisan communities and some service occupational groups seized upon the changing religious practices … which gradually came to provide a focus of organisation and identity' (p. 261). Saharanpur's craftworkers and the Deoband madrassa are deeply connected, the institution priding itself on having been built on donations from local farmers and artisans. Although tied to *ashraf* elites, the madrassa's best-known family, the Madanis, are themselves of weaver origin, and many of those living and working in the city's *mohallas* took pride in their association with the globally influential seminary. Although Nehru's campaign of the 1930s had been unsuccessful in its appeal to artisans and others to rally around a class-based identity, alternative conceptions of composite India – an India within which Muslim citizens could find a home on an equal footing – were by no means extinguished and had a profound effect upon Saharanpur during the events of the partition period, events that were closely tied with the influence of the Darul Uloom Deoband.

Memories of partition: the boy and the Maulana

When considering the coming of partition and independence, I turn to Saharanpur's Muslim craftworkers specifically, as a broader rendition of the period cannot be done justice here. Saharanpur experienced dramatic changes during the partition period in the form of inward and outward migration. The city saw one of the largest concentrations of incoming Hindu and Sikh refugees in Uttar Pradesh (Y. Khan 2003). Abdul Waheed (2006) suggests that the outward movement from such cities was dominated by the Muslim middle class who were not tied to land, like the *zamīndārs* (landowners), or held by poverty, as many artisans and peasants were. These emigrations to Pakistan of middle-class Muslims and other skilled professionals continued well after partition, large numbers still making the journey into the 1950s (M. Hasan 2019). Certainly, the stripping out of India's Muslim middle class was a generalised pattern across many north Indian states, which had profound effects for the economic position of those Muslims who remained in India (Mohsini 2010; Waheed 2006; I. Engineer 2018). However, it was not only the middle classes who were involved in mass relocations to newly founded Pakistan. In the context of cities across the north-west of India, Yasmin Khan (2003: 513–14) also describes how:

> In Saharanpur, Agra and other western districts, insecure Muslim communities were selling their goods and planning to migrate to Pakistan. This affected many ordinary Muslims, not simply those members of the elite who had an ideological attachment to Pakistan. In Saharanpur, stalls could be seen in the market selling the goods of Muslims intending to depart and, in Aligarh, one observer noted that the railway station platform was crowded with the families of Muslim artisans, primarily locksmiths, who were waiting to leave the city.

Migrations to Pakistan continued after partition, but by the 1950s the Indian government had become so concerned at the loss of skilled craft labour in Uttar Pradesh that a policy of deterrence was employed, involving coercion and incentives, in an attempt to convince artisans to stay and thus to retain their economic contribution to India (Khan 2003). For those artisans who remained, the loss of large portions of the Muslim middle class had a profound effect, with Muslims in many sectors losing control of export and wholesale, often to non-Muslim intermediaries (Unni & Scaria 2009) and leading to the positing of Hindus as businesspeople or merchants and Muslims as workers and producers across many craft clusters. In Bareilly's *zardozi* (beaded embroidery) industry, for example, wholesale and export are now primarily controlled by brokers of Punjabi origin (Unni & Scaria 2009),[2] and in Delhi the *zardozi* cluster survived, but saw a decline in demand for quality work, as much of its customer base fled during partition (Mohsini 2010). Clare Wilkinson-Weber (1999) details a similar situation in Lucknow as the city's *chikan* (needle embroidery) industry saw the 'stripping [away] of a layer of elite consumers' (p. 19) and loss of control over export and wholesale.

While a lost Muslim middle-class customer base continues to have an impact upon many craft clusters today, Mushirul Hasan (2018) has argued that as early as the 1960s shifts started to appear in relations of production in some craft sectors as Muslim artisans began competing with their Hindu counterparts for access to growing markets in India and the Gulf. These shifts, and the competition involved, led to increasing tensions as struggles for the economic control of craft industries mingled with communal tensions (Wilkinson 2006; M. Hasan 2018). Steven Wilkinson (2006) argues that this re-emergence provided some competitive advantage for Muslim wholesalers and exporters over their non-Muslim counterparts, as many of the former were themselves craftspeople and therefore had a deeper understanding of production and manufacturing processes. Wilkinson also suggests that this led, in some cases, to improvements in working conditions for labour as co-religious status with those further up the supply chain created more sympathetic relations (cf. Kumar 2017).

Saharanpur, though, far exceeds many other craft sectors in terms of Muslim control of the upper levels of the local supply chain: fieldwork surveys show that almost 90 per cent of wholesalers and exporters were Muslim.[3] As suggested by Wilkinson (2006), there were degrees to which this created relationships between workers and employers that were distinct from those in other craft sectors. Observance of the same religious holidays and recognition of Friday as the day of rest, along with the ability to appeal to religious sensibilities, offered workers some avenues of negotiation that may not have been available to those employed by non-Muslims. Just as workers could appeal to co-religious concerns, however, so employers could call upon religiosity as a means of disciplining labour through, for example, aligning hard work and productivity with notions of being a *sharīf aadmi* (respectable, gentle or pious man). Additionally, employers regularly sought to cultivate their own religious credentials in order to situate themselves as trustworthy and morally astute members of the community who could be trusted in business and trade.

The reasons for the persistence of Muslim control over the upper levels of the industry and for the relatively high percentage of Muslims in the city's population are bound into a more complex history connected with the events of partition. Midway through my first spell of fieldwork, the family from whom I rented a small rooftop room introduced me to their neighbour, Mohammad Anwar. Anwar's life had been spent working in the wood industry. Now in his seventies, he had left the family's small wood workshop in the hands of his two sons. As we sat together in the *sahn* (courtyard) of my landlord's home, he recalled how, when he was a young boy of nine or ten years old, many families in the *mohallas* began preparing themselves for departure to Pakistan:

> In the rainy season when the flood comes everything goes with it. This was just like a flood. They were like sheep and blindly went. This was the fashion at that time: everyone wanted to flee from Saharanpur. One night in 1947 all Saharanpur's Muslims took the decision to go. They had the slogan 'We will empty this place'. It was not one person but like a wave: everyone wanted to go without thinking. One night in particular the atmosphere was so bad. Everyone was running here and there without thinking, shouting 'Allah-o-Akbar [God is greater]' and making an agitation. That night everyone packed bags and prepared to leave Saharanpur out of fear. It was like a flood, and everyone was sinking in that wave without thinking whether it was good or not.
>
> All the people packed their things and the date was fixed. But then from Deoband there came an important head from the madrassa. That was Maulana[4] Hussain. He was an old man. Maulana Hussain came and told the people 'please not to go'. He said that it is our country and that we are safe here. It was only the Maulana of Deoband who stopped it; he is the reason people are living here today.

I was there as I liked the Maulana very much. He was my role model and I wanted to see him. At that time, he was very popular; every boy had great respect for him. I was studying in the madrassa of the Maulana, where he was very famous. I was alone. I was in the middle of the *masjid* [mosque] in the *sahn* and could hear the speech easily. I was near the *hauz* [pond] in the *masjid*. The Maulana was in front of me and he spoke there. I could hear everything. In the *masjid* everyone took the decision not to go to Pakistan. His speech was very impressive.

We all knew about it, as one day earlier there was an announcement and it was said that that everyone should follow what he said. The announcement was made from rickshaws by mouth, there was no loudspeaker. They did it by *bhambu* [cupping of hands over mouth to shout]. At that time, it was very bad for the Muslims. They were running here and there and wanted to sell their household things. For example, if a thing had the cost of 1000 rupees it was selling at five rupees. Things were valueless at that time. Everyone wanted to sell. It was the people from Dehradun and Jwalapur who made this situation; otherwise everyone was living here peacefully. When they came, they made the atmosphere horrible as they had been beaten.

At that time the landowners were very rich. Their caste was Ghara; they were very wealthy as they had lots of land and property. Only two peoples had lots of land – one was the Hindu Gujjar and the second was Ghara Muslim – so they never wanted to go to Pakistan. The Ghara caste decided to stay. Also, the farmers and the orchard owners did not want to leave.

The wealthy Muslims wanted to buy the possessions of the poor. The people of Haridwar and Dehradun were like refugees. We helped them and gave them food in our *mohalla*. We fixed tents on the road for them. They also went to Pakistan, but in the time they were there we gave them food. They stayed for some time and then wanted to go. Before they came here people were not thinking of going to Pakistan, but when people saw that other Muslims were going they followed like sheep. But not everyone wanted to go; it was just some people who followed those outsiders.
[…]

Some people who were originally from Saharanpur came back from Pakistan after partition as they did not like Pakistan. They had no bond and followed no rule, so they came back. They had gone there silently and never announced to the government that they were going. In the same manner they came back from there. They were not citizens of Pakistan so they could do it easily. In my *mohalla* also some people returned. There was no rule about a border so they could cross very easily if they did not like it, and they could easily come here.

Only two [factory] owners from here went to Pakistan, but in Pakistan this business is very small-scale. After 1947 those two owners went there. They started business there. Before 1947 there wasn't this work in Pakistan. At that time in Saharanpur there were four factories which were the main factories in the woodcarving industries in Saharanpur. Most of the owners stayed here.

The primary protagonist in these events, Maulana Hussain Ahmad Madani (1879–1957), was a disciple of Mehmud al-Hasan (1851–1920), who had been among the first intake of students at Deoband after the madrassa was founded in 1866. Maulana Hussain was a major actor in India's independence struggle and went voluntarily into prison in Malta to remain with his mentor after the latter was implicated in the Silk Letters Conspiracy.[5] After returning, Maulana Hussain took up a post at Deoband. No text of the Saharanpur proclamation exists. There is, however, an account written by Maulana Hussain, about a speech he made in Delhi in 1938. In the speech he argued that Islam in India was compatible with 'composite nationalism', a concept that envisioned a united and independent India, which was embodied in the fabric of the state's ideas of co-dependency and conviviality between various faiths. While recognising certain problematic areas, the Maulana argued that

> [t]he assumption that Islam and its adherents cannot confederate and interact with any other system is unacceptable. Although Islamic jurisdiction and sharia contains written views on several matters, there remain uncountable things that are allowed, and in which each person is free to act upon as per his own expediency. Among these are kingdoms, their ordinances and organisations, etc. … They [the British] do not want Muslims to participate in composite nationalism and become a united force in launching the freedom struggle that may prove the catalyst in overthrowing the British government.
> (Madnī 2005 [1938]: 133–4, 151–2)

The influence of the Maulana of Deoband was such that many who had been preparing to depart changed their minds, ensuring sufficient security to attract others fleeing the bloodshed and providing sustenance and shelter to the influx of Muslim refugees. The compassion shown to those arriving in Saharanpur by existing Muslim residents was often mentioned in the accounts of partition I collected. It was also a part of contemporary thinking on what defines a *sharīf* (noble/high-born/honourable) person and how *mehman* (guests, others) should be treated. The mass of refugees comprised those of various classes and *biradaris* (Muslim caste or community grouping), from artisans and labourers to the educated middle classes. Many initially took up residence at the roadsides and on empty grounds but gradually became more integrated within the local population. These events, then, were central to the production of the sense of 'throwntogetherness' (Massey 2005) detailed in the introduction of this book. The consequence of Saharanpur's partition history was the development of spaces which, while relatively demarcated along religious lines, were composed of Muslims from various classes, *biradaris*, social backgrounds and occupations, and of different degrees of affluence. Mohammad Rizwan, who was introduced in the opening chapter of this book, was one of those whose family, in this case his father and uncle, had fled from other areas to seek refuge in Saharanpur:

> Many years ago, in Yamuna Nagar, we had a *dilai* factory [metal forge]. That factory belonged to my father, but suddenly partition began, and my grandfather went to Pakistan. On the journey he was killed. My father's sister was also killed in an accident. My father forgot some money in his house at Yamuna Nagar. It was 1500 rupees. He forgot it as he had to run away suddenly. Then my father's sister went to his house to take that money, but those people killed her. Fifteen hundred rupees then is like 15 lakh [15 x 100,000] rupees today.
>
> My father and my uncle came to Saharanpur from Yamuna Nagar. At that time the River Yamuna was full, and they came by swimming. My uncle and my father lived in the forest on the bank of the Yamuna, as they were fearful. They had no relatives in or link with Saharanpur. They met some people who said, 'Let's go to Saharanpur, as there are a large number of Muslims there; you will be safe there'. They met in Yamuna Nagar and they told them to come, as Saharanpur was safe for Muslims. Finally, my father and my uncle arrived here, and many Muslims helped them. Some gave food and others clothes, many helped them, and my father and my uncle also married in Saharanpur.
>
> In the old days people were very gentle and helpful. Now, though, times have changed, and no one wants to help the poor.

First, they were just labour. They carried bricks, material and cement. Then they went back to Ambala [a town around 100 km from Saharanpur] for work. My grandfather was killed there, and my father was emotionally attached to the place as it was the birthplace of my father and my grandfather. Then my father built a house in Ambala and started to live there. Then, again, he came back to Saharanpur and we learned the woodwork in Saharanpur. My father lived in Ambala. We brothers came back to Saharanpur to learn this work. Each week he came here to watch over us as Ambala is close by.

Living in 'Hindustan': the mohallas since Independence

The events of partition had a profound effect on Saharanpur's *mohallas*, but the intervening years also saw a variety of economic and political changes that impacted on the city's wood cluster and on other craft-based industries across India. Often this process was twofold: some sectors saw decline and the movement of artisans into informal and petty trades, while others experienced the growing integration of artisan labour into Fordist-orientated craft manufacture. In Kanpur, for example, the textile industry saw a steep decline from the 1960s onwards, and many workers moved into informal-sector employment (Joshi 1999). Hein Streefkerk (1985), on the other hand, details the increasing integration of artisans into industrial activity during the post-colonial period, not through direct employment, but via the adaptation of their skills and the conversion of their workshops into spaces that produced goods for non-craft-based sectors of the economy. In Saharanpur the wood industry remained buoyant but became increasingly geared towards export. Mohammad Raheem, one of the largest manufacturers in the city, explained the trajectory of the family business as they moved from indirect to direct export:

> First [my grandfather] bought wood pieces and made his own work for the local market in Saharanpur. He made rolling pins for local supply. Then my grandfather met a customer from Moradabad. Slowly he started their orders; these were for export but went through that Moradabad customer. The second chance was my father's. He got a German customer from Delhi and suddenly he started exporting to Germany. That was in 1965. The importer from Germany was looking for fine work. At that time our *tikai* work [fine-grained carving] was very famous. The German came here

and saw a labourer sitting on the road. He asked about his work, as it was very good, and where he got it. The labourer said, 'I am just a labourer. It is the work of Anwar Saleem and not mine.' Then he took the customer into our workshop. My father got that order as the quality of his work was the best. Nowadays the quality of the work is very bad. After that his business started to grow and we got a second order, from Japan. It was a big deal from Japan, and we got a big order from them. After this, in 1984, I separated from my father and started my business. In 1989 I started my first business for export outside India, to go to Japan. Now, though, most of my work is to go to Europe.

While Raheem's family gained opportunities based on initial advancement in the colonial period, others had a different experience. Rizwan took me to meet his *mamu* (maternal uncle), Mohammed Shahzad Ansari, a friendly man in his sixties. He welcomed me into the small workshop where his three sons and two other boys were employed as *shāgirds* (apprentices). Above the workshop the family had living quarters. Between the two was a grate for air to pass. Through this Mohammad Shahzad called for tea and snacks. Their work consisted of orders outsourced from large producers. Mohammad Shahzad explained that they preferred this arrangement to working in the factories as they could get work from several places and keep a steadier flow of orders. Having spent eight years learning *tikai* work he began taking outsourced orders from the factories in the early 1970s. At this time there were few people in the industry, and he explained that they produced a lot for domestic consumption as well as export. Now, he said, it was different. Work came from overseas but only large factories got the orders. The small artisans, he complained, did not have knowledge or access to tools such as the internet, so were unable to engage directly with international trade. According to Mohammad Shahzad, the period when some could transition to a local capitalist class (T. Roy 1993) had now come to an end, as a new socio-economic differentiation was becoming ingrained in the community.

As we sipped tea, Mohammad Shahzad recalled that the export trade went through a particularly large expansion from about 1975,[6] when

foreigners started to come and place orders with some *kārīgars*. As a result, the industry grew quickly, and many people started to learn the trade. Some *kārīgars* started to employ many workers and became *maliks* [bosses, employers]. This only happened to lucky

NETWORKS, LABOUR AND MIGRATION AMONG INDIAN MUSLIM ARTISANS

ones who were, by chance, approached by foreigners. While there were more successful *kārīgars* from the start with larger workshops, they were still *kārīgars*. It was only from this time that the gap grew and their position in the community changed. Today it is much harder, as existing owners have a strong position and control access to the export markets. Now others can't make the same transition.

Despite this, Mohammad Shahzad's business was good and his workshop buzzed with the incessant tapping that was the constant accompaniment to woodwork. He explained that things had not always been so. In the early 1980s, following a downturn, he found himself pulling a rickshaw for a year. This, he argued, was due to an influx of workers which was not matched by a growth in work, but also due to the closing of some large sawmills by Rajiv Gandhi. At this time people started to go out of the city for work, as there was little in Saharanpur and other cities could offer better earnings. For those who stayed, things were hard, and many went into other forms of labour. Although conditions had improved since then, the rickshaw remained sitting in a corner as a kind of memento and, he said, as an insurance policy in case hard times came again.

Before this period, rapid expansion had led to the arrival of new workers from outlying villages and towns. They were commuters initially, but in some cases the influx resulted in outlying areas becoming wood-manufacturing spaces in their own right. Mehboob Ansari from the nearby town of Chilkana was among the first commuters to begin travelling into the city. Born after Independence, in 1949, he started working in the industry around 1965. He had initially worked in mango orchards, which his family took on rent from local landowners:

> My father realised that woodwork would be nice for us, so he decided to send me for work in this line. Five of us went to Saharanpur for work. We did different jobs such as *chilai* [carving], cutting and some machine work, each according to his wish. I learnt the work with my *ustād*. He was also Ansari [tailor] caste and was very nice. I had more than one *ustād* in my training until I became perfect in the work. [After finishing my training] I worked for seven years in Saharanpur, first in a factory and then in a shop. … In the factory there were six cutting machines, six people for *chilai*, some for *tikai* and some carpenters. In total there were about 50 to 55 people and four of us were from Chilkana. There were many castes in the factory. Nine or ten of us were Ansari and the rest were Teli, Kamboh

and Ghara [Muslim *biradari* names]. Ansari were the greater number; Ansari people are very gentle. [When I started my own work in the shop] it was in Sakko ko Mohalla. My partner was Qureshi [Muslim butcher *biradari*] and we set up some cutting machines. The shop was on rent and we took three machines on rent also. Then I thought it would be good to start a line [network] here in Chilkana. It was very small-scale. Here I started training some other boys. We never showed greediness, we never took money, we gave them their money and kept our profit in our pocket. Gradually the chain started here in Chilkana and the boys taught other boys. In this way the network came into existence. But, you know, after some years there were many craftsmen in Chilkana and there was not enough work, so some went again to Saharanpur for work.

While the wood industry continued to draw many commuters into the city, Chilkana still retained a local manufacturing network. Much of this work was carried out alongside agricultural production, with craftworkers moonlighting in different roles. The ability of rurally located artisans to command more than one source of income contrasted with Saharanpur itself, where craftspeople had less access to alternative sources of income and were much more reliant on wood manufacture alone. This was a point that my *ustād*, Mohammad Islam, emphasised as problematic. He complained that the influx of labour from rural areas drove down earnings, as villagers had lower expenses and other sources of income, meaning that they could work for lower rates than the city-based craftsmen, a context that was actively played upon by factory owners and other employers to drive down wages (cf. S. Sen 1999).

Other factors, such as new technologies, policy changes and communal upheavals, also interplayed in driving forms of flux and transformation within the industry. Mohammad Shahid was an elderly woodcarving *kārīgar* based in Purāni Mandi. He sat in a small workshop sandwiched between showrooms close to the entrance of the market. Here he spent his days doing various odd jobs, making a somewhat eccentric selection of objects which he occasionally sold. As we chatted, two of his friends joined us. The three elderly men cracked jokes and chuckled at my questions, although they answered kindly and with a smile. Mohammad Shahid spent many years as a cutting-machine operator and recalled how expansions in exports and the introduction of new technologies, in particular the arrival of powered large *āra* (bandsaw) and small *ārī* (fretsaw) cutting machines, affected the atmosphere in which he laboured:

When I started the work with the *ustād* I would sometimes take some work to my home in the evening and cut the wood by *ārī* machine. It was hard as there was no power and I had to work by candlelight, but I could earn a little extra money. It was very good work at the time I started.

First, just one *āra* machine came here, and in that machine they cut the wood for the partitions. Many people were influenced by it, as it can do the work in a short time. First, Syyed Hasan bought the *āra* machine. That machine was second-hand as he got it from a factory that closed suddenly. Then others thought the same. Because of the *āra* machine production in Saharanpur was increased.

The carving work is by hand, but if you want to make pieces then you go to the machine, as it can do it quickly. Until fifty years ago, if we wanted to cut a piece it took a full day. First, we did the work by hand but then after some time the *āra* machine came here and because of this production increased and our handsaw became useless. My hammer also disappeared at this time! I still do not know who took it! [The other men laughed at this joke.]

Before the machines we could cut the wood by hand. It was very interesting work to cut the wood as, while cutting, we could gossip. Fifty years ago we had lots of work and were never without. After the machines came everything became faster and the pressure was greater. This happened to the carvers too, as they had the pressure of extra wood supply and many new people came into the work.

Powered production and various ups and downs reflect the broader contradictory position occupied by craftworkers in post-independence India. On the one hand policy favoured state-orchestrated industrialisation, and on the other there was an identification of craft products as linked with the independence struggle. While the Nehruvian vision favoured the former and promoted centralised industrial planning, the craft sector remained a major part of the economy. The government provided various grants and programmes aimed at supporting traditional craft production and artisan work (Venkatesan 2009). This encouraged producers to try and ensure that they could be identifiable as craft- or artisan workers, thereby gaining access to these awards and schemes, a feature that continues today (Mohsini 2010; Venkatesan 2009). For Muslim artisans there was also access to government programmes, but this was lower than that obtained by their Hindu counterparts (Mohsini 2010). While the number of Muslims in artisan industries is high, the level of ownership and self-employment is far lower (Harriss-White 2002).

Although Saharanpur's wood industry had continued growing over recent years in terms of the numbers in the workforce and of output, a subjective sense of decline penetrated the narratives of many in the *mohallas*. For older individuals, this was woven into a nostalgia for a lost 'golden age', an affective sense that has been documented in many of north India's Muslim craft industries (Kumar 2017; Mohsini 2010). As one elderly *karigār*, who undertook brass inlay work in the *mohalla* of Khatakheri, bemoaned, 'This was golden work but now it is dust!' Nandini Gooptu (2001) connects this pattern to the broader socio-economic process of marginalisation, which creates 'a growing sense of insecurity and dislocation, and often an actual or dreaded loss of … status as independent artisans [so that the Muslim artisanal and service classes] increasingly drew upon the idea of Muslim decline and came to construct and imagine their past in terms of a proud and idealised heritage' (p. 260). Notions of a once great past are not exclusive to Indian Muslims, but also feature more broadly in discourses regarding a 'bygone age' across the Muslim world, and form an important part of the drive by various reformist movements to recover a 'pristine Islam' based on the era of the Prophet and unpolluted by the ravages of western colonialism (J. Ali 2003; F. Osella & C. Osella 2013).

Nostalgia, then, constitutes a powerful affective background within the *mohallas*, particularly for those of older generations. While these feelings are rooted in very material forms of decline, loss of status and intensifying socio-economic marginalisation, the wood industry itself is not the fading artisanal sector described in accounts of various craft industries in India (e.g. Kumar 2017; Sivramkrishna 2009; Wilkinson-Weber 1999; Mohsini 2010; N. Gupta 2011; Haynes 2012), and nor does it fit within earlier arguments focused upon the 'de-industrialisation' and 'peasantisation' of village-based artisans during the colonial era (see Gādgīl 2013 [1929]; Bagchi 1976). Although not necessarily a reflection of improving conditions for labour, the scale of the industry and the fact that it continues to attract young male recruits – men aged 18 to 34 comprise around 69 per cent of the labour force[7] – suggest that wood production in the city continues to expand, at least in terms of labour recruitment. This ongoing growth has contributed not only to the city's urban sprawl (cf. Fazal 2000) but also to the level of diversity amongst Muslim craftworkers by sucking in labour from outlying villages. Drawing on this, and on the earlier discussions of partition, the following section expands further on the contemporary constitution of the *mohallas'* residents and the woodworking labour force in terms of *biradari* (caste/group).

Stratification and biradari: a mixed scene

Biradari-based divisions can be formulated around three primary group-ings: *Ashraf* (elites claiming lineage from the disciples of the Prophet), *Ajlaf* (converts from mid-ranking Hindu castes) and *Arzal* (Dalit con-verts). This structure, though, is not as strongly enforced as is 'caste': many Islamic reformist movements emphasise the egalitarian nature of Islam and actively oppose *biradari*-based identities. At the same time, some groups have sought to reaffirm identifiers of 'caste' status in order to access resources and reservations offered by the state to Backward Castes (BC) and Other Backward Castes (OBC). This has led to the emer-gence of political and representative organisations that claim to be the voice of '*Dalit* [low-caste/untouchable] Muslims' (see Bashir & Wilson 2017; Irfan Ahmad 2003).

As with caste, the status of various *biradaris* is under constant con-struction. Imtiaz Ahmad (1978) details how in Allahabad in the 1970s the Sheikh Siddique *biradari* launched a campaign to claim *Ashraf* line-age, despite descending from Kayastha (scribe-caste) Hindus. Likewise, Ansaris (weavers) have attempted to develop an *Ashraf* descent narrative (S. K. Rai 2013), although some Ansari politicians in Saharanpur are now shifting their strategy towards claiming OBC status in order to access res-ervations. During my fieldwork, a campaign was under way for Teli (the oil-pressing caste) to rename themselves with the more regal-sounding '*Malik*'. The redefining of caste/*biradari* identity has been characterised as *ashrafisation* and runs parallel to *sanskritisation* among Hindus; it involves a reconfiguring of ritual and rules to reflect actual or attempted social mobility (Metcalf 1999). This plays out in complex ways. Edward Simpson (2006b), for example, describes how Gujarati shipyard masters of the *Bhadala biradari* used reformist Islam to challenge the influence of *Saiyeds*[8] in order to reinforce their newly established social position and gain greater control over their labour force.

Many accounts of Muslim craft industries describe *biradari* as being key to the constitution of labour forces. Mehta (1997), for example, describes an Ansari[9] weaving community in Barabanki (Uttar Pradesh) who work within the traditional confines of the caste group. Goodfriend (1983: 136, cited in Ruthven 2008: 30) suggests: 'Historically, *biraderis* with occupational specialisations also functioned as guilds, regulating access to training, transmission of trade secrets and skills and employ-ment.' The demographic make-up of the labour force in Saharanpur, how-ever, does not fit these descriptions of homogeneous craft communities.

Ansari (25.7 per cent) and Teli (31 per cent) were the most common identities subscribed to by craftworkers and others in the wood industry, but a large number of other *biradaris* were also present.[10] The founding artisans arrived from Kashmir during the Mughal era, but it was more recently that others began to engage in woodcarving and other trades. A woodcarver in a gully close to where I worked with my *ustād*, Mohammad Islam, said:

> [Before partition] the oil extraction industry was down, and many Telis moved into this [wood]work as it was then booming. They worked as labourers but over the years some have become owners and exporters. The change of caste name to Malik was not a big thing, these people just did not want to be called Teli any more. They did it to show their wealth as these people did not want to be associated with the caste.

Despite the mixed nature of Saharanpur's workforce, perceptions of certain 'qualities' pertaining to *biradari* remain:

> The character of the Ansari is to be helpful and honest. They want to progress but cannot. If an Ansari discusses a business with someone of another caste, that person will say the business idea is stupid, but later he will take the idea and do it himself, so the Ansari loses.
>   (Elderly craftworker in Chilkana)

Although the labour force was diverse and *karigārs* were usually happy to train *shāgirds* (apprentices) of different *biradaris* in their workshops, cross-*biradari* marriage was often seen as undesirable and could result in the couple being ostracised by family and community. Islam's neighbour, Farīd Malik, had a cousin standing for local election. I attended a party the cousin had organised for the neighbourhood to boost his standing and garner votes. Food was served in three sittings. Large numbers of guests enjoyed his hospitality, for which he bore a substantial cost. Farīd Malik, however, told me that he would not be elected as his cross-*biradari* marriage had damaged his reputation.

While the relative weakness of *baradari*-based identities in areas beyond marriage provides a different account from some other contributions (e.g. Mann 1992), there remains a degree of tension between notions of egalitarian brotherhood and other conceptions of community. Even Rizwan's son, Yousef, at the age of 18, was aware of these frictions:

Our parents tell us that we should marry in our own caste. This is very strict for every child in Muslim society. But I don't think this should be so as our religion does not say this. I don't think this is such a big thing in today's society. In Saudi if someone loves a girl they can marry that girl. There is no caste system there and they don't worry about Ansari or Teli.

Actually, the caste system is made by society. Some castes believe they are powerful, but others believe they are gentle. Our caste is the simplest caste. Allah sent the Prophet. He had great power and knew who was Hindu or Muslim. If you were in front of the Prophet, he could tell if you are Christian or Hindu. But he never told us about caste, so how can we believe in this. It is my wish that there should be no caste system as all men [sic] are equal in the eyes of Allah. God has not made this, but it is only humans and now they proudly say, 'Oh we are Khan' or 'We are Ansari', but this is a very wrong thing for our society.

While later chapters in this book are not structured around a *biradari*-based analysis, it aids the reader to gain a sense of the diversity of those engaged in the industry, as this is a key component in constituting the 'thrown-togetherness' (Massey 2005) of the *mohallas*. It also challenges potential assumptions, which result from *biradari* dominance in many craft industries, that the system forms a primary structuring feature. It is present, but other forces are far more significant, not least underlying communal tensions, which have, in part, contributed to the movement of Muslims of various levels of social status into the *mohalla* neighbourhoods.

Communal relations in contemporary Saharanpur: a *'bhut'* comes to call

While Saharanpur has not seen the levels of communal violence experienced in some other areas of India, such as Gujarat, moments of conflict are a periodic feature of urban life in the city.[11] Substantial tensions flared up during the debate about the Babri Masjid mosque in Ayodhya and its subsequent destruction in 1992 (A. A. Engineer 1995). In July 2014, during a return visit I made to the city, violence erupted over some disputed land in the central area of the city. The Singh Sabha Gurdwara (Sikh temple), located close to the railway station, had purchased some land to expand its facilities. However, a former Member of the Legislative Assembly (MLA) claimed that the land was in fact owned by the state *wakf* (Muslim charitable trust) board and had earlier been donated to a local *masjid*. On 26 July riots broke out and the two parties engaged in clashes across the city, in which three people died. During an earlier period of fieldwork, colour thrown at a *masjid* during the Hindu festival of Holi triggered another period of violence. Such moments may have been ignited by specific flashpoints, but they were also the result of a deeper set of tensions that lay beneath the surface of everyday life.

Stories of *bhuts* (ghosts) are common in the city, but one recent apparition was revealing. The *bhut* took the form of a large cat which attacked people during Ramadan in the summer of 2009. The *bhut* had the power to change its shape at will, transforming into human or other animal forms. The *bhut* received widespread attention, even attracting media reporters to the gullies where it had appeared. Television news reports from the time tell of a controversial 'tantric baba' (holy man)[12] coming to the city claiming that 40 ghost cats were now residing in the body of a young girl. She was forced to 'vomit' these apparitions out, after which they were buried, and the city was thus freed of the scourge (*Headlines Today* 2009). While the media presented the infestation as threatening all communities, it was the Muslim neighbourhoods that were primarily affected. This, along with the fact that the spirit, or spirits, appeared during Ramadan, led to rumours that the *bhut* had been conjured up by Hindus intent on disrupting the holy month. While it is tempting to consider such events only in the local or national context, communal tensions do not exist independently of global connections. The Indian media and sections of the political elite often make a great deal of foreign influences in the Muslim community, particularly when discussing terrorism or 'Islamification'. These conflicts are affected not just by political or religious agendas, but also by economic and global processes. Control of certain industries (Wilkinson 2006), or changing wealth dynamics, such as income generated through Gulf migration, can also give rise to frictions, which become intensified as neoliberal reforms drive precarity and uncertainty (I. Chatterjee 2009; Siddiqui 2017), albeit in ways that are often ambivalent and opaque (e.g. Osellass & Osella 2011; Oza 2012).

Saharanpur, craftwork and liberalisation

While change, transformation, precarity and insecurity have long been characteristics of craft sectors in India and elsewhere, the economic liberalisations of the 1980s, culminating in Manmohan Singh's budget of 1991, which effectively ended decades of protectionism and opened India to international corporations and finance, have impacted upon clusters such as Saharanpur's wood industry in a variety of ways. Persisting flux in craft sectors across the country continues to produce transformations that have led to increasing competition (Cunningham et al. 2005; Hussain 2016; Mohsini 2016), triggered efforts to orientate craft sectors towards global markets (Clifford 2018), and seen some sectors pushed out of the marketplace, unable to compete with mass-produced goods from elsewhere (M. A. Qureshi 1990; Scrase 2003). This is not a pattern exclusive to India. Karin Tice (1995), for example, describes how Kuna craftwork from Panama was copied and mass-produced in China, only to be sold back to markets in Central America at a cost that undercut local producers. Paul Stoller (2008) has illuminated even more complex circuits, in which Ghanaian *kente* cloth (a traditional patterned-silk clothing material) is replicated in cheap cotton in Asian-run factories in New York. The copies were copied again by producers back in Ghana who had previously worked in expensive silk. The Ghanaian producers in turn outsourced production to Benin and Côte d'Ivoire to drive down costs.

Concerns about the threat of mass production, particularly from China, were often articulated by those at the upper ends of the local supply chain, such as exporters and wholesalers. Lower-level workers and *karigārs* felt these concerns more in terms of uncertainty and anxiety, as shifts in global demand and alterations in movements of capital and commodities filtered through into the gullies and produced unpredictable downturns and upturns in demand. Yet, as I detail later in this book (see chapter 6), liberalisation and its associated neoliberal transformations are not limited to the structural context but filter through to a more subjective level, transforming (albeit unevenly) ways of seeing and being in the world amongst those engaged in wood production (cf. Jeffery et al. 2005). Additionally, pressures from global markets to drive down costs have led to reconfigurations of labour – reconfigurations which often act to suppress wages, increase flexibility and cultivate embedded forms of discipline.

Before we turn to these matters in more detail in the following chapter, recent events which have played out over the three years during which this book was being written warrant some further note, specifically those concerning the '*bhut*' of communal tension. The rise of the right, the entrenchment of the BJP in Uttar Pradesh and at the national level, the targeting of Muslims through citizenship checks in the north-east, the rescinding of Article 380 of the Indian Constitution – which provided Kashmir with a degree of autonomy – the introduction of the Citizenship Amendment

Act (CAA) and proposals for a National Register of Citizens (NRC) have further intensified not just an underlying sense of marginalisation but also expressions of fear and anxiety embodied in both explicit and tacit ways. This intensification includes an increasing desire to perform 'Indianness' through displays of loyalty to the nation and the flag. Amongst the plethora of material circulating in the numerous WhatsApp groups initiated by residents of the *mohallas*, and in other forms of social media, are images and videos of Muslims raising the Indian flag or engaging in expressions of national identity. These zealous performances of Indianness embody many of the anxieties that emerge from being the 'other' within a nation state that increasingly depicts Muslims as a threat to national sovereignty and security. Within this affective pool of circulations, however, another set of images and imaginaries is being produced which seeks to cultivate communal harmony and conviviality. Videos of local Muslim residents providing food and water to Hindu pilgrims undertaking the Kanwar

Figure 2.2   A residential gully in the wood *mohallas*. Source: author.

Yatra,[13] and images of food sharing across religious divides and of children from both communities playing together are also commonplace. As spatial slippages between material and virtual worlds open (Miller 2005), so the negotiations and contestations and forms of bordering and marginalisation play out not only in urban space but also in the machinations of digital technologies and algorithms (cf. Lowrie 2018; Chambers forthcoming).

Conclusion

This recent and older history of Saharanpur represents a complex ensemble to think through the ways in which production, capitalism and the supply chain are embedded within a Muslim craftworking community,

Figure 2.3   A young woodcarver at work. Source: author.

in which both communal and individual histories have shaped the economic and social environment. Saharanpur provides some challenges to the 'standard story' of artisanal decline and Muslim marginalisation, considerations which have been drawn out here, but which also feed through into the following chapters. Reconfigurations, changes and transformations, along with certain significant continuities, have been a part of this story. The background provided in this chapter is also essential to a historicisation of the political economy of craft production in the city today. It is to this political economy, along with the forms of embeddedness within more intimate sets of relations, that the next chapter turns, through a detailed ethnographic engagement with the wood-manufacturing supply chain.

Notes

1. Those claiming descent from the Prophet; often used by Muslim nobility and elite groups in north India and Pakistan.
2. Artisan trades dominated by low-caste Hindu labour, such as the Jatavs in Agra's footwear industry, experienced similar relations with Punjabi wholesalers and exporters (Knorringa 1999).
3. Source: author's fieldwork surveys.
4. A maulana is a scholar of Islam.
5. 'The Silk Letters Conspiracy, or Case, was a plot by a small clique of Indian Pan-Islamists located in Afghanistan, India and the Hijaz to overthrow British rule in India during the First World War' (Kelly 2013: 162).
6. As described earlier, there was also substantial export activity dating back to the colonial period.
7. Source: fieldwork surveys.
8. Saintly figures claiming genealogy from the Prophet. They occupy the highest (*Ashraf*) stratum of society.
9. The Ansari caste has two roots, one claiming descent from the Ansar of Medina, the other being weavers who converted to Islam during Mughal rule. In Uttar Pradesh the latter form the vast majority.
10. Source: fieldwork surveys.
11. These are not limited to Muslim/Hindu conflict: there has also been substantial violence between caste groups, particularly between the Thakur Rajput and Dalit communities.
12. A holy man claiming possession of mystical power, in this case a holy man of Muslim Sufi affinity.
13. The Kanwar Yatra is an annual pilgrimage in honour of Shiva. It involves carrying the water of the Ganges from holy sites along this river to Shiva temples across India. It can mean walking hundreds of miles. Each July sees large numbers of Kānvarias (devotees) pass through Saharanpur en route to cities like Haridwar and to the Himalayan source of the river at Gangotri and Gaumukh.

3
The Indian craft supply chain: money, commodities and intimacy

Figure 3.1   The Craft Fair at Noida's Expo Mart Centre.
Source: author.

In early 2012 I journeyed to Greater Noida, an isolated outlier of Delhi. Travelling on the metro to the end of the line, I took a rickshaw for the remaining 25 km, through sprawling low-level developments, to the expansive Expo Mart centre, which was hosting the Indian Handicrafts and Gifts Fair. As I had come directly from the woodworking gullies, the centre was a scene change. Smartly dressed Arabs, Asians and westerners assembled to obtain samples and place orders for multinational companies and smaller businesses. Having been unable to reach my contact, Abdul Malik, by phone, I arrived without a pass. At the first entrance, I was confronted and turned away. At the second I walked alongside a group of European buyers and passed unchallenged. It took time wandering around sections of the large tented exhibition hall, which was erected outside the main building, before I came upon Abdul's stand. I had first met Abdul in the courtyard of his factory – 'Fancy Wood Crafts' – set amongst villages around Saharanpur, two months earlier. Now he was busy meeting buyers, but he motioned me to sit at the corner of his stand while he discussed orders with two European women representing a French firm.

The Expo Mart in Greater Noida, which provides an intersection for craft industries and international buyers, is the starting point for this chapter, in which I explore the supply chain's layers of 'putting out', subcontracting and brokerage, and the connections therein. Beginning with exporters, wholesalers and large-scale factories, the chapter descends through layers of subcontracting, brokerage and smaller workshops to individual craftspeople and homeworkers. Throughout, two sets of connections are given attention: connections between people and connections constituted around money to trace the embeddedness of the supply chain from the structural to the intimate and from the global to the local. The political economy of craftwork in the city is mediated within the context of the enclaving and marginalising forces laid out in the opening of this book; this makes a particular impact by blurring class relations through the production of an increasingly fragmented supply chain within which the actors who mediate manufacture are often ambiguous, overlapped and interlocked.

The degrees of embeddedness produced have been a central narrative for understanding the 'informal sector' (e.g. Hart 1973), bazaar-based economies (e.g. Geertz 1978) and craft industries (e.g. Carrier 1992; White 2004), which are often represented as sitting at the intersection of 'traditional' and capitalist modes of production. Of course, the notion of a 'great divide' or dichotomy between pre-capitalist and capitalist economies has long been critiqued (Latour 2012), and recent contributions have illustrated the embeddedness of 'formalised', bourgeois and technologically advanced economic spaces (e.g. Ho 2009; Sassen 2005; Zaloom 2003; Granovetter 1985) along with the forms of social 're-embedding' that intertwine with neoliberal economic transformations (e.g. Mollona 2009; Shever 2008, 2012). Such critiques have led to a deconstruction of Karl Polanyi's 'great transformation', although this has tended to render everything (capitalist, non-capitalist and pre-capitalist) as embedded rather than turning back to the multiple economic rationalities which dominated earlier functionalist anthropology (e.g. Mauss 2002; Malinowski 1920). While not wishing to descend into a potted history of economic anthropology and well-trodden formalist vs substantivist debates, I use Polanyi (1968) as a jumping-off point from which to approach the supply chain. As Polanyi argues,

> Aristotle was right: man [sic] is not an economic, but a social being. He does not aim at safeguarding his individual interest in the acquisition of material possessions, but rather at ensuring social good will, social status, social assets. ... *Man's economy is, as a rule, submerged in his social relations.*
>
> (Polanyi 1968: 65; emphasis in original)

This chapter's inquiry into the embeddedness of Saharanpur's woodworking supply chain, then, draws on a universal – the argument that all economies are embedded – but is primarily focused on the particularities, internal diversities, social relations and forms of intimacy through which local production networks are mediated. Supply chains represent sites within which a variety of objects, processes, bodies, ethics, technologies and regimes are assembled in the pursuit of commodity production and wealth accumulation (e.g. Mezzadri 2016; Tsing 2016; Dolan & Rajak 2016; Carswell & De Neve 2013b). The supply chain also allows for forms of enquiry which explore the ways in which global processes fragment into the local and the particular (Tsing 2009). In this chapter, I follow Anna Tsing (2009, 2012, 2016) in arguing that global supply chains form part of the complex fabric of late capitalism, characterised and facilitated not by homogeneity, but by heterogeneity, a variety of cultural and economic niches, and diverse, often deeply embedded, modalities of labour discipline and control. An empirical engagement with the supply chain thus becomes a means by which to connect processes of global integration with local diversity, and to explore the organisational styles and subjectivities that allow global capitalism to thrive (Tsing 2009). It also enables us to track both the reconfigurations enacted by movements of capital and the ways in which capital accommodates itself to localised cultural and social formations (Harvey & Krohn-Hansen 2018).

These empirical engagements with supply chains around the globe are underpinned by an expanding body of ethnographic and other research, dealing specifically with the Indian context, which has focused on the political economy of what have been variously called supply chains, global production networks (GPNs), global commodity chains (GCCs) and labour regimes. This literature has done much to broaden our understanding of the variegated modalities, degrees of formality and informality and forms of embeddedness through which accumulation takes place and domestic and global markets are serviced (e.g. Horner & Murphy 2018; Mezzadri 2016; De Neve 2014a; Carswell & De Neve 2013b; Gooptu 2001, 2013; Cross 2010; Harriss-White 2003; Harriss-White & Gooptu 2009; Breman 1999, 2004). While the descriptive focus of this chapter does not allow scope to detail the structural debates within this literature in depth,[1] taken together these contributions illustrate the complexity of, and the ambiguity inherent in, the analysis of any network of production (however this might be theoretically imagined) within the Indian context.

Even very formal sectors, such as state-run industries, are characterised by slippages between the formal and informal as workers moonlight beyond the factory (Parry 2003). 'Formal' sites of labour may intersect structurally with informal forms of production (De Neve 2005) which enable formal sector employers to pay less because their employees' subsistence costs are underwritten by other petty earnings beyond the workplace (e.g. S. Sen 1999). Thus, structural continuity across the 'formal' and 'informal', within both economic (e.g. Narayana 2006; De Neve 2005; Breman 1999) and political (e.g. A. Gupta 1995; Agarwala 2013) contexts, produces modalities of production enabled through intersections of class, caste, gender, ethnicity, religion and other identities (Harriss-White 2003) which straddle the spheres of production and social reproduction (Mezzadri 2016). In other words, any empirical engagement with supply chains in India must deal with this diversity and take into account interlocking and overlapping modalities of discipline, control and resistance.

In the ethnographic material that follows, I seek to locate the narratives of various actors in the wood supply chain who connect the global to the local (cf. Tsing 2009). Thus, this section adds a scalar dimension to the historical context outlined in the previous chapter. Many of the actors described in the following material inhabit liminal spaces fraught with contradictions and tensions. Manufacturers and exporters occupy positions of power but also, as Muslims, experience spatial/socio-economic marginalisation (Galonnier 2012) and play out obligations to the community through performances of charity and patronage (cf. F. Osella & C. Osella 2009). *Thēkēdārs* (labour contractors) sit in an uneasy locality between workers and owners, their connections to labour often overlapping with friendship, kin and other affiliations. Artisans and workers may double as *thēkēdārs*, playing out a duality of roles. Petty manufacturers emerge precariously from the labour force only to fall back again as tenuous ventures fold under a burden of credit. Money, debt and degrees of labour bondage penetrate the supply chain at every level and intermingle with more intimate connections and embedded obligations of family, kin, friendship and neighbourhood. In a nutshell, this chapter argues that humans are indeed 'social beings' (Polanyi 1968) but that the economic can never be disaggregated from the social, just as the social cannot be severed from the economic: it is their co-constitution that is inherent to the human condition.

Kārkhānadars, wholesalers and exporters

I had got to know Abdul Malik, a *kārkhānadar* (factory owner), over a period of several months. Beginning with an interview in the court-yard of his sprawling factory, he had gradually allowed me increasing access to various sections of the production line. The invitation to come with him to Delhi for the Expo Mart had arrived unprompted, but I was grateful for the opportunity to improve my understanding of the supply chain beyond the immediate locality of Saharanpur. Sites such as Noida's Expo Mart are significant, yet rarely focused on, infrastructural projects. Funded by the Indian state as a nodal hub for accessing global markets, the centre provided a sanitised, formalised site of connection between the dust, sweat, informality and messiness of craft production, and cor-porate capital. Access was limited to those in the supply chain with the financial capacity to pay the fees for a stand at handicraft fairs and other events. In my case, it was my whiteness and the assumptions bound up in post-colonial, ethicised roles within the space that allowed my surrep-titious entry.

Many of the stalls emphasised the 'handmade' value of their items, playing on an aesthetic that commodified 'authenticity' (cf. Heller et al. 2017) and allowed international buyers to comfortably disregard systems of exploitation through the illusion of buying direct from the hands of native producers (cf. Wilkinson-Weber & DeNicola 2016). In other words, the Expo Mart comprised a key site within which the fetishisation of the craft commodity and the concealment of the underlying labour process (Marx 1990 [1867]) could be enabled. This was reinforced by the symbolic language of corporate social responsibility (CSR), a system of voluntary ethical regulation established by corporations in consultation with NGOs, international institutions, campaign groups and others as a response to consumer boycotts and protests in the 1990s over manufacturing condi-tions in the global assembly line (Dolan & Rajak 2016).

The underlying assemblages and impacts of CSR are often ambivalent (Dolan & Rajak 2016), and critiques have shown that CSR can act to stymie meaningful opposition to sweatshop labour regimes (Mezzadri 2016), create new forms of governmentality and constrain worker agency (De Neve 2014b). Although some larger factories in Saharanpur did deploy degrees of CSR within the workspace, the vast majority of the supply chain existed beyond forms of CSR intervention. Yet the language of CSR, or what Kirsch (2016) calls 'virtuous language', was a key part of the underlying discourse used by craft sellers and buyers at the Expo Mart. These deliberations were rarely explicit, but, as I watched, Abdul dropped markers of his awareness into discussions of production capacity, design availability and order fulfilment. Once the supply chain and its associated global flows had gone beyond this nodal infrastructure, however, they fragmented into the particularities and relative informality of the local, CSR often playing little part in production processes.

Abdul Malik's woodworking factory was located on the outskirts of Saharanpur. From the roadside, where one could often see a parked lorry with a shipping container attached, it looked modest. A large set of metal gates divided a length of rough brick wall that ran along the verge for 50 metres. Once I got past the *chaukidār* (gatekeeper, watchman), however, the scale of the factory became apparent. Manufacturing was organised along a production line arranged around various stages employing roughly 600 workers. The first stage dealt with raw wood, which would be cut using a large *āra* (bandsaw), a risky procedure and one that claimed many fingers and hands across the city. This was followed by spaces for *ārī* (small fretsaw) machine operators, woodcarvers, turners and carpenters. In a separate room, away from the dust of the factory floor, a dozen Muslim and Chamār (Hindu leather-working caste) women finished wood items: sanding, touching up, polishing and painting. At the other end of the room, around 15 women, along with some older men, packed completed pieces to be transferred to the container lorries for global distribution. The packing and finishing room was segregated from the rest of the factory, partly for practical reasons – wood dust and dirt could spoil the polish and the paint – but the segregation also symbolised a labour force divided along gender lines, with packing and finishing work seen as the lowest and worst-paid stratum of production.

While I return to questions of gender later in this chapter, and in subsequent material, I begin by describing the internal space of the factory in general terms and consider the modalities of production, discipline, control and contestation that constitute the production line. Manufacturers used systems of subcontracting to varying degrees, some outsourcing all work and others, such as Abdul, only some of it. However, despite limited outsourcing, a clearly demarcated space defined by high walls, the large steel entrance gate and processes of clocking in and out, the informality of the bazaar and modalities of craft production remained very much present within the factory (see also Breman 1999). The incorporation of the bazaar into this walled space meant that many of the socially embedded forms of labour discipline and control present within the gullies could also be activated within the factory context.

For factory owners, embedding the flexibility of the bazaar dealt tactically with various issues. *Kārīgars* (artisans) could operate with relative autonomy and would bring their own workers and *shāgirds* (apprentices) with them, thus handling the recruitment, disciplining, training and retention of labour. Such *kārīgars* were paid on piece rate and made their own separate arrangements with those who laboured under them. Importantly, this arrangement allowed artisans to present their labour as *apna kām* (own work) and thus retain the status of being independent rather than being relegated to the role of *mazdoor* (labourer) (see Chapter 6). *Thēkēdārs* were also commonplace – their role often blurred into that of *kārīgar* – and many brought workers with them with whom they had links through neighbourhood or family, again entrenching the embeddedness, forms of social control and informality of the bazaar within the factory space. These actors incorporated their own sets of relations with labour, but *kārīgars*, *thēkēdārs* and factory owners used a variety of other tactics to retain workers and build bonds of discipline. Chief among these was the use of advance payments as a form of *neo-bondage* which, through varying degrees of indebtedness, tied workers to employers, *thēkēdārs* and others.

Advance payments and neo-bondage in the supply chain[2]

In order to situate the significance of advance payments as a modality of labour discipline and control, it is necessary to engage with a broader literature on labour bondage and neo-bondage. The practice of giving (or pushing) and taking advance payments for work is common across low-pay sectors in India (Guérin et al. 2015), including rural migrant labour (Mosse et al. 2002), the garment industries (Carswell & De Neve 2013a; Mezzadri 2016) and construction (Srivastava 2005). While advance payments create degrees of bondage, ethnographic research shows that workers also deploy counter-tactics, for example by using migration as an exit strategy (Picherit 2012) or changing work location before the advance is repaid (De Neve 1999).

The use of advance payments is not restricted to Saharanpur's wood industry. Unfree labour, bonded labour and forms of neo-bondage remain central features of an Indian development model characterised by a highly flexible low-paid workforce, engaged primarily in labour-intensive industries (Breman 1996; Carswell & De Neve 2013a; Srivastava 2005). While there is debate regarding the degree to which neo-bondage, under late capitalism, can be seen as a continuation of older, feudal forms of bondage or as truly constituting 'unfree' labour (cf. Banaji 2003; Brass 2003; R. Das Gupta 1992; Lerche 2007; Rao 1999),[3] it can be variously reconfigured through engagements with contemporary supply chains. Carswell and De Neve (2013a), for example, discuss the decline of 'bonded' labour in agriculture, its re-emergence in power-loom work in Tamil Nadu, and the varying degrees to which it is personalised or monetised in different labouring contexts (cf. Harriss-White & Gooptu 2009; Breman 1999).

Despite these ambiguities, advance payments and other forms of neo-bondage are widely recognised as acting to undermine labour power and as stymieing class consciousness. Thus, such practices are often seen as a de-proletarianising force (Brass 1990; Carswell & De Neve 2013a; Frantz 2013; Lerche 2007) that depresses wage levels (Carswell & De Neve 2013a) and enables wealth extraction before employment has even started, by effectively charging workers to enter the labour force (Mezzadri 2016). Given this complexity, I follow recent literature by seeing advance payments not, in fixed terms, as a free/unfree dichotomy but as a continuum formed through varying degrees of coercion (Frantz 2013; Guérin 2013; Lerche 2007; Phillips 2013; Rogaly 2008). Additionally, I draw on Guérin (2013: 418) to acknowledge that advances are embroiled in broader processes in which 'poverty and discrimination remain primary "push" factors, [but] variable levels of economic and social exclusion and a diversity of labourers' constraints, rationale, motivations and forms of resistance ... also matter'.

In the context of Saharanpur's wood industry, then, woodworkers found themselves enmeshed within this continuum, within which advances provided a key tactic of coercion that enabled employers to push workers into undertaking overtime and additional work. Although employers used the system to retain labour, and workers often complained about dubious calculation of repayments, this was not a one-sided process. Both male and female workers actively sought advances to bridge times of financial difficulty and to help fund purchases or marriages. Indeed, some complained when advances were not offered, as it made these periods more treacherous and forced them to seek other forms of credit:

> Nowadays it is getting harder to take an advance from the factory. This area is poor, so we cannot take money on loan from a neighbour, as all are poor. We must take on loan only the interest money [from a Punjabi moneylender]. All the women in the area are earning just for their *roti* [bread], so the financial condition is the same, the owner never wants to give us advance money.
>
> (Shazia, a 35-year-old factory worker)

While some employers had become hesitant to offer advances, the practice remained commonplace. The amount of money workers took on advance varied significantly. Advances offered at the time of recruitment tended to be high: some informants mentioned figures of 5,000–10,000 rupees. Advances, however, were not restricted to the initial recruitment process but were often offered or taken throughout employment; they ranged from small amounts, of 100–1,000 rupees to pay a school bill or purchase food, to larger payments in the tens of thousands for weddings or other events. With the industry, including factory ownership, dominated by Muslims, these advance payments, as per Islamic principles, were not interest-bearing in the way a loan from a Punjabi moneylender would be. However, there were forms of shrouded interest present, particularly in the working of more hours than the advance equated to, a calculation that was often difficult for workers to keep track of.

Advances, then, were about more than simple bondage and played out in complex and nuanced ways (see also De Neve 1999; Guérin 2013). There were specific intersections with gender that made the experience of giving and taking advance payments different for men and women. Male workers, for example, used their mobility to evade repaying advances. Abdul, a 39-year-old intermediate-size manufacturer, explained:

> It is difficult to keep and find labour. Workers leave and don't come back even if they have an advance. They just go away and don't repay. They think about themselves and not the employer. There are plenty of orders, but I cannot fulfil them because of lack of labour.

The geographical mobility that male workers used to navigate the advance payment system was rarely an option for women. Male workers could be pressured to undertake additional overtime, or to remain employed in the factory until the advance was cleared, but it was always possible that the employer would lose both the worker and the advance through migration. By contrast, a woman who had accepted an advance had little opportunity to take the gamble, or even deploy a threat to leave the city, and was more likely to be chased up by the employer's *gundā* (thug), who could be sent to her house to pressure her to return to work. Advances, then, intersected with gendered positionalities to create an environment in which refusal became difficult, which increased the flexibility of the labour force to meet the demand of supply chains within neoliberal modes of global production (cf. Mezzadri 2016; Carswell & De Neve 2013a).

Continuing the theme of credit, advance payments and neo-bondage, the following section shifts away from larger-scale sites of production to focus on the gullies that wind off the main thoroughfares of Saharanpur's wood-manufacturing *mohallas*. These spaces are crowded with a variety of smaller, usually open-fronted workshops and – despite degrees of semi-Fordist production in the factories – remain the primary site for the bulk of woodcraft manufacturing. In the next section I continue to trace the ways in which money, credit and production intersect. I also use the following material to illuminate the variety of ambiguous actors who mediate local networks of manufacture and the interplays between production, the supply chain and intimacy.

Precarity, insecurity and money: tracing the supply chain through the gullies

Hajji was one of the 'big men' of the gully economy. He was a large-scale wood supplier and, as such, also a collector of debts. He had his hands in a variety of other, often rather insalubrious, businesses. I was first introduced to him by the rowdy group of young men who operated the workshop next door to my *ustād*, Islam. Middle-aged and plump, with teeth reddened from obsessive *pān* (betel-nut-based stimulant) use, he was quick to assert his status. Much of this he affirmed through his use of banter which, although jokey, often conveyed veiled threats and expressions of authority. When I first met Hajji, he told me that he did 'black business' and was 'a dangerous man'. On another occasion he asked if I would like to meet Shabir Ibrahim, brother of the legendary Mumbai gangster Dawood Ibrahim. It took me a few moments to recall that Shabir Ibrahim had died in a hit by a rival gang in the 1980s. His threat was clear.

On later occasions, I visited both his timber yard, and his home for dinner. He explained the challenges of having to retrieve payments, saying, 'They pay later. Usually they give the money slowly after making the wood items and selling them. It is very hard to get money from people and I am often having to put pressure on them.' Later, he elaborated, explaining that his ultimate sanction was the threat of violence and suggesting that he had deployed this on many occasions. Wood wholesalers sat towards the top of the gully hierarchy. Like the advance payments offered by employers, the credit they provided contained a cloaked form of interest. Wood was available immediately for later payment, but only at an inflated price, which allowed Islamic principles prohibiting interest on loans and capitalist modes of wealth extraction via credit to exist simultaneously.

After the wholesale stage, production continued through a variety of interlinked and overlapping connections. Khatakheri, where Hajji did most of his business, was formerly a rubbish dump, which had developed into a wood-producing *mohalla* in the 1980s. The original wood market, located at Purāni Mandi, had been established since the colonial era. While Purāni Mandi produced mainly for export, Khatakheri was geared more towards the furniture industry: its produce was consumed primarily, although not exclusively, in domestic markets. Khatakheri sold to a variety of groups and locations across the country, the largest source of consumption, both in Saharanpur and beyond, being the Muslim middle class. Purchases were made, either directly or through the showrooms, for dowry purposes[4] and for home furnishing by both Muslim and non-Muslim households. In an organisational sense, however, the markets shared the same structure, the entrance space of each being dominated by larger showrooms and wholesalers. These outlets provided the public face of the industry. Although some showroom owners had their own production facilities, most outsourced their orders to small workshops and informal networks of subcontracting.

Each day, as I sat in Islam's brass overlay shop in Khatakheri, I was privy to a huge variety of comings and goings. Rickshaw wallahs plied their way between workshops, transporting goods in various degrees of completion. Some were independent and had bought a rickshaw as an investment, charging whichever workshop required transport. Others were employed by a factory or wholesaler and brought outsourced goods to the gully. At the heart of the organisation of production were the carving shops. These units completed their own stage of production and organised others. Amongst the *kārīgars*, carving workshops would often be the first port of call for direct customers, outsourcing factories and showroom owners. From there, carvers sent items to neighbouring shops for completion of non-carving stages. A combination of higher skill and status, along with their position as orchestrators of further layers of subcontracting, placed the carving shops at the top of the gully hierarchy.

Next came the other highly specialised trades, such as brass inlay work, which involved setting thin strips of brass into finely cut grooves to form a pattern that is embedded into the wood. Then came the *mistrī* (tradesperson)-orientated trades such as carpentry, cutting and polishing.[5] In some cases carvers would recruit a carpenter or cutter to operate in their shop, and in others the work would be sent out. While carvers orchestrated most of the 'putting out', other actors were also involved. In Islam's shop we received items for brass overlay. Usually these consisted of panels or sections with the carving completed but the brass still to be added, which would later be assembled into furniture items by carpenters. Although Islam's position in the supply chain was low, he would negotiate further subcontracting with others, such as the buffing workshops, to complete his stage of the process. Across all sections of the gully chain 81 per cent of workshops received outsourced work and 52 per cent engaged in additional outsourcing themselves.[6]

At the bottom of the status hierarchy within the gullies were those jobs perceived as 'dirty work' (cf. Mohsini 2010) such as buffing, with its associated levels of dust. This is not to say that it was necessarily the lowest-paid. Indeed, Mohammad Ishan, whom Islam used for buffing, told me that he was, at times, able to earn even more than the carvers. The 'dirty' nature of the work, however, was not the only issue that led to it being seen as lowly. Ishan was already feeling the physical effects of his labour, in part because of his prodigious chai habit, the sugary liquid he often consumed instead of food to get through the long hours, but it was his lungs that suffered most. His thin frame regularly heaved with the hacking cough so common among those whose work entailed long hours breathing in wood dust. Once Ishan had returned buffed items to our workshop, small orders would be taken back to the sender by Islam or myself on his bicycle. Larger orders would be picked up by rickshaw. Furniture items would then be sent to a carpenter for assembly, often via the carver, and on to the polish shops. Small items such as boxes would be taken into the narrower lanes behind the workshop gullies. Here, the rickshaw wallahs would knock on the steel doors or shout through simple curtain partitions to the women workers inside, notifying them that work had arrived to be sanded, touched up and varnished.

Over the year and a half of my fieldwork, when I was not migrating out of the city with craftworkers most of my day was spent labouring with

Islam in his brass overlay shop in Khatakheri. Each Thursday, the eve of the Friday holiday, we would go from place to place to collect money owed by various actors who had supplied Islam with orders. The venue might be a small woodcarving unit, a larger site of production or the showroom of an exporter or wholesaler. Often, much of the afternoon was taken up visiting various order-givers who owed money. While some were quick to pay outstanding monies, frequently the response would be 'aglai hafta bhia' ('Next week, brother'). Sometimes we would receive partial payment and be told to return for the remainder, a process often repeated week after week.

It was only after a couple of months that I began to become aware of the significance of this slow drip-feeding of payments. We were in the showroom of an exporter who occupied a shop near the entrance to Purāni Mandi, the city's original wood market. Shanawas, the proprietor, had contracted Islam to add brass overlay to around 2000 money-box lids. We had completed the work over an eight-day period. Shanawas had provided an advance of 1000 rupees, the remaining 5000 rupees to be paid upon completion of the order. The previous week he had offered Islam 500 rupees and told us to return. When we did so, he upped this to 1500 rupees but would only hand this amount over if Islam would accept an order for a further 1300 money boxes. Again, he promised full payment for the outstanding amount the following week, and offered a further 500 rupees advance towards the new order. Over the following months this pattern repeated itself over and over. Islam finally retrieved the full amount for the initial order but by this time further monies were owed for other work. The primary consequence of this process was that each Thursday we would return to Shanawas's showroom. There was always some money forthcoming but also, at regular intervals, additional orders for work.

The effect of Shanawas's tactic was to create a form of 'inverted bondage' in which the employer rather than the employee was the debtor. Late payments or partial payments, then, are distinct from direct bonding (e.g. Brass 1990) and from more negotiable forms of 'neo-bondage' (De Neve 1999). As much literature focuses on systems of advance payment, little attention has been given to late or partial payment as a way of binding workers or intermediaries through modalities of 'inverted bondage'. There are some exceptions. Jens Lerche et al. (2017) describe the practice as being common also in Uttar Pradesh's garment sector, and Jonathan Parry (2013) describes systems of 'late payment' being used by contractors in a state-run Indian steel plant. Beyond the Indian context, too, there are some empirical cases. Jenny White (2004: 109), for example, describes female homeworkers in a Turkish craft manufacturing industry in which payments were withheld 'to ensure that the women would return with the materials they were given to work with in the next batch'. This, White points out, 'also had the effect of inducing loyalty, since the women always had to return and, once there, generally asked for another batch of work, rather than for final payment' (pp. 109–10). The primary contrast with advance payment-based systems of neo-bondage lies in the losses workers, artisans and others must shoulder if they want to end the relationship of bondage; abandoning the contract provider means not only the loss of a source of potential orders but also the writing off of any remaining monies owed.

Together, 'inverted bondage' and the other pressures outlined above combined to produce a high degree of precarity for all but the most established players in the supply chain. Petty commodity producers and small artisanal operations existed in a constant state of flux, in which a combination of factors could rapidly combine to cause a collapse. Two gullies along from Islam's workshop I met his friend Mohammad Aslan. Aslan had worked in the industry for over 20 years and described both his efforts to build up a small workshop and the rapidity of its collapse:

> I've been working in this line for 22 years. I did not go to school but studied under my *ustād* in a workshop near here. I saved some money as I got better at the work. Then I started planning my business. I took the money I had and took wood on credit. Initially I had three people working, but slowly this grew over three or four years. I kept taking orders and work and needed more workers to complete it. Eventually I had fifteen people working in my place. My work came from locals on a direct-sale basis, but I also got orders from people who came from Hyderabad and Kerala. They wanted samples for their showrooms and would then call for me to make more whenever an order came.
>
> The big problem was late payments. This happened often; the showroom owners would say 'Oh, I will pay you next week', or 'next month'. For this reason I had problems buying the wood and so could not meet orders. Because of this my workers left to go elsewhere. I tried to get them to come back, but they refused. It was a fast process; in three to four months my business was finished. I had debts with wood traders and for other things, but I managed to sort this by giving them the stock that I had left. After this I went to Vijayawada. I had friends working there and they organised work for me. In Vijayawada I was again labour and was just working for the owner.

Aslan was not alone in finding late payments an issue. The culture of late payment permeated every level of the industry: large and small producers alike operated in this way. Musharraf, a *thēkēdār* who lived in a nearby village and distributed subcontracted work amongst his home-working neighbours, discussed the difficulty of a position in which, on the one hand, he was a victim of late payment from those from whom he took contracts, and on the other, he was also often in a position of owing payments to his workers:

> Owners do not pay on time. Therefore, many people are leaving the industry. When the problem happens, people do not get together. Sometimes, though, the person waiting for payment, his brothers and their workers come together. Two years ago, an owner was not paying and the workers I employ came and demanded I went to him. I went and he paid some small amount from whatever was in his pocket. As I did not get all the money workers started to leave me. As a result, my work reduced. But exporters need me or people like me so eventually they approached me again and I got the workers back. ... They still do not make the full payments and keep giving me work even while they have not paid the money.
>
> A few years ago, people from France asked if I could supply them directly, but I had little capital so said no. The whole industry here is like a human being: the exporters are the brain and we are the hand. They just use their heads in the business and make the money, but we do the work. The exporters do not pay us as they are afraid that small workers will start their own businesses and come into competition with them.

Late payment, and the forms of 'inverted bondage' that were produced by it, acted not only to bond individual workers to an employer or contract provider but also to connect whole sections of the supply chain within a system that stymied labour mobility while simultaneously producing flexibility in local production networks. This section, then, has detailed specific ways in which flows of capital, along with particular forms of capital stickiness, act as central components in the local supply-chain assemblage. In the following section, I expand further on the role played by actors such as Musharraf, the *thēkēdār*, in brokering production on a daily basis. As detailed, the work of *thēkēdārs* spans both the gully spaces of small-workshop production and larger factory sites. I use this next section to entrench the descriptive engagement with Saharanpur's supply chain further into the relations based on intimacies of friendship, kin and neighbourhood.

Thēkēdārs: brokerage, mediation and intimacy in the supply chain

'Ha!' laughed Sushil. '*Uska mind off hai* [his mind is off]!' he declared, indicating a grinning young man of slim build who occupied the mat at his feet, around which were scattered various tools of the woodcarving trade. '*Woh acchaa kam nahi kar saktai hai* [he cannot do good work].' Mehboob, the target of his mockery, was quick to respond. '*Ha mera mind adha hai* [yes, my mind is half], *likin nichai full power chaltai hai* [but downstairs goes at full power],' he joked, indicating his crotch. Then, to ensure he came out on top of the banter, he continued, '*uska lund sei kutch nahi ataa hai* [nothing comes from his cock]', making a false grab for Sushil's trouser line. '*Deko bhai! Uska lund is tarah hai* [look, brother! His cock is like this]!' he continued as he picked up a chisel. Pinching the far end of the handle between his thumb and forefinger, he placed it in the erect position before gently releasing his grip and allowing the chisel to slowly droop down until its tip pointed to the floor. I had been working with Mehboob and Sushil for around three weeks in the open courtyard of a workshop employing some 30 staff. The exchange was partly for my benefit and they were quick to draw me into the joviality, Sushil shouting across to me while gyrating his hips. '*Tom bhai, tum achaa kam kar saktai hai, ha na* [Tom, brother, you can do good "work", can't you]?'

The machismo and banter that underpinned the exchange between the two was illustrative not only of the intimacy of their relationship but also of the relative egalitarianism of their friendship. Yet there was another bond between Sushil and Mehboob, that of the *thēkēdār* and the *mazdoor,* Sushil being the former and Mehboob the latter. The pair had been friends since childhood, but this relationship had developed into one also bound up in labour and work. At the same time this development had not diminished the friendship, and nor had the relationship become one characterised by mere rational calculation. To reduce their relationship to instrumentality or rational action alone would be to misrepresent the depth of feeling between the two, and would incur a risk of falling into an overly formalist rendering of informal production networks in the city.

Of all the characters in global supply chains, perhaps the most vilified, yet least understood, are the labour contractors. By many accounts they are guilty of perpetrating contemporary slavery and child labour (Phillips et al. 2011), or of being complicit in driving down wages (Mezzadri 2008; Barrientos 2008) and having entanglements with organised criminality (Picherit 2018). While I do not contest these assertions, ethnographic work has revealed a more contradictory actor (e.g. De Neve 2014a). In Saharanpur, the position of many *thēkēdārs* was unstable, and showed a great deal of fluidity between contracting and labouring roles. At times, some even occupied the roles of contractor and labourer simultaneously, and at others the role of *thēkēdār* overlapped with that of the *ustād* (master/teacher) or the *kārīgar* (artisan) (as detailed earlier in this chapter), as well as being embroiled in relations of friendship, neighbourhood and kin. Labour brokerage in Saharanpur, then, presented an image rather different from that offered in some ethnographic work on other manufacturing sectors in India. Writing on large-scale steel production, Parry (2013: 348), for example, argues that a clear separation had emerged between contractor and workers: 'the working world of contract labourers [is] differentiated from that of its regular workforce. The two kinds of workers regard themselves as distinct kinds of people and are now best seen as distinct social classes'.

While historical and localised structural contexts may create varying configurations around labour brokerage and contracting, *thēkēdārs* in Indian industries are nothing new. A body of research on labour histories has shown that they were numerous during the colonial and postcolonial eras as well as in the current post-liberalisation economy (A. K. Sen 2002; T. Roy 2008). As is the case today, the contractor's role, over history, was fluid and responded to shifting demands. Relationships with workers and employers were varied across industries, rarely being defined by the formality or informality of the sector (Chandavarkar et al. 2004). Historians have posited that labour contracting originated in the colonial period. Here, 'traditional' forms of pre-colonial authority – such as that embodied in the *sardār* (village headman) – could be transformed into the roles of industrial foreman or contractor (T. Roy 2008), a process that echoes the incorporation of bazaar-based authority into factories outlined earlier in this chapter. For some contributors the authority of the middleman, or *sardār*, is 'derived from a precapitalist culture with a strong emphasis on religion, community, kinship, language, and other, similar loyalties' (Chakrabarty 2000: 112). In this way the contractor ensures work is completed by using existing obligations. Aasim Sajjad Akhtar (2011), for example, draws on Pakistan's construction sector to suggest that the relationship between workers and contractors is based on older conceptions of patronage: patronage-based relations have been co-opted into the maintenance and control of a workforce suited to the demands of flexible accumulation (cf. K. Gardner 2018).

These discussions have been summarised by Tirthankar Roy (2008), who points to two primary discourses on the pre-capitalist origin of contractors, those focused on the 'needs of capital' and those emphasising the 'needs of labour' (p. 974). On the former – and citing the work of Raj Chandavarkar (1994) amongst others – Roy places the focus on the need to cope with labour shortages and retain workers in factory settings, such as mills, where casualisation was high and workers often absent (cf. S. Sen 1999). The contractors, with their socially embedded ties as *sardārs* or other authority figures, were best placed to ensure loyalty. However, as Roy points out, the situation could be different in other settings such as tea plantations, where unskilled work, remote locations and the criminalisation of desertion acted to retain a workforce and made recruitment rather than retention the primary issue. Here, contractors acted as the seekers of labour and as go-betweens for plantation owners who had little desire to engage in the everyday mediation of their labour force. Regarding literature attending to the 'needs of labour', and citing the work of Dipesh Chakrabarty (2000), Roy points to a more worker–agency-orientated account of contracting, in which the contractor fulfils not only the needs of capital but also those of labour by enabling workers to reduce the costs of finding work or by opening avenues to new forms of employment.

Roy's own position aligns more closely with that of Chandavarkar: he argues that capitalist development was non-linear and, in the case of contractors as well as more generally, followed a variety of trajectories which meant that the 'needs of capital' constantly had to adapt to local realities, cultural contexts and existing labour markets. Thus, Roy argues,

> The superimposition of a modern sector in the backdrop of largely traditional agriculture and handicrafts, in which the household was the main organization, the consequently weak, missing, or context-specific labour markets and quite strong social barriers to labour mobility, would have needed institutional response of some kind. That particular environment raised the costs of searching for labourers suited to mass production sites, and also raised costs of training, supervision, and welfare. These high search, retention, and training costs required different types of authorities to join together, or for one kind of authority to spill over into another sphere.
>
> (T. Roy 2008: 977)

This is not to paint a fixed image in which the contemporary *thēkēdār* represents merely a continuity from older sets of socially embedded formations. As Alessandra Mezzadri (2008: 603) points out, 'the projection of Indian social structures in the global sphere of production transforms such structures and provides them with new regulatory roles within the neo-liberal global capitalist architecture'. Additionally, more recent ethnographic work has shown that the *thēkēdār* needs more than primordial networks. Geert De Neve (2014a), for example, emphasises the role that skill and respect, gained while working at the lower levels of Tirupur's (Tamil Nadu) textile industry, play in contractor–worker relations. Successful *thēkēdārs* are able to build on the trust and obligation they have created while working side by side with others as labour. For De Neve, this trust continues to be an important means of retaining workers when individuals make the step up to contractor. It is reinforced by articulations of alternative forms of obligation, such as the use of 'narratives of friendship', to maintain loyalty among workers, an exercise in which contractors are not always successful.

At a more structural level, Mezzadri (2016) draws on literature on agrarian economies in India (e.g. Harriss-White 2003) in which rural landlords may also act as merchant purchasers and moneylenders – a point that has echoes with classical Marxist texts, not least Engels's (2007 [1845]) *The Condition of the Working Class in England* – to illustrate the consequences when multiple roles are performed by contractors in the garment sector. Specifically, Mezzadri argues that, although contractors don't usually own any fixed means of production or exploitable property, they perform interlocked roles of employer and creditor – often through the types of advanced payment outlined previously – to 'reproduce their dominant position within specific segments of the [garment] sweatshop regime' (p. 140).

Certainly, this was reflected in the gullies and factories of Saharanpur, where interlocking processes were further complicated by the prevalence of the forms of inverted bondage described in the previous section. Yet there was also a dualistic positionality running through *thēkēdār–mazdoor* relationships which blurred care and affection into control and coercion. Research on brokers in circuits of labour migration has situated forms of labour brokerage within continua of control and care (e.g. Johnson & Lindquist 2019). Writing on labour brokerage, within modalities of international labour migration from Indonesia, Johan Lindquist (2018: 94) suggests that brokerage sits in 'a complex continuum between control, exploitation, comfort, desire, trust, and care'. Likewise, Filippo Osella (2014) describes the ambiguous overlaps between reciprocity and self-interest in the context of migration brokerage between Kerala and the Gulf. Picking up from this genealogy, I argue that Saharanpur's localised systems of labour brokerage, undertaken by *thēkēdārs* and others, must be considered not only in terms of social embeddedness or capitalist structuring (although both contexts remain extremely relevant) but also through the far messier lens of emotional entanglements, intimacy, care and affection.

Sajid worked in a small factory in one of the more recently established wood-manufacturing areas. Here he undertook varnishing work, of furniture and other items. As was common in this line, payment was often on piece rates and those who had more established, ongoing relationships with employers would often double as *thēkēdārs*. Sajid's trajectory into the position reveals a variety of ambiguities, not least around the overlapping and blurred roles of *thēkēdār* and *ustād*:

> First of all, I was just labour with my *ustād*. I learned this work from the *ustād*. He was also a *thēkēdār*, like me. I am a *thēkēdār* but if some boy comes to me, he can learn the work. My condition at that time was like this. After training, though, that person can go anywhere for work.
>
> I started this work five years ago. I learned from the *thēkēdār*, but his payment was not so good, so I left and went to another person. The other *thēkēdār* told me I would get per day salary, so I worked there. Then I made up my mind that I should start my own work. I knew that my speed was slow, but I was full of hope at that time. I did work for a short time near a third person and after that I started my own work in another factory. There was no problem with my old *thēkēdār* [when I started my own work] as in this industry you can see lots of *thēkēdārs*. But before starting my own work I took permission from my *ustād* [the first *thēkēdār*]; he gave me permission for this work.
>
> In this procedure the owner is tension-free, as he gives the burden to me. From the appointment of labour to preparation of work, the owner does not have to worry. He only wants it ready on time. For urgent orders it is my responsibility to collect the workers. It is a problem and the owner doesn't want to do this. To collect lots of workers and watch all the time creates a great headache. If the workers or the owner have any problem, they complain to me. I am the link between the owner and the worker.
>
> It is very simple [to get labour] as we know every worker's number and address. Sometimes we go to their home and ask them to come. Sometimes, though, they refuse and say that they have taken advance money from their owner so cannot. In this situation, if I have an urgent need of workers, I will pay his advance money and take that worker.

Sajid's story illustrates the depth of obligation that can be built within the *ustād* relationship and how blurring this into the role of *thēkēdār* creates particularities of commitment and patronage that persist long beyond the original period of apprenticeship and employment. Yet the poaching of workers through advance payments also illustrates the challenges involved in recruiting and retaining workers. A successful *thēkēdār* also had to retain the commitment of workers in more subtle ways. Both Sajid and Mustaqim were not just *thēkēdārs*, but also worked alongside their labour force and were key players in interlinking residential areas of the *mohallas* with production spaces. This forms an important part of a relationship that must negotiate the trust of both workers and the factory owner, as Mustaqim explains:

> The owner is very intelligent and will give the work only to the person who is best. If my work is excellent the owner is sure there will be no mistake. That is why the owner chooses one person who can do all the work to his satisfaction. He gives responsibility to the contractor in whom he believes. We are two brothers and the owner keeps us as contractors. We appoint more craftsmen, but the first duty is ours. We watch every step closely as we are careful about everything. I know every worker's house so I can go very easily and ask them to come for work. I have knowledge of the people who are workers and where they live. A contractor always stays in touch with workers. This is a must so I can find them easily.

Sajid was careful not to create a distance between himself and his labour force and would often muck in to help complete orders. These moments provided both a sense of solidarity and a degree of egalitarianism. They also illustrated Sajid's own skills as a varnisher, which were now fully developed (cf. De Neve 2014a). These efforts were aimed not only at hastening production but also at legitimising his position as a *thēkēdār*. Other performative moments were more subtly displayed. Sajid would regularly bring chai and snacks for his workers, fostering a sense of care and illustrating a willingness to occupy positions that diffracted the hierarchical nature of the relationship. There were also regular assertions of friendship, and the banter of everyday work was intermingled with intimate moments of physical contact: a jovial hug, a stroke of the face, a compliment or a slap on the back.

These moments of 'on the job intimacy' were further supplemented through the creation of opportunities to develop space for intimacy and friendship beyond the workplace. For Sajid this involved taking workers out for snacks, lassi or chai or hosting individuals at his house for dinner. Such occasions were not merely instrumental. Sajid shared a similar social position with them, and the conviviality and friendship between himself and his workers was genuinely enjoyed. It was during a trip to a juice bar with Sajid and Saleem, one of his workers, that I first began to reflect on the dualistic nature of *thēkēdār*–worker relations. The three of us had squeezed onto my motorbike and just finished a laughter-filled drive across the city. The topic of conversation had been girlfriends and it appeared Saleem was particularly famous for having several at once. We teased him about having to have different mobile phones to keep track and, once seated, he showed us WhatsApp exchanges, often involving the sending of 'I love you' messages with animated flowers or pictures of movie stars. Sajid clasped an arm around Saleem's shoulders as our mango juices, topped with crushed cashew nuts, arrived at the table and exclaimed 'very sexy – very sexy man!', slapping his back as he did so.

The moment represented a continuation of the relationship I had seen between the two in the factory, blurring spheres of economy, sociality, friendship and intimacy. Given this blurring, questions are also raised regarding the nature of 'work' undertaken by *thēkēdārs*. The socially embedded nature of the *thēkēdār*/contractor role has also been recognised by others (Chari 2004; De Neve 2014a). As De Neve (2014a: 1305) points out, contractors operate in a 'complex social and material reality'. This is not a mere seepage of the economic into the social but a deeply intertwined assemblage of the two. Emotion and intimacy become part of work and work becomes a part of emotion and intimacy. A good *thēkēdār* could maintain a friendship despite its intermingling with a hierarchical relationship of production. A good *thēkēdār* could also take a hierarchical relationship of production and turn it into a friendship. A good *thēkēdār* could maintain jural (in the loose contractual sense of informal employment) and moral relationships simultaneously, running against some traditional interpretations of the constitution of friendship in anthropology (e.g. Pitt-Rivers 1973; Mauss 2002). While such notions of a clear distinction between the jural and the moral have long been critiqued (e.g. Killick 2010), the ways in which emotion itself can become a terrain of labour for contractors and other intermediaries has been little explored. Here, then, friendship and intimacy become commodified (cf. Hochschild 2012) but workers, *thēkēdārs* and others find ways to ensure that commodification does not lead to a collapse of moral reciprocity (cf. F. Osella 2014).

Not all *thēkēdārs* were as successful as Sajid. In the tightly packed gullies that constituted much of Saharanpur's woodworking *mohallas,* the intensely social and highly gendered public space produced intense and deeply vested male friendships. Yet the intensity of everyday sociality also meant that when friendships broke down the intimacy with which they were charged could erupt into difficult emotions of jealousy, betrayal, abandonment and heartache. Faisal had worked for some time in the gully where I did much of my fieldwork. The workshop to which he provided his services as a *thēkēdār* was not large. Alone in the *thēkēdār* role, he provided three carvers. The owner in turn had two others and a carpenter. Amongst Faisal's small team was Musharraf, a carver in his mid-twenties. The argument had started during a *gilli-danda*[7] game that had pitted the two against each other. Each team member placed a wager. In the final round of the match an ambiguous close call for the *gilli* (wooden puck) being out led to a major row.

It was some days later that Faisal related the incident. Indicating the now vacant spot previously occupied by Musharraf he said, '*Unhoinai fraud kiya*' (he perpetrated a fraud). The argument had led to Musharraf leaving the workshop, which placed Faisal's ability to fulfil an already overdue order in jeopardy. What was more, Musharraf had taken an advance payment with him, an advance Faisal now feared he would not see again. To add to his problems, Musharraf had also taken another worker, Abdul. Faisal's rage reflected the intermingled nature of the *thēkēdār*–worker relationship and its embeddedness in more intimate and emotional relations. Aside from his complaints about the lost advance, Faisal also fumed, '*Woh achhaa dost nahee hai! Uska dil achhaa nahi hai!* (he is not a good friend! His heart is not good!)'. Doubly betrayed as both *thēkēdār* and friend, Faisal characterised his concern not only in instrumental considerations about a loss of earnings but also in a sense of betrayal and abandonment articulated in his focus on the 'heart' as the source of Musharraf's perceived wicked act. These events played out within male-dominated spaces in the gullies and thus were also embedded in male spaces of sociality and gendered norms around masculinity. Yet the deeply embedded constitution of production networks continued beyond the gullies and into residential areas and homes, with women playing a no less ambiguous part in feeding chains of global supply.

From factory to home: women homeworkers in the supply chain

Many accounts of global supply chains situate homeworkers as the end point, the outermost reaches of localised networks of subcontracting and outsourcing. Yet what Balakrishnan (2002) terms 'the hidden assembly line' contains its own sets of socially embedded relations and forms of mediation, which add further layers of complexity and ambiguity to Saharanpur's wood production networks. In many ways these spaces reflect similar modalities to those outlined in previous sections, albeit in a differently gendered context. Like women working in factory spaces, a context I expand on in the following chapter, women engaged in homework experienced the lowest levels of income and status. Seen as 'unskilled' work, the polishing, sanding and touching up of defects on items such as boxes, incense holders and *rehals* (folding stands for holding the Quran) in fact involved a great deal of learning and skill acquisition. Yet the payment for – by way of an example – sanding, polishing and inserting a felt inlay into a decorative box could be as low as 50 paisa (half a rupee). Thus, to make the work pay, women and girls had to develop the ability to complete the work at high speed while maintaining sufficient quality to avoid rejection by the exporter, wholesaler, factory owner or intermediary for whom the orders were completed.

Among the narrow gullies that wound off the main road in the *mohalla* of Khathakheri Ayesha and I met Farhana. Although a homeworker herself, Farhana held a senior position within the gully, which was supported by her status as the longest-term resident and her connections with local *maliks* (factory owners). This position enabled her to operate as an informal *thēkēdār* by regularly subcontracting her own work to other women in the neighbourhood:

> I have worked since childhood, for 50 years. We do repair work and polishing on boxes. [Owners] give us 20, 25 or 40 paisa per box, but 50 paisa only comes for big boxes. When we have lots of work from the owner then we transfer it to other women. We are living here in the *mohalla* and we are all poor, so we always exchange work with each other.
>
> Thirty years ago, I started this practice of giving work outside. It is through our unity that we distribute the work and because of this

we can fulfil urgent orders. No one can complete the urgent order alone. Rather it needs a unity and a great number of homeworkers. Mostly they work in my home as I prefer this. I want [them] to do the work under my guidance, but if we have lots of orders then I give it to them to take to their houses. I have many contacts with factories and my work comes from many places and from Lucky's shop here. Lucky's mother's payment is very good. Thanks to the Muslims her business is growing, as she is sitting in a Muslim *mohalla*. Years ago, there were many Hindu families here, but they have all settled in the Hindu *mohalla*. Now she is the only Hindu here. Now no Hindu wants to live in the Muslim *mohalla*.

I am the oldest woman here and was the first to start this work. Because of this I am the senior in this gully. I am a famous woman here; everyone knows that I am giving work to these women. First of all, the owner wants the work done, but it is my wish if I give it to others. I can go directly into the factories for the work and the money. This is not bad for my *chāl-chalan* [behaviour, persona, demeanour] as I am going for the sake of other women. These women are helpless but if I give them work then Allah will be pleased with me. When payment comes, I distribute money among all the women.

Many times [though] it happens that one woman goes silently to the owner without my permission or knowledge. It is a big problem in this work that I can be working for 20 rupees then some other woman goes silently and takes the work for only 15 rupees. We never get angry as we know that a person gets work according to their kismet [fate, destiny]. The young girls also do the same work for their dowry arrangement.

While Farhana was keen to emphasise the charitable nature of her distribution of work, others saw things differently. Across the road lived Saba. Saba's home appeared fairly large, but several generations of the same family were crowded into the space. Her son worked as a tailor, earning a small amount. Saba, her unmarried daughters and her daughters-in-law were all involved in finishing work; Saba controlled the money and the distribution of work between them, thus embedding the supply chain within intimate relations of family and home. Previously, she had often taken work from Farhana, but she had recently decided to end the association:

I have left her work as we have to do 100 boxes in a day and get just 10 rupees for that. *Hamara wasta kahtam* [our relationship is finished]; it was my decision to end this relationship. Why should we do hard work for only 10 rupees? I told her that we are happy without her work. But now I cannot go direct to the *maliks* as she is fixed for this. She is senior in the work. She was the first lady living in this area. We come from a village. We asked her for an increase, but she refused. She tells us that 'the owner only gives me 10 paisa for each box. He never increases it so how can I give you more?' She is also very poor and has many problems, we know this. She is the senior lady in this area and is head in the gully. She is a very clever lady and when she has lots of work she comes to our house and says that she has lots of urgent orders and after our help the owner is happy, and she can finish her order on time. We are just like fools when we are doing her work. She gets benefit and is making a fool of our family.

Networks among homeworkers, then, extended beyond the initial 'putting out' stage to incorporate forms of *thēkēdār* work and the intimate relations of kin and family. Just like Musharraf and the other male *thēkēdārs* discussed previously, Farhana used ongoing performative expressions of her authority and 'care' to become and then to maintain herself as a *thēkēdār*. She was very conscious of the precarity of her position, and while she could ride out the loss of Saba's labour, she had to ensure that others did not follow in the latter's footsteps, which would have undermined her ability to complete the orders for local factory owners and wholesalers. Her work also required the repeated negotiation and crossing of gendered spatial boundaries to seek orders and ferment relationships with manufacturers and others. For Farhana, as for women who sought employment in the city's numerous wood factories, this meant negotiating gendered ideals around the spatial practices, bodily demeanour and expectations concerning the pious character of Muslim women. These ideals are effectively captured within the articulation of *chāl-chalan* (behaviour, persona, demeanour, character and reputation), a term often used by women themselves to encapsulate these concerns. It is to these negotiations, and to the everyday modalities of the craft production work undertaken by women in the city, that the next chapter turns.

Conclusion

This chapter has traced the supply chain through localised layers of sub-contracting and outsourcing. The enclaved spatial configuration of the *mohallas* played a part by physically pushing workers, artisans and others together and by clustering production into a marginalised spatial config-uration. However, the chapter has also illuminated many other intersec-tions that acted to mediate the political economy of the gullies. Under these conditions relations of class became particularly blurred. While there were clear distinctions between large producers such as Abdul and others in the supply chain, production was often mediated through relationships which overlapped with a variety of other affiliations and with forms of intimacy. In addition, it is clear that the majority of arti-sans were, in reality, labouring in conditions within which the image of the independent craftworker gave way to forms of indentured labour, neo-bondage and other subjectifying processes. As Andrew Ross (2004: 216) argues,

> Just because artisans are not factory wageworkers does not make them free, or any more capable of controlling their time and labor value … an artisan can be a skilled, apprenticed craftsman (espe-cially if he is male) who is functionally flexible in the application of those skills. But (and especially if she is a woman) she is more likely to be an off-the-books homeworker who accepts job enlargement (as opposed to job enrichment) as a matter of familial sacrifice or self-exploitation.

In accord with Ross's observation regarding gendered differentiations in craft supply chains, it was around gender distinctions that differentia-tion was most starkly felt. Of those labouring in wood production, it was women who universally occupied the bottom of the local labour hierar-chy. In the following chapter I expand on this context to detail the forms of connection and constraint that interplay within feminised spaces of production. However, I also attend to the forms of negotiation and contestation engaged in by women as they seek to express a degree of agency and, occasionally, resistance, albeit within the highly constrained and enclaved contexts that mediate women's labour.

Figure 3.2 Brass overlay work before buffing. Source: author.

Figure 3.3 Working in a large factory. Source: author.

Notes

1. For an excellent discussion see Mezzadri 2016.
2. A small amount of this section has also appeared in T. Chambers, and A. Ansari (2018), 'Ghar mein kām hai (There is work in the house): when female factory workers become "coopted domestic labour", *Journal of South Asian Development* 13(2), 141–63. It is reproduced here in edited form with the kind permission of the journal.
3. Advance payments are not restricted to the South Asian context; ethnographic work details their use in production networks in South East Asia, the Middle East and Europe (Platt et al. 2017).
4. This is a distinction between South Asian Muslims and Hindus. Whereas Hindu dowries focus on gold and money, Muslims' dowries involve more emphasis (although not exclusively) on practical items. They may include pots and pans, household items, furniture, bicycles and motorbikes, depending upon the wealth of the households involved.
5. The term *mistrī* has a more general meaning than *kārīgar*; It includes mechanics, electricians and plumbers.
6. Source: fieldwork surveys.
7. Played with a stick and a small oval of wood (the gilli). The gilli is flicked up and then struck with the stick into a predefined field. Opposing team members attempt to catch it to get their opponent out.

4
Muslim women and craft production in India: gender, labour and space

Figure 4.1 Women undertaking finishing work under the supervision of a male *thēkēdār*. Source: author.

Noor was in her mid-fifties, but her stooped appearance, missing teeth and deeply lined face had aged her well beyond her years. Noor and her family lived in the same gully as Farhana, the thēkēdār described in the previous chapter. Like many others in the area, she obtained her orders via Farhana.

The family home was a sprawling affair of reinforced concrete and crumbling thin-skinned brickwork, spread over two levels. By the standards of many in the gully, it was of a reasonable size, but the space was crowded with several generations of the same family. As was typical in many woodworking households, it was the sahn (central courtyard) that provided the site for much of the production work. Along one wall several piles of boxes were stacked, the wood bare and imperfections visible. Against the opposite wall there was a steadily growing stack of sanded, polished boxes ready for collection by Farhana, who would send them back to the outsourcing manufacturer. All the women of the household were involved in the process, as were a couple of younger girls who had started contributing to manufacturing around the age of eight to nine years.

We had arrived as a group. Over the months in Kamil Wali Gully, while working in Islam's shop, I had become increasingly aware of these spaces of hidden production but had not been able to access them because of my biological gender and spatial demarcations of public and private spheres. It was only through Ayesha, my research assistant, that I was gradually able to make contact. Ayesha had called at the household previously and had asked permission for my visit. To ensure that Ayesha's own chāl-chalan (reputation, character)[1] was upheld, we went in the company of her husband and two daughters. Noor's husband, Ibrahim, was a hawker (street seller) and pushed a small rehri (handcart) around local neighbourhoods selling onions. He departed during our conversation to return to work.

As we chatted, the women continued production. Their hands were deeply marked with the signs of their labour. Calluses from the constant sanding combined with the orange-hued staining of polish and the residue of the glue (used to insert small squares of felt into the base of each box) to produce a tapestry on the skin. The bodily punishment of long hours of sitting could be much more severe, as Noor described:

> My uterus came out from my internal body because of sitting so much. I tie some cloths and without these I cannot sit. This place is very hot and very dark, it is like a jail and we are just living here. We cannot take a break for fresh air and there is lots of dust and humidity here. If you do not believe me you can ask my daughters-in-law what my condition is from this work. I must drink water many times when I am working; my health is not so good nowadays. I have lots of problems which are due to the uterus. No doctor can cure me. They only give me medicine for it, but I never find comfort. ... It affects [me] a lot; you can see my rough hands. My shoulder became so hard it is like a stone and I cannot sleep at night for the pain. I cannot sleep in a relaxed way because of pain

and am sleepless all night as my body has become so weak. My body became useless. ... When my body stops working then I will stop the work but till then I will keep working. This does not depend on me but is according to the wish of Allah.

This chapter builds on the final section of the last, continuing the focus on female workers. Bodies in space form the primary emphasis of the chapter. This involves an exploration of the relationship between bodies and work and also an examination of the ways in which female bodies move through and across spaces of home, gully, factory and city. Two trajectories of marginalisation – that constructed around Muslim minority status and that cemented within hegemonic gender norms (Ray & Qayum 2009) – intersect in the production and reproduction of feminised sectors of the labour force. Other factors were also significant, class in particular. Those labouring in situations like those of Noor and her family were universally at the bottom of both social and labour hierarchies. In a context that often situated women's engagements with the labour market – particularly when they involved leaving the domestic space – as symbolising low socio-economic standing, it was the families with the smallest incomes that provided the labour for finishing work.

In addition, picking up from the vignette about Sabeena detailed in the introduction of this book, this chapter gives much emphasis to spatial crossings and the negotiations of reputation and character this involves. Here, I focus on the vernacular expression *chāl-chalan* (behaviour/persona/demeanour). The term articulates a complex assemblage of gendered moral and ethical circulations that regulate women's sexualities, bodies and subjectivities. It was also at the forefront of women's discourses about participation in paid labour within and beyond the home. The dynamics produced around *chāl-chalan* added additional vectors to the construction of women's bodies in workplaces such as factories and workshops. Employers could call women's morality into question and so justify forms of labour-force discipline and subjugation that exceeded what was imposed on men. Yet, despite a structural context that situated female woodworkers at the margin of the margin, women were not without agency in their engagements with manufacturing and other spatial settings. Resistance and refusal were present. Additionally, there were moments of cooperation with other women on the factory floor, and individual challenges to Muslim women's assumed position in the *mohallas* and the broader city.

Before we proceed, a further methodological note is required. As I laid out in the introduction, my involvement with the *mohallas* has always been mediated in a highly gendered context. Narrating the lives, experiences and subjectivities of women is therefore one of the more challenging aspects of this book. Gradually, curtains fell away, and over the years I have developed many close relationships with women in the *mohallas*. However, my male positionality imposed limitations that did not arise in my relationships with men. The experiences of women who labour in wood production are so distinct from those of their male counterparts that any attempt to interlace the narratives runs the risk of obscuring these distinctions. The story is gendered and, thus, so is this monograph. Finally, before beginning the chapter with a broader contextualisation of Muslim women in the Indian labour force, I must thank Ayesha Ansari for her meticulous work on this and other research outputs (e.g. Chambers & Ansari 2018). Without her, I could not have written this chapter.

Contextualising Muslim women and employment in India

Women's labour-force participation has been an area of substantive debate in Indian scholarship. This debate has been particularly concerned with declining (or at least stagnating) rates of women's participation in the labour-force (Abraham 2013; Klasen & Pieters 2015; Naidu 2016), a trend that runs counter to expected trajectories of feminisation which, elsewhere, have often been combined with wage suppression and class fragmentation (Mezzadri 2016). For some contributors to the literature, a decreasing level of female labour-force participation is attributable to positive development trends and rising affluence, while for others it represents a marginalisation of women in the labour force, as increasing unemployment, slowing economic growth and dominant patriarchal structures combine to de-feminise some sectors (Abraham 2013). This is not the pattern across the economy as a whole. Writing on garment production in Chennai and Bangalore, Alessandra Mezzadri (2012, 2016) discusses the steady feminisation of the sector that enabled local exporters to reduce labour costs by reconstructing feminised areas of garment labour as low-skilled and playing on assumptions about women's position as a secondary earner in the household (cf. Venkatesan 2010; Wilkinson-Weber 1999). She also emphasises the ways in which employment practices in the sector took advantage of locally constructed ideals of female docility and the disposability of women as employees, a combination that enabled both flexibility and gendered forms of labour disciplining. Localised configurations around gender and the role of women in the broader social context are an intimate part of global employment practices. In her classic text *Factory Daughters*, Diane Wolf (1992) described how employers in Java were able to use a degree of female autonomy within the Javanese Muslim population to recruit, while simultaneously deploying patriarchal ideology to keep wages low, as unmarried women were expected to remain economically reliant on their families.

Likewise, the (now largely defunct) jute industry saw variegated configurations around labour force feminisation in different geographical, historical and cultural settings. In Dundee, from the 1830s (before the sector went into decline in the early twentieth century) feminisation was used to drive down wages and stymie unionisation. Although women did engage in wildcat strikes, male domination of unions, coupled with forms of spatial segregation in the mills, allowed mill owners to suppress wages in feminised areas and to play women and men off against each other during labour disputes (Gordon 1987). When the industry began to relocate to Bengal in the late nineteenth century (a shift that heralded the increasing mobility of capital brought about by colonialism and globalisation), feminisation failed to emerge. This was, largely, not a result of the exclusionary practices of male workers, but rather due to the ongoing agrarian connections of the male migrant labour force, in contrast to Dundee where the highland clearances had severed links to agriculture. As a result, the needs of capital were best served by keeping women's labour in the agricultural sector, where food production could underwrite the earnings of male relatives in the mills, which enabled mill owners to pay male employees sub-subsistence wages (S. Sen 1999).

Beyond these cases, the broader literature on labour-force feminisation details how the feminisation of work (both paid employment and unpaid domestic labour) acts to marginalise women within the labour force (Drori 2000; Gordon 1987; Harriss-White & Gooptu 2009; Kabeer 2000; Ong 1988; Wolf 1992). Such processes have long justified the suppression of wages and the utilisation of gendered notions about 'physical attributes' to situate women as 'naturally' suited to, for example, textile stitching (Elson & Pearson 1981), loom operation (Gordon 1987) or keyboard work (Glover & Guerrier 2010). In turn, the skills involved in these roles are often constructed as 'low', further justifying a gendered wage gap in the workplace (Venkatesan 2010). These trends are equally present in Indian craft industries where, for example, the feminisation of *zardozi* (embroidery) work in Lucknow (Wilkinson-Weber 1999) and Bareilly (Mezzadri 2016) has been paralleled by declining wages and occupational status.

My point here is to emphasise the importance of analysing the gendering of wood-related production in Saharanpur within the context of broader structural considerations. Even starker in terms of labour force participation in India are the low levels of paid employment amongst Muslim women (M. B. Das 2005; Dubey et al. 2017). Where Muslim women are recorded as participating in waged labour, as many were in Saharanpur, the tendency is often towards 'self-employment' or 'homework' (Boeri 2018; Z. Hasan & Menon 2005; Wilkinson-Weber 1999). This is a pattern often attributed to the observance of purdah (seclusion from unrelated men, veiling). For some contributors, connecting labour-market engagements with notions of seclusion and domestic space, through home-based manufacturing, is seen as a 'choice' through which women can balance the need to earn with the requirements of purdah (e.g. Bhatty 1987). Others situate homework within purdah-orientated contexts as a restrictive practice resulting from a lack of mobility and low status that invisibilises women's labour in global supply chains (Balakrishnan 2002) and renders women particularly susceptible to exploitation and poor wages (Mezzadri 2016).

Purdah is not exclusive to Muslims in India (Jeffery 1979). High-caste Hindus, for example, can be amongst the most rigorous enforcers of the practice (Das 2005; S. Sen 1999) and it is often associated with social position, status (Chen 1995) and lifecycle (M. Das Gupta 1995; Ussher et al. 2015). Additionally, some have argued that contemporary purdah practice has been (re)shaped by the colonial experience, which has led to a blending of Brahmic (of high, priestly caste) and Victorian values among upwardly mobile Hindus (S. Sen 1999). For low-caste and low-class groups, including poorer Muslims, working beyond the home becomes symbolic of social position. However, there are degrees of agency bound up in purdah, including its evocation as a means of withdrawing from undesirable and low-paid labour (Baden 1992), its ability to create spaces of female sociality (Jeffery 1979), and its use to access certain piety-based resources and networks (Mahmood 2011). Nor should it be reified as necessarily dominant. As Zoya Hasan and Ritu Menon (2005) point out, for many Muslim women purdah is neither a primary nor a secondary consideration when it comes to decisions about work and forms of labour-market engagement (cf. Das 2005).

Yet religiosity cannot be disregarded in the analysis of women's everyday labour in wood production. Charles Tripp (2006), for example, has emphasised the ambivalences between capitalism, with its apparent gender-blindness, and Islam's emphasis on gender segregation, arguing that a 'socially embedded market was by no means gender-blind: women were regarded as a cheaper form of labour' (p. 168). Writing on factory workers in Bangladesh's garment sector, Naila Kabeer (2000) has identified similar ambivalences, whereby Islamic ideals concerning female seclusion could, on the one hand, be activated by women to carve out opportunities for employment and, on the other, led to public accusations of immoral behaviour. Israel Drori (2000: 99) describes comparable processes amongst Arab female workers in Israel and cites an informant who defends her going out to work to her father: 'I told him that I would give him respect too. I told him that I wanted to buy a stove and a refrigerator for my wedding.' Although Muslim women find ways of justifying factory work, Drori suggests that the prevalence of unemployment amongst the male Arab population is also a contributing factor. Similarly, Kabeer (2000: 140) suggests that, in Bangladesh, 'It is in this perceived erosion of the patriarchal contract, and the increasing inability of men to sustain the model of male breadwinner, that the genesis of women's entry into factory employment has to be understood.'

This body of research also hints at the variegated ways in which the bodies of working Muslim women are negotiated, contested and represented through both the interests of capital and the agentive actions of workers themselves. Saba Mahmood (2012) has made clear that, too often, 'western' or 'universalist' claims of human rights or feminist discourse paint an image of Muslim women (particularly those who subscribe to values of piety and purdah) as agentless, submissive to patriarchal systems and self-defeating in their cultural practice (cf. Abu-Lughod 2002). Mahmood asks that we move away from seeing gendered practices of modesty and piety as resulting only from external forces and instead consider how they are 'not so much an attribute of the body as … a characteristic of the individual's interiority, which is then expressed in bodily form' (pp. 160–1). Thus, we are drawn beyond cultural or economic contexts alone and into the level of subjectivity and notions of self.

Mahmood describes how, as was the case in Saharanpur, engagements with labour markets could be challenging, particularly in terms of maintaining the pious virtue of *al-haya* (shyness, modesty). The need to negotiate *al-haya* has resonances with the concerns about *chāl-chalan* that occupied the narratives of many Muslim women working in the city.

Chāl-chalan encompasses several meanings and has been variously translated as referring to one's behaviour (Ramnarain 2015), public persona
(Gadihoke 2011), mode of moving about (Jeffrey 2010), embodied norms
(Pigg 1995) and one's demeanour reflected in speech, dress and mien
(Jeffery et al. 2005). In the second chapter of her monograph Mahmood
describes the diversity of women who attended religious seminaries at
various mosques across the city. Similarly, the women discussed in this
chapter subscribed to different interpretations of day-to-day Islamic
practice and moralised their participation in paid work in different ways.
Unlike Mahmood's interlocutors, however, who came from various class
backgrounds, they were all poor, and so their participation in paid labour
was always mediated by the context of daily survival.

Women, labour and precarity: surviving at the bottom of the labour hierarchy

Earnings amongst women in the industry were consistently low: hardship, debt and even malnourishment were commonplace. While factory
work offered a marginally better income, home-based paid work was less
problematic for one's *chāl-chalan*. In either case, earnings were meagre,
generally ranging from 50–100 rupees per day for homework to 80–120
rupees per day for factory work. For some, this supplemented household
income, generating a little extra money for children or to go towards a
daughter's or their own dowry. The assumption that male breadwinners
in the household would supplement these earnings with more substantial incomes enabled employers to pay below-subsistence wages (cf.
Wolf 1992), which was a problem for those women who relied on these
incomes as the sole means of household support. Around 60 per cent of
the home and factory workers we interviewed over several months were
either widowed or divorced, and so were seeking to support a household
and children on earnings that were often below subsistence levels.

Being divorced or widowed often forced women into employment
and, because earnings from homeworking were low, pushed many to
seek work outside the house. Widows and divorcees experienced a high
level of vulnerability in terms of securing a livelihood and income, factors
that have been discussed in other contemporary (Mukherjee & Ray 2014;
Ramanamma & Bambawale 1987) and historical (S. Sen 1999) research
on India. Quantitative material indicates that divorced and widowed
women in India, along with those married to impoverished men, are

particularly present at lower levels of the Indian labour market (Afridi et al. 2016; Ramanamma & Bambawale 1987). Analysis of National Sample Survey Office (NSSO) data, for example, shows marginally more widows under 60 than married women engaged in paid labour in India (Afridi et al. 2016; Chen 1998; Kodoth & Varghese 2012) and substantially more separated women (Afridi et al. 2016).

Simultaneously, women in these situations often suffer from low bargaining power, issues of literacy and little opportunity for self-employment, which leaves them particularly vulnerable to poverty and to being trapped in lowly and precarious forms of work (Chen 1998). Broader research on South Asia also suggests that widows and divorcees are often vulnerable to sexual harassment and other forms of violence because they lack the 'protection' of a husband and need to seek employment beyond the home in a context where patriarchal ideology and victim-blaming attitudes are prevalent (Sabri et al. 2016). Although this is not a universal condition amongst women in the industry, intersections between vulnerability and marital status further emphasised the lowly position of female workers in the labour hierarchy.

The vulnerability created by the precarity of work was particularly great among those who were widowed or divorced or had sick, unemployed or (as was not uncommon) alcoholic husbands, fathers or other male family members. As their labour provided the sole household income, their bargaining power was heavily curtailed, a pattern that stood in contrast to that of many male workers, who were more able to withdraw their labour and move elsewhere. This created a justified sense of being among the most exploited in the labour hierarchy, as Zahoor, a 37-year-old neighbour of Farhana and Noor, reflected:

> The work amount is the same, but we get much less money. Even if we do lots of work, so we get less. Men always get more money compared to us whether they work or not. [Angrily] If the woman does a lot of work and is a fine artisan, she still gets less money. There is no value and respect for women in the factory.

Around two kilometres from Khatakheri were the neighbouring *mohallas* of Ali ki Chungi and Suhil Colony. In Ali ki Chungi we met Susheela, a married mother of four. Her husband worked as a fretsaw operator but struggled to maintain a consistent income, and Susheela's earnings from homework provided an important substitute. Like Zahoor, she was keenly aware of the position of women in the industry and was considering one of the few alternative income options available:

The owners become richer, but we have no union, no one listens. My mother works as a maid and will help me find work as a maid. Working as a maid will be better as it is clean work and I will not be so tired. We have no future in this industry. The men are also getting tired of this work. After some years, no one will want to do this work. From generation to generation our condition becomes worse. My husband told me that he had been doing this work from his childhood with no improvement.

This narrative of decline was prominent in the industry and featured in the stories of both men and women, reflecting the inherent precarity of everyday work and a reality that persisted despite general growth in wood production. Like Susheela, Sabina, a 40-year-old widow supporting her six children through various forms of work, described similarly limited options:

When there is no work for one to two months, I feel so bad and I have to search for other work in Saharanpur. My husband is dead, and I always need money for food. When there is no work I am working as a servant or maid. It is no different. Both bring only a little money.

The meagre earnings taken in by households were often mediated through gendered structuring in the home. Sana lived in a neighbouring gully to Gulshan and Faiza. Her husband, Mustaqim, manufactured small money boxes in a lean-to shop adjoining the house. This was piece-rate work. The boxes consisted of a wooden construction with two tin bands, a small latch and a money slot. As they lacked the carved detail of more ornamental products, the piece rates that Mustaqim could demand were low. Like others, Sana finished these items but only within the family business rather than via the networks of putting out that supplied Farhana, Noor and others. In set-ups like these women were rarely involved in handling or distributing money, as Sana explains:

My husband deals with [the money] as that is his duty. I don't take any money; all the money goes to my husband and son. All payments are collected by my son but if I need money for my medicine then I ask for it. What would I do with money? I am just doing my work! As it is our own business and not from outside so there is no question of asking for money.

The presence of a male breadwinner in the household did not always mean that women had no dealings with money. As my fieldwork continued, I started to visit the women and their families in Ali ki Chungi more regularly. Susheela, in particular, became open to my visits whether or not her husband was at home. A bubbly personality, she was greatly amused when I asked to participate in the finishing work. While I could achieve a good finish, I was never able to obtain the speed of the others and Susheela gently mocked my small pile of completed boxes, saying 'Kam jaldi karo, Tom bhai (work fast, Tom brother)'. On one of my visits, as we sat working through the stack of ornamental boxes with lids that comprised a carved section flanked by two small, flat brass elephants, I asked about the passage of money through the household. 'Pah!' She explained, 'I don't give money to my husband. Why would I give it to him'? Laughing now, she continued, 'I do not give any money to my daughter either. All the money stays in my pocket. It is for the children, for their school fees and clothes.'

Like Susheela, senior women in the households often handled earnings and organised the labour and payment of other female family members. In many cases, though, these meagre earnings were insufficient to arouse the interest of male members of the household (cf. Kantor 2002). Even where women had control over money, they remained dependent on male intermediaries, from whom payments were often late or disputed, or never materialised. Susheela said in 2011:

> The owner is very corrupt; they give money very late. We must go many times in their shop. They cannot understand our situation and sometimes they give our money one to two months late. Sometimes, though, some owners run away, and we cannot find our money. … Once we had done 10,000 boxes. The owner said to us to do some 5,000 extra boxes before payment. I thought we would get a big amount of money but suddenly he ran away from Saharanpur and we did not see him again.

Persistent poverty and gendered assumptions about women's roles combined to produce particularities in the local labour market which limited women's options to only a few types of work. Unpacking these dynamics requires not only a detailing of everyday experiences of labour but also an engagement with labour-force reproduction. In the next chapter I provide a detailed account of the ustād–shāgird (master–apprentice) system that draws most of the skilled male labour into the workforce. The reproduction of female labour was characterised by far more informal processes and often embedded within the family. It was also constructed as a naturalised and skill-less process (cf. Venkatesan 2010), although this characterisation concealed the high levels of skill acquisition required to produce to both the speed and the quality demands of the supply chain. To contextualise these very informal and deeply embedded forms of recruitment and training, the following section presents interlinked and relatively unabridged stories of women's trajectories into wood production.

Learning to labour: informal and familial recruitment

The presence of women in Saharanpur's workforce is nothing new. Susheela's mother Raisa, now in her sixties, had been working in wood production since childhood. The gully's informal supervisor, Farhana, also started as a child, pausing only briefly after her marriage. Recruitment was generally informal: older women taught their sisters, daughters, daughters-in-law, other younger relatives and neighbours. On other occasions husbands and fathers taught wives and daughters. For many this was a nonchalant process requiring no 'real learning' (cf. Venkatesan 2010). As Susheela reflected, 'It is very easy work to learn, I have no special training. When I saw my mother doing it, I learnt it from her. Nobody trained me, just by seeing I learnt it.' Susheela had paused the work after her marriage but took it up again to help support the household and pay for her daughter's education.

A short distance from Susheela lived Raisa. Keen to emphasise her piety, Raisa made clear her dedication to daily *namāz* (prayer). She was married but her husband was sick and unable to work. Thus it was her meagre income from woodwork that supported the household. Like Susheela's, her entry into the trade had been informal and had started at a young age. Now, though, she was engaged in teaching her own daughters and the daughters of others:

> [Indicating a girl of 10–12 years] When I was like this girl, I started work. This neighbour's child works with us and I pay her each week. They will eat some small snacks from this money. They are also working to save for the Gul Fair. I teach them the work. They can learn it quickly, but it takes time to become fast. See this girl [indicating 20-year-old Afsa, her brother's daughter], she is working now for her dowry. There is a box and in this she puts the things for her dowry. Her father does the same and soon she will be able to marry. Then she will be free of this work.

The dowry box was often fashioned as a central feature within imaginaries of the future for young women in the two *mohallas*. Like Afsa, women often constructed it as an end point in the daily toil of wood production. Thus it became an object that contained more than just the material items – pots and pans, a stove, plates and cutlery, etc. – that a newly married woman is expected to bring to her in-laws' household. It also embodied the possibility of a better life. These aspirations, however, were often not met. Around the corner from Susheela lived Fareeda. Married with three children, a boy and two girls, she had also learnt wood finishing from kin and had anticipated that her marriage would result in her withdrawal from wood production.

> I learnt this work from my sister. She died 15 years ago. I learnt this work from my sister's house. When I was just four to five years old, I learnt this work. I could not get an education as my childhood was spent in this work … since my very early childhood. I was married when I was just 18 years old. That was four years ago so you can imagine my age when I started this work. I was working from my mother's house before my marriage. I am working from the start of my life until now. After marriage I found that my husband did not have a lot of income, so I started woodwork here too. With only my husband's income my children could eat only half a *roti*, so it was my duty to help my husband. … No one told me to start; my husband was earning so little so I said to him '*Mujhei bahar sei kam dejiyai* [give me work from outside]'.

Yet learning to labour was not always restricted to familial contexts. Gulshan lived in a small house, also in Suhil Colony. Her house was rented, and she shared the living space, consisting of a small room and an open *sahn*, with her children and two buffalos belonging to the landlord. The house was crumbling, and the odour of the animals permeated the living space as well as the outer area. Gulshan had been living in the property since her divorce a few years ago. She had been married as a second wife, a fact that she had been unaware of beforehand. After the wedding it had become clear that the marriage had also been a form of recruitment, as her husband's family looked to use her skills as a woodworker to supplement the household income. Such practices were not uncommon, and many marriages were discussed not only in terms of dowry and family status, but also in terms of the potential skills (e.g. sewing, woodwork or knitting) that the prospective bride could bring to the groom's household in order to contribute additional income or boost the productivity of a family enterprise – a further embedding of economy in familial relations.

After a few years of marriage, Gulshan's husband had divorced her. Like many others, Gulshan did finishing work such as filling, sanding, polishing and lining of boxes, ornaments and *rehals*, and often moved between factory and home-based work. A small woman in her late thirties with a twitchy air of busyness, Gulshan hurried to prepare chai for her new guests. We were a particularly large group, comprising Ayesha, her youngest daughter, her husband and myself. We took our tea and began to chat. From time to time Gulshan shifted her place, at one point sitting next to me and declaring, 'I can sit by him; he is like my brother', a commonly used language trick which disarmed the gendered norms of the male stranger and signified increased familiarity. Once we were settled, she began her story. She talked quickly and fidgeted as she did so:

> I am doing this work from childhood, when I was 13 years old. I was doing it before my marriage because my father's family were poor. When I was small, I used to go into a factory to get the wood for the fire. In that factory I saw some women working. I watched them carefully and learnt that way. Later the owner would give me a rupee for some work. In my heart I felt some greediness for money and so I started work. My brother got angry and said that I should not go there. But when my brother went for work, I would go silently into the factory. I would come back before lunchtime. It was my trick and through this I learnt the work.

Gulshan's story was unusual, but it illustrates variegation in terms of the avenues through which women entered the labour force. For most, though, it was the bounded space of gully and home that provided the site of their incorporation into wood production. From the perspective of manufacturers, the presence of these self-reproducing networks meant that there was always a ready supply of flexible labour to complete finishing work. The supply was augmented by competition between households as each struggled to obtain sufficient work. It is to these tensions, and to other aspects of relations within the gullies, that the following section turns.

Navigating the gully economy: frictions and allegiances

The realities of everyday precarity around labour and the supply of outsourced orders meant that women's working lives often entailed efforts to obtain orders, sometimes at the expense of others. This resulted in a variety of frictions, as homeworkers competed with each other to carve out livelihoods from paltry piece-rate earnings. A few doors down the gully from Gulshan lived Faiza. Faiza's home was also simple but was of a sturdier construction and owned by the family. Her husband worked as a truck driver delivering finished wood products all over north India. When we first met, he was en route to Shimla and we spoke on the phone with him while taking tea in the house. Initially, it was a little unclear why Faiza felt the need to work. Her marriage was good, and her husband earned a reasonable wage. The marriage, however, had been controversial; it was a love marriage and her husband had been Hindu. To enable the marriage, he had converted to Islam, but others in the neighbourhood would often discuss him in derogatory terms and call his commitment to his new faith into question. While sitting in her home chatting together with Ayesha we got a window into the family's precarious financial situation when a debt collector called. Faiza begged for more time and explained that her husband was away but that they would pay upon his return.

Despite her problems, Faiza had a jolly demeanour and happily answered our questions. It was through her that we had originally met Gulshan, but on one of our later visits we discovered that the friendship had turned sour. Faiza told us that Gulshan had been undercutting her and taking work at a lower rate:

> [These days] I have no work because of Gulshan. I always used to give some work to her as I had plenty. One day she asked me, 'Who is the *malik*?' My heart is very innocent, so I told her the address of the factory. She suddenly wore a burka and went in all the factories and then one day my daughter saw that all the *rehri* wallahs[2] were coming to her house but were not bringing any work to us. I told my daughter that she is mad, as this is our *malik*'s work, this must be a mistake. I asked the *rehri* wallah why he was giving the work to that woman, as it is our work. He said, 'No, the work is for that woman.' Then my daughter got angry with me and shouted at me, saying that 'You are very innocent, mother; the times have changed. You should not help her!' ... You know I take 50 paisa for each box, but that woman has fixed 40 paisa for each. The owner is very clever, so why would he want to give me [work] at 50 paisa? Nowadays we have no conversation between us.'

Competition for work further depressed the rates that home-based workers could demand and acted as a de-proletarianising force through the advancing of individualised interests born out of precarity and poverty. Back in Ali ki Chungi, Susheela expressed a similar sentiment:

In this area the competition is too great, so work is not regular. Sometimes we have no work and we stay in our home and wait for work. … It is very bad as the work is very little, so the competition is very high. If we find work, then the piece rate is very low so there is no benefit from the work.

Precarious subjectivities combined with spatial enclavement acted to sculpt agentive actions of order seeking, and the forms of border crossing this involved, as individualised and competitive acts of self-exploitation. Here, the market and the gully were bound into one, and just as in S. Sen's (1999) Bengali jute mills or Wolf's (1992) Javanese factories it was the interests of capital that were served through this localised configuration. Recent changes in 'putting out' practice had further intensified the competitive environment, with homeworkers experiencing a perceived threat from the increasing use of women, particularly Chamār women (from a low-caste Hindu group associated with leatherwork), in factories. Gulshan, again, takes up the narrative:

Nowadays I have little work. … The owner prefers to give the work to factory women. He does not want to send work to our house as it is costly. Now many women are going to the factories. I also did some time ago but not now as my daughter is grown up. There is lots of work in the factories, but I cannot go there. Because of these women we get a lot less work in our house, but it is our own kismet [fate]. We find employment because of our kismet, not because of any Chamāri woman. Whether she is Muslim or Hindu is not a big matter, everybody finds work according to their kismet. Everyone is equal whether they are Muslim, Hindu or Chamār. It is Allah's duty to give us *roti* [bread, chapati] and employment, so we cannot blame any Chamāri women.

The evocation of kismet was commonplace and articulated a context in which women's subjectivities were bounded by economic, spatial and patriarchal modalities of structuring. For homeworkers, the gully economy allowed networks of petty commodity production to penetrate the wooden doors and curtains of the *mohalla*. Women themselves did not see this as an agentive lifeline bringing livelihoods to one's home. Instead, kismet formed an articulation of a subjective experience in which agency was often ceded to the forces and demands of production. The work came to your door not because you wished it so but because this – as well as the material conditions of labour – was the fate you had been ascribed.

Working again with Noor and her family, I asked about her dreams for the future. Her response was circumspect. '*Kismet hamko sirf yeah diya* [fate has given us only this], so there will be no change in our condition. Only Allah can change this.' It was late, and her husband, now back from his shift at the factory, echoed her statement. 'She cannot make any change. That other woman [Farhana] has all the power here, she is the only one who can make the work better.' 'Pah!', Noor scolded him. 'What can she do? Her condition is also so bad, and her health is not good.' Dismissing Ibrahim with a tut, she continued, 'Often our payment comes late from Farhana, but even she can do nothing as it is also coming late from the owner, her kismet is the same as ours.' Leaning to one side to spit *pān* [betel-nut-based stimulant] into a bowl, she ran her eyes over me sternly. '*Tom bhai, tum yeah nahi samudj suktai hai* [Tom, brother, you cannot understand this]. You can go from here to any place, but we are always here just waiting for nothing but more work.' Returning to her previous position, she continued, 'Farhana has one thing, she can go here and there to get the work and sometimes an advance. All we can do is take the work from her or the loan from Anjeet [a Punjabi moneylender], there is no other option for our *roti*.'

Debt was ever present. Noor would regularly have visits from Anjeet or other moneylenders. These were always emotional negotiations and, whether trying to acquire a loan or delay a repayment, Noor was animated in her engagements. At times this meant shouting in anger and at others wailing in despair. Noor made no secret of the fact that these displays were for show. When Anjeet had called late one evening she had managed to gain two extra days by thrusting a sick child, who she had hastily coached beforehand with a whisper of '*Bimari karo* [be ill]', into his arms. Once he had left, she turned and smiled to me, '*Deko, wo chal gaya* [look, he is gone]'. While spatially enclaved and firmly at the bottom of the labour hierarchy, women like Noor knew the rules of the game and knew how to navigate on- and off-stage performances (Scott 1990), although, as Michael Burawoy (1979) points out, these 'games' played into processes which could be self-exploiting, like the case of piece-rate competitiveness.

Emotional performances and affective confrontations were also central to negotiations with various actors in the supply chain. Farhana, the gully's informal supervisor, described how she was both the recipient and the employer of affective displays.

> When work comes from outside my home, I call all the women to come and take the work. … I get 25 paisa for polish and 25 for

repair. When I complete 100 boxes then I get 25 rupees. ... I pay them [the other women in the gully], I take money from the owner and then distribute to the other women. This is not easy and they shout at me if the money is late. Last night Noor's daughter shouted at me and that is why I had to go to the factory and shout at them, it was because of her daughter. Noor's daughter was shouting at my gate. She said, 'Give me money as I have to cook dinner and have nothing in my home.' I can understand that some women can wait, but some cannot, as they have no money and nothing in their house. I can understand that without money they have to face many problems. If my payment is late then I can arrange 35 rupees from each of my family members and then I can pay other women like Noor's daughter. You can understand that when I give her work, giving payment is also my responsibility. If I arrange it by loan or by shouting at the owner it is all my responsibility.

As detailed in the previous chapter, Farhana's movements as a *thēkēdār* involved a willingness to cross boundaries that others might not. However, there were many women who did not occupy Farhana's position of relative authority but still found themselves negotiating these crossings in order to obtain work in the city factories and workshops.

Bodies across space: negotiating home and factory

We cannot do anything and have no other option. If there is no work coming to our home, then either I go to the factory or become a beggar. What is better, a beggar's life or a worker's life? I choose the worker's life. Allah has given us hands, so we should use them.

(Bano, a 38-year-old resident of Ali ki Chungi)

In the factories there are many women working, but the work is not regular, and we often have to change factories or take in work at home. When the order is finished then our work in the factory also ends.

(Nasreen, a 31-year-old resident of Ali ki Chungi)

For many women in the two *mohallas*, working life was characterised by circular movements between home and factory work. Both were mediated through spatial configurations and in the context of *chāl-chalan*. Farhana and Gulshan engaged in border crossing beyond the *mohalla*, although not beyond the city's Muslim neighbourhoods, to find work. As described in the previous chapter, Farhana navigated the potential challenge to her *chāl-chalan* by articulating these crossings in terms of 'charitable work'. Gulshan, too, was keen to emphasise her forays beyond the *mohalla* in terms that preserved her *chāl-chalan*. Unlike Farhana, however, Gulshan's movements beyond the *mohalla* had also involved various periods working in factories in different areas of the city.

> When I started in the factory [after my divorce] the owner gave us work via a servant. He was the only one allowed into the room where women worked. There was no problem for us as we could sit comfortably. [In another factory] there was an owner who was very clever. He always gave an advance and often paid late so that workers could not go elsewhere. [That owner] always said, 'This is an urgent order, so you should work late', but I refused and only agreed to work until the evening as I had children. Also, society would think I was a woman of poor *chāl-chalan* if I worked late in the factory, as I have no husband. Society can't understand that I have no money; they always think that I am doing something bad if I'm in the factory late.

In part, it was the desire for more flexibility in the working hours of their labour force that motivated factory owners to start recruiting beyond the Muslim community in areas of feminised production. Back at Fancy Wood Crafts, Abdul Malik had begun to recruit Chamār women from an outlying village a few years previously. He was circumspect, however, about (what he saw as) the attributes of each group of workers. Some weeks into my fieldwork in the factory, he invited me to his home for dinner. The house was in a gated community next to Khatakheri. Set slightly back from most of the buildings, the place was large, with wide gates that were opened for me by the *chaukidār* (watchman). As I ate in his spacious but slightly spartan dining room I asked him about the arrival of Chamāri women in the factory. '*Deko bhai, yeah is tarah hai* [look, it is like this], the Chamāri women can work many hours and are always wanting to work overtime, but you know they are of very bad character and shout a great deal. Our Muslim women', he continued, 'are quiet, but it is hard to get them to work late.'

Most of Abdul's Chamār labour force came from the village of Mānak Mau. The village sat on the fringe of the city but was gradually being enveloped by Saharanpur's urban sprawl. Like that of many villages around the city, its population consisted of a fairly even split between Muslim and Hindu residents. Women from both groups commuted into the city to work in the wood factories, but generally made the journey with others of their own community. Amongst these was Sabra, a divorced Muslim woman of 36. She lived with her three children and her aging mother. Her brother lived in Dubai, where he worked in a juice factory. Sabra's family were in the process of building a new house, the money coming from Dubai. Yet Sabra still opted to work in the wood factories in order to improve the family income, a decision for which she was teased by the boys in the village, who would often whistle at her as she went by. Sabra had worked in the factories for six years. She was acutely aware of the questions this would draw about her character, but was firm in her justifications:

> Oh, there are no facilities for women [in the factory]. There is no separate place; whether the women follow the veil system or not they never wear a veil in the factory. It does not matter whether the woman belongs to a respectable family or that her *chāl-chalan* is good. If we say that we need a separate place or a veil the owner always shouts at us to go back home and says that they need workers, not the veil or the burka. He needs work until 6pm. … Nowadays the times are changing and so it is better that I keep silent on these issues. If we belong to a respectable family or if our character is good, we should keep quiet in the factory. If women say anything about our problems, there will be a great dispute. If any woman's *chāl-chalan* is good, she will not talk to another man. She should live separately from the men. I know that the atmosphere in the factories is very bad. It is my rule that I never want to talk to any men.
>
> When the woman is in her house it is very respectable, but when a woman goes outside there is no respect in this society. I cannot prove, if I am outside, that my *chāl-chalan* is good and that I am *pāk dāman*.[3] It is our bad conditions that mean we have to go to Saharanpur each day. I know that the veil system is very necessary in Islam. Sometimes in the factories the men are really very rude. Some men address me like a dog: 'tu'.[4] I never talk to men in the factory as I know that they are shameless. Sometimes there is fighting between men and me. The men tell me that I am not very smart or pretty. They say, 'If you are *pāk dāman* then go to your home. If you belong to a respectable family, you would not come to the factory.' I have to bear this blame silently. If I did not, my job would be finished.

The bringing up of working women's morality, sexuality and spatial practices was not something women had to navigate only in social spaces; it was also activated as a form of discipline and control in the factories themselves. Negotiating access to factories was often challenging, and even more difficult when we attempted to engage with female workers. Nisar Colony adjoined Purāni Mandi. The area had long been a wood wholesale market but had recently seen the development of increasing numbers of medium-sized manufactories. Kazim Crafts was one of these sites. Ayesha and I had contacted them by phone and arranged to meet the owner, Rashid. A large, heavy-set man of rotund build, Rashid was not an easy character. The interview we had hoped to conduct was quickly refocused onto our activities and Rashid bombarded us with questions. Often, he would cut off our attempts to answer by delivering his own view on what the answer should be. When we finally managed to steer the conversation to the employment of female workers in the factory, he was mocking in his condescension. '*Kyo unse savaal puchna chatai hai, wo kutch nahi jantai hai* [why do you want to speak to them, they know nothing]?' 'You can speak to me, I can give you all the answers you need,' he continued. 'Those women are characterless, they don't come here for work but only for sexual pleasure.'

His remark, while not the view of all factory owners, reflected questions of character and morality that hung over many female factory workers in the city. Shazia, a 35-year-old widow, remarked, 'In the factory the owners, male workers or contractors are often rude to us and make comments about us, saying that we are like a loose woman or they may say some sexual things to us.' Faiza, a 50-year-old married woman, described how:

> For the younger girls, the factory can be very bad, as the owner or some other man sometimes tries to touch them or to start some affair. Her character will be ruined, and people will say that she is *gandā* [dirty], then maybe it will be hard for her to marry and people will laugh at her.

In late December 2011 I was coming to the end of my first month working in Abdul Malik's factory. This had involved participation in various stages of the manufacturing process, but my male positionality had initially confined me to male-dominated spaces of the factory floor. Over time, however, access to areas where women were primarily employed, such as packing and finishing, started to open up. I was working with some of the female packers during a slack period, when they were approached by Abdul. He acknowledged me with a grin, before turning to Farida, a young woman in her mid-20s, stating, '*Ghar mein kām hai, āj wahā jāo!* [there is work in the house, go there today!]'. Farida nodded, replying, '*Hā ji* [yes, sir]', before bundling up her possessions and leaving. As she set off the others giggled. Later, Noor, one of the older female workers, explained, '*Abdul hameshā us-se apne ghar bhejhte hai* [Abdul always sends her to his house]'. There was a questioning tone in her voice and a smirk that insinuated some degree of immorality in her move to the private space (cf. Chambers & Ansari 2018).

Younger women, in particular, found that their engagements with factory work resulted in imputations of dubious character. These were reinforced by rumours of affairs between favoured workers and factory owners, not all of them unfounded (Abdul himself had married a former worker as a second wife). The degree to which such rumours were the subject of speculation depended on the youthfulness of the woman concerned (cf. Parry 2001). Stage of life, then, made the factories less problematic for older women, at least in terms of sexual harassment or consequences for their respectability (cf. M. Das Gupta 1995; Ussher et al. 2015), but not necessarily in terms of lost agency or control of one's labour. While differentiated by factors such as lifecycle, the disciplining effects of these discourses around the sexual morality of female workers had deeper structural implications. As Mary Beth Mills (2017: 316) argues in the context of research from across Asia,

> As discursive constructs, figures of feminine immorality alert us to the ideological support that locally gendered symbols and gender hierarchies provide for expanding modes of capital accumulation and neoliberal governance across the region. … At the same time, these figures encode and dramatise the unsettling moral and material demands that, as marginalised subjects of national development regimes, many ordinary Asians must navigate on a daily basis.

In the case of Saharanpur's wood-manufacturing sites, the imputation of feminine immorality not only acted as a structural justification for low wages and status but also enabled forms of bodily discipline on the factory floor. Abdul employed some women directly, but others worked under Faisal, a *thēkēdār*. Faisal supplied labour during times of higher demand for finishing work. While this labour included some older men, he primarily employed women. During a particularly busy period he reprimanded one of his female workers for not keeping her eyes on her work, saying, '*Kya tum boyfriend ke lie dekh rahe hain*? [are you looking for a boyfriend?] *Apanee aankhen neeche rakho, kaam karo*! [keep your eyes down, do your work].' It was a moment in which gendered notions of Muslim women's femininity, questions of sexual morality and patriarchal workplace hierarchies were brought to bear in the production and reproduction of constructed ideals of Muslim women's docility in bodily form (cf. Foucault 2008 [1979]).

In this context, the refusal by some women to engage in factory work, despite the potential for improved earnings, is as much tied up with a lost sense of agency and control over one's own body as it is connected to concerns around female seclusion, purdah and *chāl-chalan*. Faiza, whose fractious relationship with Gulshan had seen the two falling out, summed up the various factors that contributed to decisions to avoid factory work:

> It is respected work as we are doing this work in our home. If we go to factories, we have no respect in society. She [my daughter] always wants to hide our identity in school and not show that we are labour so she has always wanted me to leave this work, but I try to convince her that there should be no shame in hard work because we are not asking for money like a beggar. We are eating our *roti* in a respectful manner. Our society blames women if it sees them work in a factory or with an unknown man, but they cannot understand why we may go. I may go for a job or my *roti*. Our society is blind; they never think it may be possible that a woman has some problem and that is why she is outside. In the factories they treat us like servants, and we must follow every order; here we are always working hard but there is no man watching us and telling us what to do.

The evaluation of the pros and cons of engaging in factory work was not based on economic gain alone but required consideration of a variety of factors. While factory work provided a higher and potentially more stable income, it did not necessarily negate some of the other problems faced by homeworkers. Women in Saharanpur's factories were often treated as a flexible labour force. While some were directly employed, others worked through male *thēkēdārs*. As with homeworkers, however, this arrangement often lacked the close bond present in many male worker–*thēkēdār* relationships, in which links of neighbourhood and similar social position created a degree of mutual trust. Many of the problems and risks faced by homeworkers in the gullies were also present for female factory workers labouring under *thēkēdārs*. Fareeda, a 40-year-old factory worker who resided in the same gully as Noor and Farhana, related:

> They even run away with our payment; it has happened many times to me. The contractor is very bad and always runs away with our money. The owner is not responsible for this incident as the *thēkēdār* takes the money, so the owner is free from any fight. … The *thēkēdār* always pretends that he will give us money next week but then tells us it will be the following Friday. The *thēkēdār* is a scoundrel so we cannot trust him … If we go to the owner's office he shouts, 'I have not appointed you; you should go and search for the *thēkēdār*.' He tells us that it is not his responsibility.

This is not to say that all *thēkēdārs* were 'scoundrels' but rather that switching from homework to factory work did not necessarily represent a move away from systems of subcontracting and their associated insecurity and precarity. Likewise, shifting to factory labour did not negate divisions that were driven by competition for work. Similarly to Sabra, Farah lived in Mānak Mau and made the daily commute to Abdul's factory, where she worked alongside Chamār women. Communal divisions present in the village were often reproduced within the factory space, and Chamār and Muslim workers would take their lunch separately and occupy different sections of the finishing workspace. Farah explained the lines of demarcation between the two groups:

> [In the factory where I work] Muslim women are few, but Hindu women come there in great numbers. The low-caste women like the Chamāris go there too much. Sometimes there is a fight between us. The Chamāri women have everything, they live at a good standard and they have a house and money. They only go for the work to get money for their fun and enjoyment. The poor Muslim women go because of their poverty. Some are widows, some go because their sons do not give them any money, but the Chamāri women only go for 'timepass'. One Chamāri woman is going with her young girls; she has a house that the BSP [Bahujan Samaj Party] government gives them as they are of the same caste. She has no need of work, but we have many problems and get no help from the government.

Despite these divisions we did find moments of unity. For some workers the presence of Chamār women had provided an opportunity to challenge factory owners. Sitara from Ali ki Chungi was a 50-year-old factory worker. Some 15 years ago, when her children were small, her husband passed away. After completing *iddah*[5] she took a job in one of the city's largest factories but found conditions not to her liking. The work was hard, her hands, often bled from the *rigmal* (sandpaper), overtime was compulsory and payment often late. She eventually moved to a smaller factory, where she works today. As in Abdul's factory, Chamār and Muslim women ate separately but Sitara described how, gradually, the women had started to speak up together and to develop an appreciation for each other's position:

> Now we are raising our voice and asking for 120 rupees per day. There is no union, but we have some unity. Now we have taken the decision that we will not work for less than 100 rupees per day. We will only work if the amount is 100, 110 or 120 rupees. In saying this, we are both Chamāri and Muslim. But you know the Chamāri women are responsible for this increment. You know the Muslim woman is timid, she cannot shout or raise her voice, but the Chamāri women can. They raised their voices and we followed. Seeing the Chamāri women doing this gave us confidence. Now we are with them in this fight, but we do not know if the owner will give more money.

This is not to suggest weakness or timidity on the part of Muslim women, but the situation is, in part, tied up with a degree of political ascendancy undertaken by Chamārs and other Dalits through political mobilisation in Uttar Pradesh and other areas (Ciotti 2006; Witsoe 2016; Govinda 2017). While such movements remain constrained in the context of caste oppression, variegated forms of agency and activism have increased in these communities (Govinda 2017). The BSP's emergence as a major player in the state-level politics of Uttar Pradesh from 1989 has also played a part in cementing degrees of confidence and aspiration in the community.

Yet a dismissal of female Muslim workers as only being led by others who are less constrained by the expectations of purdah, *chāl-chalan* and other notions of female seclusion, piety and modesty would be a serious misrepresentation. In her wonderfully detailed account of the lives of young Muslim women in the *bastīs* (slums) of Kolkata, Kabita Chakraborty (2016) details how media, technology and shifting constructions of self are embedded in affective circulations intersected by Bollywood culture and globalising forces. Specifically, Chakraborty emphasises how

Bollywood influences and other factors interplay in young women's ideas about romance, love and intimacy. Various globalising circulations are also a part of the ways in which Muslim women construct themselves vis-à-vis the labour market. Let's be very clear: agency in this context is highly constrained. The ethnographic material presented in this chapter has demonstrated the multiple enclaving and enclosing forces that female workers experience. Yet Sitara's story begins to hint at moments of collectivisation that challenge established hierarchies based on female subordination, external and internalised forms of bodily discipline and, very importantly, class.

These moments were not limited to the factories, with their potentialities for connecting to other subjectivities which, while no less gendered, constructed their female positionalities in terms that allowed greater levels of workplace confrontation. In the gullies, too, the very networks that facilitated processes of outsourcing also offered moments of care, organisation and, albeit to a limited degree, resistance. In the spring of 2014, Farhana had brought an order to the gully from a new manufacturer with whom she had not done business before. Her networks of *mohalla* workers, including Noor and Zahoor, had completed the order in a couple of weeks. During a later period of fieldwork in the summer of 2014 I made a return visit to Noor and her family. Tension had been building for some time as the manufacturer, a man called Ishmael, had still not paid the outstanding money. This meant that Farhana had not been able to pay the other women in her network. As was characteristic of her forthright style, it was Noor who took the initiative. Through numerous phone calls and visits to other women in the gully, including Farhana, she harnessed the building anger into action on a sweltering Monday afternoon in early August.

Noor, together with several other women, began by taking their grievance to Farhana. Farhana pleaded her case, reminding them that she was in the same situation and that she was not able to pay them until the owner paid the outstanding sum. The discussion was conducted in respectful terms in the *sahn* of Farhana's house but was impassioned and lively. I had tagged along with Noor and Ibrahim, her husband. Ibrahim and I sat to one side and I had occasionally to whisper to him to get updates, as the pace of the discussion meant my level of Hindi struggled to keep up. Eventually Noor declared, '*Theek hai, ham vahaan jaayengee* [okay, we will go there]', referring to Ishmael's factory. Noor was usually very guarded about revealing the locations of her suppliers for fear of being undercut by others, but on this occasion the length of the delay, coupled with the fact that this was the only order she had received from Ishmael, meant that she relented. The group, now comprising most of the female woodworkers in the gully, around twelve in total, donned their burkas and piled, along with a few male relatives, into three rickshaws.

Once at the factory, the women pushed their way into the courtyard and demanded their payment from Ishmael. He initially refused, while the male workers laughed and shouted from the sidelines. Gradually, however, the vehemence of the argument began to draw a crowd and Ishmael looked increasingly uncomfortable with the situation. It took over an hour of shouting, threatening and cajoling for him to succumb and hand over some of the outstanding payment, promising the remainder the following week. Three days later I had to make my departure from the city, but over the phone Noor confirmed that full payment was eventually received. '*Wo hamase dar luktai hai* [he is in fear of us],' she stated. 'He will not give any orders to Farhana again, but we have our money because of our strength.' While such direct confrontations were rare, this account of the event – along with other ethnographic material presented in this chapter – helps to challenge dominant representations of Muslim women in the labour force (and of Muslim women more broadly) as passive victims of embedded systems of production, patriarchal ideals and norms of female seclusion. Such factors are prominent in structuring the lives of women in Saharanpur's *mohallas*, but forms of counter-conduct are by no means absent.

Conclusion

This chapter has elucidated the gendered construction of the supply chain by emphasising the ways in which women's labour is mediated through notions of femininity, women's docility, patriarchal structures and spatialising practices. This is a labour force that is invisibilised both at the level of international divisions of labour and within the local supply chain. The chapter has illuminated the complexity of relations amongst women woodworking in the residential gullies of the city's Muslim *mohallas* and the complex negotiations of character and personhood that are involved in traversing the spaces of home, *mohalla* and factory. Across all sites of production, Muslim women are firmly rooted to the bottom of the labour hierarchy and experience the starkest forms of exploitation and subjugation. But this chapter has also detailed moments of contestation and resistance that form an important part of the gendered labour dynamics of the wood supply chain.

From here the book moves to the publicly visible gullies which make up the larger arena of wood manufacture. Comprising numerous open-fronted, small-scale workshops, these are male-dominated spaces of sociality and work. The shift in focus back to the localities where the majority of my fieldwork was spent begins with a discussion of learning to labour, specifically the *ustād–shāgird* system that forms the primary structure through which the city's male labour force is reproduced and craft skills are passed on. Women do feature elsewhere in this book, but the material that follows is very much focused on the male life worlds that, as a consequence of my male identity, formed the spaces of deepest engagement throughout the research. I hope, though, that this chapter has gone some way towards avoiding the kind of exclusively male narrative that is often a feature of ethnographic research undertaken by men in gender-segregated contexts.

Figure 4.2 A *thēkēdār* delivering items to be finished by homeworking women. Source: author.

Figure 4.3 A gully near Ali ki Chungi. Source: author.

Notes

1. Not an easily translatable term but broadly speaking it means character, reputation or 'how society sees you'. It carries a great deal of weight and strength and is used mostly, although not exclusively, by, and with reference to, women.
2. A *rehri* is a four-wheeled cart. *Wallah* in this case refers to the person pushing it (basically a delivery man).
3. A colloquial expression meaning literally 'pure shawl', but here it means purity of character.
4. In Hindi 'tu' meaning 'you' is generally only used for animals or children (usually when they are being told off). It is the lowest in terms of respect, 'ap' being the most formal (for example for parents, teachers or elders) and 'tum' being the casual form used among friends or equals.
5. *Iddah*, the period of mourning for a new widow, lasts four months and ten days.

5
Apprenticeship and labour amongst Indian Muslim artisans

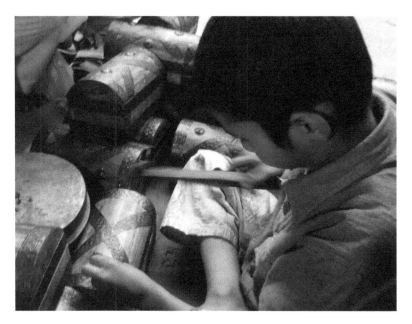

Figure 5.1 A young apprentice at work. Source: author.

Islam became not just an informant and friend but also my ustād. I could see pleasure, and slight amusement, in his eyes each time I addressed him as such. Although brass overlay work had been deskilled (following the introduction of pre-cut brass) and looked to be a modest undertaking, I soon realised I had much to learn. Initially, I was allowed only to carry out simple tasks. Islam drilled holes in the brass shapes, cut tacks from brass wire, laid out the design and hammered a tack lightly into each hole, just enough to clutch the wood underneath. Gripping the tacks with tweezers, I then nailed the tacks into the wood with a small hammer. Even this humble job proved difficult. The thin wire tacks were fragile. I bent many of them and had to pull them out and start again. Often the tacks required a small head. This was achieved by adjusting the hammer angle from side to side while tapping, and so spreading and flattening the top of the tack.

Initially I struggled, and Islam showed me items that had come back ruined from the buffer's shop. The lack of a head had led to the buffing machine ripping off the brass designs, meaning they had to be scrapped and started again. None was wasted, however. Bent tacks were returned to the pre-cut brass manufacturer where they could be traded for a discount off Islam's next purchase. The size of the tack head had to be adjusted to the condition of the wood. If it was dry, the head could be small, giving a smoother finish to the design, as the tack gripped naturally to the grain. Damp wood required a broader head, as moisture lubricated the material, which allowed the tack to come loose during buffing. To begin with, I had to ask Islam, 'Kya yah lakri gila ya suukh hai? [Is this wood wet or dry?]'. Slowly, however, I started to get a feel for the material, to understand the subtle differences in texture and appearance, depending on the moisture level.

It was not just technique that I struggled with. My body did not adapt well to long hours of sitting and working. The shop was small, and we sat opposite each other on the stone floor, which was only covered with a thin hemp sack. We removed our shoes and used our toes and feet to steady more awkward pieces of wood. I found I often shifted position and by the end of the day my lower back was screaming. I was reminded of a story told by an old friend, a tailor from Mussoorie. When he was a boy his father started to teach him the work. For weeks he sat cross-legged in the shop only watching what his father did. His mother complained that this was a waste of time and that, if he was not working, he should do something else. His father, however, explained that he was learning the most important skill: to sit. I told this story to Islam and explained that, as a boy, I never learnt 'to sit'. He chuckled and reminded me, each time I stood up groaning, that it would have been a good thing to learn this.

It was a couple of months before I was allowed to do anything more complicated. I was pleased when Islam presented me with a board of wood, upon which brass shapes were laid out, and a hand drill. Here, too, my touch proved heavy. I often made the holes too big, which meant that the tacks would not hold. Frequently, the bit stuck during drilling, rotating the brass. Patiently, Islam showed me how to approach this with a combination of speed, to avoid sticking, and delicacy, to avoid oversized holes. It was longer still before I was introduced to the most difficult stage of brass overlay work. Designs were composed of floral or abstract shapes. These ended in curved brass leaves with an engraved stem pattern consisting of three scores starting together at the base and opening out towards the tip. We undertook this with a fine-tipped chisel. The brass leaves were delicate and my fear of damaging them resulted in the grooves being barely visible. Islam encouraged me to apply force. Often I punctured the brass but slowly I started to get the weighting of each blow. The grooves had slightly rough edges and I compulsively attempted to brush the stray shards with my finger. Islam quickly stayed my hand, explaining that the shards could become embedded in the skin and that they would disappear during the buffing process anyway.

As our friendship grew, we spent more time together away from work. I often went to Islam's home and was introduced to his parents, brothers, wife and three children. His father, who made sweet wrappers, smoked beedies (cheap cigarettes) and talked through missing teeth, which made him hard to understand. Islam's mother was highly visible in the home space. She greeted me warmly each time, placing her hand on my head by way of blessing. The other women remained mostly in the sahn (courtyard), where food was prepared and household chores completed. Islam and I usually sat together in a rear bedroom. The younger women averted their gaze as I passed through the communal space. On one occasion I was sitting alone while Islam was at namāz (prayer). His mother entered and requested that I help repair a music player. I followed her to the next room where the women were. They giggled and asked me questions while I fiddled haphazardly with the machine. I got the feeling that the broken music machine was being used as an opportunity for them to get a look at me. I felt uncertain whether I was supposed to be in the space and averted my gaze before exiting. I did not mention it to Islam but a few days later he asked if I thought the machine could be fixed. The more I got to know the family the more some of the curtains fell as relations became increasingly informal.

Although familiarity allowed a degree of informality, Islam was diligent in his religious practice. He always made time for namāz and sometimes I joined him. As well as completing namāz, Islam wore the kurta-pyjama (a light collarless suit, usually white) and did not shave his beard. As our friendship grew, Islam occasionally expressed his concern regarding my lack of religion. He never did so out of a desire to convert me, or for his own satisfaction, but through a genuine concern that his close friend might not join him in the afterlife:

The Quran is the word of God, but you are my best friend. I do not give you any pressure, but you should investigate. Let's go in Jamaat [Islamic evangelising tour or gathering] and there some foreigners can explain to you. They came because they believe in Allah. Many people convert to Islam as they get an idea about Allah's power. I am very much worried about you that you will burn in fire if you have no faith. Tom, you are my best friend and I do not want to see you in the fire. ... I never want to convert you, but I am telling you this as you are my best friend.

Islam was also keen to school me in other aspects of Islamic practices and broader cultural norms, and so became a cultural as well as a craft ustād. He instructed me how to perform namāz and the correct procedure for vazu (pre-prayer washing procedure). When we attended the masjid (mosque), he prayed next to me, ensuring that I followed his movements. While some of his tuition was orientated towards formal occasions there were also numerous smaller adaptations that he encouraged me to make. These included instruction in how I should bathe and maintain my body hair, and small corrections on those occasions when I stumbled in the application of everyday behaviours. Islam's desire to draw me into more pious forms of daily practice was amplified in part by his involvement in the Tablighi Jamaat (which expressly preaches embodied norms and routines as a path to becoming a good Muslim), but it also intermingled with his position as my ustād and (increasingly as time passed) my friend. Yet Islam was not the only ustād in the gully and, while some applied similar moral frameworks to their engagements with shāgirds, in certain other workshops social life revolved around hanging out, drinking alcohol and, at times, frequenting prostitutes. Here, the lessons I would have learned would have been very different, and status would have been acquired not only through the development of craft skills but also through willingness to engage in these pursuits.

Introduction: the carpenter's apprentice

In her children's short story 'The Carpenter's Apprentice', Monisha Mukundan (1999) tells the tale of Mohammad, a young boy who is about to start the day on which his *ustād* will allow him to undertake his first wood join on the building scaffold where they labour. That morning Mohammad's friends come to take him to an elephant fight. When he says he cannot join the festivities they taunt him. His friends work as stonemasons and scoff at the temporariness of the scaffold, derisively telling him that the stone flowers they fashion will last for eternity. His master, *Ustād* Pira, overhears the conversation. Later he moves to reassure Mohammad, telling him, 'Every bit of work is important. If we didn't build the scaffolding, in the best way we can, there would be no building, no base for marble decorations. We helped to lay the foundations of the building, and the building rises only because we are here' (p. 32). Mohammad's downtrodden spirit is revived, and the story concludes with an emphasis on the affection he feels for his *ustād* as he takes his tools and, surrounded by the carpenters, declares, 'I'm ready!'

Mukundan's story reflects classic notions of master–apprentice relationships. The *ustād* acts as protector, patron and teacher. The *shāgird* gives respect, affection and, once sufficiently trained, his labour. This chapter combines my own embodied experience of undertaking an apprenticeship in the wood industry with reflections on the stories of those for whom woodwork provides a livelihood. Through these ethnographic insights, I illustrate how the *ustād–shāgird* (master–apprentice) system is embedded in the broader political economy, labour force reproduction and forms of self-making. *Ustād–shāgird* systems are not relics of a pre-capitalist past, and nor are they static and unchanging within contemporary modalities of capitalist production and development. Rather, they are bound up in complex circulations shaped by the demands of the supply chain, shifting cultural practices, religious and other moral frameworks, reconfigurations in the status of younger men and contestations around knowledge.

Apprenticeship in Saharanpur, I argue, is not a cleanly defined space of skill acquisition and well-established hierarchical structures as presented by Mukundan and others (e.g. Burki 1989); rather it is a complex assemblage of forces which at times align and at others conflict. It is also a space of multifaceted emotions (cf. Gieser 2008; Simpson 2006a), from love, intimacy, care and respect to anger, betrayal, jealousy and distress. Additionally, the *ustād–shāgird* system cannot be detached from the spatial context of the *mohalla*. The forms of enclavement and bordering outlined in the introduction and in other chapters of this book interplay with long-duration processes of craft labour reproduction. These constraints limit access to other pathways of knowledge acquisition, further feeding into the reproduction of the workforce. However, it also creates a sense of identity and belonging for those entering wood trades, through which subjective and material forms of socio-economic marginalisation can, to a degree, be countered (cf. Willis 2017). Holistically, this draws the chapter into attending to both disciplining and agentive aspects of apprenticeship as well as the variety of connections through which it is constituted and reconstituted.

Conceptualising apprenticeship: craft and beyond

Contemporary debates on apprenticeship have focused on two broad areas. The first questions the processes through which craft and other forms of knowledge are transmitted and the ways in which cultural and religious structures impact this transmission (e.g. Schmoller 2017; Stoller & Olkes 1987; Marchand 2010; Simpson 2006b; Gieser 2008; Bloch 1991). The second considers the role of apprenticeship within the broader political economy and the forms of change that 'traditional' modalities of knowledge transfer are experiencing in the contexts of colonialism, globalisation, industrial capitalism and neoliberalism (e.g. Gooptu 2018; Sanchez 2012; Epstein 2008; Sennett 2008; T. Roy 1999; Braverman 1998). These two areas of focus are not mutually exclusive; hence this chapter considers them concurrently.

Research on apprenticeship in craft industries reminds us that there are effective forms of education beyond formal schooling and that knowledge is tacitly embodied, not only verbally transmitted (Portisch 2010; Venkatesan 2010; Simpson 2006a; Dilley 1999; cf. Bourdieu 1990). It also reveals apprenticeships as a key site in processes of social and hierarchical reproduction (Simpson 2006a). Trevor Marchand (2008: 246) illustrates that apprenticeship is not just about learning but also about structuring 'the practitioner's hard-earned acquisition of social knowledge, worldviews and moral principles that denote membership and status in a trade'. As Michael Herzfeld (2004) puts it, apprenticeships are served in a 'total social context' that involves creation of persona as well as imparting of skills. Apprenticeships are often highly gendered. Thus, in male-dominated industries such as Saharanpur's woodworking cluster, apprenticeship is also a key site for the production of masculinities as well as a liminal space of transition from boyhood to manhood (f. Mellström 2017; Parker 2006; Willis 2017). Beginning with political economy and questions of labour process, in the following material I consider knowledge transmission, the role of cultural and religious (Islamic, in particular) factors in shaping apprenticeship and the forms of continuity and change taking place within the system.

In his classic text *Labor and Monopoly Capital*, Harry Braverman (1998) argues that craft labour is increasingly divided and routinised through incorporation into capitalist modes of production. For Braverman this is about more than efficiency and cost; it is also a means by which control is exerted over workers through the appropriation of craft knowledge. This has the effect of creating a relationship of dependency, as labour no longer holds intellectual knowledge of the whole production process.

Thus, some moments of counter-current aside, deskilling becomes the dominant pattern across sites of production globally. In earlier chapters of this book we have seen moments of deskilling (the segmentation of brass overlay work and the representation of feminised areas of production as skill-less, for example), but we have also seen the persistence of *ustād–shāgird* relations even within the walls of factories. While this persistence is partly bound up in modalities of resistance to industrial modes of production and capitalist temporalities (a point I expand on in the following two chapters), it also allows factory owners to use pre-existing *ustād–shāgird* systems to discipline and control labour. Writing on carpet weaving in Agra (Uttar Pradesh), Tirthankar Roy (1999) emphasises the blurring of the role of *ustād* and labour contractor in factories owned by Europeans (cf. Prasad 1907; Watt 1903: 436). T. Roy (2013) later expands on this to describe the emergence of dual systems within industrial manufacturing in India which incorporated both artisanal modes of recruitment and training (a pattern that blurred the roles of *ustād* and contractor) and more centralised models of labour control. It is the concurrence of the two, rather than the replacement of the former with the latter, that enables the most effective disciplining of labour.

Beyond the factory context, the role of *ustāds* in contemporary supply chains is equally ambiguous. Roy Dilley (1999: 41), for example, describes a weaving master in Senegal spending 'most of his time hawking finished cloth around the traders at the market [… with] apprentices [… being] guided by an elderly client weaver and a fully trained young man'. These master weavers, Dilley suggests, used networks of obligation, generated through training apprentices, to increase spheres of influence within the marketplace. Often, the master was, in effect, an employer whose concerns were primarily securing business deals, wheeling and dealing in the bazaar and extracting labour value from apprentices. As Dilley found in Senegal, in Saharanpur most apprenticeships took place within spaces that were deeply embedded in the gullies, neighbourhoods and familial networks of the *mohallas*. Apprenticeships were always part business deal and part reciprocal arrangement, but they were also shaped by influences emanating from Islam.

Here too, Dilley (1999) points out the importance of connecting apprenticeships, within Muslim-dominated craft industries, with Islamic principles of learning and scholarship. Dilley draws parallels between apprenticeship amongst artisans in Senegal and the repetitive learning practised in Quranic schools. This is a point outlined in more detail by Trevor Marchand (2013) in ethnographic material detailing the lives of minaret builders in Yemen. Here, he echoes Dilley by arguing that apprenticeship often involves 'learning without understanding', a process like that of children reciting the Quran without understanding the words.[1] For Marchand (2013), the completion of an apprenticeship with the minaret builders paralleled the three stages to Islamic enlightenment: Islam – submission to or the embodying of religious practice; Iman – the cultivation of faith; and Ishan – the 'level at which one's intentionality is fully absorbed in, and guided by, spiritual faith and understanding' (p. 23). In craft terms this final stage is the point at which 'thoughts and actions are absorbed with the drive to reproduce the "beauty" of the craft over which he has acquired mastery' (p. 74).

As Seyyed Hossein Nasr (1990: 10) reflects, 'Islamic sp[i]rituality is … related to Islamic art through the manner in which the Islamic rites mould the mind and soul of all Muslims including the artist or artisan'. Citing Ibn Khaldun, Titus Burckhardt and Seyyed Hossein Nasr, Marchand (2013) continues by discussing the lack of division between the categories of 'art', 'science' and 'craft' and suggests that the emergence of these distinctions is a European phenomenon. Decline in the status of craftwork in India (Mohsini 2016; Kumar 2017) and its associated forms of learning can be understood, then, not only within the context of socio-economic marginalisation but also against the background of a constructed severing of craft from technology, science and art, a process that relegates the artisan to the status of petty commodity producer (cf. Marchand 2013).

Against this background Marchand (2010) conceptualises apprenticeship in terms of mimesis (the mimicking of reality). This conceptualisation differs somewhat from phenomenological approaches that emphasise embodied practices over language in the transferral of skills (e.g. Ingold 2000). Mimesis, however, focuses on the transmission of 'experiential truth', with cultural meaning being communicated linguistically (Gieser 2008). Within Islamic scholarship on education, a similar foregrounding of language is present. Syed Muhammad Naquib al-Attas (1977) emphasises the centrality of speech in his reflection on education in Islam, arguing that it is 'the capacity for understanding speech, and the power responsible for the formulation of meaning' (p. 3) that make people rational. Like Marchand, al-Attas identifies differentials between Islamic and European understandings of 'rational man' [sic], specifically the tendency within European secular philosophy to separate *intellectus* (intellect) and *ratio* (rationality). This separation, al-Attas (1977: 2–3) argues, is problematic for Islamic notions of humanity, which foreground the harmonisation of *intellectus* and *ratio* captured in the concept of *aql*, 'a spiritual substance by which the rational soul (*al-nafs al-nātiqah* …) recognizes and distinguishes truth from falsehood'. The focus on *aql*, as lying at the core of what makes us human, leads al-Attas to situate education within Islam as being about more than knowledge and skill transfer alone. Instead, he sees education as defined through *ta'dib*, which brings together the disciplining of mind, body and soul (cf. Abdalla et al. 2018):

> [Education is the] *recognition and acknowledgement, progressively instilled into man, of the proper places of things in the order of creation, such that it leads to the recognition and acknowledgement of the proper place of God in the order of being and existence.* … Since meaning, knowledge and education pertain to man alone, and by extension to society, the recognition and acknowledgement of the proper places of things in the order of creation, must primarily apply to man's own recognition and acknowledgement of his proper place – that is, his station and condition in life in relation to his self, his family, his people, his community, his society – and to his self-discipline in actualizing within his self the recognition by the acknowledgement. This means that he must know his place in the human order, which must be understood as arranged hierarchically and legitimately into various degrees (*darajāt*) of excellence *based on the Qur'ānic criteria of intelligence, knowledge, and virtue (ihsān)*, and must act concomitantly with the knowledge in a positive, commendable and praiseworthy manner.
> (Al-Attas 1977: 16; emphasis in original)

In this context, then, apprenticeship within Muslim craft industries is a disciplining process that spans the economic, social, embodied and internal spheres. To posit all modes of contemporary apprenticeship in Saharanpur as constituted through Islamic influences alone would, however, be a reification of Islam and a homogenisation of apprenticeship across Muslim-dominated craft industries. Many of the aspects outlined above are present and, as more recent ethnographic material shows, apprenticeship is not limited to the reproduction of skills but is also intimately involved in the crafting of subjectivities and ways of being in and seeing the world (*nazriya*). However, the ways of being and ways of seeing that emerge are by no means homogeneous, and, along with the influences detailed previously, are shaped through colonial encounters (the forms of intervention outlined in chapter 2, for example) and more recent modes of incorporation into complex global supply chains that weave their way into contemporary modalities of apprenticeship in the city.

In ethnographic research amongst dhow (boat) builders in Gujarat, Edward Simpson (2006b) emphasises the importance of considering Islamic influences on the construction of *ustād–shāgird* arrangements.

Simpson situates this construction in a shifting context in which, for example, newly dominant caste groups have cemented their position by aligning themselves with Islamic reformist movements and ideals. He also details more affective aspects of the apprenticeship process which inaugurate individuals into nuances of '[l]anguage and the gestures of language … through which friendship and camaraderie are communicated' (p. 66). Early experiences of apprenticeship are, Simpson argues, as much about humiliation and being the 'butt of every joke' as they are about learning skills. For Simpson apprenticeships are not based just on mutual relationships but on the 'drama of apprenticeship' and the violence inherent in it. This leads him to critique the notion that apprenticeship is primarily about learning.

Instead, Simpson argues that profit motives drove many *ustāds* (cf. Dilley 1999) and that, for apprentices, apprenticeship was often seen as a 'means to other ends' such as foreign adventure or personal advancement. Writing about artisans in Crete, Michael Herzfeld (2004) likewise details the master–apprentice relationship in highly fractured terms intersected by the reconfigurations and pressures of global markets as well as by changing status and identity. For Herzfeld apprenticeship often walks a fine line between learning and the theft of designs, ideas and customers (cf. Meagher 2006; Gowlland 2012; Turna 2019). Following Herzfeld, Simpson and others, the ethnographic material in this chapter shows that apprenticeship did not only involve learning one's place within the social fabric of the gully, the *mohalla* and the broader community but also contained various conflicts and divergences. Building on this, I illustrate the ways in which apprenticeship interplays with the spatial context of the *mohalla*, the (re)production of the labour force and the cultivation of *kārīgars*' subjectivities. While involving forms of discipline, the embodying of practices, and degrees of enclavement within the *mohalla* and its networks, apprenticeship also provided a 'durable identity and set of relationships' (Carrier 1992: 546) which interplayed with the intense social fabric of the gully and neighbourhood (cf. Gowlland 2018).

Apprenticeship in Kamil Wali Gully: aspiration and enclavement

In the previous section I gave considerable attention to a broad contextual background which brings together numerous intersecting considerations. This was essential in order to establish the multiple factors shaping contemporary *ustād–shāgird* relationships in the city. In Kamil Wali Gully, as elsewhere in Saharanpur, apprentices were numerous. Some were young boys, some in their late teens. Some were taught by considerably older masters and others by those of a similar age. Most started with simple jobs: fetching tea, sweeping away wood shavings and running errands. Many would spend the whole day in the workshop earning little more than tea and lunch, although paid apprenticeships were also emerging. Early on in my initial fieldwork I met Imran, an experienced carver whose childhood polio had left him with deformed legs. He occupied a position of some authority in the gullies because of his political ties with both the Samajwadi (socialist) and Communist parties. These activities had given him a sense of broader structures and he situated apprenticeship within the lifecycle of the artisan, a lifecycle he saw as being constituted through exploitation:

> Children are learning how to work from just eight years old and never get time to study. They are making plain wood into gold but never get any money for it. [Indicating children of around 8–10 years old in the room] They learn the work from this age. Parents send them out to bring a few rupees back, people have no choice in this. We are trapped here in the *mohalla* and only the wood-work provides our *roti* so what else can they do? The children learn this work for many years, but the exporters take the labour of their hands for their own luxury. We know all about the wood-work but only they [the exporters] can understand the money.
>
> Sometimes the labour inspector comes and says the children should not work. We say 'yes' but once he is gone the children start work again. There is no choice. [Indicating some incense holders] The children made these. They go to the shop and try to sell them to the owner, but he only gives them two rupees for it. The children can maybe earn 100 rupees per month. An artisan must learn for six, seven or eight years but after this they just work their whole life for the exporter or factory owner. If the artisan is old, then the owner just throws him out of the job with no pension and, at best, gives them just two to three thousand rupees advance. Although this work does not require a [formal] education it does need a brain. If you have a degree or are an engineer, you cannot do these things, but these people are getting nothing for it. It takes a good artisan to put the brass in the wood but look at this man [indicating an elderly gentleman], now he just works as a *chaukidār* [watchman] and they [manufacturers, exporters] show no respect for his knowledge as an *ustād*.

Even in the early stages of inauguration into the trade, children became familiar with informal forms of subcontracting and with the idea that one's livelihood relied on the exporter, wholesaler or factory owner. Formal education was not absent, although the quality of the schools in the *mohallas* was notoriously low and many children engaged in forms of craftwork or apprenticeships alongside Hindi-medium schooling. Islam's young nephew would often join us at the brass overlay shop in this way. His apprenticeship was not of a formal nature. Indeed, in some ways it was not an apprenticeship at all. He earned a little pocket money and enabled his uncle to complete orders when demand was high. He showed little enthusiasm for the work, however, and often sought ways out of his obligation. A favourite trick was to convince his uncle to let him run some errand or other and stretch out the time away as far as possible. Islam was tolerant of his behaviour and recognised that the work was little more than 'timepass' for the boy. He saw little future in brass overlay work and so was not keen to train family members fully. When we discussed his aspirations for his two sons, he expressed his desire that they become *mistrīs* (skilled tradespersons in other than craftwork) and undertake apprenticeships in a mechanics shop or with a builder. The woodwork trade, he said, was dead and there was no future for them in becoming *kārīgars*.

Across the gully was the carving shop of Nafees, Waseem, and Imran and his brother Monis. Here three *shāgirds* were employed. The high level of skill involved meant that all three expected lengthy apprenticeships. The four men were strict but nurturing with the boys. Mistakes were made. On one occasion the youngest of the apprentices, Imran, allowed his chisel to slip and blunt on the stone floor. Waseem was angry and gave him a clout around the head. The boy was upset and continued to work with tears welling in his eyes which, despite his best efforts, occasionally fell onto the partly carved wood. At day's end, however, Waseem put an arm round his shoulders and joked, 'The problem is your brain is blunt like this chisel,' and with an affectionate squeeze added, 'Don't worry, we will make it sharp.' Next door to Islam's shop was a workshop occupied by five young men. Brash, rude and bantering, these were not the mild-mannered and diligent craftsmen across the gully. Here, too, there was an apprentice. However, Shamshad was not a demure boy. A friend of Shahnawaz, the owner, he was of a similar age. Although Shahnawaz was technically his *ustād*, the relationship between the two was unlike that in Mukundan's short story. When I asked how the arrangement worked, Shahnawaz replied, 'Yes, I am his *ustād*, it means I can fuck him whenever I want.' Shamshad was quick to respond, 'If he could only get his cock to work.'

These contrasting engagements reflect the variety of learning arrangements present in the gullies. They may involve formal relationships or more informal approaches where mates train mates. Environments in which the *ustād–shāgird* system operates vary, which creates additional layers in the relationship. The person of the *ustād* may take differing forms. The *ustād* may himself be an employee and in turn employ a *shāgird*. As Abdul, a workshop owner in a neighbouring gully, describes, 'I give the artisan who works for me [in my workshop] a piece rate and he employs other people from that money under the *ustād–shāgird* system. In this way I do not have to worry about the training.'[2] As payments were often made on piece rate, the *kārīgar* could improve his own earnings by training a *shāgird*. At times *ustāds* left the training to experienced workers in their employ or doubled as *thēkēdārs* in the factories and workshops of others. In the context of Saharanpur, then, the definition of what it was to be an *ustād* or a *shāgird* was fluid and did not reside simply in 'classical' conceptions of apprentice and master.

Despite this variation, the *ustād–shāgird* system remained the primary mode of skill transfer and labour force reproduction (71 per cent learnt their trades through the system),[3] with others learning from family members or seeing themselves as not having had formal training. There had been some attempts by the state government to institute formal training centres for woodwork. One of these had been established in the local government-run wood-seasoning plant but prospective woodworkers had little interest in the programme, and suggestions that it could enhance the skills of existing *kārīgars* were widely mocked. In the 1970s the nearby Darul Uloom Madrassa at Deoband had, for a time, attempted to induct its religious students into craft trades, including woodcarving. This was less about providing livelihoods and more about using former students to propagate the influence of the ulama (scholars of Islamic law) amongst *kārīgars* and others. Barbara Metcalf (1978: 119), in her study of religious education at the madrassa, describes how:

An abortive innovation on the part of the school was the inclusion of training in crafts and trades. There was hope that students, thus trained, could support themselves in villages and small towns and, simultaneously, share the benefits of their religious training with their neighbors. This would, no doubt, have furthered the influence of the ulama, but the plan came to nought because the students deemed such work unsuitable.

While more formal training courses were often rejected, the forms of socio-economic and spatial marginalisation experienced by those in the gullies fed through into perceptions of alternatives to a training in the wood trade. These limitations were not founded merely in subjective ideas of what constituted a valid imaginary of future employment. At the opposite end of Kamil Wali Gully was the workshop of Waseem. Now in his late fifties with two adult sons, he had, when the pair were children, aspired to cultivate a route for them out of woodwork. His imaginary was one shaped in the context of middle-class ideals that associated modernity, social mobility and status with high-tech skills (IT in particular) and a formal (English) or internationalised education (Misra 1961; Upadhya 2009; Sancho 2015). I got to know Waseem well during several periods of fieldwork. In the spring of 2012, I took a fishing trip with him to a nearby canal. I was interested in better understanding the aspirations he had harboured for his sons when they were young, as he was one of the few woodworkers I met who had invested in formal education to such a degree.

Waseem sighed and, with a suck of air through his teeth, responded, 'Tom bhai, I did not want them to have to work like me. Always there is struggle in this work and we never know if there will be any work the next week. You have seen our condition here, there is no hope in the woodwork any more.' Twitching his fishing rod absent-mindedly, he continued, 'I wanted them to have the metro-city life. I had been in Delhi and Mumbai for work and seen how the [middle-class] people were there. I wanted them to be like those people.' Although Waseem was running only a small unit and employing two or three non-family members, his petty bourgeois position had allowed him to meet the costs of a secondary education in an English-medium school for his sons, while his only daughter had received lessons at the madrassa. Once the sons had graduated, he sent one, Faisal, to a local institute for computer training and the other, Farooq, to inter-college to undertake a diploma in business and commerce. The following day, back in his workshop, he emphasised the fruits of his investment by gesturing towards his two sons who, now both in their early twenties, sat on the floor engaged in woodwork. The eldest son, Faisal, explained:

> I did a computer course in software. Now, though, I do not remember how to do those things, so I could not change to that work. When I finished the course, I tried to get work in the company line in Saharanpur but there were no jobs. In Delhi, too, no one would employ me. Others have had a similar experience. I don't mind having to go back to the wood line: both types of work are good, and this is my own work [*apna*

kām]. … After not getting a job I went to Chennai for some time to do woodwork. Now I am working here again with my family.

The story illustrates the disconnect between aspirations towards middle-class forms of self-making and the structural realities of ongoing caste, religious and ethnic marginalisation. As Henrike Donner and Geert De Neve (2011: 18) argue, 'the gap between the representation of class as relational and the lived experience of class in terms of exclusionary practices has become more significant'. In this case, Waseem's assumption that middle-class ways of being were the outcome of investment in education was tempered by the structural realities of a social context in which a young Muslim man from a *mohalla* in Uttar Pradesh made an unlikely candidate for white-collar employment.

The gap between educational outcomes and the aspirations of young men has been explored in a comparative context by Jeffrey et al. (2004). Focusing on two marginalised groups, Muslims and Chamārs, they deal with increasing access to education in the context of decreased employment opportunities for a newly educated youth (cf. Jeffrey 2010). They suggest that gains from education are not just about obtaining work but are also tied up with notions of status and development. These notions encourage young men to 'fasten onto conceptions of transformation through education' (Jeffrey et al. 2004: 975–6). Focusing on rural areas, they argue that 'Muslim young men have been more capable than Chamars of managing contradictions in narratives of educated distinction, as evident in their pragmatic attitude toward failing to obtain salaried work' (p. 975). Indeed, both Faisal and Farooq were philosophical in their evaluation of the situation they found themselves in. Reflecting on life in the *mohallas*, Faisal continued, 'Here I have my friends, I know all the people and the way things are. In the BPO[4] I would have been alone and maybe it would not have been a good life.'

Faisal's point is an important one and it hints at the ways in which the *mohalla*, and its associated networks of (gendered) sociality, offer a sense of comfort and familiarity. The experiences of Waseem and his family also influenced the subjectivities of others as they considered possible and imagined trajectories for themselves and their kin. I had been introduced to Waseem by Rizwan, a skilled carver, who operated a small workshop directly opposite Islam's brass overlay shop. Rizwan and his family became very close friends, to the extent that during more recent fieldwork trips to the *mohallas* I have always stayed with them in their rented room on the roof of a wood workshop. It was Rizwan's uncle and father who had swum up the river from Yamuna Nager to the relative safety of Saharanpur during partition. Of a slightly stocky build and in his mid-40s, Rizwan operated his workshop along with his sons, who, in 2011 when we first met, were aged 17, 14, 11, 10 and five years. Yousef, the eldest, was already a proficient woodcarver and the others had good capability. The youngest, five-year-old Ishmael, was yet to start learning but he would often be in the workshop mimicking his brothers and father by knocking away at small offcuts of wood, albeit without a chisel.

Rizwan was not from a woodworking family. After partition his ancestors had settled in Khatakheri, which was at that time a small village outside the main city. As the area developed into a wood market his father decided that Rizwan should enter the trade. Close to the family's small room was the stall of an elderly man, Irfan, who sold *pān*,[5] cigarettes and sweets. I would occasionally purchase individual Gold Flakes (a cigarette brand) from him, and when in the company of Rizwan I began to notice the reverence with which he spoke to the old man, always prefacing a new discussion with *Ustād ji* (master sir). It was only later, while interviewing Rizwan towards the end of my first spell of fieldwork, that I realised that Irfan had also been Rizwan's *ustād*:

> I went to the *pān wallah* you can see near my house. I went into his shop. At that time, he was a master *kārīgar*. When I started to learn this work, I first took only tea and water. I never got any salary; I was just a spot boy.[6] I was 12 or 13 years old. When I was learning, my *ustād* only called me to bring tea and nothing else, but after two years he gave me some tools and started to teach me the work.
>
> [My *ustād*'s work] came from *mukhya ji*.[7] He was a construction contractor but when the woodwork started, he went into this line. That contractor took the wood from the *mandi* (Purāni Wali Mandi) and made it in his place. My *ustād* took all his work from this contractor who then sent all the finished items outside Saharanpur.
>
> My *ustād* made some of the carved trim for furniture. These were small, as the double bed was not in fashion and there was no sofa. At that time people were simple and had no idea about sofas and double beds, they could never imagine this furniture. Only in Khatakheri did this first come. Khatakheri is the centre for modern furniture.
>
> When I started with him, I thought that one day I would be perfect in this work. At that time, we could find two rupees in a week but some years later I could find 90 rupees in one month, then 120, then 150, but finally it became 250 rupees in a week. That was my salary when I started but after reaching 250 rupees [as a worker] I started my own work. Then I could earn twenty to twenty-five rupees per day, but it was my own work so this was better.

Similarly to the modalities of supply chain mediation outlined in chapter 3, Rizwan's *ustād*, and therefore Rizwan, found themselves embroiled in patterns of authority that drew on other forms of hierarchy, in this case the role of the *mukhya* as a labour contractor.

Rizwan's own role within complex circuits of labour mediation was limited to his family, his sons providing a labour force that operated within familial obligations. As we chatted about his son's incorporation into woodwork, he cited Waseem as an example of why this offered the best opportunities for them and the family. 'Look at Waseem. He spent so much money on his sons' education but now they sit there like us doing this woodwork. It was a great loss for him. It is better that they learn this work; with this work you can go anywhere … . Maybe Yousef will go to Saudi.' There were, however, some forms of education beyond an apprenticeship under him that Rizwan was keen for his sons to undertake. All five of the boys, along with his youngest daughter, seven-year-old Nasreen, studied the Quran Sharif in a local madrassa. For Rizwan this was not only about educating them in scripture but also about shaping their character and personhood. Rizwan felt capable of training his sons in the trade and providing them with skills and discipline. In his view, for them to become '*sharif*[8] this secondary education was essential. For Rizwan the notions of becoming a craftworker and of crafting a 'good Muslim' were inseparable (cf. Mohsini 2010).

In April 2012 I invited Rizwan's eldest son Yousef to the small room I rented for the duration of my initial fieldwork in the city. By this point, Yousef and I had also become close friends and he would often seek to spend time with me, taking me out for evenings around the city to hang out with his friends. Now 18, he was keen to talk in depth about his life story and we spent the evening sharing a meal and discussing his memories of growing up in the industry:

> J: My father always worked outside Saharanpur. Do you know about paralysis? My father has this problem in his hand. Suddenly it became useless and there was no movement in his hand. Because of this tragedy I left my study.
>
> T: In what class did you study?
>
> J: I only studied in the madrassa, not in the school. After I left the study, I started to learn this work for one month with an *ustād*; it was in Khatakheri. He was my first *ustād*. I learnt this work for one month there and then my father recovered some movement in his arm, so I started work with my father. Since then I have

been continuously working with my father. Then we started some work from outside Saharanpur. It was labour work that came from the small factories.

T: Was it your own place, where you sat?

J: No, it was nobody's property, but it was government property under the water tank. As no one was coming in that place it was safe for us. There was a big tree and we did our work under the tree.

T: Was there any problem?

J: No, we had no problem, as we never paid rent money for that plot, as it is a government plot and there was no enquiry at that time. We had just one problem, as we had no roof over our head and if the rain came we had to pick up all the wood from the place. After this work we made a partnership with another man, but that person was dishonest, he did some fraud.

T: How was he a fraud?

J: For example, if you and I start some combined business and you see some great profit in this business, you will push me out of the business and say, 'Who are you? Get out of this business!' It was a very harmful business for us. After this we started our work from a hut [chhappar] near our house. It was a government place too. It was also a free place for us; we had no payment to make to anybody. Then one day a person came to us and proposed that we should do work in his workshop. So, we worked for four months in his workshop then, again, another person proposed that we moved to his workshop and we accepted his proposal. He offered us more money.

T: What was the condition of the wood industry then?

J: Yes, it was quite good.

T: What was your age at that time?

J: At that time, I was just 10 years old. I started this work at the age of 10. We made mudhas [cane stools] at this time. Then, again, a third person came to us and offered us more money to go to his workshop. The third person told us that his business had stopped suddenly because of some great loss and that he wanted to start again. He said that he had no customers for his work but asked us to join him to help start the business again. We started his work, but he was very lazy in payment and did not want to give us money for the work. He always gave us problems and then my father took the decision to start his own work. Then we took a shop on rent, appointed a carpenter and after some time bought a shop. It was small but all of us worked there. My uncle also worked with us in the same shop. My father taught the work to my uncle and after some time he went out of Saharanpur and we felt very alone in our business. In that period, we made our own work and after collecting some money we took a workshop on rent for our work. It was quite a big workshop and we worked there. At that period our business was growing and one customer came from Malaysia. Another also came from Saudi. Suddenly our business became very good.

T: What was your age then?

J: I was just 14 years old. Then, again, we took one workshop on rent and now we had two factories on rent and our business was growing day by day. We had lots of orders and were very busy at that time. But suddenly our carpenter told us that he was going outside Saharanpur. We gave him permission but after he went suddenly our business decreased. He was a very fine carpenter and did good work for our business, as a good artisan is the basis of any business. After he left, suddenly our business stopped. We looked for another carpenter but never found one. Also, the wood became very expensive, so we closed our workshop. Then we started our own work and we had one order from Rizwan bhai in Mumbai. In this period, we had to face the problem that wood was suddenly costly, but the price of furniture was very low. Villagers are responsible for this low rate as they fixed a low rate for the wood items [to complete orders in the village areas]. As they take the wood from the forest or the jungle they can make furniture at a low rate. Their production costs are low so they can fix the low rate, but it makes a big problem for us. Our neighbours also cut the wood from the forest and made the furniture for a low cost. Because of our neighbours our business stopped.

At the age of 18, Yousef had already witnessed many of the ups and downs of the industry and experienced first-hand the precariousness of livelihoods in the sector. His relationship with his father was deeply bound into wood production. Rizwan was kindly and affectionate towards all his children. He also exerted forms of discipline both around general behaviour and in terms of maintaining their labour and keeping the production that the family relied on going. Of course, the intertwining of familial relations with labour and work is nothing new in craft or informal sector industries, and is seeing a re-emergence in many post-industrial and post-liberalisation contexts (cf. Mollona 2009; Shever 2008; Stensrud 2017). In the years following my initial fieldwork, as Yousef got older, there were more moments of tension between him and his father, as Yousef's expectations regarding the relationship and his position in the hierarchy of production had shifted. These moments of resistance were expressed primarily through ignoring phone calls from his father and disappearing with friends for long periods, a point of ongoing frustration to Rizwan. In the following section I expand on conflictual relations within *ustād–shāgird* relationships, and explore the forms of obligation and patronage that they embody.

Islam's story: conflict and patronage

Islam did see value in formal education. He opted to send his six-year-old son, Saud, to school and intended to do the same for his other two children. Islam himself had had relatively little schooling and had started as a *shāgird* at the age of 14. His induction into brass overlay had not, however, been the single trajectory of apprentice–journeyman–master that is often associated with artisanal training. Instead, it had been a far messier process, involving various *ustāds* and trades:

> When I was growing up, I thought 'I cannot study any more, so I should start working.' There was no benefit to timepass, so work was necessary. I went for work making women's heels. In this work there was much dust and it was harmful to the lungs, so my family told me to stop. Then I started buff work but also there were problems with dust. After one year I stopped. Then I started the brass work on wood. My *ustād*, Abdul, gave me 10 rupees for this work. He taught me the brass work for many years. It took five to six years.
>
> All the work was done by hand. First we made some *tikai* design on the wood, then we filled it. Now, though, it is very easy work; if anyone wants to learn he can learn in a month. Now we can complete a sofa in a few days but at that time it took one to two months as all work was done by hand. My *ustād* took a large sheet of brass and we made designs on it. At least five people were necessary for this. One made the design and the other was cutting. Two to three would fix the brass onto wood. Now, though, I can do this work alone as I can buy brass ready cut. After this we would shape the brass after it had been cut. We called this process 'band'. Then slowly I started some cutting work.
>
> At that time, we were five boys learning with the *ustād*. There was also the *ustād*'s brother. After some time, he built a separate shop. Then he called me to come to his shop for work, so I changed my job and stopped the work with the *ustād*. My *ustād* gave me 1500 rupees but

his brother offered me 2000 rupees [per month]. When I was working with him, I was cutting the patterns. I made a rule that I would give 150 rupees for my home and secretly save 400 rupees [per week] to start my own work. After this I made my own shop in my *mohalla*. At that time, I had everything and completed it all in my shop. Then my *ustād* came and shouted at me, 'What are you doing? It is not good! Come to my shop!' He was angry as I knew every part of his business, so he was fearful that I could compete with him in the business.'

Islam's experience of apprenticeship, then, had been somewhat conflictual. Significantly, it had involved engagements with a variety of trades and workspaces within areas of craft production. In many ways, this aspect of his apprenticeship had been a part of his preparation for later phases of employment that incorporated high levels of precarity and uncertainty. By the time Islam started his small brass overlay shop, his subjectivity had already been cast as that of the flexible worker willing and able to move trades and meet the shifting demands of the supply chain. Additionally, the common practice of poaching *shāgirds* – as done by *thēkēdārs* who attempted to lure away each other's workers – indicates the increasing commodification of the *shāgird*'s labour value. The trained or semi-trained *shāgirds* were a useful acquisition. With the initial low-value stage of early learning completed, these young men provided a ready source of labour that could be obtained at relatively low wages.

Like the experiences of women detailed in the previous chapter, this situation was based on certain gendered assumptions. The assumption in this case was that the earnings of *shāgirds*, as unmarried boys and young men, were still largely underwritten by older male members of their household. As with women, this assumption allowed the payment of below-subsistence wages but also created a demand for their labour. This situation contrasts somewhat with patterns of *shāgird* commodification in some other craft sectors. Writing on the city of Koforidua in Ghana, Kobena Hanson (2005: 164) describes how 'the token "drink money" that once formed the basis of the apprenticeship contract has now been replaced by exorbitant cash payments. Apprentices have to pay huge sums of money – fees – or face expulsion from training'. Rather than the apprenticeship itself becoming a commodity, as with Hanson's case, in Saharanpur it was the labour value offered by the *shāgird* that was increasingly commodified.

Alongside moments of conflict and increasing degrees of commodification there was a deep-seated sense of patronage in many relationships between *ustāds* and *shāgirds*. *Ustāds* would often furnish their *shāgirds* with tools and even help them financially to establish their own workshops.

Abdul had been angry at the time of my *ustād'* Islam's supposed betrayal but the two later repaired their relationship and became close friends. The buffing work Islam engaged in before moving to his *Abul's* shop provided a relationship with a former *ustād* that proved useful beyond the period of training. Uttar Pradesh's politics had, until shortly before my initial field-work in the city, been dominated by the Bahujan Samaj Party (BSP)[9] and its charismatic leader Mayawati, who gained a majority in 2007. During my fieldwork the situation changed. Elections were scheduled for the spring of 2012. In the run-up the streets of the city were filled with con-voys of vehicles and people proclaiming their support for various parties.

The results saw the end of domination by the BSP and the election of Mulayam Singh Yadav's Samajwadi party.[10] This pleased several of my friends, who had felt isolated by the caste-based rhetoric of Mayawati and saw the Samajwadi party as more representative of the Muslim community. For Islam, in particular, the election result had an effect. For some time he had been trying to obtain a BPL[11] ration card.[12] These are notoriously dif-ficult to get. During the election Islam's former buffing *ustād*, Juned, had been elected to Saharanpur's *Nagar Palika Parishad* (city council) on a Samajwadi ticket. Now, after Islam and I had failed to make any headway at the government office on the opposite side of the city, Islam activated the patronage of his former *ustād*. This began with a phone call to Juned in which Islam repeatedly emphasised Juned's status as *ustād* while appealing for his assistance. Within half an hour Juned arrived at the government office. He immediately set about a demonstrative performance of his influence by berating the official and demanding that the BPL ration card be issued. The official's attitude became demure and he quickly agreed to Juned's petition.

There were multiple factors bound up in this moment, of which the activation of patronage based within the *ustād–shāgird* relationship was but one. Juned's new position was, in part, cemented by his ability to exert (or at least be seen to exert) influence over state bureaucratic structures and bureaucrats themselves. This display of *sifarish* (leaning on someone to get something done) was also a means through which Juned was seeking to legitimise his position as a *neta* (leader, politician) in the *mohallas* (Chambers forthcoming). Alongside this, though, obli-gation towards Islam as his former *ustād* was also visible. Despite the performative display and the promise to complete the application on the part of the official, the card itself was never forthcoming, a reminder of the limitations of the influence and the ability to make effective claims from the state amongst low-level *netas* originating from the Muslim *mohallas* of the city. Islam and Juned's story is also a reminder that *ustād–shāgird* relations cannot be segregated from other social and hierarchical structures. Rather, the system is deeply interwoven into the sociality and politics of the *mohalla* as well as being intersected by broader political and economic contexts. In the following section I continue the focus on forms of hierarchy but also trace the ways in which the naturalised authority of the *ustād* is challenged and transformed within the gullies in the context of the increasing status and confidence of younger men.

Youth, haste and pace: transformations in apprenticeship

> The old Muslim men wanted their children to learn this work, as they thought it was fine work for their children. The old men had no idea that this industry will change and there is no future for their child. Now we feel very sorry for the new generation to whom we gave this work. Now people can understand that there is no future for this work, we are only *mazdoor* [labourer].
>
> (Ameer Ahmed, an elderly woodworker in Purāni Mandi, 2011)

Rizwan's *mamu* (maternal uncle) Mohammed Shahzad Ansari, who was introduced in chapter 2, bemoaned the transformation in *ustād–shāgird* relationships. Like Rizwan he had undertaken his apprenticeship on 'drink money', or in his case chai and snacks alone; now, though, he had to pay his two apprentices a small salary of around 1000 rupees per month. 'These days,' he said, 'no one is learning the carving work for the art; they are just learning it to get money. Now they want to learn fast and are not careful in what they do.' Complaints about the impatience of *shāgirds* to complete their training were commonplace amongst more senior *ustāds*. These complaints intersected with a broader narrative of decline and a loss of skill-related status in the industry. 'Now', Shahzad continued, 'the young boys just want to finish their apprenticeship and start their own business, but they cannot see that rushing means they will never be a master of the woodwork and know the art.' When Ameer Ahmed, the elderly *kārīgar* whose quote opened this section, expressed his despair at there being 'no future for this work', he was not suggesting the end of the industry. Instead, like Shahzad, he was highlighting a sense of lost status and skill as well as the intensifying alienation produced by increasingly fragmented supply chains and a transformation in the *nazriya* (way of seeing the world, subjectivity) of those engaged in apprenticeships today.

In Kamil Wali Gully, as I undertook my apprenticeship in Islam's shop, there were numerous small conflicts between *ustāds* and their *shāgirds*. Many were minor and were part of the day-to-day disciplining of *shāgirds*, like Waseem's whack around the head. On occasions, though, they would become deeper and involve disagreements of long duration. Amongst the workshops in the gully was one belonging to Imran. In his early sixties, experienced and known for the quality of his carving, Imran was universally addressed as '*ustād*' by others in the gully. He had, at the time of my arrival, one *shāgird* working with him. Azim was around 20 years old and had been with Imran for about five years. Imran taught Azim as he had been taught by his *ustād* in the 1980s and expected the same level of respect he had given his own *ustād*. Azim was always deferent towards Imran and the two seemed to have a reciprocal arrangement. It was a shock to Imran, then, when Azim suddenly upped sticks and left Saharanpur to work with a group of friends in Mumbai. Imran was furious about the departure, complaining to Islam and myself, '*Wo taiyaar nahin hai!* [he is not ready]'. Of even greater frustration to Imran was Azim's return some six months later. Along with two friends, with whom he had travelled to Mumbai, he established a workshop in one of the nearby gullies. For Imran, this elevated a situation of abandonment to one of betrayal, with Azim now producing carved items in direct competition with him.

The point I want to make through these examples is to situate transformations within the reproduction of artisan labour within broader labour-market dynamics that foreground the malleability, flexibility and haste of youth over skill and experience. Such reconfigurations are not limited to the contemporary context. Paul and Laura Bohannan (1968), for example, have illustrated the ways in which capitalist transformations can reconfigure age-based hierarchies. With high-end carving work on the wane and its gradual usurpation by lower-skilled production for export markets or the domestic furniture market, an extensive period as a *shāgird* no longer held the same value as it had in the past. This is not to say that there was no market for high-quality work: Imran remained busy with plenty of specialist orders. Rather, it was the availability of ready livelihoods requiring lower skill levels that tempted many *shāgirds* away from lengthy apprenticeships.

Short-term economic gain, then, was a part of the story, but there were other factors at play in the actions of Azim and others, including the hastening of transition to manhood. Some weeks after Azim's return I asked him why he had cut his apprenticeship short. He responded, '*Waha mei jessai batcha ta* [there I was like a child]'. The breakdown in the relationship between Imran and Azim also reflects broader transformations which, supported by representations in media and other affective sources, reify youth – young men in particular – as cultural heroes and entrepreneurial neoliberal actors (Sukarieh & Tannock 2014). When Imran and others completed their apprenticeships, the acquisition of craft skills and the status acquired through a lengthy period of training were key markers of masculine adulthood. While these markers were not absent, increasingly, young men and boys in the city had other means through which to construct themselves as men. Migration was one, a point I expand on in later chapters. Others included the establishing of a business or the use of consumption practices. The latter included the cultivation of ideal body types, specifically the muscular form of the Bollywood hero.

Alongside the wood shops, tea stalls and *masjids*, a plethora of gyms had developed. These spaces were often fronted by large posters of Bollywood heroes such as Salman Khan and Shahid Kapoor, and many young men in the *mohallas* dedicated time to the pursuit of these images of masculinity. These practices often went hand in hand with steroid use, and Dr Masood, a local medical practitioner, joked to me that many of these young men came for a muscle injection on a Monday and their *shakti* (power) shot on a Friday. The latter referred not to an injection for physical strength but to medication used to counteract the erection problems that can be a side effect of steroid use. Using also the latest fashions – available inexpensively as ready-made garments in the local bazaar – young men reproduced the ideals of masculinity portrayed in movies and other media to construct a sense of maturity and status.

Before expanding on several of these points in the following chapter, I turn to a final narrative from Sajid, another close friend who lived in the same *mohalla* as Islam. I first met Sajid while taking dinner at Islam's house. Tall and slim with a chipped front tooth, he was in his mid-20s. Unlike most of the friends I met during fieldwork he had a good level of English and was keen to practise. Sajid was particularly driven to gain education by attending various institutions, and worked hard to acquire a variety of skills in the garment and wood industries. Ready-made garment production – alongside informal occupations such as hawking or shop-keeping – offered one of the few alternative livelihoods in the *mohallas*, and I met several people who flitted between the two, following the ebbs and flows of the market. Sajid was unusual amongst the many individuals I met over many years of engagement with the city, as he did manage to find work beyond these areas. A short spell as a low-level accountant was followed by two years in Saudi Arabia as a driver. More recently he completed training as a health and safety supervisor and worked somewhat sporadic contracts decommissioning industrial sites. Although he was no longer in the wood industry, he and his family had long made their livelihoods within woodworking trades. Sajid's childhood and young adulthood had been dominated by woodwork. His story, recorded before his departure to Saudi in 2014, is revealing, as it draws out more affective concerns regarding the choosing of a less experienced teacher of a similar age over the traditionally desirable master *ustād*.

> I used to buff until I was 17 years old. Then I decided to learn the woodcarving as I used to love that work. When someone talks about [carving work], he talks very deeply. Other people think, 'Oh, what an art' and 'How did he make it?' I used to think, 'Oh wow, it is nice work. Maybe I should try.' Then I joined a teacher for woodcarving. He used to study. He worked and studied. I used to go there at night after finishing my buffing work.
>
> That *ustād* was younger than me, he was two years younger. My second *ustād* was only five years older. Because of this we could have good communication. If you are of the same age, you can have good communication. If one is much older, the mind will not connect. People used to learn for eight to ten years, but now the child comes, and they give one year and then think that you have enough knowledge to do work. If I go to an older teacher he will take five years minimum as he thinks with his mind. So, I joined the younger one as he knew that I will be able to finish quickly.
>
> Then my *ustād* went to Mumbai. I had finished tenth class[13] and sometimes had a gap in my buffing work. Then my exam was about to come, and I studied for some time. Then I started with the third carving *ustād* in Khatakheri. He was nice. He was a villager. He had good humanity in himself and he taught me as a brother. He was also five years older. I went for a full day and then would work at home. I used to work at home as I had responsibilities. But then the company my *ustād* worked for changed the rules for carving. The owner told the *ustāds* that they should no longer have *shāgirds* as he wanted to employ only directly.
>
> So, my teacher sent me to another company. Then we were two, me and my friend who had come from Saudi after working there. I had been sent to the company for a job as we had learnt as much as needed. There I was working for a *thēkēdār* not an *ustād*. We went there and we talked about our salary. It was necessary for us as we had learnt enough but it does not mean we will do this work all our lives.

Conclusion

This chapter has sought to detail the intersection of *ustād–shāgird* systems of learning and skill acquisition with a variety of processes. Many of the arguments presented here are present in other ethnographic work that details apprenticeship-based learning in a variety of craft industries globally. The primary contribution has been to bring them together within the specific empirical context of Saharanpur's wood *mohallas*. The chapter has also laid a bedrock for material expanded upon later in this book. Azim's abandonment of his *ustād*, for example, begins to take on a deeper resonance when we consider the significance of male friendships in driving imaginaries, aspirations and desires amongst artisans and others in the *mohallas*. This is detailed in chapter 7, but is essential if one is to understand the patterns of labour migration that have emerged in recent years. In the preceding material I have often focused on transformative processes, but it is also important to remain conscious of continuities. Despite the increasing status of young men over older *ustāds* and the shifts in skill levels brought about by incorporation into global chains of supply, there are still many young men who see out a full apprenticeship. This is particularly the case in carving, though less so in other trades such as carpentry and brass work, where skill levels are not as high. It is this theme of change and continuity that forms the foundation of the following chapter, which also brings the focus on connections and circulations into a more affective context.

Figure 5.2 Apprentices working on a bedhead. Source: author.

Figure 5.3   The author during apprenticeship. Source: author.

Notes

1. In Saharanpur, and across the Muslim world, children recite the Quran Sharif in Arabic. However, this recitation is not accompanied by the learning of Arabic itself. Thus, outside Arabic-speaking areas, learning to recite the Quran does not necessarily require an understanding of the content. Although this may seem counterintuitive to some, the position of many Islamic scholars is that the Hadiths (specifically those detailed by Abdullah ibn Ma'sood) state that it is the repetition of each word that brings blessing upon the pronouncer, not the meaning that the word conveys.
2. Although this allowed him to pass responsibility, he complained, 'If the labour inspector comes I explain this [that he is not the employer], but still he fines me [for employing child labour]'.
3. Source: fieldwork surveys.
4. Business Process Outsourcing. This covers a whole range of outsourced activities from call centre work to human resource management and accounting. It is commonly abbreviated to BPO and is often associated with working to overseas time zones (e.g. working for a BPO outsourcing for a US company often requires working US 'daytime' shifts.
5. A stimulant blended from betel, areca nut and tobacco. It is chewed.
6. A phrase borrowed from the film industry (in this case Bollywood). The boy who operates the spotlight is the lowliest employee on a movie shoot and has a reputation for often being harshly treated.
7. Chief or principal. Here it refers to a village leader ('*ji*' is added for respect).
8. Noble, honourable, high-born or eminent. The word has connotations of an *Ashraf* lineage but is used in Saharanpur to describe someone of good character.
9. Roughly translated as the 'People in Majority Party'; its main support was from lower castes.
10. Literally 'Socialist Party'.
11. Below the poverty line.
12. These below-the-poverty-line cards give some degree of access to free healthcare in government hospitals.
13. The 10th Board Exam, or Secondary School Certificate, marks completion of secondary school.

6

Neoliberalism and Islamic reform among Indian Muslim artisans: affect and self-making

Figure 6.1   Posing with a high-end motorbike at Saharanpur's annual Gul Fair. Source: author.

'My hero!' Sajid declared, holding aloft a copy of Steve Jobs's authorised biography. We were sitting in the small entrance room of his house discussing books he was reading to improve his English. 'Oh, why?' I asked. 'He made his business himself and did so many great things. We should all try to be like him, then we too can be a success,' he replied. Although not everyone shared the same affection for Steve Jobs, the notion of making it, through establishing one's own business, or obtaining a sense of apna kām (own work) within the configurations of the bazaar economy, was a desire reflected throughout the gullies of Saharanpur's woodworking mohallas. Later that evening we sat drinking chai, having just finished dinner, when there was a knock at the door. Sajid shouted, 'Con hai? [Who is it?]' The response declared the presence of a Jamaat at the door. The three smiling men who entered the room shortly thereafter wore their beards long and their trousers short. All were on a forty-day khurūj (proselytising tour). They went through a ritual I had seen several times before, reminding Sajid of the basic tenets of daily Islamic practice and encouraging him to consider engaging in khurūj himself.

This chapter is about affect and self-making. In this context I engage with two very different projects that seek to instil forms of subjective and material transformation; one is bound up in globalising discourses rooted in neoliberalism, which situate 'the entrepreneur' as the ideal neoliberal actor, and the other is rooted in the no less global work of the *Tablighi Jamaat*, which seeks the re-crafting of Muslims to (re-)establish the reformist ideals of a Muslim life during the time of the Prophet. Both projects, I argue, use affective tools to propagate their ideas and to create spaces within which the transformation of subjectivities and embodied practices can take place. Both make appeals to the heart. However, while the former attempts to cultivate modalities of subjective transformation from the inside out, the latter does so from the outside in. Thus, the production of 'entrepreneurial' subjectivities primarily concerns the internalisation of neoliberal governmentality (Ferguson & Gupta 2002), a governmentality that seeks to produce the flexible, self-reliant, entrepreneurial and enterprising worker. The *Tablighi Jamaat*, on the other hand, begins with everyday habits and practices – ways of dressing, washing, eating and praying – to produce, over time, a pious Islamic subjectivity. The purpose of this chapter is not only to explore tensions and conflicts between the two projects but also to draw out points of interaction and overlap, particularly where these concern engagements with work and labour in the *mohallas*.

Producing affect: neoliberal self-making as global craft

India has undergone substantial economic liberalisation since the mid-1980s, a process that was cemented in 1991 by the then finance minister Manmohan Singh's budget. The changes this enacted ended a long period of protectionism and import substitution and opened the country's economy to global markets. Since then, there has been much debate about the supposed benefits or negative effects of liberalisation. Early on, during my first period of fieldwork, I asked several friends and informants about the changes I expected them to have seen. Generally, however, little in the way of immediate impact was felt in the gullies, in contrast to some other sectors, such as state-owned industries, which saw a substantive reduction in scale and a large movement of secure labour down the labour hierarchy and into precarious and informal employment (Breman 2004). For those in the wood gullies, forms of neoliberal economic restructuring were often experienced as continuity rather than change. This is not to say that discourses advancing neoliberal ideals have not found their way into the *mohallas*, or that neoliberal governmentality (Ferguson & Gupta 2002) has had no impact. Instead, what I term 'threads of affect' act as a carrier of ideology, positing neoliberal ideals within images of the self and within ways of being in the world.

To trace these threads of affect, which act to carry ideology into the woodworking shops, it is necessary to draw on conceptualisations of an 'affective pool' within which a variety of emotions are called into action in the service of divergent projects. Affect, Yael Navaro-Yashin (2012: 24) argues, moves us beyond the subjectification of governmentality to engage with an 'affect-subjectivity continuum ... that attends to the embroilment of inner and outer worlds, to their codependence and co-determination'. In this sense, then, attention to affect draws us further into considerations of the role of the imagination. Affect challenges us to consider a milieu of circulations within which subjects are enmeshed (Richard & Rudnyckyj 2009: 59). It extends engagements with capitalism beyond labour provision alone and asks that we consider appeals to collective dreams and aspirations (Cross 2014) or to a 'commitment of the spirit' (Boltanski & Chiapello 2005). It also constitutes a 'new' frontline in struggles between labour and capital that contains both novel modalities of control and the potentiality for emerging forms of resistance (Hardt & Negri 2000; Tsing 2009). In short, affect theory is the awareness that 'ideals "out there" get "inside" to shape our desires' (Elias et al. 2017: 8).

When applied to ethnographic contexts concerned with work and labour, affect theory draws in the role of emotional responses among workforces and others which may, for example, foster a sense of individual responsibility, competitiveness and productivity as mechanisms of labour-force control (Rudnyckyj 2009). Thus, female Wal-Mart 'associate' workers in America's Midwest may be motivated through appeals to family values and Christianity to accept precarious employment and drive up corporate profits (Moreton 2009). Those anticipating the arrival of a Special Economic Zone in India may experience 'feelings of responsibility, autonomy and ownership [which translate into] dreams and desires ... allied with the goal of profit making' (Cross 2014: 101). On the other hand, former state-sector workers in China may resist the government's attempts to remake them as 'entrepreneurial subjects' through counselling sessions and 'kindly power' by evoking emotional displays of anger or by 'acting mad' to avoid punishment for deviant acts of resistance (Yang 2010, 2014; cf. Ong 1988).

The production of entrepreneurial subjects, then, is intimately bound up with calls to the emotional and affective level. Simultaneously, craftwork has been increasingly foregrounded within global discourses as part of an entrepreneurial development model that aligns the craftworker with the enterprising subject capable of forging their own path 'out of poverty' (cf. Barnes 2018). Often facilitated by microfinance and other initiatives, workers and others have been actively encouraged to become self-reliant and enterprising 'craft' producers. Such interventions have been criticised as producing modalities of labour market engagement which are inherently precarious and no less, perhaps even more, exploitative than Fordist-orientated labour regimes (Prentice 2017; Elyachar 2005).

This state of affairs is not limited to the global south. In insightful work, Laurie Ouellette (2017) has connected these dual emergences of 'craftwork' and 'entrepreneurialism' to neoliberalism in America's beauty industry. Here, she ties the growth and feminisation of the sector to the reification of aesthetic labour in the media, citing US shows such as *Nail Files*, *Nail'd It*, *Blow Out* and *Shear Genius* which actively cultivate an ideal of self-enterprise, entrepreneurialism and 'craft' while concealing the drudgery and exploitation that constitute the realities of much salon and beauty work. Craft modes of production (or the aesthetics of craft, at least) – along with their associated temporalities, spatial dynamics and social embeddedness – are experiencing a resurgence under post-Fordist late capitalism (Gibson 2016). Within the rubric of late (neoliberal) capitalism and development, the artisan or craftworker in 'traditional' craft industries occupies no less ambiguous a position (Schmidt 2018) than the programmer, creative worker or hairdresser (Ouellette 2017; DeNicola 2016; Holmes 2015; Sennett 2008).

In the Indian context, such considerations have played out in complex and variegated ways. Indian media have been rife with the idealisation of entrepreneurial figures, much emphasis being given to powerful 'rags to riches' stories of people who have been eulogised as, for example, 'defining the new India' (e.g. *India Today* 2015). Bookstalls and magazine counters are populated by the mugshots adorning biographies of Mukesh Ambani, Bill Gates, Lakshmi Mittal and Steve Jobs. Such accounts form an aspirational narrative that is repeatedly presented as part of the tale behind many individuals within business elites and politics (not least the country's Prime Minister, Narendra Modi) and have become commonplace in Bollywood films and television (Mankekar 2015). These images are by no means restricted to India, and there are many everyday critiques which, for example, have led to workers in some areas of the private sector associating the 'neoliberal entrepreneur' not with a heroic image but with corruption and criminality (Sanchez 2012). Yet the landscape of Indian social life has increasingly been embedded within the symbolism of an 'enterprise culture' (Gooptu 2013), a set of affective circulations reflected in Sajid's idolisation of Steve Jobs.

This extolling of successful people has been accompanied by a variety of shifts associated with the steady march of liberalisation under way since the 1980s. Government jobs at various levels, previously the aspirational domain of labouring elites (Parry 1999; Holmström 1999; Breman 2004), are increasingly undermined by collaboration between the state and the private sector to informalise employment across the Indian economy (Gooptu 2013: 14). Simultaneously, structural alterations have seen a degree of state withdrawal, although this has primarily incorporated the termination of state-run industries rather than the ending of welfare or clientism (T. Roy 2007; Routray 2017). Many occupying roles in state-run sectors have endured either privatisation or loss of employment, resulting in the uptake of 'informal' work. These changes, however, have more often been experienced as a descent down the labour hierarchy (Breman 2004) than as the enabling movement into entrepreneurial enterprise suggested by some libertarians (e.g. De Soto 1989; Prahalad 2009). Both new and older forms of 'self-employment' conceal underlying types of wage labour that provide little real 'independence' (Breman 1996) and, as with the transformations in other sectors globally, are no less grounded in the labour process than Fordist forms of economic structuring.

The everyday experience of labouring in the gullies, whether as a carpenter, carver, brass worker or buffer, was characterised by inherent precarity. Work would come and go. Periods of *mandee* (recession) were common and often interspersed by times of intense labour that involved working late into the night. During my time in the brass shop, and over various visits since, I watched as several slowly built businesses employing small numbers of workers folded over a matter of weeks. A temporary fall in orders meant workers could not be retained, debts for wood taken on credit could not be repaid and demand for rents from landlords, who owned most of the gully shops, led to eviction (see also chapter 3). Such insecurity was not new. Many of the facets of what has elsewhere been characterised as neoliberalism represented continuity rather than change in the *mohallas*.

Some time after my initial fieldwork, Islam, too, closed his small shop and found himself working as a *mazdoor* (labourer) in a nearby factory. This led to several years of regular relocations within the city as he drifted from one job to the next. Artisans often spoke of themselves as independent business owners engaged in *apna kām* (own work). As with the aesthetic of 'craft' in the beauty industry (Ouellette 2017; Holmes 2015), the complex networks of subcontracting within which daily labour played out meant that for many the reality of *apna kām* was often closer to that of *mazdoor* (labourer) than *kārīgar* (artisan) (cf. Mohsini 2016; Breman 1996). At the same time, however, *apna kām* formed a central articulation in forms of self-making. Thus, the term, its usage, and intersections within the affective circulations outlined above require a vernacular interpretation.

Apna kām: 'entrepreneurialism' in the mohalla

Carla Freeman's (2014) vivid account of entrepreneurial self-making amongst middle-class Barbadians illustrates the ways in which the rise of an entrepreneurial ethic interplays with colonial legacies and cultural traditions, giving projects of entrepreneurial self-making historical and cultural specificities. Just as broader processes of neoliberal restructuring are bound up in degrees of 'contextual embeddedness' (Brenner & Theodore 2002) and variegated forms of neoliberal governance (Ferguson & Gupta 2002; Ong 2006), so the cultivation of an entrepreneurial ethic is fermented within particularised contexts. While seeing the 'entrepreneur' as embodying 'neoliberalism's heroic actor: supple, flexible, and keenly responsive to market fluctuations, always prepared to retool and retrain to advance in uncharted directions' (p. 17), Freeman (2014) indicates that 'entrepreneurialism' also represents 'a subtler, generalized way of being and way of feeling in the world' (p. 1).

While I sat for eighteen months or so in the workshop of my *ustād*, Mohammad Islam, the value of independence, embodied in the notion of *apna kām*, was repeatedly emphasised. This could be framed in various ways. Working on *tikka* (piece) rates, for example, enabled flexibility in terms of when and how one worked. Many woodworkers expressed a preference for this over *tankhwa* (salaried) arrangements, a perspective that can be seen as a critique of Fordist labour regimes (cf. De Neve 2014b). This preference was often articulated in terms of 'independence', 'freedom' or 'flexibility'. At the same time, the desire for forms of labour identifiable as *apna kam* among *kārīgars* and others led many larger manufacturing units to incorporate various aspects of the bazaar economy, along with its forms of embeddedness, into the factory space. As described in chapter 3, this offered manufactory owners the opportunity to delegate processes of labour retention and control to *thēkēdārs*, *ustāds* and others. However, it also enabled workers to conceal the *mazdoor*-status of factory work by articulating piece-rate-based forms of payments and, albeit limited, degrees of control over work-time within the factory as constituting *apna kam*. Thus, those who would otherwise be seen as *mazdoor* by their peers, neighbours and friends could lay claim to a degree of independent *kārīgar* status even while labouring within the distinctly wage-labour-orientated space of the factory.

As Islam explained, there was much to be wary of in switching to factory work. When Islam became a *shāgird*, learning brass overlay, the work had high status and generated a good income. At that time brass was cut by hand using a fine-pointed chisel and a hammer. Within a couple of years, things changed. One successful brass worker purchased large cutting machines and began to manufacture pre-cut shapes. Overnight the work deskilled as a new niche was added to the supply chain, which led Islam, speaking in 2011, to seek alternatives:

> A friend told me about a factory where I could get 150 rupees a day. There was checking for every worker. The gatekeeper wrote when we arrived and there were foremen who always watched us. We couldn't rest even for one minute. It was difficult for me because I had been doing *apna kām* but there I was just a *mazdoor* (labourer). I had to queue to collect my money like a servant. We often got our money very late and after rude treatment from the owner and the foreman.

After some time, Islam opted to return to his shop, preferring this to working as a *mazdoor* in factories 'like a servant' and citing the need to 'make time for society'. The desire for *apna kām*, then, was rooted not only in concerns with status but also in more communal considerations around fostering social connections.

As detailed in chapter 3, many smaller workshop owners would muck in, labouring alongside their workers. Clearly, there were performative components within these practices. They not only boosted production but also enabled employers in small workshops, who occupied a similar and equally precarious socio-economic position to their employees, to display humility, thus maintaining a close relationship with workers and decreasing the chances of them leaving. Even in larger units, it fostered degrees of closeness and a sense of shared interest in the goal of profit making. However, there were further justifications for these activities. When considered in the broader context of the bazaar, mucking in also allowed owners of workshops to show themselves as hard-working, entrepreneurial and industrious in the eyes of others (cf. Basu 1991). Within variegated systems of interlocking and subcontracting, reputation mattered, and showing willingness to dirty one's hands was tied up with ideas of good character and respectability – being a *sharīf aadmi* – which encouraged others to do business with you.

At the opposite end of Kamil Wali Gully was the workshop of Naseer. Considerably larger than the operations surrounding Islam's small workshop, Naseer's unit employed 25 workers and consisted of a covered workshop area, containing a couple of fretsaws and other powered tools, along with a large open courtyard used mainly by carvers and carpenters. Naseer described the ways in which he saw his engagement in the daily labour of carving as essential to maintaining his reputation among others in the bazaar:

> If the owner is lazy and sits around all day, people will think he is not good. They will think that he does not care about his business and will not go to that person with any order as maybe it will be late. It is good to work. Now some owners just sit and spend their time buying motorbikes and fashion, but these people are *faltu* [useless]. They cannot be trusted; maybe they will take your money and spend it on a bike or some other thing.

Naseer's comments regarding some, usually relatively young, workshop owners symbolised a marked shift in the means through which entrepreneurial success was constructed and displayed. Many younger petty producers had embarked on a revision of the imagined ideal, framed through a shift from production to consumption. These consumption practices were not merely about style, fashion and wealth but also tied in with presenting oneself to others in the bazaar as successful and entrepreneurial. At the entrance to many small workshops a large new motorbike was prominently displayed. The motorbike had become the symbol of success. Fareed, one of this new breed of petty producers and owner of a high-end Honda Karizma, situated himself in contrast to Naseer:

> We have to dress very smartly; it is very important. Both local and international buyers are coming, and we should present ourselves as a respectable person if people are to do business with us. It is not good to dress in dirty clothes. We need to be smart and handsome in this age. We need to be like the businesspeople if we are going to make money.

This not only traces an emergence, but also illustrates that a shift from labour- to consumption-based identities is not necessarily a result of transformations from Fordism to neoliberalism (e.g. Bauman 1999) but can also play out in contexts of relative continuity. David Graeber (2011) has highlighted the need to challenge the often assumed disassociation of production and consumption. Instead, he argues for a focus on the 'production of people', including those who base their relationship with the material on consumption and those who do not. What was occurring, in the wood gullies, was a foregrounding of consumption as a means by which to achieve the same goals around self-making that were previously attained through engagement in the toil of daily labour. Just as mucking in potentially attracted orders through the display of craft skills and by showing dedication to work, so ostentatious displays of wealth, through consumption, were aimed at attracting business by displaying success. The latter, however, can be conceived as a form of 'aesthetic labour'. While this is a concept usually used to link women's employability and roles in workplaces with the consumption of beauty products and services (e.g. Ouellette 2017), there is a shared connection, as both contexts lead to the cultivation of subjects whose contribution to capitalist modes of accumulation interconnect spaces of labour and consumption. This (re)configuration also hints at forms of penetration into a marginal locale by more affective notions that align ideas of style, fashion and ostentatious consumption with business success and entrepreneurialism.

Of course, the effect is to simultaneously conceal structural transformations which add additional vectors of wealth extraction and precarity, specifically through credit and debt. While many of the new breed of stylish, young, petty bourgeois workshop owners attempted to separate themselves from the supposed backwardness of the labouring owner, their position was no less precarious, and the perfect storm of debt, vacating workers and lack of orders could collapse an operation, just as Islam's friend Aslan experienced (see chapter 3). In other words, despite attempting to construct themselves as 'entrepreneurs', many of this new breed of petty manufacturers existed at the same level of precarity as the *kārīgars* they employed. What is more, profits often created earnings that were not much above those of a salaried *kārīgar*. However, a portion of the small profits achieved also had to be sunk back into the work of self-presentation. Motorbikes such as Naseer's Honda Karizma were particularly symbolic in this regard. For most, the outright purchase of a high-end bike was beyond their means. Thus the motorbikes were usually obtained on credit and repossessions were commonplace. As I got to know Naseer a little better, I asked him about the recent repossession of his Honda Karizma. 'It is like this', he explained. 'I get the latest bike when money for an order comes through and I can afford the deposit. I make the payments as long as I can, but often I need the money to purchase wood or other things. It is very difficult; you never know when things will fall apart.' Later he laughed when I asked him about displaying the bike. 'Ha! Your thought is correct, that [the bike] was a showpiece,' he exclaimed, indicating the spot where the bike had been before its repossession.

The subjectivities of Naseer and others were not, then, the carefree subjectivity of the entrepreneur but were riven with the anxieties and contradictions of uncertain and precarious subjects (Ortner 2005). Of course, craftworkers in the city did not draw merely on an imported ethos founded in 'western' notions of neoliberal enterprise but also on a variety of cultural, religious and historically constituted moral frameworks. Artisanship has long espoused a degree of independence embodied in the person of the journeyman (Sennett 2008). Likewise, Islamic influences interplay to give *apna kām* prominence. Some years ago, Mattison Mines (1972: 342–3) argued that there is such a deep-seated sense of labour ownership amongst Muslims that even executives 'complained … about their dependent status and noted that their relatives would hold them in greater esteem if they were self-employed'. Patricia Sloane (1999: 16) describes how 'entrepreneurship has become the main vector of ethnic, religious, and moral worth' for many urban Muslims in Malaysia, and Filippo Osella and Caroline Osella (2009: 207) point to the presence of an 'entrepreneurial ethic', one which they argue is counterbalanced by a deep-seated 'community orientation' embedded in charitable almsgiving amongst Muslim business elites in Kerala. Yet, as this chapter shows, constructions of 'entrepreneurial selves' and of a pious Muslim identity come together in variegated, and at times competing, ways.

As Salwa Ismail (2013: 107) suggests, forms of economic organisation within Muslim communities cannot be thought of in terms of an 'Islamic economy' alone (cf. Kuran 2004) but also embody 'the tensions and contradictions of the structural transformations associated with economic liberalisation and privatisation'. These ambiguities play out in a variety of ways and intersect with the interests of capital in the gullies to produce subjectivities that are, on the one hand, cultivated through the pressures and spatial structuring of the *mohallas* as a margin and, on the other, not delineated from discourses and affective circulations that cast particular subjects as an aspirational ideal. The evocation of entrepreneurialism is, though, not the only cultivated desire routed through circuits of affect into the gullies. In the following section I explore the role of reformist movements, specifically the *Tablighi Jamaat*, in cultivating subjectivities and forms of self-making.

The *Tablighi Jamaat* in Saharanpur: a brief introduction

In Saharanpur's gullies, as in other Muslim neighbourhoods, the ways in which religious reform was orchestrated were changing. While negotiation of reformism has long been a circulatory process (Feener & Sevea 2009), the influence of *Ashraf*-dominated ulamas was being replaced by more informal forms of proselytisation. A major contributor to this development was the emergence of the *Tablighi Jamaat*. The movement allows individuals to involve themselves according to economic means. Therefore *Jamaats* regularly set out from *masjids* in Saharanpur to nearby villages. These groups were formed not of scholars, but of labourers, farmers and artisans who took what time they could spare to participate for three days or longer. At the other end of the scale, the city was visited by multinational *Jamaats*, consisting of members from all over the world, including Africa, Europe, America and the Gulf. These groups generally started their journey from the large *markaz*[1] at Nizimuddin in Delhi, where participants from different countries were placed together under an amir (leader) and allocated routes to travel. Reformist Islam forms a complex tapestry, filled with contestations and negotiations within and between groups (F. Osella & C. Osella 2013), but broadly speaking Islamic reformism can be seen as referring to 'projects whose specific focus is the bringing into line of religious beliefs and practices with the core foundations of Islam' (F. Osella & C. Osella 2013: xi).

Jamaati activities are global, but it is Saharanpur, or at least the nearby town of Deoband, that sits at the historical centre of the organisation. Maulana Muhammad Ilyas,[2] the *Tablighi Jamaat*'s founder, gave his devotion to the Deoband madrassa before establishing the movement in the town of Mewat following his second hajj in 1926 (Ali 2006). Its foundation was laid in a period during which various Hindu groups were seeking to 'reconvert' Muslims who had a Hindu lineage.[3] Maulana Muhammad Ilyas felt that the madrassa system was too slow in challenging this and in driving reform of the masses (M. Ahmad 1991). These concerns led the *Tablighi Jamaat* to take a different approach to reformist work. Rather than containing religious authority within the walls and scholarship of madrassas, the *Tablighi Jamaat* sought to disseminate it among the masses by involving 'lay participants' (Metcalf 2003). This is achieved by participation in *da'wa* (missionary work)[4] and through the *khurūj* (religious tour).[5] The *khurūj* takes place over a period lasting three days, forty days or four months. It is the forty-day period that is considered an ideal minimum for new initiates as it allows enough time to develop a religious consciousness away from material and economic concerns or familial and local traditions (M. Ahmad 1991). It is the purification of the participant, as well as preaching to other Muslims, that forms the primary purpose of the *khurūj* (J. Ali 2003).

At the core of the organisation's philosophy is the idea that religious authority is borne by each Muslim, irrespective of social standing. This belief places responsibility on all Muslims to broaden their knowledge regarding Islam and to share this with others (J. Ali 2003; Metcalf 2003). As Mumtaz Ahmad (1991: 517) suggests, 'The exclusive focus of attention of the *Tablighi Jamaat* is the individual. In the belief that an individual can sustain his moral character even in the context of a hostile social environment the *Jamaat* does not seem to have concerned itself with issues of social significance including the reform of political and social institutions'. Francis Robinson (1999: 13) takes this further, arguing that Islamic reformism should be seen in terms of broader change among South Asian Muslims, which 'involved a shift in the focus of Muslim piety from the next world to this one. It [made] Muslims … increasingly aware that it was they, and only they, who could act to create a just society on earth'. The principles upon which the *Tablighi Jamaat* is founded give a central role to notions of individual morality and behaviour, the obligation to teach others and the duty of each individual to be 'effective in the world' (Metcalf 2003). The *Tablighi Jamaat*, however, also gives a great deal of emphasis to the next world. Marloes Janson (2014: 1), for example, cites a pious member of the movement in the Gambia stating, 'Life is a test /*Akhira* (the hereafter) is the best.'

This is not to exclude *Tablighi Jamaat*'s collective and communal aims. Certainly, a common identity and the associated sense of belonging and comradeship were important aspects in drawing my brass overlay *ustād*, Islam, towards the movement. Writing on Southern Thailand, for example, Alexander Horstmann (2007) describes how the movement provided communal safety during periods of violence in the region. The apolitical nature of the *Jamaats* meant that they were tolerated by the state more willingly than other Islamic movements. Horstmann suggests (p. 126) that communal markers, embodied in dress and practice, created distinctions between Muslims and other groups which were previously less clear. The global nature of the *Jamaat* also represents a change in the way in which Muslim communities perceive themselves in relation to those elsewhere in the world and redefines the boundaries around notions of friendship and kinship:

> In Southern Thai communities, foreigners from India, Bangladesh, and Pakistan were traditionally perceived as strangers ... who needed to be ritually incorporated and related to the community and their ancestors before they could become accepted members. The [*Tablighi Jamaat*], however, has introduced highly mobile *Jamaat* from as far away as Jordan, and the locals thus become cosmopolitans overnight and call their Muslim guests (*kheak*) brothers who share the same beliefs. The local concept of kinship is extended on a global Muslim level, whereby Southern Thailand has become part of the [*Tablighi Jamaat*'s] transnational Islamic landscape.

Personal stories form an important part of the *Tablighi Jamaat* activities. Each individual who participates in a *Jamaat* is expected to leave an account of their experience (either written or oral) with the *masjid* from which they set out. It is from these personal accounts that Metcalf (2003: 142) draws to suggest that they iterate the desire of members to bring others into the fold of true Islam, those who strayed often being seen as victims of other influences. Most importantly, she suggests, the stories show the 'seriousness and importance Tablighis give to their work, coupled with the divine blessing they confidently expect for doing it'.

In daily life, too, individuals initiate profound changes as a result of their engagement with the movement. Against the background of the violent upheavals during and following the Gujarat riots of 2002, Jasani

(2008) describes the story of Suhanaben. Following her initiation into the *Tablighi Jamaat*, she became increasingly conscious of her piety. Not only did she seek to be modest in her daily practice and attend to her *namāz* (the prayer undertaken five times daily), but she also gave away her beauty salon, fearing it to be *haram* (against Islamic law). Suhanaben went on to become active in counselling other women, both in relation to coping with the stress of daily life following forced relocations to ghetto areas and in relation to their Islamic observance.

The dramatic change that follows becoming a '*Jamaati*' impacts on the way in which individuals narrate their stories, often laid out in terms of before and after their 'conversion', although '[c]onversion does not refer here to the transition from one religion to another, but to the turning towards a new form of piety' (Janson 2006: 45). In addition, a tradition of archiving each individual's story at the end of a tour emphasises how the movement itself contributes to the creation of a 'narrative culture' (cf. K. Gardner 2002), which interacts with other ways of telling present within the society of an individual's upbringing. It is against this background that I turn to my *ustād* Islam's story in order to illustrate an individual's perspective on belonging to the *Tablighi Jamaat* and the personal significance and importance it can hold. For Islam, his 'conversion narrative' was constructed as a self-making project, one which involved a prior, liminal and reformed self.

Islam's story: re-crafting a craftworker[6]

> I was different from other boys. We all went to other cities for enjoyment and ate chow mein. Then I grew up and came to my *ustād* [who taught me brass-overlay work]. When I was with the *ustād* my friends became model-style. They were rich and educated. They became a different type and did some wrong things. I was a *namāzi* boy[7] since my childhood. I wore jeans and t-shirt, but I never left the *namāz*. I played cricket and am fond of this. Some friends went every day to the cinema. They were also troubling girls and touching them. When I saw their bad habits, I refused to go with them in public places.
>
> 'After *isha namāz*[8] and *fajr namāz*[9] every day there was a special speech for the *namāzi* people in the *masjid*. Some special people like the mullah put pressure on us to join the *Jamaat*. They said that if we join we will find heaven after death as the world is not for ever but eternal life is after death so they said that we should try for

this. They also told me that I should follow the rules of Muhammad as this is sunnah.[10] The *Jamaati* people told me not to follow girls and not to watch movies. ... The *Jamaat* told me to learn the rules of Islam, to go for *namāz* and read the Quran. They offered that I should go in the *Jamaat*, but I always rejected their proposal and said that I will go later as I have work. But one day I decided to go there and started to collect money for *Jamaat*.

I collected 7,000 rupees and gave 2,000 rupees for my family and kept the other 5,000 rupees. At that time my friend Mehboob was at my shop so I was not worried about my business. But if I were all alone in the shop then I could not go in the *Jamaat*. [After the *Jamaat*] I kept a beard and started to wear kurta pyjama and left the jeans. ... Before *Jamaat* when I went to Mussoorie and Dehradun I had no idea about the Islamic rule. I could watch women but now I know all about my Islam. I have changed my brain and my heart. If I go to Mussoorie and Dehradun I go for natural beauty, not women's beauty. ... You know in Saudi Arabia, in Mecca and Medina all the women are in the veil and follow that rule very strictly but in Sahastra Dara[11] girls and boys would bathe together but now it is shameful for me after *Jamaat*.

Now I like the Islamic rule very much; I often go in the *Jamaat* and hear the religious stories. I realise that this is our reality and life. Our *namāz* and our Quran and our clothing should be fine according to Islam, as these three things are our religion and also our life. I can give you one example: if I am an employee under any boss I will do hard work there, as he is my master so I should be loyal and honest for him as the job gives me an income. Our life is under Qayamat [Judgement Day]. A person can live 50 to 60 years in this world and after death there is no importance for worldly things.

When I go for the *Jamaat* there is a head called 'Amir'. He is like the military head of the *Jamaat*. He makes all the rules and distributes the work. He told us who will make the food and who will wash the pots. He told us that two people should cook food and two others can learn the book. Once a *Jamaat* came from Australia and the rules were the same for them. The Amir takes all the decisions for the *Jamaat* work. He was a mullah-style person and very educated in the Islamic rules. He has a big crowd of followers in his *markaz*. ... Once we went to Agra. He made all the rules in Agra and told us in which area we should go for making speeches on Islam. He told us that in Agra we should go in a Muslim *mohalla* and to change people's minds so they follow the rules of Islam. Sometimes many *Jamaat* go to America and also to the UK. The *Jamaat* goes to every part of the world and also, they come to India from many parts of the world. ... In Kashmir, Mumbai, America and England, also in India the *Jamaat* comes and goes. It is the circle.

The *Tablighi Jamaat* in Saharanpur

Just as Islam had instructed me on daily practice, so he made suggestions to others. While Islam's position at work was low, being a *Jamaati* allowed him to recover status on religious grounds.[12] Early one Friday, following prayers, Islam, Naseer (our friend from the workshop directly across the gully, who would also be my companion during migrations across the country – see chapter 8) and I set off on my motorcycle to the *durgha* (Sufi shrine) at Kiliyar. The *durgha* was famous as a place of cleansing for those possessed by spirits and was popular with both Hindus and Muslims. 'Exorcisms' took place in the *sahn* (courtyard), which contained the tomb of Alauddin Sabir Kaliyari, the thirteenth-century Sufi saint to whom the *durgha* is dedicated, and a *masjid*. The process was dramatic. We watched a teenage Muslim girl with self-inflicted scars upon her arms convulse and writhe while close by a Hindu boy threw himself repeatedly to the ground, screaming numerous curses. Upon *azan* (the call to prayer) all the action ceased. Bodies were cleansed and calm prevailed as the crowd dispersed for *namāz*. Islam emphasised this as an example of the power of Allah, but also warned that some wrong practices occurred here. As we entered the tomb of Alauddin Sabir Kaliyari, Naseer opened his palms to begin praying. Islam was quick to stay his hand and explained that he should 'pray only to Allah'. Islam was also hesitant to join in with *namāz*, saying that the mostly Barelvi-aligned participants made mistakes in their method of prayer. Instead, he prayed a short while later with a few other men who also followed the Deobandi tradition.

In the locality of his workshop, too, Islam used his position as a *Jamaati* to enact some degree of authority, reminding others of correct daily practice and encouraging them to join *namāz*. While some did, others met his call to '*namāz paro*'[13] [do your *namāz*] with ambivalence, responding '*Kam hai Bhai* [There is work, brother]' or '*Waqt nahi hai* [There is no time]'. One afternoon in the second month of my apprenticeship Islam asked me, in a concerned tone, what others said about him. I was unsure of his meaning. He explained that they might ask why I was sitting with him instead of in the other shops as he was not so educated. He enquired whether others referred to him as 'mullah'.[14] I shifted awkwardly, as I had heard the term used, and in a disparaging way. Although I admitted this, I reassured him that most used the more respectful suffix 'mullah ji'.[15] As a self-making project, Islam's new-found *Tablighi* identity offered a means through which to re-represent himself within the sociality of the bazaar. It also opened certain economic networks. *Tablighis* were present at every level of the industry and, as with kin, friendship and neighbourhood-based connections, craft production embedded itself into networks of shared piety and religiosity. This gave Islam preferential access to a small number of additional out-sourced orders based on the *Tablighi* involvement he shared with some wholesalers, manufacturers and exporters further up the supply chain.

For Islam the *Tablighi Jamaat* held great importance both in terms of his reverence for his religion and the hereafter, and because it produced an affective sense of belonging and connection. Islam told me about his first *khurūj* four years earlier. He had travelled for forty days, a liminal period that culminated in a large-scale meeting in Bijnor attended by thousands.[16] For Islam this was an event that stirred a strong emotional response. He described the warmth and comradeship he felt in the company of *Tablighis* from across India and beyond. For Islam the *khurūj* opened a cosmopolitan space that offered a sense of connection to a global Islamic community. This sense of belonging extended beyond periods of *khurūj* and provided possibilities for instant rapport with strangers. In the spring of 2011 we travelled to G B Pant hospital in Delhi in order for Islam to undergo a heart scan (see the following chapter). After completing checks at the hospital, Islam was keen to visit the *markaz* at Nizamuddin.[17] As we travelled on the bus two Bangladeshi men boarded. They were carrying sleeping bags and small packs. This, along with their observant clothing, identified them as heading for the main *markaz* to join a *Jamaat*. Despite never having met Islam, they immediately greeted him with '*asalaam alaikum*' (an Islamic greeting) and a warm rapport was rapidly established based on shared outward appearance.

The multinational nature of the movement also influenced Islam's outlook. Unlike many of his friends, who had laboured in other areas of India or the Gulf, Islam had not migrated for work. His journeys had only been with the *Jamaat*, and their duration was restricted by his economic situation. The presence of numerous *Jamaats* passing through Saharanpur from across the world, however, offered him opportunities to engage with those from the Americas, Africa, South East Asia and Europe.

Early one evening Islam called, asking me to come to the *masjid* as an international *Jamaat* had arrived. Upon entering we were pleasantly surprised to encounter again our Bangladeshi friends from the bus. I visited the *Jamaat* twice, on the first day with Islam and on the second with our mutual friend Rizwan. Chatting to several members of the group, who had travelled from Europe, Africa and elsewhere in Asia, I was struck by the different ways they proselytised and how their narratives of 'conversion' intersected with 'ways of telling' (K. Gardner 2002) cultivated in differing cultural and educational backgrounds. A German-born *Tablighi* of Turkish origin proselytised through a rendition of his own story of transformation through involvement with the *Tablighi Jamaat*. It was a narrative that centred on the individual and the self as the main actor. Thus, he related how he used to drink, take drugs and engage in other *haram* practices. The beginning of his involvement with the *Tablighi Jamaat* was situated as a moment of salvation and self-transformation, which he held as an example of why I too should consider Islam. In contrast, an East African traveller proselytised through a narrative from which the self was absent. Instead, he focused on scripture, relating tales memorised from the Quran. In part, this focus reflected his Quranic schooling, but it was also mediated through differing ways of seeing one's place in the world.

While members of the *khurūj* came from numerous countries, and the narratives they told were shaped within variegated cultural contexts, shared forms of mien, dress and practice created a sense of united purpose and connection. While unable to engage in an international *khurūj* himself, Islam was able to activate his own embodied practices to connect, despite lack of a shared language and degrees of cultural distinction. Later, Islam expressed his pleasure at being able to meet others from across the world, even within the provincial and marginalised gullies of Saharanpur's woodworking *mohallas*. While Islam enjoyed meeting *Tablighis* from various countries, it was those from Saudi who impressed him most:

> Until some years ago there were only one or two *Jamaats* in India but now it has changed and in lakhs the *Jamaats* come and go. There is no place in the world where the *Jamaat* cannot go. Some time ago one *Jamaat* came from Saudi to Khatakheri. I forgot [to tell you], otherwise you could have met them. All were Arab people and were very handsome and beautiful people … . If I am in Saudi, then I cannot do any bad thing, it is a very great place and to meet them was a very good thing.

Now, during Eid, Islam, and some others who entered the *Jamaati* line, dressed in what they termed 'Saudi style'. This consisted of a long *thawb*[18] and a coloured turban wound round the topi,[19] which marked them out from those who wore the plainer Indian style of white kurta and turbanless topi. The attire had initially appeared in Saharanpur after being brought back by migrants arriving home from Saudi Arabia. Now, though, the *thawb* and other garments associated with 'Saudi style' were easily available in the local shops, with the designs run up alongside the latest styles of jeans and shirts in the city's numerous backstreet ready-made garment workshops. A couple of days later I returned to the *masjid* with Rizwan. Again, we sat and chatted with the same *Tablighi* group after evening prayers. When we left, however, Rizwan was more circumspect regarding the visitors, telling me, 'They are very good, but you know they are also very rich.'

The *Tablighi Jamaat*, reformism and work

Becoming a member of the *Tablighi Jamaat* impacts on status and position within Saharanpur's tight-knit gullies. For factory workers, being observant means time away from manual labour to attend prayers and to snatch a few moments socialising with others. For 'independent' producers, such as Islam, it may provide access to a broader set of networks through which orders and work can be procured. Unlike some other reformist movements, however, the *Tablighi Jamaat* does not attempt to cultivate forms of personal transformation in the everyday environment. The *khurūj*, for example, is fundamentally about the removal of the individual from the corruptive influences of labour, work, business, community and family. As Mohammad Islam recalled of his forty-day *khurūj*,

> The Amir told us that praise of Allah is the most important thing and that work is the second thing for the person. We cannot keep connection with our family or house when we are in *Jamaat*. There is no worldly talking in the group; we have no permission to discuss family problems in the *Jamaat*. He tells us about Islamic rules only. He tells us about the Quran and *namāz* and about some moral books. There is no worldly talking about business or work. There is no gossip about tasty food. The Amir never told us to eat interesting or tasty food, he only told us about the life after death. He told us what will happen after our death. If our [religious] work is good, then we will find heaven.

This is not to say that the *Tablighi Jamaat* separates itself from economic activity beyond the period of *khurūj*. In an echo of work outlined earlier in this chapter regarding an 'entrepreneurial ethic' within Islam, Marloes Janson (2014: 87) describes how *Tablighis* in the Gambia sought to escape 'professional careers that might "corrupt" them, [and] were often led to establish their own businesses ... . They valued such businesses highly because the Prophet used to trade and trading is easily combined with *tabligh*'. For individuals such as Islam a 'professional career', beyond factory labour, was never a possibility. Yet the desire to give time to *khurūj* and other *da'wa* work intermingled to further embed the value of *apna kām*.

In 2014, a couple of years after my initial fieldwork in the city, I returned to Saharanpur for the summer season. Islam had already told me, by phone, that he had been forced to close his small workshop in Kamil Wali Gully because of a lack of orders, which he ascribed to *mandee* (recession). He complained that his new conditions of labour made it difficult for him to engage in *da'wa* work as the factory owner would not grant him the flexibility to take time away for anything other than *namāz*. In a small gully across Khatakheri's main strip I met Kabeer, a woodworker in his late teens whose unshaved beard still had the wispiness of youth. Like Islam, Kabeer had become involved in the *Tablighi Jamaat* and we discussed the intermingling of his *Jamaati* activities and work in the small rented woodturning shop where he laboured as sole proprietor:

> Sometimes it can be hard, but it is my duty to Allah that I should make my *namāz* and do the other things. I get up at 5am to do the religious work. At 9am I start this work but also pray five times per day. I work until 9pm at the maximum but as this is *apna kām* I can take time away when I need to do *da'wa* or if I want to go for a three-day *khurūj*. I do not find it hard to balance. I go for *Jamaat* three days in every month, so 27 days for work and three for *Jamaat*. In this I satisfy my heart. I do the lifestyle things, wear short trousers and do my *namāz*.

Kabeer's concerns primarily surrounded the creation of time for *Tablighi* activities. For some, however, membership of the *Tablighi Jamaat* allowed the cultivation of degrees of respect within the broader fabric of the bazaar economy. A short distance away, I met Ahmed, a friendly man in his fifties, who ran a small workshop employing around 10 staff. Initially I spoke to one of his senior employees, who was quick to praise his employer, even in his absence: 'He is the only one who always pays on time. Many owners do not give money when they say they will, so the workers take revenge by running away when it is busy.' Later I asked Ahmed a little more about the way he operated his business. Ahmed's engagement with the *Tablighi Jamaat* had drawn him not only into reconfiguring forms of personal practice but also into cultivating an awareness of Islamic business, a set of ideals he described himself as following resolutely:

> I never take the workers' money and always pay on time. Because of this the payments to me always come on time. This is Allah's gift. I always get money up front from the buyer; buyers are willing to do this as they know I will always keep my promise and deliver on time. I also remind them what is written in the Quran and the Hadiths, as they should follow Allah's word in business also and not cheat or make any fraud. Whether the work is small or big I never get a problem in payments, thanks to Allah. Because of my belief I do not allow credit; people say that business cannot be done without credit, but I am doing it. I do not take credit, but I also do not make my workers work under credit. Because of my timely payment my workers trust me and so I do not get the problem many other owners have with workers running away.

To a degree, Ahmed's invocation of Islamic business practices allowed him to negotiate relations of 'inverted bondage' which permeated many of the supply-chain relations in the bazaar. The trust Ahmed created through his observance of Islamic business principles meant that some of his workers remained with him for many years, an unusual situation in the gullies where labour was usually transient. This is not to say that all of those who were involved in the *Tablighi Jamaat* were as observant. Indeed, Shahnawaz, the owner of the small unit where Naseer, who had joined us on the trip to Kiliyar, worked, was condescending towards the pronouncements made by some *Tablighis*. 'Oh,' he said in a mocking tone, when I asked him if such individuals were more reliable, 'they tell you all about Islam and the rules, but when you come and ask for the money you are owed they are just the same as the others; they just wave their arms and say, "I don't have the money today, come again tomorrow."'

While most craftworkers were not directly involved in the *Tablighi Jamaat*, and there were some who openly mocked the organisation's activities, forms of piety and observance of daily ritual and practice were not limited to its members. More broadly, the construction of a *sharīf aadmi*, laid out earlier in this chapter, was often bound up with adopting outward signs of observant practice. Rizwan had only had tacit engagement with the *Tablighi Jamaat*, having attended a three-day *khurūj* some 10 years before. Like Islam, though, he had cast off his 'jeans pants', adopted the kurta and wore his beard long. It was the mutual articulation of being a *sharīf aadmi* that lay at the core of Rizwan's close relationship with 'Hafez Bhai', a trader from Mumbai. In his early sixties, friendly but serious in nature, Hafez had first met Rizwan during a business trip. In Mumbai, Hafez ran a successful wood-manufacturing business that supplied furniture but also created sections of movie sets for Bollywood films. Shortly after meeting him, Hafez encouraged Rizwan to join him in Mumbai. Although Rizwan returned to Saharanpur they continued a business relationship. This bond was reinforced by their shared sense of religiosity and its associated moralities, which meant trust could be more easily assured (Kuran 2004).

For Rizwan the careful cultivation of this relationship and the emphasis on his observance had achieved an economic as well as a social end. The notion of being *sharīf* was bound up not just with respectability but also with outward daily practice. Following unspoken rules of business in the gully and being known to be a 'good Muslim' allowed Rizwan and others to be seen as people with whom business could be done. Reputation mattered to Rizwan and he was always careful to cultivate it. The family lived in two small rented rooms of a very basic standard, cooked over an open fire and had little more than a couple of beds, some cooking equipment, an old TV and woodworking tools. Despite this, Rizwan was generous with his hospitality and his charitable giving. While visiting distant relatives who were experiencing greater hardship, Rizwan was quick to give money and, as is customary, would always present the eldest child with a few notes when visiting the houses of friends or relatives. Even the family's inverter[20] was given by Rizwan to the local madrassa.

For Rizwan, as for many of those discussed earlier in this chapter, the overriding concern was to maintain a sense of *apna kām*, however embedded this might be within relations of bondage and employment. 'Does having your own business help someone to be a *sharīf aadmi*?' I asked one evening as we sat out on the hessian-covered bed frame on his rooftop. 'Oh,' he responded, 'you can be *sharīf* whatever work you do; it is only a question of how good your heart is.' He paused to reflect and then continued, 'But to have your own work is very important: if we are just *mazdoor* [labourer] then there is no way to go up. The *mazdoor* becomes stuck; maybe his business will not go down but also it cannot go up as the *malik* [boss] takes all the benefit.' Pausing again to briefly reprimand his youngest son Ishmael, whose kite-flying antics had taken him too close to the edge of the roof, he continued, 'In the factory you can be *sharīf* but you cannot be a *kārīgar*, and people will say, "Oh, he is a good man but he is a *mazdoor*," and feel pity in their heart for that man.'

Conclusion

This chapter has discussed two very different projects that used divergent techniques to cultivate forms of self-making: the entrepreneurial self, cultured through affective images, discourses and ways of being, and the pious *Tablighi* self, formed through an embodied, practice-based approach. While substantially different, both exist in the context of globalised networks that wind their ways into the spatially and economically marginalised gullies of Saharanpur. The *mohallas* are, in many ways, an enclaved and, to a degree, ghettoised margin, but they are also embedded within global projects and circulations which foreground particular ways of being in the world. In terms of the political economy of craft production, both neoliberal ideals grounded in notions of 'entrepreneurialism', and *Tablighi* representations of the pious Muslim, intersect with artisanal values to foreground *apna kām* as the preferred mode of self-representation. As we have seen in the previous chapters, however, representation and material conditions may be contradictory. In the following chapter, I continue to focus on more affective contexts, but shift the emphasis to the role of affective and informal networks rooted in male sociality, in mediating labour and (building towards the final two chapters) in migration. These are networks constituted, in part, as a result of spatialisation processes that create material conditions conducive to intense forms of connection, albeit in a context often characterised by relative poverty. Linking to this chapter, I also explore the ways in which these networks are, to some degree, reinforced by Islamic ideals of (Muslim) brotherhood, but foreground the broader category of 'friendship' as the primary site of enquiry.

Figure 6.2 Men dressed in 'Saudi style' during Eid. Source: author.

Figure 6.3 Sweets being sold during Eid. Source: author.

Notes

1. A centre from which *Jamaats* depart, usually attached to a mosque.
2. Maulana Muhammad Ilyas also taught in Saharanpur Mazahirul Uloom seminary for a period.
3. Primarily the Meos of Mewat.
4. *Da'wa* is focused on practice among Muslims rather than on conversion of others.
5. Often called a 'tour' but literally meaning a sortie or patrol, this being drawn from language associated with the notion of jihad (Metcalf 2003). Structurally there are similarities with certain aspects of Sufism, although the movement is not particularly in favour of Sufi traditions (F. Robinson 1999). Like Sufi structures, these groups are organised under the leadership of an amir who will guide the group and organise its day-to-day running.
6. Aside from translation and basic editing I have left this as Islam told it. It was his request that I do so and the translation and editing were done in consultation with him on a return trip.
7. A boy who prays five times a day.
8. The evening prayer, the last of the five daily prayers.
9. The first prayer of the day, performed at sunrise.
10. The Islamic way of life.
11. A waterfall near Dehradun.
12. The dual status of Islam and others is not a situation exclusive to Saharanpur. Simpson (2006a), for example, describes a reform of economic and social status through the trope of reformist Islam in the shipyards of Gujarat.
13. The literal translation of *paro* is the instruction to 'read or study', but the meaning here is 'do'. *Paro* is used rather than *karo* (literally 'to do') out of respect for the act of *namāz*.
14. A reference to the leader of a mosque, but in this case used to denote someone who fancies himself to be such but does not hold sufficient religious authority.
15. The addition of 'ji' denotes respect. The term 'mullah' is commonly used in Saharanpur as a descriptor for anyone who wears a beard and kurta, irrespective of whether they are involved in the *Tablighi Jamaat*.
16. Large-scale meetings are now common across South Asia. Recent gatherings in Bangladesh have seen the largest coming together of Muslims anywhere in the world (excluding hajj) (Siddiqi 2012), and the *Tablighi Jamaat* has attracted some of the largest congregations of Muslims in the USA and Europe (Metcalf 1996).
17. A Muslim neighbourhood in central Delhi known for its Sufi shrine. It is also the site of India's main *markaz*.
18. An ankle-length gown commonly worn by men in the Arabian areas of the Gulf.
19. Literally 'hat' but here referring to the Muslim skullcap.
20. A device connected to a car battery that switches between charging and powering according to the supply or non-supply of electricity.

7

Friendship, urban space, labour and craftwork in India

Figure 7.1   Young men hanging out while working. Source: author.

The argument had come about by accident. Having spent six weeks in Saha-ranpur during a short fieldtrip in the summer of 2015 examining state-issued documents, cards and paperwork (Carswell et al. 2019; Chambers forthcoming), I retreated to the mountains near Mussoorie with the aim of escaping the heat and carrying out comparative work in a village. I had said goodbye to friends in Saharanpur, my former ustād Islam included, and had moved on, both physically and mentally, to the new site. In the past, towards the end of my longest period of fieldwork, Islam and I had made a trip to Mussoorie and the nearby town of Dhanaulti. The trip had further cemented the already deep sense of friendship and affection we had developed for each other. We had laughed about the khataranāk rasta (dangerous road) along the mountain ridge to Dhanaulti and joked together about friends back in Saharanpur, times in his brass shop and mountain life.

Now, though, I returned to the region alone and trekked out to a small village beyond the cascading waters of Kempti Fall where I had some old friends. Research in Saharanpur had revealed a connection between marginality and documents, cards and other forms of paperwork bound up in lengthy periods of waiting and being made to wait, in tenuous and highly mediated relations with the state and in a constant sense of having to prove one's Indianness. I was interested in comparing the rural spaces of the Himalayas, an area often painted as marginal to the state, with the forms of marginality in the Muslim neighbourhoods of urban Saharanpur. It quickly became clear that it was the urban centre and not the rural periphery that, in this case, embodied the starkest forms of marginalisation. As I had done in Saharanpur, I asked informants in the village if they could show me the documents, cards and other forms of paperwork they had been issued by the state. In the mohallas this had consisted of a handful of documents, but in the house of Sandeep, a local bus driver, the contrast was stark (see Figures 7.2 and 7.3).

Figure 7.2   A craftworker displays his cards and documents issued by the state. Source: author.

Figure 7.3 'Sandeep', a Hindu resident of a village in the Garhwal Himalaya region displays his cards and documents issued by the state. Source: author.

The experience was another reminder of the multiple trajectories that forms of marginalisation can take, as well as the ways in which they can become embodied in material form. But this is not a chapter about the state or about rural/urban comparisons. The reason I digress to the Garhwal Himalayas is to relate another story tied to my previous trip with Islam. A few days into my stay in the village I got a phone call from Islam to say that he was in Dehra Dun and on his way to meet me in Mussoorie. I was somewhat taken aback by the unexpected call and, apologising profusely, said that I could not leave the village at this time and travel back up the mountain to the old hill station. Islam sounded deeply upset and replied, 'Hamarai muzum mei ham dost ko waqt detai hai [In our belief/culture we make time for friends]', before hanging up the phone. Islam had always been big of heart, generous, loving and kind, but easily upset. We had had brief quarrels previously and I expected this to blow over. During the following months, despite numerous attempts, he would not take my calls. I was very saddened as our friendship had thus far been sustained despite geographical distance. I was also acutely aware that, for Islam, I had betrayed certain expectations around our relationship.

This chapter is about male friendships in the gullies and workshops of the woodworking *mohallas*. It is a chapter shaped, in part, by my own gendered experiences of the field which became deeply rooted in networks of male sociality. The incident with Islam was mediated within a broader context intersected by relations between researcher and informant as well as class, ethnicity, wealth and gender. My friendship with Islam was not identical to his friendships with others in the gullies, and nor was Islam's understanding of the rules and obligations of friendship universally subscribed to by men and boys in the *mohallas*. Yet it did reflect an intensity present in the types of male sociality that formed a highly significant part of *mohalla* life. Against this background, the chapter makes four primary arguments. First, the spatial configurations of the *mohallas* – the forms of enclavement, bounding and bordering they involved – were active in producing the social intensity of life in the gullies, a life that was further framed by norms of gender segregation. Second, the intense sociality of the *mohallas* was deeply bound up with labour, work and production. While we should remain aware of interwoven dualities of discipline and control, friendship networks, I argue, provided spaces of mutuality, reciprocity and support vital in navigating the precarity of work and the spatial demarcation of the *mohallas*. Third, and linking to broader literature on labour in India, the focus on friendship challenges the foregrounding of kinship and caste – prevalent in many empirical accounts – as the primary mediator in forms of labour-force engagement. Finally, against a background in which modalities of resistance are constrained, I explore the ways in which friendship-based networks intersect with contestations around the control of time and with the desire for *apna kām* outlined in the previous chapter.

The introduction of temporal considerations also forms a critical area of exploration in beginning to build outwards from the city by turning to modalities of migration and the subjectivities of woodworkers who travel across India or to the Gulf. The affective and informal networks and forms of gendered sociality detailed in this chapter are, I argue, essential to an understanding of the emergence of extensive connections of migration (both within India and in the Gulf) that are dealt with in the final two chapters of this book.

An understanding of forms of urban friendship has emerged from a growing body of research on conviviality (e.g. Kathiravelu & Bunnell 2018; Nowicka & Vertovec 2014; Wise & Velayutham 2014). It has focused primarily on forms of bridge building across difference and thus attends to inter- or multicultural friendships and other relations. There are degrees to which this plays a part in the *mohallas* (see Chambers 2019). The male sociality of the public sphere constituted a set of convivial relations that crossed certain boundaries, in particular those of *biradari* (caste, community) and, to a somewhat lesser degree, class. Thus the *mohallas* were not only constituted through communalism but, as discussed in the introduction to this book, also a space for connection and community building (cf. Chandavarkar 2009). This community building was embodied within what Doreen Massey (2005) terms a 'throwntogetherness', deeply rooted in the history of the city as a site of refuge during partition and in spatial pressures that have pushed somewhat disparate groups of Muslims together (see chapters 1 and 2). While degrees of bridging across difference were present, strongly bonded relations were often confined to the broader Muslim community, exceptions being found mainly amongst the more affluent residents, whose financial status and education opened access to cosmopolitan spaces and networks.

My focus here is not on the weak ties of conviviality. Instead, the chapter emphasises the strong ties and intimacy of close friendships. In the introduction to a special issue on urban friendship, Pnina Werbner (2018) draws out an emphasis on 'weak ties' in much of the literature, including that on conviviality. In part, she suggests, this has been influenced by Georg Simmel's (2013) essay 'The metropolis and mental life', first published in 1903, which exposes the dualities of urban worlds as, on the one hand, enabling the loosening of social constraints and, on the other, leading to 'flattened subjectivities', alienation and the devaluation of the social world. Thus the city is often seen as offering many acquaintances but little in the way of strong ties forged through kinship or close friendship. Importantly, however, Werbner also identifies various ethnographic works – James Pritchett (2007) on the Lunda-Ndembu in Zambia and Mattia Fumanti (2016) on urban Namibia, amongst others – that show that, particularly in poorer, marginalised urban neighbourhoods, close-knit networks of friendship can be a central feature of urban life. Such networks, Werbner continues, offer resources, support and potentialities, but can also be enclaving and productive of class, gender and ethnic distinctions.

I follow Werbner, but also show how the materiality of the *mohalla* and the structuring effects of wood production had a profound influence on the types of sociality that were produced. While itself deeply entwined with the urban spatial context, craftwork has often been described as being embedded in strong affective networks. James Carrier (1992: 553), for example, has argued that unlike industrial production, which 'is seen to be impersonal and regulated by abstract forces such as "the market", [craftwork] is seen to be personal and regulated by personal forces like "affection", "creativity" or bonds between people'. Likewise, Clifford Geertz (1978) saw bazaar-based economies as fundamentally entrenched in personal interconnections. As we have seen, however, Saharanpur is no less a part of complex webs of global production and capitalist supply chains than is the factory floor. Additionally, anthropological research in high-tech and corporate spaces has shown that they are no less embedded in cultural tropes and social networks than are the artisan or the village (e.g. Ho 2009).

This is not to dismiss the particularities of the Indian context, craftwork or the specificities of Saharanpur's history and cultural make-up. Nicholas Nisbett (2007), for example, has emphasised the significance of friendship groups as a crucible of social reproduction in India as important as those of family and kin. Nisbett, in his research on call centre workers in Bangalore, argues that the 'friendship group, however temporal, is a well-established sphere for the negotiation of identity and status' (2007: 948). In an industry dominated by a young male labour force and in an arena that was highly gendered it was these friendships that occupied much of the social energy of young (and older) men in the city. The importance ascribed to friendship at times even surpassed that given to family and kin. This could be seen not just in day-to-day social activity but also in patterns of affiliation and recruitment within workshops. It has long been argued that caste and kinship networks in India are a primary means of labour recruitment and control (e.g. Chakrabarty 1988). In some cases, this has led employers to utilise narratives of kinship to exert authority over workers with whom they have no familial relation (De Neve 2008). In many sites of labour this association has been borne out in the empirical evidence (Harriss-White 2005; De Neve 2008). In Saharanpur, however, even though a large proportion of respondents had relatives working in the industry (65 per cent), relatively few laboured in the same location as their kin (21 per cent).[1] Likewise, patterns of recruitment did not take place primarily through kin-orientated networks but through friends and acquaintances.

Ethnographic literature dealing with friendship in India has illuminated a complex realm that can be both supportive and exploitative (Dyson 2010; C. Osella & F. Osella 1998). In work on the relationship between women's friendships and agricultural labour in rural Himachal Pradesh, Jane Dyson (2010) suggests that friendships can be conceived as containing opportunities to counter powerlessness and form a basis for mutual support, but also acknowledges that they are significant in the reproduction of power relations. Similarly, Caroline and Filippo Osella (1998: 189) argue that friendship can create a space within which existing hierarchies can be 'subverted, reversed, denied and re-affirmed in episodes of personal interaction'. As is shown in ethnographic material presented later in this chapter, male friendships in the gullies also contain these dualities. This situation reflects some of the material presented earlier in this book (chapter 3 in particular), but here I take the engagement deeper to draw in what Osella and Osella (1998) call the 'micro-politics of friendship'. In the *mohallas*, this was an inherently intimate and, at times, sexualised politics as young men negotiated the boundaries of their masculinity and sexuality. In more recent research on male–male relations in Kozhikode (Kerala), Filippo Osella (2012: 532) points to the significance of what he terms 'homosociality', within which 'expressions of same-sex desire are hidden from the public gaze, while intense male friendship is reinscribed as a(n Islamic) moral value'. Osella's characterisation of male sociality in the Kozhikode bazaar holds many echoes with Saharanpur's gullies. Osella describes how:

> The apparent informality of such intense male sociality is maintained through a specific male aesthetic of enjoyment, rooted in the particularities of the neighbourhood's matrilineal system, a historical orientation towards bazaar economy, local politics of status distinction and a religious rhetoric of brotherhood and gender segregation.
> (2012: 535)

Egalitarian notions of friendship run strongly through Islamic discourse (K. Gardner & Osella 2003) and, while friendship was certainly not only constituted through Islamic ideals, narratives foregrounding its importance were present. Legitimate criticisms of the anthropology of friendship have emphasised its Aristotelian – and therefore Eurocentric – origins (Desai & Killick 2010; Pahl 2000; Carrier 1999), leading some to question if it can be deployed as a category beyond the Euro-American setting (Desai & Killick 2010). Yet friendship within Islamic philosophy takes an equal, or even more central, position. Building on research in Pakistan, Magnus Marsden (2005) points out that friendship, like many other areas of life, such as business, education and family, is conceived as bound up in meanings surrounding the notion of a 'Muslim life'. Shelomo Goitein (1971: 485–6) suggests that the pre-Islamic Arab world was dominated by connections of kinship until the arrival of Islam, when friendship took on new meaning:

> Formal friendship, *suhba*, came into the Arab world with religion, with the Islam of Muhammad. Conversion was conceived as a personal bond between the new believer and the founder of the religion. … From that time on, spiritual bonds of the greatest variety became the base of sustained personal relationships transcending family attachments, the strongest being those connected with Islamic mysticism known as Sufism.

In the madrassas and *masjids* of the city, ideals of brotherhood and the embodying of egalitarian ideals which usurped caste, *biradari* and caste were often preached.

Margrit Pernau's (2017) seminal work detailing the 'history of emotions' among north Indian Muslims provides a detailed foundation for situating constructed elements of emotion and friendship. Pernau (p. 21) reflects on an article published in 1880 in the *Tahzību-l Akhlāq*.[2] The article focuses on a gift from Allah which gives 'men [sic] an enthusiasm (*josh*) for meeting others and establishing bonds'. The author, Pernau continues, draws on both Islamic and Enlightenment traditions to locate this enthusiasm within affective notions of love and compassion (*muhabbat, hamdardī*), emotions which, while naturally produced, must also be cultivated to 'form the basis of civilisation' (p. 22). Importantly, when discussing compassion Pernau points out that it 'is a social emotion, but not necessarily an unequivocally benign emotion. It serves to construct a community and to negotiate its boundaries, but it is also a tool of exclusion and helps fortifying the communities' internal hierarchies' (p. 21).

The friendships discussed in this chapter are often constituted within the bounded space of the Muslim *mohalla* but, as literature concerning other settings across India suggests, do cut across difference to some degree. The potential for fragmentation of hierarchies, Osella and Osella (1998) point out, runs counter to Dumont's (1980) situating of hierarchy as the central defining feature of Indian cultural life. A variety of more recent contributions have reinforced this position. Nicholas Nisbett's (2007) study, for example, illustrates the formation of cross-caste friendships amongst call-centre workers that embodied both a strong sense of egalitarianism and loaded affective content. Amit Desai (2012) describes what he terms 'ritual friendship', in which male bonds are affirmed through *prasad*,[3] in which the notion of *prem* (love, affection) was posited ahead of caste-based distinctions. Craig Jeffrey's (2010) account of unemployed former students in Meerut relates a scene in which friendships formed on street corners and in tea stalls reached across old divides of caste and, in his case, religion. For Jeffrey these actions formed an 'intimate culture' that fostered the building of trust and solidarity. In Saharanpur, expressions of *pyar* (love) formed a central part of the way in which friendship was articulated. As Jeffrey (2010) found, nonchalant banter and expressions of affection were central to building deep affiliations. At the same time, the gendered construction of labour spaces, sociality and the face-to-face informality of relations in the bazaar played important roles in shaping labour networks, as did notions of shared

religious identity and reformist discourses. Many aspects of male sociality (banter, flirting, teasing, joking, etc.) are discussed in the following
material and have been detailed in ethnographic material from across
India (e.g. Osella & Osella 1998; Jeffrey 2010; Nakassis 2013).

However, there are specifics that I draw out which make friendship
in the *mohallas* somewhat distinct. The *mohalla*, I argue, comprised a
space of gendered hyper-sociality which produced a sense of comfort,
familiarity and belonging in a space that was often characterised – from
the outside – by idioms of non-belonging and foreignness. While friendships themselves were constructed around expressions of egalitarianism
(cf. Osella & Osella 1998), unlike those among middle-class youths in
Meerut or Bangalore (Jeffrey 2010 and Nisbett 2007 respectively, who
focus on lower-middle-class young men), they did not draw in the same
diversity of identities. Additionally, the spatial pressures and forms of
demarcation of *mohalla* life – along with the avenues of labour force
reproduction outlined in chapter 5 – acted to enmesh male sociality
deeply within the political economy of craft production. In what follows
I give some emphasis to forms of sociality amongst young men but also
draw in accounts of friendship across the lifecycle of male *kārīgars* and
other craftworkers in the *mohallas*. To do so I incorporate three stories
centred on particular individuals and groups.

Male sociality and the contesting of space: Yousef's story

The area around Kamil Wali Gully comprised various spaces of social
interaction: tea shops, gyms, street corners, the shade of a tree, the
stall of a cigarette vendor or just the gully itself. These spaces not only
offered but materially enforced regular moments of social interaction.
Throughout my fieldwork in the city, moving through these spaces could
be a convoluted and lengthy process, involving numerous stops for tea
and conversation. While, in my case, the extent to which these social
interactions delayed intended progress was somewhat increased by my
outsider status, it was a familiar rhythm for craftworkers and other residents. Workshops themselves embedded a similar social value in their
material construction. Almost universally open-fronted, the workshops
represented a fluid space between the gully and the site of labour. Even
those men who undertook work in their own homes would often do so
in a room open to the street, or even on the front step of their property.
Sociality, then, was always invited and was physically ingrained within
the built environment.

The range of relationships present in the workshops was wide, but in a significant number of these spaces those who laboured together were constituted around friendship groupings. In some cases, relations in the workshops involved employed workers who, although they did not have a social relationship with the employer, would recruit each other to work in the same place. Some workshops were run more collectively, as had been the case with Shahnawaz (see chapter 6), and had formed around friendships forged in neighbourhoods during childhood or in other workplaces later in life. Just as in chapter 5, where I discussed the socialisation of *shāgirds* into 'pure' and 'impure' practices, so the occupants of the workshops tended to coalesce into groups who shared similar interests and spaces of sociality. Those who attended the gym together would often form working partnerships. Likewise, those who regularly attended the *masjid* fell into labouring parties. Relations, however, were by no means exclusive, and regularly overlapped.

Often, I went out with Rizwan's eldest son Yousef to join his friends. Once away from the household, with its familial constraints and obligations, Yousef could be boisterous and highly entertaining. Rizwan always encouraged this time for Yousef, telling me that *ghūmnāi* (roaming) was important for him to build his own connections in the neighbourhood and beyond. Yousef's network of friends was already extensive. He still worked with his father, but the networks that formed almost organically in the tightly packed gullies were the scene of intense connection building. Although fluid, the groups of young boys and men with whom Yousef spent his spare time engaged in a great deal of mutual exchange, including the sharing of money, clothes and other resources (cf. Osella & Osella 1998). This exchange was underscored by intimate physical contact, such as leaning on each other, cuddling, hand holding and tickling.

The Maussian roots of friendship studies within anthropology are well documented (Desai & Killick 2010; Sahlins 2011; Pitt-Rivers 2016), and many accounts distinguish friendship as comprising non-jural and egalitarian forms of reciprocity that disrupt power-producing elements of gift exchange. C. Osella and F. Osella (1998: 191), for example, show how, amongst young male groups in Kerala, 'intense physical contact and sharing affirm egalitarian principles, breaking down social distance'. They also identify 'the risky play of flirting' (p. 200) as a key site of masculine performance. Empirically, I begin by focusing not on cross-gendered aspects of flirting but on the ways in which the flirting and teasing of with women slips into processes of reciprocal exchange amongst young men. For Yousef and his friends this reciprocity was primarily conceived around the sharing of risks and dangers (*khatra*). One of the primary arenas within which this took place concerned romance and the navigating of gendered divisions within the *mohallas*.

Jaheer, universally known as Chottu ('young', 'small', 'boy') because of his petite build, was one of Yousef's closest friends and the two were often seen in each other's company. Abdul, another of Yousef's close group, was quite a contrast to Chottu. Stocky and muscular, he was fond of sessions in the gym. Along with many of Yousef's friends, he was also an avid chaser and teaser of women. This activity took two forms. The first involved searching for 'girlfriends' within the *mohalla*, and the second involved flirting with and teasing young women beyond the *mohalla*. Relations with the opposite sex in the *mohallas* could be a risky pursuit, not least because of the crossing of gendered spatial divisions it involved. Chottu related how he had assisted Abdul in his pursuit of a girl residing in a nearby gully:

> Today I went with Abdul to his girlfriend's house. She told him that she was making *aloo paratha* [fried bread stuffed with potato] and that he could come. Then I went there straightaway to take the *paratha*. She was waiting at the gate and said, 'Salaam'. As Abdul is like my brother it was okay for me to speak to his girlfriend. We help each other like this in love affairs. He cannot go there directly as her parents will beat him a lot if they see him. It is risky for me too but at least if they impose some ban on me Abdul will still be okay. It always happens in love affairs that parents beat the boyfriend. In Abdul's relationship everyone has agreed to the marriage, but the girlfriend's father is very rude and does not agree with their relationship. But Abdul is also a very rude person and has told everybody that he will marry only that girl. The girl is also very strict in this and has said that she will marry only Abdul, but her parents do not know.

The flirting engaged in by Yousef and his friends is reflected in urban life across India and plays out in similar ways within communities of differing religions, classes and castes (e.g. C. Osella & F. Osella 1998; Donner 2008; Chakraborty 2016; Grover 2018). It has also long been a part of the intimate life of the *mohallas*. However, emerging technologies and the increasing availability of social media have transformed the ways in which flirting took place (cf. Chakraborty 2012). Reminiscing about his own youth, my *ustād*, Islam, described:

> At that time, it was a very difficult period for having a girlfriend. The boys waited at the college gate just to watch the girls walking by. They might follow a girl they liked but there was no mobile and

it was hard to find a place to meet. These days the boys can meet a girlfriend by mobile phone. When I was young there was a girl in my neighbourhood who I liked. I watched her for a whole year a year and then finally I sent her a letter via a small boy. We sent letters back and forth through local children but then her family moved away and there was no way to stay in touch.

It was mobile phones and new forms of social media that Yousef primarily used to mediate relations with women in his *mohalla*. Handsome and charming, he was successful at acquiring 'girlfriends'. In the evening he often sat on the rooftop having whispered phone conversations with those whose numbers he had surreptitiously acquired. The use of WhatsApp allowed these conversations to become more of a face-to-face affair. At times, he would beckon me over and ask me to converse with the young woman on the screen, an introduction that often resulted in much amusement.

If attempting to establish relationships with the opposite sex within the *mohallas* contained degrees of *khatra*, the risks were amplified in other areas of the city. Trips across town could involve flirting with 'college girls' (a term broadly covering women in their late teens or early twenties). This kind of flirting was, as C. Osella and F. Osella (1998) observed, a difficult area to negotiate and interpret in the fieldwork context. Yet I became involved. Thus, on a trip to the cinema next to the city's main clock tower, I found myself thrust to the fore as the group (on this occasion consisting of Yousef, Abdul, Chottu and three others) recruited my services to begin a conversation with three young women in the foyer. Although they had hoped that my foreign status and the degree of exoticism this embodied would produce a positive response, my cack-handed efforts were met with laughter but little success.

Here, though, flirtations intersected with the spatial demarcations of the *mohalla* and played out across divides of religion and class. For young lower-class Muslim boys and men, engaging in flirting activity that is commonplace across the country could – in the context of right-wing Hindu nationalist discourses – be recast as a provocative act. During a later phase of my fieldwork, Yousef's friend Abdul landed himself in trouble in this regard. While working in Udaipur, Abdul had charmed a young Hindu girl in the local bazaar and even proposed marriage. Before returning to Saharanpur, Abdul had phoned her to say that the relationship was over. Abdul anticipated that this would be the end of things. It was quite a shock to him and his family when, a couple of weeks later, she turned up at the door of their house, having made the train journey from Udaipur. In tears, she expressed her love for him and her desire to marry. Abdul's father was furious. Not because of his flirting – it was generally accepted that young men would do that – but because her presence brought the family into danger. The young woman was rapidly ushered back to the railway station and bought a ticket home. Later, his father, Musharraf, told me that her family might have called the police and that they could have been thrown in jail or beaten.

The micro-politics of flirting, which can involve active and agentive performances by both women and men (C. Osella & F. Osella 1998), were here also inscribed with the politics of communalism and with negative constructions of young Muslim men (cf. Salem 2016; Abhik Roy 2004; Shaheen 2003). Yet the male groups who dominated the public spaces of the *mohallas* were also engaged in defining, shaping, negotiating and contesting boundaries. Atreyee Sen (2012) describes the agglomeration of various *mohallas* into the sprawling slum of Sultanpur in Hyderabad. Her ethnographic material illustrates how the configuration of Sultanpur is shaped through spatial claim-making by residents. Sen focuses on *mohalla mardangi* (male pride) among young men and boys who exert youthful authority in defence of the Muslim neighbourhood and police its spatial definitions, including Muslim women's engagements with the public sphere. The forms of 'vigilantism' described by Sen were not present to the same degree in Saharanpur, but the (often invisible) borders of the *mohallas* were informally maintained by young men and others.

In Saharanpur, there were concrete forms of border making conducted by non-state actors, although these entangled with state processes. On the edge of Hasan Nager was a small fenced public park with some scrappy grass and a children's playground. The amenity was put in as a wealthier, primarily Hindu, neighbourhood began to develop on land adjoining the *mohalla* of Khatakheri. For some years the park was used by both communities, but in the spring of 2016 a residents' committee in the adjoining neighbourhood began to campaign to have those residing in Khatakheri excluded. Familiar articulations of othering were invoked: unruly behaviour and the threat posed to women and girls whose modesty and chastity must be protected formed the primary argument. In turn, this act of border making was contested by residents of the *mohalla*.

Young men and boys, in particular, sought to resist the new boundary. In the summer of 2016 Rizwan's son Yousef and I pulled up by the park on my motorbike to call at his friend's place. The friend was not at home, and our conversation quickly turned to the contested space. Yousef described how, a few weeks before, some boys from the *mohalla* had been chastised by residents of the neighbouring area for being in the park. That night an unauthorised lock had been placed on the gate by the residents' committee of the wealthy neighbourhood. However, this only served to increase the number of boys hanging out in the park after dark. Before the incident the park was a space of little interest, and *mohalla* boys would only occasionally go there. The arrival of the padlock had reconfigured the park as a site of contestation and now many climbed the gate at night to resist the new border. The state, then, was active in shaping an imagined border but it was also constituted through everyday politics that pitted the 'civilised' outside (or inside, as with gated communities) against the residents of another space. At the time of writing, the appeals of the residents' committee to the state demanding the legitimisation of their bordering practice has gone unheeded and the spatial contestation remains unresolved.

Two primary points emerge from this engagement with the everyday activities of young men in the *mohallas*. The first illustrates the ways in which male sociality becomes intertwined with urban space, forms of enclavement and moments of contestation. The second concerns the importance young men give to these relationships and the affectively loaded constitution of male sociality in the city. While forged in youth, these relationships do not terminate with the attainment of markers of maturity, such as marriage.

Friendship, labour and work: forming crews

The closeness of these bonds and their constant reinforcement through favours and exchanges contributed to the building of tight friendships. In a neighbourhood where the economy was 'nested' in the everyday (Kudva 2009), these relations soon translated into connections of labour, recruitment, business and production. As Barkat, a 32-year-old buffing *thēkēdār*, explains,

> They [the people I employ] all live here [in my neighbourhood]. I have known them since childhood as our height and age is the same. We played together in childhood, so I know them very well. They are my friends too; we often meet together to go out and for tea or the cinema. If some worker cannot do our work, he can honestly and frankly tell me, and I never mind it.

Geert De Neve (2014a) describes the role friendship plays in the maintenance of workforces in the small production houses of Tamil Nadu's textile industry, suggesting that *thēkēdārs* used 'narratives of friendship' to maintain loyalty among workers. This, De Neve argues, was not always successful; the apparent strength of such bonds, emphasised by *thēkēdārs*, was not necessarily reciprocated by workers. Labour would still jump ship or abandon the *thēkēdār*, even taking an advance with them. In chapter 3 I described similar dualities and ambiguities in relationships in the gullies. Here I expand on this account to connect the more enabling aspects of friendship-based networks of work and labour in the wood industry.

For my *ustād*, Islam, despite his membership of the *Tablighi Jamaat*, non-*Jamaati* networks based on bonds forged in workplaces and the neighbourhood remained his main source of employment, support and mutuality. One of his longest-running friendships was with Mehboob. The two had grown up in the same *mohalla* and often hung out together when Islam was still donning his 'jeans pants' (see the previous chapter). When he first left his *ustād* and caused upset by starting his own business (see chapter 5), he initially set up his workshop with Mehboob. As with many business relationships in the gullies, their partnership was fluid, a pattern reflected in groups of friends such as those detailed in the previous section. The two were close and often made work-related decisions together. By the time I arrived in Saharanpur, Mehboob had managed to build a petty manufacturing business, without Islam, making boxes for export. A year after my initial fieldwork, when I returned to the city, Islam admitted that his own business was struggling. A couple of months after my second departure he informed me during a telephone conversation that he had had to shut up shop. Once again it was his friendship with Mehboob that came to the rescue. Within days of Islam closing his small shop, Mehboob offered him a share in his own business. The extent of support provided by Mehboob far outweighed what Islam could reciprocate, in the short term at least.

While some affiliations were drawn along lines of respectability, '*sharīf*' or forms of religiosity, many were also born out of the types of tight social relationships people formed in neighbourhoods and gullies while growing up. Relations of production, then, took different forms. Particularly striking were the various types of collective working that took place. Groups of men regularly formed themselves into teams or crews who operated together to increase their work capacity, to improve their position of negotiation or their ability to undertake a greater number of production stages. The teams in Kamil Wali Gully formed around a variety of identities, many of which have been discussed in the preceding sections. In a small workshop across the main road from our brass shop a group of eight men had managed to lever their cutting machines into the tight space. All were from an outlying village and all were of the Teli *biradari*. The team had formed itself around kinship-based affiliations and village networks. Elsewhere, however, teams formed around other commonalities, which, as discussed earlier, included religious observance and a fondness for other pursuits (drinking or going to the gym, for example).

A little way down Kamil Wali Gully from Islam's shop was a metal doorway leading into an open courtyard where several *ārī* (saw) machines were situated. The space was rented collectively but the machines were owned by the individual operators. The work was on piece rate and the cutters could demand a reasonable amount in comparison with some other sections of the production process. The machines were reliant on Saharanpur's decidedly dodgy power supply, which meant that the operators were often idle and tended to work late to make up for lost time. It was during these power outages that I headed down to their workshop to sit and chat, drink tea and smoke *beedies* (cheap cigarettes). Our conversations had to be dropped suddenly whenever the power returned. Orders usually arrived from the carving shops, which may have received work directly from a customer or as an outsourced order from one of the showrooms. The carving shops used a pre-cut stencil[4] to draw the design on the wood. The shapes were cut into this before it was returned to the sender, who added carving work. Although each man owned his own machine, the group worked both independently and collectively. This flexibility meant that they could handle large and small orders. The operators used a collective approach to working in order to strengthen their position within the gully economy. Others were engaged in similar practices.

Nafees, Wasim, and Imran and his brother Monis, the group of skilled carvers whose young *shāgird* had been the recipient of a clout round the ear (see chapter 5), also worked together in an informal team, sharing their profits. The group was flexible, and members came and went. There were times when some headed for work outside the city, but they were always welcomed back. The relations between the men, aside from the two brothers, were mostly based on acquaintance and friendship. They had known each other from youth, or had worked together previously. Nafees, Wasim and Imran had all spent time in the Gulf. Wasim had been the first to go and had recruited the other two. Although the three who went to the Middle East had known each other, their bonds of friendship were strengthened in the dormitory environment of the furniture-making factory in which they worked in the Gulf. As with the *ārī* machine operators, the collectivity of their operation allowed them to produce in larger quantities and handle more substantial orders. It also meant that they were able to manage risk better. As Nafees pointed out,

> If one of us has a problem with money or does not have enough to purchase wood, we help with this. Then if sometime I have this problem I know they will help me too. We have known each other for many years and are all respectful of this.

Islam lived about two kilometres from his workshop. One afternoon, when there were no orders to complete, we went to talk to a group of young men working near his house. When I met Nizamuddin Ansari and his three friends they were sitting in a small open-fronted workshop attached to Nizamuddin's brother's house. All were carvers and were employed adding designs to chair legs that had been outsourced from a nearby workshop. They were younger and less experienced than the team in Kamil Wali Gully. They were not related, and all four were of different *biradaris*. As we chatted, two of them departed, along with Islam, for their *namāz*, but the others remained to work and talk with me. Nizamuddin and his friends explained that their arrangement took them into various spaces of work, but always as a group:

> This place [their current workshop] is our reserve place, we can come any time. We have double the benefit as we can work in the factory or in this place. Twenty days ago, we were doing work in a big factory. Before going there, we were taking work from anywhere, it came from different places. At the moment the work is very low in that factory but after some time we plan to go back there. We are doing work on a contract basis so it is not fixed, but [as we can move] it means work is regular. When the work is low in the factory we can move into this place and when the work increases again in the factory we can go back there. We can go anywhere to get the work.
>
> There are four of us and we always go together into the factories, but we do not take anyone else. [Last time also] we all went together into the factory. There are always four of us but sometimes we have arranged one carpenter between us, because we took a contract in that factory so we had need of a carpenter and a polish *wallah* as well. We formed a group because we wanted to be able to do all the work in one place.[5] We already knew that there was lots of

work there. We directly went there and asked for work. The rate is very good in that factory, so we took the decision to do work there.

We decided together to go there for work. We always do work together because we are best friends. We can chat and make jokes. We will not go into a factory if the owner says he needs only one worker, we always go together. There is no boss, we are all equal. We cannot start our work alone. We are not friends from childhood, but we first met in a factory and worked in the same place. Our friendship started there. We have been friends for six years.

A while ago we went together for work to Haryana, in a place called Kaithal [about 130 km from Saharanpur]. There all of us friends went together. We were all four in a group there. We were working on carving on a Mandir. There were only four of us working there, and the owner gave us the work. We got good money from there, it was very good. The payment came from the Mandir organisation. The priest gave it to us.[6]

For Nizamuddin Ansari and his friends, the decision to create a team gave them a sense of companionship and belonging. As with others I met, the emphasis was on the idea that work-time passes with greater ease when you are part of a group. In an environment in which long hours were the norm, it made sense to overlap work and social time. However, there were more practical elements to their relationship. Not only could they handle larger quantities of work when labouring away from the factory, they could also increase their bargaining power when negotiating with owners on rates and conditions. Additionally, Nizamuddin's account reveals the significance of friendship networks in connecting to patterns of migration beyond the city. Before turning to this in the next chapter, I expand on the significance of informal and affective friendship-based networks by considering the ways in which they can, at times, act to forge everyday forms of resistance rooted in contestations about time.

Crafting temporalities: time, friendship and 'resistance'

Much of the previously discussed literature on artisanship and craftwork deals with temporal materialities and considerations of worktime – particularly the slippage of 'work' and 'non-work' time. Similar descriptions are present in analytical engagements with precarity in the global north, where 'the temporality of life becomes governed by work. … [There are] long working hours [and] "bulimic" patterns of working in which periods with no work can give way to periods that require … round-the-clock working' (Gill & Pratt 2008: 17, 25). In many ways this emerging temporal structuring echoes the constitution of artisanal or craft-based production, familiar to those in Saharanpur, more closely than Fordist modes of industrial manufacture that they have replaced elsewhere. In his classic text *Time, Work-Discipline, and Industrial Capitalism*, E. P. Thompson (1967) describes the arrival of the clock, aligned with industrialisation, as leading to the segregation of work and life through rhythmic systems of clocking on and clocking off. For Thompson this represented a loss of control and the demise of an age in which temporality was governed by nature, by the seasons and by day or night.

Others, too, have emphasised the importance of considering differentiated cultural temporalities in contexts of capitalist/non-capitalist and coloniser/colonised. In his early work on Algeria, Pierre Bourdieu (1963) – drawing on Edmund Husserl's phenomenology – outlined the temporal practices of Algerian Kabyle peasants and the disorientating effects of capitalist temporalities imposed by the French coloniser. For the Kabyle, Bourdieu argues, time is seasonal, socially regulated and collectivised, and the Kabyle associate slowness with care and thoughtfulness, in contrast with colonial or capitalist constructions of time which favour speed and haste. Time, for Bourdieu, is central to the structuring of consciousness but is also a means of subjectification and domination (cf. Auyero 2011, 2012).

While a simple rendition equating Kabyle understandings of time with those of Saharanpur's *kārīgars* would be a crude homogenisation, Bourdieu's and Thompson's contributions point to the value of ethnographic explorations of temporalities of work and labour. Thus, tracing the temporal aspects of woodworkers' engagements with workplaces and supply chains offers an opportunity to consider more than discipline and control. It also allows us – in a context in which organised labour movements are non-existent – to draw out aspects of conflict between labour and capital embedded in contestations around time. Against a background of broader circulations aligning craft with entrepreneurialism, which posit 'artisanal' modes of working as an idealised form of flexible, precarious and 'independent' labour (see chapter 6), this focus also offers potential insights into places and spaces where craftwork-like temporalities represent a (re-)emergence rather than a continuity. Often missed in E. P. Thompson's text is a concluding note in which he reflects on a possible future re-emergence of temporalities that are again unregulated by clock time within capitalist societies:

> if the purposive notation of time-use becomes less compulsive, then men [sic] might have to re-learn some of the arts of living lost in the industrial revolution: how to fill the interstices of their days with enriched, more leisurely, personal and social relations; how to break down once more the barriers between work and life. (Thompson 1967: 95)

In the woodworking *mohallas*, 'time' was an area of everyday contestation between *kārīgars*, craftworkers and their (direct or indirect) employers. The temporality of craftwork often required long hours of labour. However, many craftworkers actively resisted clock-time and preferred the relative independence offered by *apna kām* (however amorphously constituted), citing the need to make time for 'society' as well as for work. For many, this meant time for family, attending events such as weddings, and the cultivation of neighbourhood- and friendship-based networks, an investment in social capital that provided a critical resource in times of need. For others, dedicating time to 'society' was also tied up with a desire to engage in religious pursuits, charitable activities or missionary work, as had been the case with Islam (see the previous chapter).

Back in Abdul's factory (discussed in the opening of chapter 3) I worked for some time alongside Shahnawaz. Shahnawaz was a broody character in his mid-thirties. He had married late but now had two young sons. His wife, Ayesha, was a very different personality, irreverent and humorous; she would tease me a great deal whenever I visited and enjoyed making a show of bossing Shahnawaz around. Like many workers in the wood industry, Shahnawaz had moved employment location many times in his working life. Shahnawaz was a fretsaw operator, a highly skilled trade which took some years to master. Learning the fretsaw was beyond the scope of my available fieldwork time, but I regularly sat in this section of the factory and watched as the operators swung and rotated the wooden pieces back and forth following the pre-marked patterns. Speed was a key part of the fretsaw-operator's skill set and, with the saw remaining static, the operator had to combine it with a high level of accuracy in following the faintly marked designs.

At the time, Abdul Malik was pushing the fretsaw operators to work longer hours, as a large order was due for completion. He used a combination of coercive and disciplining practices, from offers of overtime pay to the invocation of outstanding advance payments. A salary-based contract meant that Shahnawaz and the other fretsaw operators were obliged to work nine hours per day, but Abdul was now a regular presence in the section to ensure a high pace of output, as other sections could not complete their tasks until the fine cutting work was done. During tea-break and prayer times, Shahnawaz's already broody demeanour was becoming increasingly glowering. 'Kissai kai liyai waqt nahi hai, bhai [there is no time for anyone, brother]', he muttered to me over chai. 'Aj kal is kam sei tension hamesha atai hai [these days there is always tension from this work]', he continued.

A few weeks later, after I had stopped working in Abdul's factory, I heard that Shahnawaz and some of the other ārī operators had left. I tracked them down to a small backstreet location where Shahnawaz and four others, along with a couple of additional recruits, had set up their own unit in a small and cramped rented space. Here, they were taking orders collectively and working together on their completion. Conditions were little different from those in the factory; indeed, the small space and lack of light made work even tougher. Income was now much less reliable and Shahnawaz reckoned his earnings were substantially less, which was further compounded by the sporadic nature of outsourced work.

There was a feeling amongst the group, however, that these losses were worth bearing to recover a sense of ownership and control over time. Later, in Shahnawaz's house around a kilometre away from the workshop, we discussed his view of the new arrangement. 'Now,' stated Shahnawaz, 'if I must go for some family business or if there is some other work to be done, well then, I can go. My friends [who I work with] will not mind as they know that I will also help them if they have to do some other work.' He paused to take a handful of namkeen (savoury snack). 'In this way,' he continued, speaking through the spiced snack, 'we are not servants of some malik but can arrange our work to suit our needs. Kam mushkil hai, likin hamari waqt hamari waqt hai [work is hard, but our time is our time].'

The 'freedom' from factory time, combined with communalised working, offered greater flexibility. However, this is not to say that Shahnawaz and his colleagues were free from other modes of discipline. Returning to the bazaar meant a return to the circulations of credit and systems of delayed payment outlined in chapter 3, and required irregular working hours. When a large order was due, the group would work through the night, rotating and cutting the wood by the dim light of a few underpowered bare bulbs. The temporality of work had changed but was also impacted by material influences. Abdul's factory incorporated a large generator capable of running the entire assembly line. For Shahnawaz and his friends, Saharanpur's unreliable electricity supply now became a non-human mediating factor in the rhythms of work. During such periods of load shedding Shahnawaz and his colleagues would sit idle, smoking *beedies* and chatting. The end of these periods would require a hasty return to the machines, 'lost time' being made up by working late into the night.

In the literature on temporality in South Asia, 'waiting' has taken a prominent position, particularly the ways in which it intertwines with imaginaries of the future (e.g. Gardner 2018; Carswell et al. 2019; Cross 2014; Jeffrey 2010). Writing about young people in Uttar Pradesh and Uttarakhand, Jeffrey and Dyson (2016) have emphasised the ways in which the pre-eminence of capitalist institutions and the uncertainty and insecurity of life for many in India – particularly members of marginalised communities – create a present-centred subjectivity. This subjectivity, they argue, constrains imaginaries of the future and conceptualisations of longer-term social change, what Jeffrey and Dyson term 'prefigurative politics'.

Likewise, Laura Bear (2014: 6), building on both Marxist and anthropological traditions, has emphasised the unstable nature of future-orientated temporalities under neoliberalism. She argues that 'modern time' is characterised not only by 'unprecedented doubt' but also by 'divergent representations, techniques, and rhythms of human and non-human time'. Importantly, her argument leads Bear to situate temporal practices as bound into 'attempts to develop legitimacy and agency' (p. 19). This focus asks us to consider not only the regulating and disciplining processes of, for example, bureaucracies, workplaces and capitalist time but also the differentiated forms of time mapping at both individual and inter-subjective levels.

Such temporal constructs were, in the context of Saharanpur's wood industry, mediated through artisanal histories, labour insecurities, precarious work, constructions of the ('entrepreneurial') self and circuits of capital and debt. They were also highly gendered. This differentiation was primarily constructed around 'value'. Men's time was seen as precious, as something to be conserved, as being bound into ideals of the male breadwinner and therefore to be dedicated to paid labour or social activity (see Carswell et al. 2019). Women's time was seen as expendable, as surplus and as something to be filled. Despite constraints on spatial mobility it was often women, particularly in poorer households, who would undertake the laborious work of queuing, waiting and negotiating at government offices, ration shops and other sites of state interaction. Bano, a 32-year-old woman, married to a lorry driver and engaged in piece-rate woodwork, explained.

Men ... tell us they can do just one work, either earn or waste time. Our brothers and husbands never have time for this [government work]. It is not good for us. We have responsibility for home and children. We have lots of work, but instead we have to go for the rations or try and make applications at government offices for things we never get.

Bano's statement reveals more than just gendered considerations about the practicalities of interactions with the state, in which men and women juggle different responsibilities (Carswell et al. 2019). Women themselves emphasised the burden that undertaking these 'time-wasting' tasks added to the multiple demands of domestic and paid labour. This sense of wasted time was echoed in men's articulations of the paid labour engaged in by women, such as those featured in chapter 4. Often, this work was described by men as 'timepass', an expression usually applied to activities undertaken to fill vacant time.

Time and temporality, then, were experienced through intersections beyond that of the marginalised Muslim artisan working at the lower end of the labour hierarchy. Yet while partly enabled by their male positionality, the efforts of Shahnawaz and his friends to gain control of their labour time, and the forms of collectivisation this produced, reveal time as a key site of contestation between labour and capital in the woodworking supply chain. Their ability to gain such control was also bound up in relations constructed around notions of friendship which mediated a more egalitarian set of working arrangements. While their move to a communally run workshop did not separate them from broader relations of production it did suggest that glimpses of a 'prefigurative politics' (Jeffrey & Dyson 2016) at the margin are possible, even if such moments are limited by broader structural constraints. It also indicates the value of investing in the development of strong friendship bonds. Thus, Islam's disappointment with my own failure to meet the expectations he placed upon such relationships was not limited to his own character but was part of a context in which friendship and the resources it offered mattered beyond the basic need for human companionship.

Matters of the heart: friendship as a subaltern resource

Islam had, and still has, a heart condition, something he has had from around eight years of age. A small hole in one of his heart valves meant that he often suffered from angina and found it hard to engage in more physical tasks. The condition was manageable, although he had to purchase medication on a regular basis. During my time with him a local doctor advised that he should go to Delhi for tests. Mehboob, Islam and I made several trips through the night in order to join the queue at the large government-operated G B Pant Hospital. Each time, the journey was wearing. We would take a late-night train, arriving after only a couple of hours' sleep. The morning would be taken up with repeated queuing, during which we were able to sleep a little more on the hospital floor. The initial ultrasound scan involved the insertion of a scanner into Islam's oesophagus to view the back of his heart. As the doctor manoeuvred the tube, Islam gripped my hand tightly and groaned. After a series of trips and several rounds of tests the doctors recommended an operation, cautioning Islam that otherwise his angina and periods of weakness would continue and that, in the longer term, there could be a risk of cardiac arrest.

Islam was fearful of the process and on the journey home we discussed the pros and cons of having the operation. For Islam, the prospect threw up many problems. There would be costs, and there would be a lengthy period of convalescence during which he would be unable to work. The first priority for Islam on our return to Saharanpur was to activate the networks of friends he had built up during a lifetime in the *mohallas*. Money was requested and various amounts were offered. This was on the basis of *karz*, an informal interest-free loan. There was an expectation of repayment, but it was always vague and long-term. Rather, it was a sense of obligation and broader forms of mutuality embedded in networks of *wasta* (social capital) that provided the primary motivation for these offers. These networks would need to provide more than just financial assistance. Islam would have to bring four people with him to give blood donations for the operation to go ahead (cf. Street 2009).

For Islam and his family there was real concern about the risks involved. Islam was unsure whether he should continue with medication instead of undergoing surgery. On a Thursday evening he called together at his house many of those who had made offers of support. There were 14 of us in total: Islam, his father and two brothers, his former *ustād* Abdul, Mehboob, several other friends from the neighbourhood and myself. Our discussion went on long into the night and each individual had their say on the topic. While I was in favour of following the doctor's advice, it was eventually decided that Islam should forgo the operation. This collective process of decision making within extended groups of kin and friends was one I often came across in the course of my fieldwork. In Islam's case it involved a major issue, but it was also common around far more mundane concerns. Amongst these was the prevalence of collective decision making about migration, which, for many men in the *mohallas*, was a mundane and uneventful process naturalised within a culture of migration that had developed amongst the *kārīgars* and associated trades in the gullies.

It was a matter of the heart that, some three months after the phone call with Islam, provided the prelude to the recovery of our friendship. Sitting in a café in the UK city of Brighton, I found my thoughts drifting to Islam, as they often did. Feeling particularly low and missing my old friend and ustād, I sent a text. The message was brief, simply stating 'dil mei bahut dard hai [there is much pain in my heart]'. My meaning had been metaphorical but Islam, perhaps drawing on his own struggles with his heart condition, took it as literal. The panicked phone call that followed not only re-established contact but provided affirmation of the depth of affection and care between us that persisted despite our earlier falling out, described in the opening of this chapter.

Conclusion

Julia Elyachar (2010) has argued that apparently nonchalant activity in poor neighbourhoods of Cairo, such as social visits, can be seen as an investment in *wasta*.[7] This itself represents a form of informal labour, as it allows access to resources, mutual support and networks of work and recruitment. This 'labour', Elyachar argues, is not for immediate economic remuneration but to increase influence within an embedded economy and to provide a safety net in times of hardship. Elyachar continues by arguing 'that practices of sociality have outcomes, and that those outcomes are essential to the political economy' (p. 454). Simone (2004) makes a similar point in the African context, suggesting a notion of 'people as infrastructure', in which 'economic collaboration among residents seemingly marginalized from and immiserated by urban life [forms an] economy of perception and collaborative practice […] constituted through the capacity of individual actors to circulate across and become familiar with a broad range of spatial, residential, economic, and transactional positions' (pp. 407, 408).

There is, I argue, a structuring quality to the apparently everyday forms of sociality discussed in this chapter. In chapter 3 I provided a structurally orientated account of the political economy of craft production. It would be problematic to see the forms of intimacy and sociality presented in this chapter and in some earlier material as a clear-cut form of resistance. These friendships are enabling in various ways, but they also contribute to the provision of a flexible labour force that disciplines

Figure 7.4   A carver working on a sofa back. Source: author.

itself through mutual obligations rather than necessarily developing oppositions to capital and exploitation. This is not to say that sociality of this type is not itself a structuring force. To dismiss it as only a consequence of economic conditions or an instrumental survival strategy would limit any analysis. With this in mind, I turn to an exploration of how the forms of sociality detailed in this chapter feed into structuring patterns of migration from the city.

Notes

1. Data was gathered from 180 respondents in workshops and factories. There was little difference between the two (22 per cent and 20 per cent respectively).
2. Pernau states that the author's name is missing but suggests it is probably Saiyid Ahmad Khan.
3. A ritual of gift giving to an idol at a shrine or temple.
4. This is made by and purchased from a designer. The designers are particularly skilled and often highly regarded in the market. They are also few in number.
5. Here the team collectively take on the role of *thēkēdār*, by bringing in additional labour whom they pay.
6. Adapted and edited from interview transcript.
7. An Arabic term meaning 'relationship' or 'employing a middleman'. It is also used in Urdu-speaking areas of India. *Wasta* consists of trust- and reciprocity-based networks constructed around '[t]ribal values of family [and] social solidarity[,] reinforced by Islam's strong emphasis on … family, social solidarity (*takaful al Ijtima'i*), and mutual assistance. … *Wasta* exemplifies the personalized approach to social and political life' (El-Said & Harrigan 2009: 1238).

8
Internal migration in India: imaginaries, subjectivities and precarity

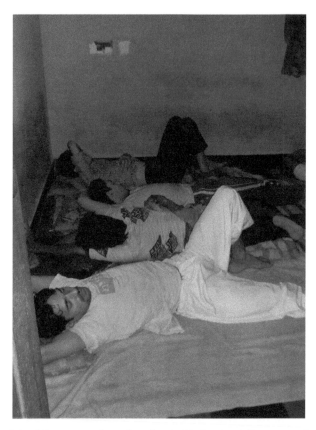

Figure 8.1   Migrant workers sleeping in Hyderabad. Source: author.

On a Wednesday morning in August 2011 outside Saharanpur's railway station, following the Eid holiday, Faisal gathered with friends to travel to Udaipur in Rajasthan in search of work.[1] Many had returned to Saharanpur from elsewhere before Eid. Eid, along with weddings and other festivals, contributed to the circular nature of migration and offered an opportunity to exchange information. The friends' discussion focused on the delayed train. Usman, the least optimistic, suggested, 'Oh, we should go in a few days. There is still enough money to enjoy after Eid for some more time, let's leave now and go to the bazaar. We can go after Friday [the Muslim holy day].' Eventually the decision was made, and the tickets were returned. This ambivalence towards departure was commonplace, and friends in the wood gullies would regularly call off trips at short notice. Likewise, departures could be impulsive decisions to travel substantial distances across the country made at the drop of a hat. Migration was no carefully planned strategy conceived and imagined over weeks or months, but a familiar process easily accepted and quickly abandoned. Rizwan summed this up when recalling an earlier journey to Madras:

> My friends took me to Madras. If you are my friend and you come to my home, and I suggest some place to go, like a garden, you go. My friend came and recommended it to me, so we went there. It is the tradition or link of Saharanpur's business that a friend who has been in some place advises us about the work there.

This chapter is about internal migration in India and follows the experiences of (mostly young) men as they migrate from Saharanpur's woodcraft gullies to various areas of the country. Within this context the chapter makes four primary arguments, all of which continue into the following chapter, which focuses on migration beyond India to the Gulf. First, the chapter argues that migration from the city can only be understood by considering the histories through which the woodworking *mohallas* developed and the forms of male sociality detailed in previous chapters, a sociality that acts as a key mediator in the fostering of patterns of movement within and beyond the *mohallas*. Second, the chapter contends that the huge variety of migratory connections present in the city's Muslim neighbourhoods offer a representation divergent from much of the literature on Muslims in Indian cities (particularly in the north of the country), which focuses primarily on enclaving and marginalising forces (e.g. Gayer & Jaffrelot 2012). Third – and expressly linked to the framework of marginalisation and connectedness outlined in the introduction of this book – the final two chapters show how forms of marginalisation and enclavement penetrate beyond the material context and become mobile, thus acting upon the subjectivities and imaginaries of migrants even as they transit various geographical spaces. Finally, this and the following chapter illustrate the importance of considering the relationship between migration and the imagination, a relationship that is constituted not only in terms of rupture and disjuncture but also through continuities that operate across material, affective and subjective levels.

A variety of factors drove migration from the city. Economic concerns were a part of this landscape, but so were more affective considerations such as the desire for adventure, the hastening of manhood and the influence of friends. Conditions were a factor in the migration decisions made by those in the gullies, but the constant in the lives of migrants from the city was the presence of friends who were already at the destination or with whom they travelled. The idea of migrating to a place where one would know nobody was perceived as pushing at the boundaries of the imaginable. In part, this was pragmatic; concerns about exploitation were intensified when migration became associated with isolation. However, the sociality and intimacy of the gullies, and the friendships in which young men invested so much time, formed a social realm that was itself mobile, a familiar world that could travel with the migrant from place to place. The structuring effects of informal and affective networks in the gullies of Saharanpur continued into forms of migration that stretched to every corner of the country.

Tight bonds and male sociality acted to create emotional and material particularities in the ways woodworkers engaged with migration. For the men and boys of Saharanpur, imagining the future was very much a collective act. Plans were laid, and aspirations expressed. This was often a group pursuit as young men whiled away their time together, during or between work, daydreaming of business plans or of making trips out of the city for either recreation or work. Once hatched, such projects could be rapidly enacted with little sense of upheaval or rupture. As quickly as they were established, so also they could be abandoned. A late train, bad weather, the return of an old friend or just a change of heart could result in cancellation and the return of recently purchased tickets. Just as minds were often changed and plans cancelled, so migration itself was engaged in, with a similar degree of ease and ambivalence.

Internal migration in India

Internal migration within India is one of the country's big stories. The estimated number of internal migrants has been steadily climbing for decades, reaching around 453.6 million in 2011, an increase of 139 million from a decade previously and a figure that brings the total percentage of India's population engaged in migration to just over 44 per cent (Kundu 2018).[2] Along with Bihar, Uttar Pradesh has long been one of the primary sending states, outward flows of migration often being associated – within various representations – with high levels of backwardness in the development of the two states (Malhotra & Devi 2016; Nandy 2019). These are substantial figures, but internal migration in India remains a relatively unexplored category, 'despite irrefutable evidence that movement, both within rural areas and between villages, towns and cities, has always been, and continues to be, a central feature of life within the subcontinent' (K. Gardner & Osella 2003: vi). Over recent years both quantitative and overview-orientated research (e.g. De Haas 2010; Bhagat 2010; Castaldo et al. 2012; Abbas 2016; Mishra 2016), along with ethnographic contributions (e.g. K. Gardner & Osella 2003; Gidwani & Sivaramakrishnan 2003; Parry 2003; Majumdar 2017; P. Rai 2018; Daehnhardt 2019), has started to address this lack of empirical data.

There is, however, very little in the way of research focusing on the experiences of Muslim internal migrants. Earlier contributions engaging with migration amongst Indian Muslims (both contemporary and historical) have primarily concentrated on international migration and on regions in the south of the country (e.g. S. Ali 2007; F. Osella & C. Osella 2009; Verstappen 2017) or coastal areas with lengthy historical connections to the Gulf (Simpson 2006b; Green 2011) (for exceptions see A. Chatterjee 2017; Thapan et al. 2016; Rogaly et al. 2003). When migration by north Indian Muslims is discussed, it is often dealt with in the context of enforced migration into bounded urban spaces resulting from violence, communalism and marginalisation (e.g. Saberwal 2010; Jasani 2008; Seabrook & Siddiqui 2011; Contractor 2012; Jaffrelot & Thomas 2012; T. Alam & Kumar 2019), albeit to varying degrees (Heitmeyer 2009b; Williams 2012). (For a quantitative critique see Susewind 2017.) For many working-class Muslims across the country, however, experiences of migration are (comparatively) mundane and involve journeys in search of work and livelihoods across India. Although often less rupturing than the types of upheavals detailed in the literature cited above, labour migration still includes the potential for a variety of transformative processes. Yet, as the following sections show, the extent to which transformations may occur is also mediated by forms of continuity. This draws us into thinking not only about the material conditions of migration but also about the ways in which experiences and expectations constructed around migration interplay with the imaginations of migrants and others.

Imagining the imaginable: imagination, migration and subjectivity

A growing body of work explores the role of the imagination in migration. While not dismissing 'the economic', these studies discuss how imaginaries of migrants are an important 'non-economic' consideration (Halfacree 2004; Smith 2006; A. P. Marcus 2009; Radhakrishnan 2009; Coles & Walsh 2010). For Saharanpur's craftworkers, movement, migration and connectedness were all part of everyday life. Even though labour migration from the city only began in earnest in the early 1980s, following a downturn in the wood industry, craftworkers accessed networks that extended to every corner of India and the Gulf. The rapid formation of these networks and the ease with which craftworkers transitioned into being a migrant community create an image of migration different from that in accounts that represent it as a 'disjuncture' (e.g. Ong 1988; Mills 1997; Cwerner 2001) or a 'rupture' (e.g. Griffiths et al. 2013). It was the pre-existence of the possibility of migration in the imaginations of those in the city that smoothed this transition. As Mohammad Mehboob, an elderly craftworker, framed it,

> We were ready to leave for work; we are craftworkers, and we often moved workshops and went to nearby towns. So, to go further was not such a big thing. … We could imagine it already.

The imaginaries of migrants from the city were shaped through a variety of factors, including prior histories of migration held in the collective memory, a religiosity that created a sense of connection to other places, the importance given to holders of knowledge of localities within India or beyond, and ideas of personal change or transformation. The imagination is not only a part of conceiving migration. Imaginaries are shaped, changed and even transformed by migration itself. Imagining departure, going elsewhere, returning and imagining again form a constant process in which the self is crafted and re-crafted and through which more collective visions are forged and re-forged.

Although I foreground the imagination of migrants in this and the following chapter, I do not dismiss structural considerations. The materiality of migration is intimately involved in the shaping of migrant imaginaries. As laid out in the introduction of this book, I build on Tim Ingold's (2013) conceptions of the relationship between the imagination and the material, a relationship that he sees as being cyclical and intertwined. Ingold evocatively illustrates a blurring of the real and the imagined. The imagination, he argues, is active in carving out 'paths' or 'ways'. Imagining is not an act of absent-minded pondering but instead directs engagements with the material and is shaped through such engagements. Ingold is primarily concerned with production, but migration, its effects and its connections are also formed by the imagination and simultaneously active in shaping the imagination in a self-perpetuating process. This is not to suggest an organic or independent progression free of constraints, structural conditions and regulatory frames. Instead, there are possibilities for migration to cultivate new subjectivities or forms of consciousness that may offer challenges to normalised hierarchies, structures or inequalities. There are also various ways in which the imaginations of migrants can be subverted, co-opted, influenced and structured to meet the demands of labour markets both domestically and abroad. These processes intersect with the structural constraints of various migration regimes as they seek to serve the needs of capital across geographical space.

Amira Mittermaier (2010), in her work on dreams and imaginaries in Egypt, shows that the imagination, or at least how the imagination is conceived of, and the role it is seen to play, is both culturally diverse and non-static. Mittermaier's work draws attention to cultural specificities and asks that we consider how cultural contexts shape not only what is imagined (or not imagined) but also how imaginaries may be defined or conceived within a given context. It also intersects with a broader body of work on migration and the imagination which attends to various facets of the imaginations of migrants. A historical imagination, for example, considers how histories of mobility and pre-existing connections (either travelled or imagined) contribute to the contemporary movement of people (Comaroff & Comaroff 1992; Shaw 2002). Here, connections formed through colonial activity, circuits of trade, conflict or alliances live on in cultural and social practice. Shaw (2002), for example, details how the rituals and images of the Temne in Sierra Leone have been shaped through historical engagement with the Atlantic slave trade, the memory of which has become incorporated into cultural and social practice.

Work on the 'religious imagination', in the context of migration, emphasises the role of religious identity, networks, pilgrimage and travel in shaping the imagination. The narratives within this research involve both physical and temporal movement, such as a journey of the soul, a transformation in subjectivities or a shift to a purer and more pious form of being (J. W. Fernandez 1982; Eickelman & Piscatori 1990; Johnson & Werbner 2010). Others have attended to the types of 'spatial knowledge' that individuals, groups or communities may possess which allow images of other places to form (A. Marcus 2009), images that may be outward-looking (Massey 1994) or enclaving (Schulten 2001). Here, a 'geographical imagination' may embody power or status in which the holders of geographical knowledge are revered and so cultivate the imaginations of others seeking similar prestige. Within the imaginaries of potential migrants, the 'geographical imagination' can become 'a projection of migrants' conceptions of place ... embedded in the minds of those who wish to leave ... in search of their "dream"' (A. Marcus 2009: 486).

These approaches all seek to understand how the imaginations of migrants are shaped, and thus how this impacts on experiences of migration. Others have focused on how migration itself affects the imagination and fundamentally changes what may be imaginable. Contributions dealing with the 'social imagination' envisage migration as holding the potential to drive new forms of resistance or social transformation while simultaneously being sought to be controlled by states and others through media, spectacle and drama (Appadurai 1996). Here migration invokes revolutionary potential, although in a post-structural rather than a vanguard context (Gaonkar 2002). In terms of migration, it explores potentialities within increasingly de-territorialised or trans-global imaginaries, which hold emancipatory possibilities that 'imagined worlds' may enable subversions of and challenges to established hierarchies and relations of power. Thus, increasing mobility creates new forms of instability capable of freeing the imagination from pre-existing social controls (Appadurai 1996).

Within much of this literature, migration is seen as fostering new horizons within the imaginations of those involved, which leads to the emergence of new subjectivities that situate migrants as vanguards of change (De Haan & Rogaly 2002) or as the embodiment of cosmopolitanism (Gidwani & Sivaramakrishnan 2003). Such cosmopolitan ideals are identified as enabling increased cultural versatility, a sense of the 'spatial diffusion of ideas' and 'a *geographical imagination* secured by notions of discrete, self-evident places and subjects awaiting transformation through the cultivation of a universal ethos' (Gidwani & Sivaramakrishnan 2003: 343). Horizons may broaden, but this broadening is not to confuse the cosmopolitan nature of craftworkers in Saharanpur with increased social mobility. Subaltern cosmopolitanisms play out at various levels of hardship and affluence. As Pollock et al. (2002: 6) argue, 'Cosmopolitans today are often the victims of modernity, failed by capitalism's upward mobility, and bereft of those comforts and customs of national belonging. Refugees, peoples of the diaspora, and migrants and exiles represent the spirit of the cosmopolitical community.' However, not all of those who traverse borders or engage in travel fit the cosmopolitan mould (Werbner 2008). Thus, in his discussion of 'demotic' (of the people) cosmopolitanism in an Indian steel plant, Jonathan Parry (2008: 327) argues that class positioning is critical in shaping the 'imaginative horizons of workers' and that '[r]egular company workers in the *public* sector steel plant are most cosmopolitan' while 'workers in *private* sector factories are more likely to be encapsulated by kinship, caste and regional community' (emphasis in original).

It is essential to consider how the imagination can act to limit what can and cannot be conceived, creating acceptance, compliance and even docility. As David Harvey (2000) reminds us, cosmopolitan connections are also fundamental to globalised production and consumption. A 'cosmopolitan imagination' may echo ideologies of globalisation and act in the stratification of labour markets (Castles 2012). Merely identifying it within the imaginations of a community or labour force, however, does not automatically facilitate the production of 'progressive political agendas' (Gidwani & Sivaramakrishnan 2003: 362). In the context of labour migration, Mary Beth Mills (1997: 41) argues that the 'potential exists for the production of new meanings and practices in the resulting disjunctures between dominant meanings and lived experience, and between *imagined* possibilities and limited opportunities' (my emphasis). As Mills points out (citing Ong 1991), migrants' encounters with, for example, capitalist wage labour do not necessarily lead to the proletarian resistance imagined in classical models. Similarly, Aihwa Ong (1991) focuses on rupturing aspects of migration amongst rural female Malaysian migrants whose imaginings of life in the city are not met by the realities of industrial production. Here new forms of resistance are conjured up as women become possessed by spirits to express the distress they feel at the conditions they find themselves in. While indirect forms of resistance may emerge, they are connected more to the shock of a dramatic change in life than to a sense of consciously challenging injustice or exploitation.

Throughout this literature, whether focused on enabling or exploitative aspects of migration, the emphasis is on change, transformation, rupture or disjuncture. Migrations create shifts in the imaginations of those involved in the process: the self is transformed, the social reconfigured, the hierarchy challenged, or the body and the person shocked. The imagination, however, is not shaped only through change. Nor do shifting material contexts necessarily foster transformative processes at the subjective level. Rather, there are various forms of continuity that persist within both the material and the imagined. Throughout my time in Saharanpur, the most emotional aspects of my fieldwork were bound up in male sociality and its associated expectations, intimacies, comfort and obligation.

In the crowded and mostly masculine spatial context of the gullies, sociality regularly overlapped with business and production. Young men and boys entering the industry did so in a context bound up in friendships fostered through childhood and youth in the equally congested residential areas that wind off the main spaces of production. Banter, warmth, arguments, fallings out, reconciliations and intimacy were a constant background to the emotional context of the everyday. This terrain was not limited to Saharanpur but was very much a part of migrant life in other areas of the country. Journeys were usually made in small groups, work and life on the road playing out in necessarily intimate environments. Beyond the domestic context, the labour camps of the Gulf held much that was familiar. Dormitory rooms were usually occupied by men of similar social backgrounds and the everyday intimacy and sociality of life interplayed with the imaginations of migrants to instil a sense of familiarity and comfort rather than rupture or disjuncture.

There are other continuities. In the context of a developing culture of migration in Hyderabad, Syed Ali (2007) shows how migrants may be seen on return as heroic, and that migration itself has triggered forms of social change. He also points out that migrants' preference for, for example, Saudi Arabia as a destination is tied up with degrees of familiarity with areas of Jeddah that strongly resemble Hyderabad. Ali argues that migration has become so normalised in the city, particularly within the Muslim population, that the counter-cultural act is no longer to migrate but to choose not to migrate. Saharanpur had also seen the emergence of a 'culture of migration' that had normalised domestic migration and, as migration to the Gulf continued to grow, the degree to which a returnee might be seen as exceptional was dissipating. This sense of normalisation was not limited to the period after the emergence of current flows, which began in the 1980s, but cemented in older memories embedded within the collective imaginary of the city's Muslim population. Before returning to the descriptive material that evokes the more emotional concerns underpinning the imaginaries of migrants, I turn to the historical context, a context that is also active in the imaginations of potential, current and returning migrants.

A brief history: the 'rupture' of partition and the 'continuity' of artisan mobility

Migration from Saharanpur began in earnest in the early 1980s. The woodworking industry had been growing, sucking in labour. Eventually, new legislation[3] aimed at closing sawmills, and increased competition from elsewhere, led to a decline. The resulting surplus of labour meant craftworkers turned to other sources of income both within and beyond the city. For some, this meant a shift into informal activity, as in the case of Rizwan's *mamu* (maternal uncle), Mohamed Shahzad Ansari, described in chapter 2. For others, it meant looking further afield. Here, the routes and networks used were varied. Mohammed Abdul, Islam's former *ustād* (see chapter 5), made his first trip out a couple of years after Mohamed Shahzad Ansari started pulling his rickshaw. This opportunity came through kinship and by accident. His *chacha* (paternal uncle) worked in Saharanpur's large cigarette factory and was transferred to Hyderabad. Upon arrival, he observed the presence of a furniture industry. Abdul's *chacha* had a son, Azim (Abdul's cousin), who had recently completed an apprenticeship as a woodcarver. Through his father, Azim relocated to Hyderabad to seek work in furniture production. It was this cousin who suggested that Abdul, too, should join him working in the city. Thus, Abdul made the trip to Hyderabad, and while he only stayed for six months others followed, opening a migration pathway that today involves thousands of workers. Although not solely a result of Abdul's own migration, the emergence of some neighbourhoods in Hyderabad where large numbers of woodworkers from Saharanpur can be found is a direct consequence of earlier movements by workers such as Abdul.

Others were drawn to various areas of India by the relocation of the industry away from Saharanpur as workshop owners and exporters sought business elsewhere. Ameer Ahmed, a craftsman in his eighties, told me how his son ran away to Mumbai. He did not follow relatives but went to work for an exporter from Saharanpur:

There are many exporters who were basically from Saharanpur but have now settled in Mumbai. If they need workers, they come here to take them. They told my son about work in Mumbai. If the worker is better off in Mumbai, why would they come back? If they have problems, though, they return. The exporter gives advance money and the cost of the journey.

It was not just those originating in Saharanpur who recruited labour. The reputation and skill of craftworkers also started to draw interest from elsewhere. Many owners in Saharanpur complained that it was hard to retain labour. One bemoaned:

There is demand for workers all over India. Some workers work for me for 5,000 rupees a month, but they can get 8,000 rupees elsewhere in India, so they go away. In this season I lost 50 per cent of my staff like this and have only managed to replace 25 per cent.

Economic factors, then, were important, as craft workers began to seek work beyond the city. The stories of returnees and the ideas and styles they brought back also shaped the imaginations of others. Early migrants obtained status and social capital upon return and their new-found 'geographical knowledge' was often sought by others. The easy acceptance of migration is not rooted merely in the imagination or in an emerging migratory culture. While forwarding a 'culture of migration' as the primary facet driving outward movement is useful, it often ignores the unequal relations embedded in such processes and makes a pretence towards ideological neutrality which may shroud links between movements of labour and neoliberalism (Halfacree 2004). It also posits migration as emerging within a relatively ahistorical context and gives little account of previously trodden pathways and histories of connection.

For those in Saharanpur, the willingness to migrate can be located not just within emerging cultures but also in experiences related to Muslim identity, the history of the wood industry and the dramatic change experienced in the city during partition (see chapter 2). Jonathan Addleton (1992), working on Pakistan, links easy acceptance of migration to the Gulf with the upheavals of partition, which left a 'legacy of unsettlement' that ensured a willingness to accept further movement. As Addleton found in Pakistan, the collective memory and 'communal imagination' (Comaroff & Comaroff 1992) of Saharanpur's Muslim population holds a migratory experience far more 'rupturing' than relocation for work. 'Unsettlement' not only resides in memories of partition but also connects with the long histories of artisan mobility outlined in the second chapter of this book. It is in this broader historical context, much of which continues in the corners of the communal and individual imaginations, that migration from the city needs to be understood.

Re-emerging mobility was also contained within persisting cultural traits, such as an emphasis on the importance of *ghūmnāi* (roaming), which pre-dated recent large-scale labour migration. For young men, such as Rizwan's eldest son Yousef, migration was a rite of passage (cf. F. Osella & C. Osella 2000; Monsutti 2007; Marchand 2015). Rizwan regularly headed discussions, at the household level, about sending Yousef further afield. Instrumental considerations were in play, but Yousef's view was also one of excitement. Many of his friends had been out, and he looked forward to time away working with pals and seeing other areas. For many young men in Saharanpur migration had become normalised to the degree that it represented a rite of passage into manhood. Indeed, evidence suggests that migration itself may speed the journey to maturity (F. Osella & C. Osella 2000).

Alessandro Monsutti (2007: 169), for example, describes the journeys of young Afghan men migrating to Iran for work as 'conceived as a necessary stage in their existence, a rite of passage to adulthood and then a step toward manhood', a factor echoed in the imaginations of young men such as Yousef. Returnees gained prestige with peers and were acknowledged within the family as having achieved a transition. Thus, after Yousef's first trip, Rizwan's language with his eldest son changed. A kindly but commanding tone was replaced with the more informal *bhai* (brother), denoting (or suggesting) a degree of egalitarianism in their relationship. For Monsutti, migration provides not just an avenue to manhood but a means of broadening social networks beyond kin and family. For Saharanpur's craftworkers the broadening of networks was not just about facilitating migration or business but was also critical to survival in a fundamentally precarious occupation. Migration had become defined as a liminal period through which manhood could be achieved, but the degrees of transition that were possible and imaginable had shifted with the normalisation of migration. The boy could become a man, but, the returnee was no longer seen as the hero.

Not everyone in the industry was involved in migration, but, in a reflection of national figures, almost 40 per cent of those I surveyed during my fieldwork had worked outside Saharanpur at least once. After I started work with Islam, it did not take me long to realise the extent of outward journeys and migrant networks. The scope of possible destinations was particularly impressive; workers and *kārīgars* described trips to Nagaland, Kashmir and Kerala as well as to larger cities such as Mumbai, Delhi, Kolkata, Hyderabad and Chennai. Much of this migration was relatively short-term (see Table 8.1).[4]

The type of work done varied between locations. In Rajasthan, particularly Jaipur and Jodhpur, the work was mostly handicraft, supplying the tourist trade and export markets. In Kerala, the production was of furniture for domestic and export use. Hyderabad also involved furniture production, but here it was mostly for local consumption, particularly for Muslim wedding dowries, but also for general household use by both Muslim and non-Muslim families. Elsewhere, larger factories, particularly those without direct links to export markets, used *thēkēdārs* as intermediaries to recruit skilled *kārīgars* and other craftworkers from Saharanpur. Although there was a great deal of diversity in these networks, the prevalence of avenues of migration embedded in the friendship-based networks described in the previous chapter carried through into quantitative data gathered during fieldwork in the city (Table 8.2).

There were degrees to which migration was also bound into identity-based networks. While workers and *kārīgars* described working in a variety of arrangements and for employers, *thēkēdārs* and others of reasonably diverse backgrounds, many expressed a preference for Muslim employers, a pattern which follows through into the quantitative data (Table 8.3). Additionally, the presence of employers in various areas of the country who themselves originated from Saharanpur (Table 8.4) added a further degree of entrenchment to networks based on degrees of shared identity.

Table 8.1 Length of time spent away during the most recent migration.

Length of time	< 3 months	3–6 months	6–12 months	1–2 years	> 2 years	Don't know
Migrant workers/ craftsmen (%)	20	39	11	3	17	9

Table 8.2 Person who had recruited the respondent to a factory or workshop for migrant work on their most recent trip.

Primary recruiter	Relative	Friend	Owner	*Thēkēdār*	Other
Worker/craftsman (%)	21	30	10	23	16

Table 8.3 Religion of those employing workers who had migrated from Saharanpur, as stated by respondents regarding their most recent migration.

Employer's religion	Muslim	Hindu	Christian	Other	Don't know	Invalid*
Migrant employee (%)	56	22	4	1	12	8

Note: * Covers those who worked on a self-employed basis during the period of migration.

Table 8.4 Origin of those employing workers who had migrated from Saharanpur, as stated by respondents regarding their most recent migration.

Employer's origin (town or city)	Saharanpur	Other	Don't know	Invalid*
Migrant employee (%)	40	40	12	8

Note: *Covers those who worked on a self-employed basis during the period of migration.

As suggested in Table 8.1, most contemporary migration was circular: migrants returned at regular intervals and many engaged in ad hoc patterns of work and flitted between Saharanpur and various other locations around the country. In almost all cases migration was urban–urban, although this included small towns and cities as well as the larger metro centres. While they were not influenced by the seasonal effects of agriculture seen in rural-to-urban or rural-to-rural migration, cycles were constituted around religious holidays, Eid al Fitr and Eid al Adha in particular. Such occasions also became essential opportunities for the exchange of information about work opportunities in different areas of the country and for future migration plans to be imagined, often with others. Migrants also returned throughout the year because of weddings, deaths or illness, or to see friends and family; such events sometimes resulted in the informal recruitment of kin, neighbours and friends.

To situate this in a more ethnographic context, I turn to the life stories of two friends from the city: my old friend Rizwan, and Naseer whose postponed departure from the railway station opened this chapter. I begin each section with interview material gathered at the end of my initial year and a half of fieldwork in the city. The interviews are abridged and edited from original transcripts, but remain faithful to the narratives presented by the two men. These are followed by a more descriptive account of separate migrations I undertook with Rizwan and

Naseer throughout my fieldwork. The two stories draw out the arguments around which this chapter is constructed by illuminating the role of affective networks, the forms of familiarity and continuity these networks embody and how migration is intersected by degrees of marginalisation and connectedness. In addition, Rizwan and Naseer's migration histories illustrate the haphazard nature of migration from the city, the high degree of precarity present and the everyday concerns of migrants as they considered possible destinations and negotiated conditions in localities around the country.

Rizwan's story: in search of *apna kām*

Rizwan had made his first trip out of the city a couple of years after Indira Gandhi's assassination in 1984, to work with his *mamu* (maternal uncle) who made carved table legs in Punjab. This early foray was followed by a longer trip to Mumbai, a journey that was influenced by a recently returned friend:

> In 1986 I saw a boy who went to Mumbai. He was my first friend to go out of the city for work. Now he is dead. He went to Mumbai. When he came back, he looked just like Amitabh Bachchan.[5] Everyone wanted to walk with that man and to know about Mumbai. They asked him if he had met some hero; he was just like a hero and said he had seen every hero and heroine. Everyone wanted to know how the hero and heroine dressed. It was a status symbol to walk with that boy as he knew the Mumbai life. He was the first boy to go [from our group of friends]. Others went because they hoped to become a hero like him. When I came back, many people asked me about Mumbai. They asked me what the life was like and what heroes were like. I told them that I saw many heroes and heroines. I went to see a shoot; the hero was Sunny Deol.
>
> Now many people go, so it's not unique, but at that time even if a person went to Delhi, it was a famous thing. People knew nothing about Delhi and Mumbai, but now it is common. In the old days, people were simple and polite. The men wore sandals, not shoes, and rubbed oil in their hair. They wore pyjama. People were simple at that time. It was different compared with today's style. This fashion continued till 1988; after that everyone wanted to make their hair like Amitabh Bachchan – me too.

I have been to so many places now that I can't count them all. The hardest place was Madras [Chennai]. I had many problems there. It was a language problem; we cannot understand the Madras language. It was very hard as we could not even ask for a glass of water. No one could understand what we wanted there, and we could not understand what they were saying to us. Also, the food was not so good, and we could only get rice and no *roti*. Everyone wants to eat just rice there. We could not find *roti* in Madras. The temperature was also very hot for us. I cannot tolerate the temperature there. The main problem was that we had to buy water if we wanted to drink. The water is not good there, so you have to get it in a bottle.

We can go to every place in India very easily. In every city you can find some Saharanpur workers. ... We can find workers of Saharanpur very easily. Right now, I could call friends in ten different places in India and know what the work is like in that place and if it is good to go there.[6]

There was, then, more to Rizwan's migration history than simplistic, and much criticised, models of economic 'push and pull' (Harris & Todaro 1970). His narrative also reflected a desire for adventure and social status (cf. Shah 2006) as well as certain ambivalences about becoming a member of a migrant community (cf. Ferguson 1999), embodied in his identification of people in pre-migration Saharanpur as 'simple and polite'.

Rizwan's engagements with migration continued throughout my initial period of fieldwork in the city and for several years afterwards. During Ramadan in 2011, we gathered at the house of Rizwan's *saali* (wife's sister) in a neighbouring *mohalla* and discussed Rizwan's plans to head out of the city after Eid. A family friend, Ishmael, had also joined us. Rizwan contemplated the pros and cons of travelling to Mumbai. Ishmael was hesitant; he said, '*Rizwan bhai, abbi dārhī walla kē li'ē suffer khatarā hai* [For those with the beard the journey is not safe].' At that time there was trouble in Muzaffarnagar, on the main line to Delhi, a reminder that migrant pathways, like spaces within the city, were communally constrained. Despite this, Rizwan finally decided on Jodhpur, where he had heard good work and wages were available.

A few days before his departure, Rizwan and I sat on the rooftop of the two rooms the family rented. Here we had celebrated Eid a couple of weeks before. Now, in the dusky heat, as his children played with kites, we discussed his dreams for the upcoming trip. He told me that all the tension was now gone, as it would be a successful trip. He hoped that they could make something in the region of 10,000 rupees a month in Jodhpur, about 4,000 rupees more than in Saharanpur. Rizwan had given up the workshop he rented in Kamil Wali Gully in preparation for departure and told me that in Jodhpur they would be able to engage in *apna kām*. At the time Rizwan did receive direct orders from customers at his workshop in Kamil Wali Gully but often undertook work outsourced by others. His acceptance of such work was tied to his desire to escape *kirāya* (rent) and build a small house. During Eid, when the family sat to pray before breaking fast, his youngest son, Ishmael, asked, 'What shall I pray for?' Rizwan instructed him, '*Ghar kai liye mangnao* [pray for a house].'

While Rizwan prepared to leave with his wife and children, his oldest son Yousef had gone ahead, along with other members of an informal team. The team comprised a carpenter, a cutting-machine operator and a polisher, all friends of Rizwan, whom he had convinced to join the venture. Rizwan hoped that they would be able to establish a collective business, although he recognised that much work would still come on a subcontracted basis from larger producers. Reflecting on this during an earlier interview, he identified more affective considerations:

> The journey to Jodhpur is very long, so if Yousef goes with others he can have fun on the journey. If we are a team we can have a better time together when we are there, as we will not be alone. As a team, we can have some gossip. It is better for us if we are in a group, as we have a significant majority if we are a larger number.

I anticipated joining them in Jodhpur, but within a couple of weeks the family returned. Upon my enquiring, Rizwan explained that conditions were bad as there was no latrine and they had to go in the fields. The work was also below what was expected and the factory owners, from whom they had received subcontracted orders, treated them like *mazdoor* (labour). A couple of days after their return we sat in the summer evening heat taking chai in the improvised *sahn* of his small rooftop room. As we discussed the situation, it became clear that the networks that had provided Rizwan with information about working conditions had been too successful during the Eid holiday. Thus, many others had also heard of the riches to be gained in Jodhpur and made the same trip once the Eid celebrations were over. A situation of labour shortage, in which the craftsmen could demand reasonable rates, was suddenly reversed by an influx after Eid, which led to a labour surplus. Under these conditions there was no chance of establishing a position of *apna kām* (see chapter 6).

Rizwan was no stranger to this situation and was quick to set his sights on Ludhiana, where he had a relative running a small business. This time I joined them from the start. Once again, Yousef went ahead. We set off with Rizwan's second son, Abdul, on the early morning passenger train as the first chills of autumn eased the journey. Rizwan intended that the rest of the family would follow once they were established. Upon arrival, we found Yousef already working in the employ of Imtiyaz, Rizwan's *humzulf* (wife's sister's husband). Imtiyaz had been in the city for about ten years and had a workshop in a side street populated by woodworkers all originating from Saharanpur. The craftsmen were well established: some had been there for thirty years. Although Rizwan was happy for himself and his sons to work under Imtiyaz initially, he was keen to get his own business under way. Imtiyaz introduced him to Vijay, a neighbouring Hindu wholesaler, who offered Rizwan a place on the step of his *malding* (decorative wooden strips) showroom in exchange for a share of Rizwan's profit. Yousef, Abdul and I took up residence on the step, displaying items we had brought, and began to work on others in the hope of some sales. It was not long, however, before Vijay requested that we add some carving effects to the *maldings* and Rizwan began to grumble about being co-opted as a *mazdoor* rather than engaging in the *apna kām* he had hoped for.

Initially, we slept in the *sahn* outside the front of Imtiyaz's home. Later we shifted to a rented room nearby where we slept on plyboards on the floor. The neighbourhood was a contrast from the wood *mohallas* of Saharanpur. Mainly consisting of Hindus and Sikhs, the community had a very different feel. The difference also encroached on the home of Imtiyaz and his family. His wife prepared food in an open-fronted *sahn* and took little notice of the rules of purdah, regularly visiting neighbours to chat and drink tea with her head uncovered. The family seemed settled in the area and had good relations with their Hindu and non-Muslim neighbours and friends. For Rizwan, however, the setting became a concern, and he discussed shifting to a Muslim neighbourhood some 8 km away. This he intended to do before the rest of his family relocated, as he was particularly worried about the lack of a *masjid* where the children could study the Quran Sharif.

As the weeks wore on, Rizwan became more frustrated with the setting and with his increasing reliance on Vijay. Eventually, in October 2011, he abandoned the venture and returned to Saharanpur. Over the following year, further trips were attempted. An effort to go to Mumbai was cancelled as he could not recruit a carpenter. Rizwan and Yousef made it to Hyderabad but again returned as they had not found enough work. It became something of a joke in Kamil Wali Gully, as they regularly said 'Goodbye' and we replied, *'Tikay, aglai hafta milaingai* [Okay, see you next week]'. Rizwan took the various attempts in his stride, and I was endlessly impressed by the family's ability to ride out the costs. Eventually, he decided that these attempts were futile, and after arranging *karz* (an interest-free loan) from a friend restarted business one gully away from where I had first met him.

In recent years Rizwan and his family re-established themselves in Saharanpur. With his growing sons able to take on more work, Rizwan could attend to greasing the wheels of business in the bazaar. His climb back to a position that gave an impression of *apna kām* (see chapter 6) remained precarious, and, like most of those who ran workshops, Rizwan remained embroiled in complex networks of subcontracting. The precarity of labour both in and beyond the city was further highlighted by the fate of Rizwan's one-time sponsor, Imtiyaz. Imtiyaz was always fond of the bottle, and his drinking began to affect the success of his wood shop in Ludhiana; it was not long before he experienced a trajectory of rapid decline similar to that related by Islam's friend Mohammad Aslam (see chapter 3). By 2014 Imtiyaz and his family were living in impoverished conditions back in Saharanpur. Rizwan and his family continued with their workshop but were always subject to periods of *mandee* (recession). During Eid and on other occasions Rizwan still asks his children to '*dua mei ghar kai liye mangnao*' [in your prayer ask for a house]. When I made a return visit in the summer of 2016, Rizwan's wife quietly told me of her frustration with her husband's fondness for risky endeavours and of her desire for a more stable life. Whenever she complained, Rizwan would respond '*Yah Allah ke haath mein hai* [It is in Allah's hands]'. She then shrugged her shoulders and uttered a proclamation common among women in the *mohallas* (see chapter 4), '*Yah hamaari kismet hai* [This is the fate we have been given]'.

Rizwan's story reflects the problematics of spurious claims that link migration with entrepreneurial success (e.g. Naudé et al. 2015; Wahba & Zenou 2012; Murphy 2000). It also illuminates the extent to which migration, for Saharanpur's craftworkers, had a high degree of unpredictability and was often a haphazard process. Jonathan Parry (2003) has drawn similar parallels amongst Indian steel plant workers in Bhilai (Madhya Pradesh). Parry criticises the notion that migration can be regarded as a 'strategy'. Instead, he suggests, 'migrants may see themselves less as strategisers than as gamblers playing in a high risk game of chance[, this being symbolised in] the often haphazard, spontaneous and opportunistic way in which the decision to migrate is taken' (p. 220). For Bhilai's steel plant workers, migration had become bound up in a rupturing experience tied in with a decline of the state steel industry. For Saharanpur's woodworkers, migration was also messy and unpredictable: failed relocations were commonplace. The extent of the networks available to workers from the city meant that migration was often not imagined as a gamble to the degree described by Parry.

Naseer's story: the taste of water

Like Rizwan, Naseer was an experienced migrant. His first trip had been as a young boy of about 14. There were many echoes between Naseer's migration history and that detailed by Rizwan; concerns about the taste of water, affective considerations, and aspirations bound up in projects of self-making were all present. Naseer's story also emphasises another intersection central to this chapter: the presence of forms of continuity that persist, at both the affective and the material levels, across the spaces of the *mohallas*, during journeys to other areas of India and in migration destinations.

> My friend was working in Ramgarh [Rajasthan]; he called to ask me to come, so I went there to work with him. I spent four months there, but it was not good for me, and my health became poor, so I came back. Next, I went to Kerala for three months, but the food was terrible, and I did not like it. The food system is very different from ours: they did not like *roti*, and their vegetable is raw coconut. The water was good in Kerala but not the food. In Rajasthan, though, the water was very bad. The taste was very different; it was *kara pani* [salty water]. No one can drink a glass of water if we mix salt in it, so how can we drink that water? We believe that water is essential; if you go somewhere and the water is not suited to you, you get ill. We like the water of Saharanpur. We never get ill from this water as it is sweet. I never adapted to the water of Rajasthan and fell ill from it.
>
> In Kerala, we had a room and did our work in the room, which was on rent organised by a Saharanpur person. He was based in Kerala but came back to Saharanpur to take on some workers. I had no relationship with him. He just wanted some workers, so we went there. I found this work because I had a friend and that friend also had a friend in Kerala. At that time I was in Saharanpur, and my friend told me, during Eid, that his friend wants some workers in Kerala. So my friend asked if I wanted to go and I agreed. We made contact with my friend's friend. Then we went with him to go there.

The room was near the factory, and so we could bring the work into the room. It was easy for us. The owner always sent the work there. The main problem was that we had to make our own food.

After this, I worked in Saharanpur for three years in a small workshop on a contract basis. Then I came to Hyderabad for work and spent six years there [not continuously]. The food was good, and the water was sweet. At that time my ten friends were living in Hyderabad. They phoned me and told me that the work was very good here. I had a friend in Saharanpur. He was a carpenter, and we decided to go together. The ten friends were living in Dilshad's house, and Dilshad sent the money for the travel. Sometimes I came back after six months but sometimes after one year. I just came back for Eid and sometimes for weddings. Once, I came back for my own marriage and did not go back for a long time.

I spent three years with my wife, but some time ago I went back there. Sometimes they [the owners] would give me 5,000 to 10,000 rupees advance to come back. When I am in Hyderabad, I live with friends in the room Dilshad provides. It is mostly okay, but sometimes we fight, like when we tease some person or called them a donkey then the fighting would start from a joke. Like when one boy made a joke about another boy that he is becoming a body-builder, then the fight started. If some boy did not do his cleaning work, or if some boys want to sleep and others do not, this is the main reason for fighting. Now I have no problem living with friends. When we are together, we can feel nice as we can share our secrets and problems. We rarely fight with our friends; otherwise we live together with love. Like in Dilshad's factory, you can see that we live happily with our friends.[7]

Naseer's emphasis on food and water was of significance. A variety of contributions show that what people eat and drink, particularly in South Asia, forms an integral part of communal and regional identity and is often 'imbued with symbolic and cosmological meanings' (Mookherjee 2008: 58), meanings that may be contested by different political, corporate and social groups (Solomon 2015; C. Osella & F. Osella 2008). For Muslims, the consumption of meat, for example, can be seen as a source of strength, by those within the community, or as a symbol of violence and pollution, by some outside (Chigateri 2008). For craftworkers, too, there is a specific aesthetic to food. Naseer and his friends started each day with a breakfast of milk and eggs. In part, this was tied to the gym-going activities of some in the group. It was also bound into embodied relationships with daily labour; milk and eggs were seen as giving people the ability to endure long hours of work (cf. C. Osella & F. Osella 2008). The purity and sweetness of Saharanpur's water, and other dietary preferences, were often emphasised by migrants, and this acted as an ethnic marker that created an elastic connection to home (cf. Rabikowska 2010; Hage 2010; Bielenin-Lenczowska 2018; Ratnam 2018). On the road, too, collectivised forms of migration allowed craftworkers to re-create an affective sense of 'home' through shared cooking and the reproduction of *Saharanpur ka khana* (Saharanpur food) (cf. Ratnam 2018). Tendencies to seek out Muslim employers, or employers who themselves originated from Saharanpur, further ingrained this aesthetic, as dietary preferences were likely to coincide.

Sharing of food with workers was also a means through which employers attempted to forge links and degrees of obligation with their labour force. Before Eid, I had joined Naseer in Hyderabad, where he was working with another group of friends in the workshop of three brothers, all of whom originated from Saharanpur. Their father had come to the city in 1983 during the early period of labour migration from Saharanpur. He had gradually built a business, using contacts at home to bring stock and recruit labour. After 30 years, he returned to Saharanpur, saying, 'It is where my heart is', leaving his adult sons to run the business. Although the brothers were born and bred in Hyderabad, they identified themselves as being 'of Saharanpur'. On a later visit Shamshad, the youngest, articulated distinctions he saw as existing between those from the north of the country, Uttar Pradesh in particular, and the south. 'South Indians', he said, 'think only of themselves, but those from UP feel only love.' Shamshad said that 90 per cent of their labour came from Saharanpur, as locals did not possess the skills required, but also that their *nazriya* (way of seeing the world) was different. Those who came to work for the brothers became a crucial part of their social world and often shared time, as well as food, with their employees.

Success stories, like that of the three brothers, are by no means universal, yet such tales acted to reinforce the hope that, through migration, economic and social mobility might be achieved. Naseer reflected:

> I can reach a higher position, but it takes time. It may not be possible. Money is necessary so I must work outside Saharanpur. I can do it in the future, but now I am not ready. It takes one lakh [100,000] rupees to start. I want to make my own business in the woodcarving industry. Otherwise, I plan to set up a business in which there is less investment but also good earnings.[8]

The dream of 'making it' through *apna kām* played an essential part in shaping the imaginations of migrants, but here more emotive factors were also in play. Musharraf was the most senior and most colourful member of the group. Tall and handsome, he had spent most of his adult life migrating, partly to escape family, including his domineering and occasionally violent father. The loosening of familial constraints enabled by migration allowed him to engage in activities that would have been more difficult at home. These included drinking alcohol. Musharraf was keen to show me pictures of Goa and regaled me with stories of drunken antics and western 'girlfriends'. He played to a crowd, for whom such tales cemented his status and cultivated the imaginaries of younger members of the group, who were impressed with his worldliness. Despite this, and like the rest of the group, Musharraf always migrated with friends or to places where contacts were already working. While economic gain played a part, he was also concerned with the idea that migration only becomes worthwhile in the company of others. 'Without friends', he said, '*akelāpan* [loneliness] would make this very difficult'.

The brothers' workshop was in a small backstreet behind a large steel gate and consisted of a partly covered courtyard filled with unused wood and half-finished furniture items. Naseer's *tala* (workspace) was under a corrugated roof from which hung a fan. He added carving to panels, then passed these to the carpenter for fitting before a couple of polishers finished the items. In the meantime, I practised basic designs that Naseer sketched out for me onto pieces of scrap wood. Conditions in Hyderabad were rudimentary but held forms of comfort. Ten wood-workers and I shared a single room, located at the front of the employer's house, with thin mats covering the concrete floor. Here we ate, socialised and slept. Next door was a grubby toilet room with just enough space for a bucket shower. Initially, we worked long days, often finishing late. Ramadan, however, heralded an earlier finish, which allowed time for socialising. While the facilities were basic, the atmosphere was intimate and relaxed. The group were close and friendships deep. Banter and jokes were constant, but there were also physical warmth and compan-ionship. Musharraf sat cuddling up with Abdul, who he nicknamed *Gora* (pale, white) because of his complexion, and joked, 'He is my best friend, girlfriend and wife.'

The intimacy and male sociality that underpinned everyday life in the small workshop in Hyderabad very much represented a continuity with the gullies of Saharanpur, albeit with a little less social or familial constraint. This sense of continuity was vital, as it created familiarity and comfort. As an emotional component of the migration experience it pushed woodworkers to engage with environments that were different, but did not represent a step change from the rhythm and feelings involved in working in the gullies. The imaginations of migrants may have been shaped by ideas of adventure, self-making, coming of age and status, but at a more emotional level there was also the seeking of familiarity, comfort and safety. Thus the experiences of those migrating from Saharanpur could act in enclaving ways that ran counter to ideals that tie migration to normative projects of cosmopolitanism or a reconfigured social imagination.

The conviviality, comradeship and intimacy which persisted despite occasional arguments were the source of belonging and comfort, and a familiarity sought by those far from home. They became a part of the negotiations and tactics used by workshop owners to retain their labour force. The three brothers who ran the workshop often spent the evening in the workers' quarters, playing cards and socialising. While work on emotion or affect, in terms of labour spaces, has focused on appeals to the 'spirit' or 'heart' of workers through technologies deployed in the formal sector, (e.g. Rudnyckyj 2009) Shamshad and his brothers were also aware of the importance of cultivating the more emotional aspects of the working environment. As well as offering affection and providing them with periods away from family, the time invested in socialising with their workers acted to narrow distinctions of affluence and built friendships that intermingled with the employer–employee relationship. The importance placed by workers on conditions beyond those defined by economic and material concerns was an essential part of fostering commitment and loyalty in their labour force. Barbara Harriss-White (2001: 6) has argued:

> relations between men are carefully, almost 'naturally', constructed so as to nurture co-operation and control – control over other men within and outside the household. It is by means of this control over men that control over capital is concentrated. Co-operation conceals control.

Each worker kept notes, in a small book, of items completed by himself. Later these books were checked by Dilshad: piece rates were often the primary source of conflict between the brothers and their employees. Despite their best efforts at diffracting relations of labour through narratives of friendship and other emotive appeals, tensions relating to record keeping, and other complaints, led several of the group to discuss alternatives as we returned to Saharanpur for the Eid holiday. The period after Eid proved challenging for the brothers, as they struggled to convince sufficient numbers to return. On a visit some months later Shamshad complained, '*Mazdoor jesse kabuter, woh ider uder jatei hai. Unko pakarnai bahut mushkil hai* [workers are like pigeons; they go here and there. It's very hard to catch them].' Musharraf did not return, and complained that Dilshad often gave a lower rate than agreed. Dilshad, in his turn, accused Musharraf of taking an advance and leaving without repaying it. While the class divide was not as stark as in large factories, in the areas of advance money and payment differentiations conflict became more defined. The eventual departure of key members of the group led several others to follow, as a desire to remain together drove a somewhat haphazard pattern of migration amongst the workers.

After Eid, it was some time before people started to leave Saharanpur, citing a local expression, '*Agar jeb mei paisai hai, Eid kutam nahi hota hai* [Eid doesn't finish as long as I have money in my pocket]'. Eventually, though, Naseer set off to Udaipur with a different group of friends. Like Rizwan he was quick to return. His decision to abandon Udaipur partly stemmed from the familiar problems with food and water, but on this occasion the main problem was being engaged in the manufacturing of Hindu *murtis* (small shrines). This, Naseer felt, was *haram* (against Islamic law or practice). While some of those he had travelled with stayed, happy to produce *murtis,* he returned. Naseer then spent a month working for a Hindu factory owner in Chandigarh before heading to Kamareddy, a town three hours north of Hyderabad, where I joined him. Again, we worked with friends who were already there. Unlike in Hyderabad, the owner, Mohammed Javid, had no historical link to Saharanpur. He had started as a wood wholesaler, but when his business went bust he set up in furniture production with a local carpenter. Five years before he had been approached by a man called Tariq, who had come with a small team from Saharanpur. Javid realised that the new workers were more highly skilled and worked faster and longer than locals. He split with his partner and became solely reliant on labour from Saharanpur. Although Tariq and his team moved on, Javid retained a network of contacts in Saharanpur that originated in the initial group.

Two other workers joined us after a couple of weeks. They had come from the workshops of the brothers in Hyderabad and, having spoken to Naseer and others by phone, decided to relocate. The workshop was small, consisting of an open yard with a tarpaulin-covered area on one side. We slept on site in a room at the rear. The labour force consisted of three carpenters and two polishers, Naseer being the only carver. Most ranged from their mid-teens to their mid-twenties, but one worker, Suheel, brought his young brother. Waseem was 13 and working away for the first time. He did not receive money directly as he was learning the polishing trade and was therefore technically in the employ of his elder brother as a *shāgird*. His labour contributed to the piece-rate earnings of his older brother, who provided him with a small amount of pocket money. When I first met Waseem in December 2011, he was shy and unsure of himself. Holding the older workers in awe, he often sat quietly in the corner when there was a rest from labour. When I visited again in April 2012, not only had he grown, but he was cocky and sure of himself. In the absence of his family, it was this group of young men who were influencing and shaping his character, as well as providing companionship and affection.

With Ramadan now a distant memory and the wedding season in full swing, work was constant. Naseer allowed me to do some basic carving on final pieces while he did the complicated parts. We worked long hours to complete orders. There was time for a quick visit to the gym each morning, but after that we often worked until midnight. Javid reassured his workers by saying that it was not long until the end of the wedding season, reminding them of the money they were earning. They received piece rates but didn't take the full money each week, preferring instead to take 500–1,000 rupees for expenses, extracting the rest as a lump sum when they departed. Naseer felt that although there was more to do in Hyderabad, Kamareddy was a better set-up. This was largely down to *kharch* (cost), as the small town offered lower living expenses and Naseer liked the area in which the workshop was located.

In Kamareddy it was mostly Muslims who populated the neighbourhood, which, unlike many cities in the north, was relatively affluent (cf. Gayer & Jaffrelot 2012). Like Saharanpur, it was also a site of reformist activity, mainly that undertaken by the *Tablighi Jamaat*. As had been the case in Hyderabad, we were visited on occasion by *Tablighis* undertaking *da'wa* (missionary) work. The craftworkers would listen but were usually condescending towards the eulogising undertaken by those engaged in the organisation once they had left. Only Ishmael, who had worked for Javid for about a year before Eid, gave more attention to reformist activities. Towards the end of my time in Kamareddy, a significant event was organised in the area featuring sermons by various Islamic preachers. Most of the neighbourhood turned out, and the streets had a festival feel. For Naseer and the other craftworkers, however, work continued as usual. While we could hear the sermons over the amplified speakers, for those busy in Javid's workshop, this sound was set against the ongoing noise of production. Afterwards, I asked Naseer why they had not joined in. '*Oh,*' he responded, '*yaha kai renai walai bahut ameer hai, unkai function hamari liyai nahi hai* [the people who live here are rich, their function is not for us].' While connections of migration took craftworkers to every corner of the country, the subjective experiences of migrants from Saharanpur were often configured through various enclaving pressures. At times these were configured around the broad marginalisation of Muslims in India, but they could also be crafted through divisions along regional and class lines which constructed woodworkers as low-class and affiliated them with stereotypes of the 'UP *wallah*' as backward, uneducated and polluting.

Conclusion

This chapter has begun the process of carrying through the exploration of marginalisation and connectedness, detailed in the previous chapters, into networks of migration. The empirical data presented here offers a very different image from that presented in much of the pre-existing literature on north Indian Muslims. Saharanpur's *mohallas* are not only defined by inward movements into increasingly segregated spaces but are also constituted through a myriad of networks of migration which are sculpted – in part – by the affective networks of male sociality that have been detailed in previous chapters. Focusing on the relationship between migration and the imagination has allowed the narrative to consider both change and continuity. Coming of age, the loosening of familial ties and projects of self-making all feature here. Simultaneously, there are various continuities that carry through from the *mohallas* into sites of migrant life. These include a high degree of precarity, degrees of bondage, and male sociality and intimacy, along with a sense of spatial, social and economic marginalisation configured within intersections of class, religion and place of origin. Continuity is also present at a more emotional level: conditions of work and sociality often echo those present in the gullies of Saharanpur. This continuity creates a sense of familiarity and comfort but can entrench the forms of enclavement and marginalisation that emerge from material and structural factors. In the final empirical chapter of this book I draw these threads into international migration, extending the exploration of woodworking networks beyond the Indian domestic context to the construction sites and dormitory blocks of the Gulf.

Figure 8.2 Workers in Kamareddy. Source: author.

Figure 8.3 Employers socialising with their migrant labour.
Source: author.

Notes

1. Some material in this chapter has previously been published in T. Chambers (2018), 'Continuity in mind: imagination and migration in India and the Gulf.' *Modern Asian Studies* 52(4): 1420–56. It is reproduced here with the kind permission of *Modern Asian Studies*.
2. Based on 2011 census figures, the most recent available.
3. The informant did not specify which legislation this was, but it appears to have been the 1980 Forest (Conservation) Act.
4. This is problematic: as gathered in Saharanpur the data is less likely to cover long-term absentees.
5. Amitabh Bachchan and Sunny Deol are Bollywood actors. Rizwan's term 'hero' refers to such actors and is a common descriptor in India for Bollywood stars.
6. Adapted and edited from interview transcript.
7. Adapted and edited from interview transcript.
8. Mohamad Faisal, 2011.

9
Labour migration between India and the Gulf: regimes, imaginaries and continuities

Figure 9.1   Migrant workers in Dubai. Source: author.

Finding Gulfam was not easy as I struggled with the building Gulf heat in May 2012. My newly acquired UAE SIM card was playing up and our calls were often cut off. I knew he was somewhere in the sprawling sub-metropolis of Mussafah, a vast industrial area on the outskirts of Abu Dhabi. Having made the trip from Sharjah, a neighbouring emirate, I could only think to join the line dominated by South Asians at the central bus station. Sure enough, when it did pull in, and the scramble for seats began, I was relieved to see the bus board displaying 'Mussafah Workers' Village'. The forty-minute ride on the crowded bus took us away from the glass-clad skyscrapers and tree-lined multi-lane thoroughfares of downtown Abu Dhabi, across the Khor Al Maqta waterway and through a desertified infrastructural gap – populated only by a large highway intersection – that acted as a line of demarcation between the city and those whose labour built it. Still unable to reach Gulfam, I stayed on the bus until the end of the line, passing through a maze of construction yards full of heavy equipment and roughly hewn dormitory blocks. Here, machinery, supplies, materials and construction workers themselves were 'stored' side by side, ingraining the social position of migrant labourers within the cosmology of the urban landscape.

Upon my disembarking from the bus, a crackly conversation allowed me to give Gulfam my location and I hunkered down in the limited shade available as the afternoon sun radiated overhead. It was not long before I started to attract attention. First, a couple of men from Hyderabad stopped to ask what I was doing. Then four men from the Pashtun region of Pakistan approached me and were thrilled when I answered in Urdu. My presence was clearly unusual. They asked about the UK and what brought me to Mussafah. I explained about my time in Saharanpur and that I had come to meet a friend. They asked me how Pashtuns were seen in Britain and my views on the war in Afghanistan. I, too, was curious. They told me they were working in the construction sector. They came from the same village and had found work in the Gulf through a co-villager who had travelled previously. One, Ajmal, had been there for 10 years, with only brief returns to await a new visa. Like most construction workers in the Gulf, they were locked into two-year contracts with an option for a third year. Several came time and again, sending money back to families while fulfilling various contracts.

As one hour turned into two, and then three, I watched the comings and goings at the small, hot and dusty bus stand, occasionally chatting to workers, then sitting and observing. It felt as though the whole of South Asia was passing through the kerbside of scrub and sand: Pashtun and Sindhi men appeared wearing distinctive topis (hats) cut to shape at the front. Observant Indian and Pakistani Muslims exited vehicles. Several buses were driven by Sikhs. A man I presumed to be Filipino, in shorts and sandals, kicked the dust idly. Legions of men in trousers and shirts, with hard hats and tiffins (lunch tins), chatted in Hindi, Malayan, Tamil, Urdu and Bengali as they were disgorged from streams of transport returning from the city. In this vast storage yard on the outskirts of one of the Gulf's grandest metropolitan centres, a scene of subaltern cosmopolitanism was being enacted. While I found the scene fascinating, the heat was becoming oppressive. I was grateful when, after more crackly phone calls and help from a Chennai-born taxi driver, I finally met Gulfam and we headed together to the dormitory block where he had been posted.

This chapter engages with transnational migration from India and is structured around five primary arguments, some of which were partially developed in the previous chapter. The first is that contemporary migration to the Gulf Cooperation Council (GCC) region[1] from Saharanpur must be understood in the context of longer communal histories of migration, movement and connectedness. Second, migration to the GCC is deeply woven into patterns of movement within the Indian domestic context; thus contemporary emigration to the Gulf cannot be effectively understood without engaging with migrants' prior histories of mobility within India. Third, the affective and informal networks detailed in previous chapters are significant in shaping both structural factors and subjective experiences of migration to the GCC from the woodworking *mohallas*. These networks facilitate migration but also produce a sense of familiarity and comfort that can act to conceal some of the conditions of exploitation within which GCC migration takes place. Fourth, and continuing from the previous chapter, I argue that migration from the city involves ongoing processes that alternate between the real and the imagined, the domestic and the international, and origin and destination, processes that lie at the core of the cyclic production of migrants' imaginations, subjectivities and experiences. Finally, and linking to the overarching focus of this book, I contend that continuities from labour at home, during migration in India and when migrating to the GCC act to replicate conditions of enclavement and marginalisation which persist despite substantial geographical movement and degrees of cosmopolitan connectedness.

Migration to the GCC region is dominated by the *kafala* system, which restricts workers' periods of stay, requires a *kafal* (sponsor) – to whom a worker is tied – and excludes the possibility of citizenship. Since the oil boom of the 1970s migration to the GCC has become a central livelihood strategy and a key income source for migrants and their families across South Asia and beyond (A. Ahmad 2017; Jain & Oommen 2016;

Rajan 2016; Adhikari & Hobley 2015; Kollmair et al. 2006). Expanding migration to the GCC has led to wealth creation – often through remittances (Genc & Naufal 2018) – but also to transformations in the social fabric of sending areas, including reconfigurations in kin, class, gender, caste-based relations (F. Osella & C. Osella 2000; Gamburd 2000; Parreñas 2005; Punathil 2013; Adhikari & Hobley 2015; Rafique Wassan et al. 2017; Chambers 2018) and even modalities of gift exchange (Campbell 2018). Although many pre-existing hierarchies endure (Rafique Wassan et al. 2017), the emergence of large-scale patterns of migration to the GCC has had ambiguous transformative effects across South Asia and beyond.

In India, remittances have funded local development (Azeez & Begum 2009), financed property acquisition (Varrel 2012) and paid the costs of education (S. Ali 2007; Mathew 2018). These benefits have been weighed by problems of absent family members (Zachariah et al. 2001; Ugargol & Bailey 2018), tensions between communities with varying degrees of access to migrant pathways (M. Hasan 2018) and potential for loss resulting from the precarious nature of working arrangements in the GCC (Chua 2011). High degrees of precarity became further amplified by common legal and illegal practices, including the confiscation of passports, fee extractions, theft of wages and breaches of contract (cf. Buckley 2014). Tight restrictions placed on labour migrants engaged in areas such as construction, paid domestic work and other semi- and unskilled jobs have led some activist organisations, academics and media outlets to consider the *kafala* system as a form of 'neo-slavery' (Jureidini 2010; Manseau 2007) or as bonded labour (Frantz 2013). As with the neo-bondage discussed in chapter 3, however, degrees of bondage within the *kafala* system are better conceived within a continuum than within a binary framework of free and unfree labour (B. Fernandez 2014).

Of late, a great deal of attention has been given to Nepalese workers, particularly those involved in Qatar's World Cup preparations (e.g. Pattisson 2013; A. Gardner et al. 2013; Dorsey 2014; Millward 2017; A. Gardner 2018; Donini 2019). Criticism has been levelled at employment conditions and poor health and safety, which have led to high injury and fatality rates (Aryal et al. 2016). Reports have also focused on conditions of work, emphasising vulnerability and indentured aspects of contracts under existing labour laws (A. Gardner 2018). Before a focus on Nepal emerged, research on labour migration from India to the GCC concentrated mainly on the south of the country, including the states of Kerala, Tamil Nadu and Andhra Pradesh (e.g. Bristol-Rhys & Osella

2016; Gardner 2010; S. Ali 2007; F. Osella & C. Osella 2000, 2011; Prakash 1998). These areas have long-standing connections to the Gulf, particularly Kerala, where maritime trade and Arab settlement constitute an important part of the state's economic and cultural make-up (F. Osella & C. Osella 2003, 2011; Radhakrishnan 2009).

Conversely, Uttar Pradesh and other northern states have received little attention in this regard. Although it is a more contemporary phenomenon, Uttar Pradesh has seen migration to the GCC increasing rapidly. The state registered 191,341 emigrants to the Gulf in 2012 (Sasikumar & Thimothy 2015: 6), compared with 27,428 in 2004 (Ministry of Overseas Indian Affairs [2007]: 39; Jain 2016). Figures for 2013 and 2015[2] suggest that numbers exceeded 200,000 in these years (Wadhawan 2018: Figure 3).[3] Overall, nationwide, Uttar Pradesh now accounts for 25 per cent of total emigration clearances for overseas labour (Ministry of External Affairs [2019]: 316). As a result, migration to the GCC from Uttar Pradesh now exceeds that from Kerala, Andhra Pradesh and Tamil Nadu,[4] and the percentage share of GCC emigration continues to climb (Wadhawan 2018). Like the previous chapter's discussion of internal migration amongst Indian Muslims, this chapter of the book provides an ethnographic contribution aimed at addressing this empirical shortfall within the migration literature. First, though, I attend to a broader body of research which allows for the development of a theoretical understanding surrounding the implications of migration regimes, such as that embodied within the *kafala* system.

GCC migration and the *kafala* system: imaginaries, structures and temporalities

In considering migration in the *kafala* system I follow Aihwa Ong, whose notion of 'graduated citizenship' offers a significant step in bettering our understanding of migration regimes across Asia. Here, Ong argues that

> preexisting ethnoracializing schemes (installed under colonial rule) are reinforced and crosscut by new ways of governing that differently value populations according to market calculations. Thus, while low-skilled workers are disciplined, elite workers and members of dominant ethnic groups enjoy affirmative action and pastoral care.
>
> (Ong 2006: 79)

While the *kafala* system applies to all migrants in the GCC, regardless of their origin, the regulatory and material experiences of the scheme are strongly differentiated along class, gender and ethnic lines. This differentiation is particularly marked in terms of distinctions between European and non-European migrants (Walsh 2018; Fechter & Walsh 2010). Amongst South Asian migrants, too, various intersections exist. In ethnographic research on Dubai, Ahmed Kanna (2011) and Neha Vora (2013) have both shown how middle- and upper-class Indians make effective claims to the rights and privileges of citizenship even in the absence of legal citizen status. Often, the construction of class differentials among South Asians in the GCC is overlaid by ethnic distinctions that reflect those experienced by Naseer and his friends in Kamareddy (see previous chapter). While Keralans, for example, move into health, education and skilled middle-class jobs, the experiences of migrants from Uttar Pradesh often diverge widely from those of many of their south Indian counterparts and are embedded in hierarchical patterns that carry through from the Indian national context, a context that, as mentioned in chapter 8, constructs some northern states such as Uttar Pradesh and Bihar as backward, unclean and riddled with criminality. This portrayal of Uttar Pradesh, Bihar, Jharkhand and other states can then be used to justify the subjugation of migrant workers from these states within the national context, a process that is reproduced at the transnational level.

Migration regimes bound into modalities of graduated citizenship are also underpinned by more mundane everyday practices that act to discipline and subjugate the bodies and subjectivities of labour migrants through forms of structural violence (cf. A. Gupta 2012). Entering GCC labour markets embroils migrant workers in a context that simultaneously facilitates neoliberal economic desires, by producing flexibility and low wages, and imposes a high degree of governance through the regulation of workers' bodies, activities and movements. This regulation starts before departure, with prospective migrants undergoing medical examinations and blood tests, an exercise in bio-power that subjugates and disciplines the prospective migrant (cf. Foucault 2008; A. Qureshi 2013). Sajid, whose idolisation of Steve Jobs at the opening of chapter 5 had marked out his 'entrepreneurial' credentials, was more reticent in his summation of two years spent in Saudi Arabia. After his return in 2017 we discussed his pre-departure trip to Lucknow to obtain medical clearance at a Gulf Approved Medical Centres Association (GAMCA) facility. The trip involved lengthy periods of waiting, itself a disciplining act (cf. Conlon 2011; Auyero 2012; Carswell et al. 2019), before the procedures were undergone. Reflecting on the process, Sajid remarked, 'They take our blood before we go and then, for two years after our arrival, they take it again.' His initial mention of blood referred to its physical removal, but its ongoing 'extraction' was intended as a metaphor for the exploitation of migrant labour, and articulated the subjectifying and marginalising forces he had felt during the trip.

These processes, together with the highly constrained configuration of *kafala*-based migration regimes, have, in some cases, led to migrants being represented as naïve, passive victims who are 'trafficked' through networks of brokerage and restrictive regulative pathways (e.g. Castles 2011; Afsar 2009). Despite the best attempts of GCC states to formalise migration regimes, various informal practices are commonplace. Remittances, for example, are regularly repatriated to countries across South Asia via the informal *hawala* system (Malit et al. 2017), and the *Azad* or 'free visa' system, which involves a *kafal* sponsoring a visa for fictive employment, is used by some migrants. Under *Azad* arrangements, the *kafal* extracts commission at the time of issue, and often as a monthly fee, during the migrant's employment within whichever GCC state the visa is valid for. While embedded in layers of informal exploitation, the 'free visa' system allows migrants to enter the GCC labour market as 'free agents' who can, in theory, work where they like, thus avoiding the bondage of *kafala* (Pessoa et al. 2014). Additionally, ethnographic interventions have shown a more complex scene riven with ambiguities, contradictions, informalities and resistances that enable migrant workers to express agency in a variety of ways (e.g. A. Ahmad 2017; Mahdavi 2016; Johnson & Werbner 2010). Here, subjective experiences are articulated by migrants themselves, who tell stories not only of exploitation, but also of care, affection and intimacy (A. Ahmad 2017; Mahdavi 2016; Osella 2014; cf. Lindquist 2018).

Spaces of care and mutuality are, of course, highly gendered; male and female low- or unskilled migrants are channelled into very different spaces of labour market engagement. Over several years of researching in Saharanpur, I have not come across any women from the Muslim *mohallas* who have engaged in migration to the GCC. In other areas of India, however, particularly the south – and in countries like Sri Lanka, the Philippines and Indonesia – women's migration is commonplace amongst Muslims and non-Muslims alike. Here, ethnographic research has been particularly nuanced in drawing out agentive aspects of female migration, which is often characterised by greater levels of isolation and marginalisation grounded in limited labour market options as well as in ideals of purdah and gender segregation.

In detailing the experiences of Sri Lankan Muslim women in the GCC, Rapti Siriwardane (2014), for example, describes how female workers encountered Arab women wearing the *abāyah* (body-covering loose-fitted cloak), a garment they often adopted themselves. Siriwardane's informants did not to see the garment as a stifling or restrictive intensification of *purdah*. Instead, adopting practices and dress 'possessed an agency of its own; an agency that women hoped they could sustain or replicate upon returning home' (Siriwardane 2014: 18). In the Gulf, too, becoming more pious enabled some female domestic workers to legitimise time away from their employer's home to attend religious gatherings, escape isolated working conditions and connect with other women engaged in the domestic sector (Johnson et al. 2010; A. Ahmad 2017). Negotiations such as these with employers and others situate migrant workers not as merely passive subjects but as active in shaping economic, social and Islamic spaces. As Dale Eickelman and James Piscatori (1990: 5) suggested some years ago, 'contemporary labour migration … has facilitated changes in religious institutions and practices at least as important as those inspired by earlier generations of elite Muslim intellectuals in the Middle East and Indian subcontinent'.

In the context of the male migrations detailed in this chapter, two primary points emerge. First, there are various continuities in the subjective experiences of migration undertaken by craftworkers and others from Saharanpur's *mohallas* that persist at both the material and affective levels (Chambers 2018). Advance payments, forms of brokerage, modalities of neo-bondage and degrees of unfree labour (see chapter 3) are not exceptional conditions for those arriving in the Gulf region but are often seen as a 'normalised' set of labour relations which, to a degree at least, echo those of home. Nor are the labour camps necessarily experienced in terms of rupture, as the spatial arrangements and the persistence of highly gendered male sociality represent an affective continuity from prior involvements in migration within India.

Second, the affective and informal networks that were so prevalent in Indian domestic migration and within the wood gullies of Saharanpur persist – despite degrees of formalisation and restrictive labour market regulations – within migration to the GCC region. As was the case for female domestic workers (Johnson et al. 2010; A. Ahmad 2017), it is these networks that offer the greatest possibilities for expressions of agency and mutuality. Simultaneously, however, I suggest, attending to the affective context of male migration from Saharanpur to the GCC shows how such networks can be stifling of resistance by creating a sense of familiarity and comfort. In other words, the GCC labour market actively plays on the expectations and experiences of migrants, many of whom have prior histories of domestic migration which act to shape their expectations and experiences of migration further afield.

Despite these dualities, the friendship-based affiliations discussed in preceding chapters are an important structuring factor in influencing patterns of migration beyond India. Quantitatively orientated research has traced patterns in the data on migration to the GCC which suggest a greater prevalence of friendship-based and informal networks amongst Muslim migrants to the region. Drawing on quantitative data from Kuwait, Shah and Menon (1999) identify disparities between migrants from different countries. Sri Lankans tend to use agents, with only around 13 per cent obtaining work (and visas) through friends or relatives. This contrasts sharply with Pakistan (56 per cent) and Bangladesh (39 per cent), where informal networks are much more prevalent. Shah and Menon make the further link that this is directly related to the dominant religion of each country.

Indeed, they found that of all respondents who had come through friendship and kinship links, 77 per cent were Muslim; other groups tended much more towards the use of recruitment agents and formal routes. Andrew Gardner et al. (2013) also illustrate the presence of more informal networks amongst Muslim migrants in Qatar: around half of their respondents came through family (21 per cent) and friends (22 per cent). While further research would be required to make a concrete assertion regarding connections between the informal and affective networks present in Saharanpur and large-scale differences in patterns of migration to the GCC, it is fair to say that webs of kinship and friendship are often an important part of navigating borders, contracts and regulatory processes (Vertovec 2009). By friends and informants in Saharanpur they were broadly seen as preferential to avenues dictated by more formal forms of mediation and brokerage.

While labour migration from Saharanpur to the Gulf may be relatively recent, it has been built on older networks as well as being shaped by contemporary migration regimes. The *kafala* system is itself constructed in the context of a longer history of movement within the Indian Ocean region. Created to regulate pearling dhow (boat) crews from coastal areas of South Asia who were seen as potentially polluting to Arab culture, it was only later formalised to control migrant labour in the 'post-oil' era (Longva 2019). Any attempt to contextualise the historical narrative of migration from Saharanpur, then, cannot limit its scope to 'India' alone. To acknowledge this, I draw on research that identifies the presence of a 'methodological nationalism', research which challenges entrenched views of 'state' or 'nation' as a natural category (Beck 2007; Wimmer & Schiller 2002). Likewise, notions of 'area', such as South Asia, have been contested as often being themselves imagined or created within scholarly and colonial contexts (Van Schendel 2002). Historical and geographical explorations reveal more fluid landscapes that push us to 'imagine other spatial configurations, such as "crosscutting" areas, the worldwide honeycomb of borderlands, or the process geographies of transnational flows' (Van Schendel 2002: 647). This is not to disregard the significance of 'place'. Nodal cities have long been particularly important in this regard. Thomas Blom Hansen (2014: 283), for example, points out:

> When the need for labour of all kinds grew dramatically in the Gulf from the 1970s onwards, the colonial networks and pathways were already well established, and Mumbai was the first place to which Arab employers went in search of labour and other services.

To begin steering this chapter towards a more ethnographic engagement, I turn to one such 'nodal' city, Mumbai, and to a series of events that were related to me as having taken place in the mid-1980s.

Gulf migration from Saharanpur: a brief history

In the late summer of 1985 two men met in a hotel room of the grand colonial-era Taj Intercontinental Hotel in Mumbai. One of them was out of place in the palatial surroundings. Habib had arrived straight from the woodworking shop in Mumbai where he laboured as a woodcarver. Having arrived from the provincial city of Saharanpur a few years before, Habib was struggling to feel at ease in these new surroundings. The other man, Abdul Noor, was much more familiar with such spaces. A successful businessman, merchant and broker from the Gulf state of Qatar, he had long plied his trade across the Indian Ocean and built up considerable wealth. Just a few days before, Abdul Noor had approached the owner of Habib's workshop and left instructions that if any artisan wished to return with him to Qatar, they should visit the hotel the following day. It was with some hesitancy that Habib decided to chance a visit:

> I first went [to Mumbai] in 1978. One person, Abuzar, worked with me in Saharanpur. Now he is in Qatar. He went to Mumbai and worked near the J J Hospital. The name of the workshop's owner

there was Ali Hasan. That owner sent Abuzar back to Saharanpur to bring workers. Now the system is different, and we do not need links for work. If we have the owner's address, we go directly. Now we do not need anyone as we have many networks.

Mumbai was like Dubai at that time; everyone wanted to ask questions [about it]. They asked about climate and lifestyle. They wanted to know the problems too. Nowadays if anyone goes away it is not such a big deal. At that time no one went to the Gulf and certainly not by air. Only two brothers [from Saharanpur], Tahir and Tayyub, went by ship to Dubai.

I got the work in Mumbai through my friend Abuzar. In Mumbai, there's one place called Gram Bhavan. There I started work. The place was owned by Ali Hasan, but the work was *apna kām*. It was my responsibility to buy wood, labour and electricity but the profit was split fifty-fifty with the owner. I spent eight years in this way and earned good money. In 1986, I think, a customer came from Qatar. His name was Abdul Noor. I was not there but the owner gave me his card and told me that I could meet them in the Taj Mahal Hotel. They needed two artisans and if I was interested I could go. It was my good luck that I had applied for and received my passport, but I was fearful as I thought they could hurt me. But I could see that people who came back from the Gulf had many good clothes and money in their pocket. It is human weakness that we also want a life like that.

So, I put on my best clothes and went to the Taj Mahal Hotel. The doorman did not want to let me in. He asked me lots of questions. I gave him the card and told him my purpose. He called that person and asked them if they wanted to meet me. They said yes and I was allowed inside. They asked me lots of questions about my experience. They told me that I would be doing carving and other work. They asked my address and I gave them my card.

Some time later they came to our shop and watched everything we did. When they were satisfied with my work, they said that I could go. I talked about the salary in Qatar. It was my demand that I wanted 1500 riyal in Qatar. They offered 1000 riyal but said if the work was good it would increase. I rejected their proposal as I would have to leave my country and family for little benefit. People can leave their family but only if they get benefit from it. At last the agreement was fixed for 1200 riyal. Finally, then, I left Mumbai to go to Qatar.[5]

Habib related this tale to me during the spring of 2012. Having recently returned from a lifetime of trips to the Middle East, he was at that time resettling into his native city. He had reached the age of 60, the point at which migrant workers are no longer allowed into the Gulf. As he reflected on his life story, I was struck by the symbolism of the meeting in the Taj Hotel and the various axes it represented. On the one hand there was the figure of the merchant and broker representing a long history of trading ties across the Indian Ocean which pre-date both the post-globalisation era and the colonial period, on the other the artisan from a landlocked north Indian city recruited through historically embedded but largely informal networks that intersected in the 'nodal city' of Mumbai (Hansen 2014). Finally, the hotel itself embodied the spectre of colonialism as a further mediating factor in Habib's early migration. Like Rizwan's recollection of his motivations for travelling to Mumbai (see the previous chapter), the way in which the Gulf was imagined and the forms of self-making that Habib saw it as potentially enacting were key factors in his migration story.

While Habib was not the first from Saharanpur to travel to the Gulf, he was among the earliest. Since Habib's first trip to the Gulf in 1986, Saharanpur has seen a rapid burgeoning of migration to the region. As many made the trip and brought back stories, both migrants and potential migrants were aware of the precarity and riskiness of migration to the GCC. There were many relative successes (the absence of any such would quickly stymie the imaginations of others), but there were also examples of failure and loss. Fear, or the 'nightmare', is as much a part of the consciousness of potential migrants as is the 'dream'. The 'nightmare', in the context of the Gulf, is one not just of financial loss but also of isolation, entrapment and *akelāpan* (loneliness), concerns that become intensified in a context – the *kafala* system – in which the ability to up sticks and leave an employer is curtailed.

Habib, like Rizwan before his first trip to Mumbai, had been influenced by his own imaginings, based on the style and exoticism brought by migrants returning to Mumbai from the Gulf. Images of returning migrants in Saharanpur differ greatly depending upon the perspective from which others view them and on which part of the GCC region they have visited. A wholesaler in Purāni Mandi reflected:

> If they go to Saudi, they come back with high moral and religious values, but if they go to other parts of the Gulf they return with low values. Either way they don't want to work in [the Saharanpur wood] industry as they consider the wages to be too low and look

instead to go back outside. They don't invest in this industry either, but just buy property and try to go abroad again.

There is a degree of reality in these imaginings, even if they may be somewhat amplified by those creating them. Over his lifetime, Habib had visited several Gulf states and was clear regarding the distinctions in his experience:

> Dubai is a free port, so it is not strict, but Saudi is very strict. Qatar is also not so strict but not as easy as Dubai. It is in the middle. In Saudi many things are banned. When it is *namāz* time, a big van comes, and the owner gives us instructions to go for *namāz*. It is the company who send the van to make sure all the workers go. There is no alcohol in Saudi, life is simple and straight, and we cannot do any impure thing. Some people who go to Dubai want to drink alcohol and do bad things. … Only some people who go abroad are successful. The reason is that if a person earns 500 rupees in Dubai then he can drink and use 500 rupees on bad things. He never thinks about tomorrow and never thinks about family. He never saves 200 rupees for his family. He just does wrong things in Dubai.
>
> But many people are very polite, and if they earn 2000 rupees in a day they save good money for the family and not for their own amusement. A worker can only work until he is about 58 and then his physical power will go down. If his lifestyle is healthy and he eats fruit and drinks milk he can work for a long time, but a worker never finds this lifestyle. Many live a bad lifestyle and drink, and smoke hashish and cigarettes. So, the machinery of a human body goes down day by day because of these bad habits. As they do this, and also do not eat good food and work too much, life is short. Many people drink too much tea or have illegal sex, so they maybe only live till they're 40.[6]

Habib's story reveals two interwoven strands that appear in discussions of these different destinations. The first is wrapped up with a sense of morality, the good migrant who puts family first and sacrifices his own comfort, versus the bad, who seeks opportunities for personal fulfilment and his own pleasure. This Habib links with how the consumption of certain foods, drink and carnal pleasures have a negative impact on the body of the worker. In his terms, to be a strong and good worker, lifestyle and consumption patterns are important. [This is also a feature of life in Kamareddy, where Naseer and the others consumed milk, fruit and eggs after morning visits to the gym, both to aid the physique and to give them 'strength' for work.] In the second strand Habib links these differing lifestyles with the contrasting spaces of Saudi and Dubai. While Habib emphasised a number of distinctions, he also described many similarities across the GCC region. 'Work in the Gulf', he said, 'is always the same. Wherever we go *ham sirf mazdoor hai* [we are just labour]'. It is to the variegated experiences of returning migrants that the following section turns.

Success and failure: migration experiences and the *mohalla*

The stories related to me by friends and informants over several periods of fieldwork in Saharanpur have been diverse. Not always articulated through the rubric of exploitation that dominates many accounts, the stories of returnees challenge us to rethink what is seen as being most significant from a more emic perspective. The processes involved in becoming a craftworker – a lengthy apprenticeship, forms of self-making bound up in labour, patterns of sociality and conceptions of becoming skilled – were reflected strongly in many stories of migration to the Gulf. Habib had been recruited specifically because of his craft knowledge. For many, a move to the Gulf meant not only the possibility of extra earnings but also the potential undermining of carefully acquired skills and a descent into lower-status forms of labour. Shamshad was an acquaintance of Rizwan who had returned from Saudi Arbia about three years earlier. He had adopted a more Arab style of dress and regularly dropped Arabic words into his speech to mark out his credentials as a Saudi returnee. He was keen to emphasise the purity of Islam in the country but also expressed his concerns regarding the recognition of his skills as a carpenter:

> There were many rules there from the Quran and these had to be followed. These laws were good, and people were happy because of them. I was provided with accommodation, which was good as we were given an air-conditioned room in which only two to three men slept. My passport was taken from me for a two-year period for safe-keeping, as they told me that I was not able to keep it safe myself. I felt it was a good place as people did not lie and they were good Muslims who always went for *namāz*. For the first three months it was not good, though, as I was just doing labour, but then they noticed my skill and put me on carpentry work. It would have been

very hard to continue working as labour but when they started me as a carpenter I could show that I knew this work well. I came back because of family and wanted to return, but I got married and had some family problems. Also I could not raise the money to go back a second time, but still, to this day, I hope to return.

For others the experience of deskilling had been more persistent and was a primary driver in decisions regarding possible returns to the GCC. Faqir was in his early thirties. Like Habib, he had been recruited during a period of internal migration to Mumbai. For Faqir, too, it was a lack of recognition of his status as a *kārīgar* that formed a primary concern.

I was in Saudi for two years. I was working in Mumbai about nine years ago, when I was about 23, and was approached by a couple of tourists from Saudi who asked me if I wanted to go for work. I thought this was a good idea, but I had to raise around 24,000 rupees for agent fees. I managed to get the money together from friends and relatives and left. When I arrived, the company's driver was waiting for me at the airport and took me to the factory. I had been told that I would be doing carpentry but when I got there, I found that it was cutting plywood.

The factory was located in the middle of the jungle away from the city and two kilometres from the nearest road. It was a large factory and all the work was machine work. The company I worked for had about ten factories and the one I was in had ten to twelve people working. The people I was working with were either from Pakistan or from Misor [in Egypt]. All were Muslim. It was hard for me as many spoke Arabic, although the Pakistanis spoke Urdu. The salary was 11,000 rupees per month, which was what I had been told but this was not much for going such a long way. For the first three months I was not allowed out of the factory as this was part of the contract, but after that I was able to go roaming on my day off. I made some money but not as much as I had hoped. The worst thing was having to cut the plywood. I am a *kārīgar* and told them this, so to work as labour is not good.

Having recently returned from Abu Dhabi, Islam's friend Abdul was far stronger in his derision at the treatment he received.

People there are like dogs, as they made me do all sorts of other jobs, like cleaning toilets, which are below my skill. They were very rude and treated me like labour only. I stayed only three months and then had to get out of there quickly. I will never go back. But because of this I lost a lot of money, as I had already paid for the agent.

Round the corner from Islam's shop was the showroom of Mohammad Dilshad. His friend Kalim had recently returned from the Gulf. A little younger than Dilshad, he was slim and stylishly attired. While we talked, he idly fiddled with a new mobile. Although his outward appearance suggested a degree of success his story of migration was mixed:

> I was in Dubai for two and a half years. Before going I worked in Goa. I am in the polishing line. Now I am 26, but when I went I was 23. The agent was not so expensive compared to some others as I did not pay for the visa, only the flight. The agent told lies, though. He charged me 16,000 rupees for the ticket, but it cost only 12,000 rupees. I had a visa for three years and they took my passport to keep for the first two. The agent told me that I would get fifteen hundred dinar a month, but it was only a thousand dinar. I was in a room with six other people from Uttar Pradesh. The company made a deduction for the room and for the taxi from the airport. We arranged food ourselves and ate in the room together.
>
> Each day we worked ten hours, but there was also overtime. We got paid extra for it, but it was not our choice. We got one day off. We would spend some time in the room relaxing and chatting. Always we made some good food on Friday and went for *namāz*. After that we went roaming in Dubai. It is a very expensive place and it was hard for me to buy things and to get about. Although it was costly, I liked roaming. The best things were going to the beach and eating burgers.
>
> For Ramadan the company gave free food, but outside of this our monthly outlay was something like two hundred dirham [the currency of the UAE] [not including deductions taken by the company]. After all the costs and things, I could save about twelve to thirteen hundred rupees per month. I sent this back via Western Union to my mother. She put all the money in the bank and slowly I got half a lakh [50,000 rupees].
>
> After returning I started business in the showroom line. I made a partnership with a friend and went to Lucknow to make a showroom. In Lucknow the expense was great, and it was hard to sell things as we were not in a good location. I had a great loss there.

Because of this I am thinking of going back [to the Gulf]. When I worked in Goa, I had one friend from Saharanpur. He has been in Dubai for eight years and I will arrange to work with him. This time it will be better as he can fix things. Last time I had many problems because of the agent. Now I will have a direct contract with the company, and they will send the plane ticket. This is thanks to my friend.[7]

The presence of more informal networks of brokerage has received little attention, but existing ethnographic research shows that they are central to the navigation of migration regimes in the GCC (C. Osella & F. Osella 2011) and elsewhere (Lindquist 2012). My research for this book did not extend to an engagement with migration brokers and agents themselves, but even within the more formal kinds of brokerage research has shown the cultivation of more affective connections to be important (F. Osella 2012; Lindquist 2012). Significant in this context is Kalim's desire to use informal avenues that parallel the patterns of brokerage within India that have been outlined in the previous chapter. Here, it is often the case that those acting as the broker, in this case Kalim's friend in Dubai, don't see themselves as such. Yet, just like those in Javid's workshop in Kamareddy, described in the previous chapter, actors like Kalim's friend can be key mediators who allow GCC employers to recruit additional labour, and prospective migrants to gain information on conditions of employment before they engage in the risky and costly process of entering into the 'bonded labour' arrangements of the *kafala* system.

As in Rizwan's story (see previous chapter), Kalim also saw migration as a potentially enabling route into *apna kām*. His tale of a failed effort to obtain the status of showroom owner echoed many of the narratives of precarity detailed in previous chapters. While Kalim's story was one of mixed results, others had experienced far greater losses. Eager to help in my quest for information, Dilshad suggested that I should talk to another man who was peddling from a goods rickshaw, loaded high with half-finished chairs, on the opposite side of the road from where we had been chatting. Nasir Ddin was a man of short stature approaching middle age. The grey in his hair was concealed with a liberal application of henna and his simple shirt and trousers were flecked with sawdust:

I went to Bahrain in 2004. Before going I was a barber and had a shop. It was not big and was on rent, but I had chairs, scissors and other equipment. My cousin was working in the Gulf already and doing well. You see pictures of smart Arabs in the paper and think that if you go you will become like them. It was expensive so I sold my barber equipment to pay 35,000 rupees to an agent. He arranged the work, visa and plane ticket. I arrived [in Bahrain] at 8pm but there was no one from the company to meet me. I had no money but waited all night in the airport with nothing to eat. The next morning a driver finally came.

I worked in a hardware store. I was the only worker and was general labour. I just carried things and put things in customers' cars. At night I slept in the shop. The agent told me that I would get a salary of 10,000 rupees per month, but it was 6,500 rupees. The work in the store was okay but I could not save anything. In Bahrain my monthly outgoings were about 1,500 rupees, so I could send back only 5,000 rupees each month. (This was enough for household expenses, as I am also married with three children.) When I realised this, I wanted to come back, but the owner had my passport. Anyway, I had no money for the plane ticket. After two years I came back but had little savings so could not do anything. The only thing was to buy a second-hand rickshaw for 6,000 rupees. I lost all my things here and now I am 36 years old but am only pulling this rickshaw. If any person asks me if they should go to the Gulf, I tell them not to.[8]

Later Dilshad described how Nasir's story contrasted with that of the cousin who encouraged him to go:

When he [Nasir] came back he was crying a lot, but you know his cousin stayed there for eight years and made very big money. Now his cousin is back and has a big house. Now people say that he is like his cousin's dog.

Nasir's experience embodies the potential risks of a system that ties the migrant to the employer and to a fixed-term contract. It also adds a further reasoning to the fear of *akelāpan* (loneliness) that resonated in many stories of migration. On a later occasion Nasir described the crippling isolation he had experienced, saying, '*Har raat main rota tha* [Every night I used to cry]'.

Nasir, then, represented one of the worst-case scenarios, the failed returnee who, in his case, was reduced to the metaphorical status of his cousin's dog. In ethnographic research on Kerala, Osella and Osella (2000) identify four categories of returnee migrant: the *gulfan* – the young migrant who returns between trips or has just relocated; the *kalan* – an anti-social figure who uses his Gulf wealth only for his own interests; the *pavan* – who is over-generous and gives too much away; and the 'mature householder' who holds substantial wealth but also supports others, often in clientelist relationships. Osella and Osella point out that the *gulfan* must negotiate a path between the three possible routes of *kalan*, *pavan* and mature householder. Echoing their research in Kerela, Nasir embodies the 'failed *gulfan*', a pitiful figure to whom all three paths are closed.

The *gulfan*'s position in Kerala, and the potential trajectories that followed time spent in the Gulf, differed from some aspects of the young Gulf returnee in Saharanpur. Osella and Osella describe the successful *gulfan* as defined by conspicuous wealth and consumption, a position which makes him a desirable potential groom. During discussions with various informants in Saharanpur, prospective marriages of daughters to Gulf returnees were articulated in a far more measured frame. This was particularly so in the case of those who had been more than once: many relatives expressed concerns about arranging marriages of daughters and sisters to such men, as they feared that they might return to the Gulf leaving their new wives 'abandoned'. Here, the potential status acquired through migration rubbed up against notions of male guardianship, duty to family and the *chāl-chalan* of left-behind wives. This friction produced ambiguities in the potential progression to mature householder, as the Gulf returnee was seen as an unstable presence within the social structure of the *mohallas*.

The flow of Gulf money into the *mohallas* had also disrupted urban cosmologies and situated Muslim neighbourhoods as represented by pollution and backwardness. During my initial period of fieldwork in the city an article appeared in *The Times of India* about Muslim 'ghettos' in the town of Azamgarh (eastern Uttar Pradesh).

> [p]eople of this town have been going out for more than 100 years. Initially, they travelled to places like Malaysia and Singapore. In the 1960s and 70s, they went to Bombay. Then came the great Gulf rush. Those who managed to get out of the ghettos not only made a life for themselves, but also pumped money into the town. With the state almost absent from all spheres of life … it's the remittances from migrants which are sustaining and fuelling growth here. … 'Almost every family has someone working outside. It's because of the money sent by them that the Muslim community has made some progress in education and jobs,' says Umair Siddique, a researcher

at Shibli Academy. 'Now our boys go out for education and good jobs and not for menial work.'[9]

The money is visible in certain pockets here and there. In a town where every government building … looks like a relic, there are some swanky new ones. Most of these are private schools, hospitals, and madrassas. Local intelligence officials talk of Salafi winds sweeping the area because of financial and moral support from the Gulf. But the people see the madrassas as educational institutes, particularly those which also provide some vocational training.

(Saxena 2011)

Here the narrative is one of Gulf migration providing a route out of the ghetto and away from persecution. The article finishes with the sentence 'For those who want to avoid trouble and mention in the police records, there is only one shot at redemption: the escape from Azamgarh.' As in Azamgarh, the effects of incoming money from the Gulf were visible in Saharanpur. Large new houses had started to appear in the Muslim *mohallas* and migrants' children were attending schools that were out of the reach of those working locally. These transformations also disrupted urban hierarchies and provided a point of friction for those who saw the *mohallas* as the space of the dangerous, Muslim 'other' (cf. M. Hasan 2018). A couple of times a week I would go to write up my field notes in a chain coffee shop on the other side of town. Here I met Anil, who ran a nearby jeweller's. He invited me to his home for dinner, during which he reproduced many of the most negative representations of Indian Muslims perpetuated in the media, in some political circles and elsewhere: the dangerous and demonic Muslim whose loyalty to nation and right to citizenship was dubious at best.

Of the increasing amounts of money arriving from the Gulf, he argued that they were either being wasted on ostentatious consumption, by Muslims whose backwardness made them incapable of prudent investment, or channelled into the building of madrassas which were, for Anil, the ultimate threat to Indian security. Anil's characterisation was one fermented within the rhetoric of the Hindu right, but religiosity was one of a series of factors that intermingled in the producing of imaginaries and memories of the Gulf. In the following section I develop a more nuanced engagement with the stories and images of the Gulf circulating in Saharanpur to build on the previous chapter and draw out the role of the imagination in shaping the subjectivities of migrants, prospective migrants, returnees and others.

Imagining the Gulf, remembering the Gulf: circulations and the imagination

It was Saudi that proved the most common destination among those from Saharanpur. This may be tied up with economic demand. As the location of Mecca and Medina, it had a further appeal. Although most migrants were unlikely to be able to complete hajj, there was usually the chance for *umrah*.[10] Sajid, the 'entrepreneur' and former Saudi migrant mentioned in chapter 6, had expressed his desire to go not just for work but also to visit the holy sites. Similarly, Rizwan had Saudi in mind for his eldest son Yousef. While he was in two minds about the benefits of working overseas, he saw Saudi as the preferred location as it would allow Yousef to learn more about Islam, and ensure respectability. Unlike many in the gullies, my *ustād*, Islam, had never engaged in labour migration, in part because of health issues that limited his ability to travel. His involvement with the *Tablighi Jamaat*, however, had cultivated a sense of connection in his mind to the Gulf, particularly to Saudi Arabia.

While embedded partly in historical and religious imaginaries, Islam's sentiment illustrates how ongoing circulations continued to shape the imaginations of those in the city. Images conjured in the minds of migrants and potential migrants are by no means fixed but are played out through affective circuits of movement, religiosity, objects, styles and media that blur what the Gulf is and how it is seen (Radhakrishnan 2009). The person of the Gulf migrant may be imagined by others in multiple and simultaneous ways, at once embodying the experienced adventurer, the pious Muslim, the abandoner of duty and the person of questionable morals. A young man returning from Dubai and boasting of drinking and women may be seen as having adopted loose morals by some in the *mohallas* and sway the imagination away from the benefits of such a destination, as was the case for Rizwan with regard to his son Yousef. For others, the very same tales may further the returnees' status in their imaginations and inspire a desire for emulation.

Such tales could be mediated in various ways. The images conjured by returnees, for those thinking of making the trip and for others, were not told in a context free from the politics, concerns and social norms of the *mohallas*. One afternoon, across the gully from Islam's workshop, I sat chatting to Ifran, who had recently returned from Saudi. He was not full of tales of adventure and success but instead painted a bleaker picture, arguing that the (Saudi) *maliks* treated the workers '*kutte kee tarah*' [like dogs]. As we chatted, we were joined by the imam of the neighbouring madrassa. I had known the imam for some time and, while stern, he was an affable character of rotund frame in his late fifties. At the very moment of the imam's arrival, there was a notable change in Ifran's tone. He switched from his scathing account of conditions in Saudi to a far more positive tenor which gave emphasis to the respectful religiosity they were taught and the purity of Islam in the Kingdom.

Attendance to these nuances of stories told and imaginations forged reflected, in the varied accounts of returnees, the ways in which tales may be revised according to the cultural context, the company one is in and the life stage of the migrant (cf. K. Gardner 2002). Tales of exploitation and opportunity, sacrifice and glory, confinement and adventure, ambivalence and ambiguity all feature. Younger men tended towards positive interpretations. Experiences were often couched in terms that built status among peers. In Purāni Mandi, a group of young men made ornamental newel posts. I would stop at their shop occasionally for tea and a chat. They were always bantering and often included me. They introduced me to Usman Malik. He had recently returned from Kuwait and was full of bluster and boasts as he ensured that his friends and others in neighbouring shops were aware of his worldly experiences. As a *tanga* (horse-drawn taxi) passed, he mocked the driver for the backwardness of his vehicle. His friends laughed and applauded as he revelled in his new image. Later, however, a nearby craftsman told me, 'Of course it is all lies, he [Usman] has only been working as a servant to some big *malik*.' Older returnees, such as Habib, were often more circumspect.

> It is not a beneficial system for us, but it is not so harmful either. I spent my life away. I spent 18 years outside and I earned a lot of money, but I am like a stranger in my own country now. My goodwill is finished now. No one can recognise me. My circulation of work is finished too, and I am like a new person, so I have to start from step one. Yes, I spent my life out of the country, but I am happy as my family spent their life in comfort. If I worked in Saharanpur, then I could earn two to three hundred rupees per day and some days none. When I was outside I could send money every week. We spent a happy life and lived comfortably with lots of money. The life insurance is also there because of the money sent from outside. It is true that we can earn here, but we cannot save even a rupee as the salary is very low. In the Gulf we can earn twenty to twenty-five rupees in a month. When a man goes to the Gulf, every day his family wants more and more things. Our wives think that if we work here, there is little money, so they have little desire, but if we work

outside then their desire goes up and up. When we are outside we are always under pressure, as the family always calls asking for this thing or that thing.[11]

Migration can be seen as a process aimed at building social networks beyond the confines of kin and neighbourhood (Monsutti 2007). However, in the very act of committing to these new connections, migrants may lose access to the original networks that they set out with the intention of broadening. Habib's early migrations had been undertaken at a time when a Gulf returnee held undoubted status as an exceptional or even heroic character in the imaginations of others. With the increasing normalisation of migration to the Gulf, Habib had seen a steady decline in status that paralleled the gradual erosion of his 'circulation' in the *mohallas*. Towards the end of my fieldwork, I dropped in to say a final goodbye to Habib. His son, Faisal, answered the door and explained that Habib was away on *Jamaat*. Habib's earnings had funded a religious education for his three sons, and they had encouraged him to undertake the new journey. His son continued, 'We have told him that now it is time to leave this useless work [in the Gulf] and to turn to the important work of *da'wa* and *khurūj*.'

Faisal's words were indicative of his own religious positionality but also reflected broader societal shifts in the ways in which migration to the Gulf was viewed and imagined. In some sending areas, such as Kerala, prolific Gulf migration and the presence of powerful affective circuits has led to a shift in the national consciousness of migrants; many no longer consider the Gulf a foreign land (Percot 2006). In parallel with Syed Ali's (2007) identification of a 'culture of migration' in Hyderabad, Saharanpur had seen the increasing normalisation (and therefore de-exceptionalisation) of Gulf migration. However, with the more recent emergence of Gulf migration in Uttar Pradesh and other areas of north India this normalisation is still very much in formation.

Important distinctions were associated with the materiality and types of labour engaged in by migrants from Saharanpur that created differences in imaginings and experiences of the Gulf. While much migration from Uttar Pradesh to the Gulf is circular, for labour migrants the *kafala* system and the segregation of the labour camps from cities and cosmopolitan centres meant that there was little chance to establish roots. As for circular migrants elsewhere, these constraints left little possibility of assimilation or incorporation (Levitt et al. 2003). This enclavement, however, was not necessarily seen in negative terms by those contemplating migration to the Gulf. As with internal migration (even more so given the risks involved and the inability to change employer or to return), the primary concern in the minds of potential migrants, who were used to travelling and working with others in the city or elsewhere in India, was a fear of isolation. Not only could isolation make you more vulnerable to exploitation, it could also change the imagined experience of life overseas from one bound up in the camaraderie, male sociality and intimacy – familiar to internal migrants – into a period dominated by a *kēlāpan*, as Nasir Ddin had found. Thus, Rizwan reflected on his concerns about using an agent to find Yousef work:

> You know the agent is expensive and we do not have money for this. I do not think it matters for the work as the agent can also arrange good jobs, but it is better for Abdul to go to some factory where there is someone already, as otherwise he could be alone in some place.

This was not mere supposition. Mohammad Abdul ran a small shop, having returned after several trips. He explained that both he and his eldest son went for work in Saudi. Their work was arranged through an agent and was to be in a furniture factory. While this became truer for Abdul, the owner decided to use his son as a gardener in a distant farmhouse. Abdul explained that his son often cried to him about having no one with him. After three months Abdul went to visit his son, and, seeing his condition, pleaded with the owner to allow him to relocate. Eventually it was agreed that the owner would get another gardener and allow Abdul's son to move. The latter has since returned to the Gulf, but this time he made arrangements of an informal nature with people the family knew through their *mohalla*. This story draws the thread of this chapter back towards reflection on the more affective aspects of migration. As with the previous chapter, on internal migration, a deepening of the ethnographic detail requires a shift in focus away from the narratives of potential migrants, migrants, returnees and others in Saharanpur towards a more experiential account that shares in the everyday experience of migrant life in the Gulf. It is the attention to a more emotional engagement with migration that provides a contribution beyond much of the existing material on migration and the imagination.

Following arrival: the dormitories

Obtaining numbers of migrant workers in the area is difficult. However, the *Gulf News* (Stratford 2006) describes 'Al Mussafah [as an] area where an estimated 12,000 workers often share cramped rooms containing up to 20 beds'. Recently it has been earmarked for development, which may see the relocation of migrant labour (Bajić-Brković & Milaković 2011). Mussafah is strategically located on the other side of a creek and is geographically very much segregated from Abu Dhabi proper. I had never met Gulfam before I arrived in Mussafah, having been introduced to him by phone through a mutual friend in Saharanpur. At that time, he was in Sharjah working for a company fitting interiors in new buildings. Just before my arrival he was transferred to Abu Dhabi. Gulfam was older than I expected. While I imagined a younger man during our telephone conversations, he turned out to be around 40, with greying hair and a full frame. Gulfam was the foreman of a group doing interior fittings, mostly carpentry, and had 15 men in his charge. For him this was a step down. In Saharanpur he had owned a furniture business. It was not particularly large, but he described how he used to be his own master. Financial problems led to a decline of his business and eventually he was forced to shut down. It was this that drove him to look for work in the Gulf as a way of acquiring sufficient capital to start again.

We made our way, along with the company driver, to the dormitory block. Situated between a couple of shops and a construction storage yard, the block consisted of a steel gate which opened into a courtyard with doors to the rooms on three sides. Gulfam's room was the first on the right. I tried to lay my bedding on the floor but Gulfam insisted that I take his bunk. The room was shared with five others, but Gulfam told me that in some rooms there were two men sharing a bed. Despite this, conditions were slightly better than those I experienced while migrating with workers in India. Each room had a rickety air-conditioning unit and the bunks had mattresses. There was a kitchen, containing numerous stoves, which became crowded, hot and full of the smell of a variety of South Asian cooking, during mealtimes, as the burners were fired up. The men made their own food, often sharing this duty with their room-mates. Rooms naturally divided into national groupings brought together by a common language and shared taste preferences. Yet in many ways it was a cosmopolitan space. Bangladeshis, Pakistanis and Indians joined each other in the courtyard to play football, chat and share jokes. Behind the dormitories there was a substantial toilet and shower block which was a world apart from the small facilities in Hyderabad and Kamareddy. The accommodation was not provided by the Jordanian-owned company for whom all the residents worked, but was leased from a company that specialised in dormitory accommodation.

My initial impression was that many facilities were provided, but when we began to pack up to return to Sharjah it became clear this was not so. Apart from the bunks, air-conditioning units and toilets, everything was loaded onto a lorry, including mattresses, cookers, gas cylinders, a couple of fridges and even carpet tiles from the floor. Gulfam explained that all these items had been bought by the workers themselves. Some, such as cookers and cylinders, had been purchased collectively by the inhabitants of a room, while others, such as mattresses, had been bought to provide a little comfort. While there were some distinctions, the material arrangements and conditions felt, in the context of my previous migrations with friends in India, familiar. Friday still provided a day of respite and an opportunity to go roaming in the city or just laze around in the dorm.

While I could access the camp, the worksite was out of bounds to me. The hours were long, and overtime often demanded by the employer. However, the rhythm of the day was not greatly different from that in Hyderabad or Kamareddy. The evenings were spent in the dormitory or in the communal courtyard onto which our door opened. Of the five men with whom Gulfam shared the dormitory, four were also from Saharanpur and, with one exception, had arranged work at the site through informal channels that were largely an extension of migration networks within the domestic context. Just as Rizwan could call on others in various corners of India, so potential Gulf migrants were more and more able to make links to work through friends, neighbours and others who were already in or had returned from the Gulf. There were material advantages to a more informal passage: it enabled migrants to cut out costly agents. Faisal also hailed from Saharanpur but had organised work through an agent, eventually paying out about 90,000 rupees in advance to secure a three-year contract.

The fifth resident was Junaid, from a village near Lucknow. He was the most experienced of them all, having spent 15 years abroad, returning home only to obtain new contracts. For Junaid, like Musharraf in Hyderabad, life had become defined by migration, and he said he preferred this to life at home. The others joked that this was because his wife was 'buhuut mota' [very fat], jesting that 'Junaid bhai pasia nehee mil suktai hai kyoki uskee beebi sub khatee hai [Brother Junaid cannot make any money as his wife eats it all]'. As with the worksites in India, it was more than the mere materiality of conditions that provided a degree of continuity far from home. The banter, conviviality and intimacy of life in the camps very much reflected that of migrant destinations in India. All the occupants of the room had engaged in internal migration before setting off for the Gulf, and these experiences provided a primary reference point for their expectations of migration beyond the domestic context. While the Gulf may be imagined in a variety of ways, the experience of being there was bound up in degrees of familiarity as much as it was in difference.

The men of this dormitory shared a language, tastes in food, and interests. Evenings were spent engaging in the same kinds of jovial intimacy and occasional disagreements that were present in domestic destinations. The conditions often described by media outlets and others as cramped and dirty are material familiarities for those who reside in them, and are reasons beyond structural concerns why workers themselves often accept the arrangements they find themselves in. Yet in seeking comfort and familiarity, workers in the Gulf shaped in their everyday lives an imagination that contrasted with ideals of a vanguard or cosmopolitan migrant. As set out previously, continuity can create forms of enclavement rather than necessarily opening transformative horizons. This is partly structural, as spatial segregation is a prominent part of the urban landscape, but there was also a degree to which continuity was actively sought out. While the dormitory courtyard provided a space of relative cosmopolitanism, there remained a degree of ethnic segregation among the workers, and more intimate time was always shared with those of a more familiar background.

My time in the dormitories of Abu Dhabi was limited. Unlike in India I was unable to obtain permission to work. By day I was mostly alone as the workers headed out to the sites where they were fitting internal decor. They showed me photos of stylish apartments they had worked on. The rooms contained fittings and fixtures that would not be out of place in any fancy catalogue. The lobbies were grand, with tall ceilings and airy spaces. They also showed me snaps from the public beach in Dubai. They were particularly keen on a photo of Abdul, one of the men with whom we shared a room, in which the background scene contained a western woman in a bikini. The photo was staged to surreptitiously capture her image. The moment took me back to Hyderabad and a trip to a shopping mall with Faisal and Usman. They were regular visitors to the mall, which is attached to an IMAX cinema, but the ways in which they, unlike the hordes of middle-class Indian shoppers, could experience it were limited. We looked in the windows of the shops, rode the escalators and sat in McDonald's for a few minutes without ordering anything. Like the skyscrapers on which Gulfam and the other men worked, and the foreign women they illicitly photographed, much of what has been conceptualised within the context of cosmopolitanism and modernity could be seen but not touched.

Conclusion

This chapter has drawn the narrative of the book across transnational space. It has traced various continuities from the gullies of Saharanpur to the Gulf, continuities that play out at both the structural and the subjective levels. Previous chapters in this book have detailed the reproduction and socialisation of labour in the wood industry. Likewise, labour relations and workers' subjectivities in the GCC cannot be conceived only in the context of arrival in the region or even the initial moment of engagement with disciplining processes such as medical testing and waiting. Instead, the cultivation of migrant subjectivities and imaginaries is constituted over a long duration. The 'marginalised' or 'bordered' subjectivity produced in the bounded spatial context of the *mohalla* is rendered mobile and persists across national and transnational spaces. Migration is a biographical and contextual process; thus the resistances and transformations it may produce need to be understood in these terms, as do degrees of compliance, discipline and control. If the local craft labour force in Saharanpur is constituted through early socialisation into the industry, which creates familiarity with particular sets of labour relations, then the subjective experience of GCC labour markets can only be understood through a holistic account of labour force reproduction across transnational space.

While this chapter has emphasised forms of continuity, it has also (building on the previous chapter) attended to change and transformation, to the shift to adulthood that migration may accelerate, to the forms of self-making it enables and to the role of the returnee in bringing back new-found styles, stories and status. Additionally, the chapter has shown how the imagination is cultivated in an inter-subjective context as well as through material and affective forces. It is critical, however, to temper our enthusiasm for the potentiality of migration as an agent of social change and to remain conscious of the realities and imaginaries of migrants themselves. This is not to dismiss all potentiality. The account I have provided in this and previous chapters covers a single ethnoscape. Writing on migration from Kerala to the Gulf, Michelle Buckley (2012) points out that there have been strikes amongst construction workers in the Gulf, which took place despite spatial configurations, an ethnically divided labour market and regulatory frames aimed at controlling workers. The imagination always contains potentiality, but migration is by no means an automatic catalyst. Marginalised subjectivities and the forms of enclavement that formed a spatialising background to life in the *mohallas* extended across geographies of movement and mobility,

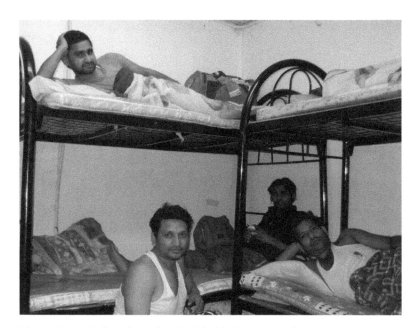

Figure 9.2 A dormitory in Abu Dhabi. Source: author.

Figure 9.3 Naseer looking on over a shopping mall in Hyderabad.
Source: author.

shaping expectations, imaginaries and experiences of work, conditions and environments in both India and the GCC region.

Notes

1. Currently consisting of Saudi Arabia, Kuwait, Bahrain, Oman, Qatar and the United Arab Emirates.
2. Based on Emigration Check Required (ECR)-status migrants.
3. Indicators for 2017 show a decline in emigration from Uttar Pradesh and elsewhere; the reasons for this are not clear (Wadhawan 2018: Figure 3).
4. Southern states have seen stagnation or decline in total numbers of GCC migrants: Kerala from 104,101 (2010) to 66,058 (2014); Andhra Pradesh from 72,220 (2010) to 53,104 (2014); Tamil Nadu from 84,510 (2010) to 83,202 (2014) (Ministry of Overseas Indian Affairs [2015]).
5. Edited and adapted from interview transcript.
6. Edited and adapted from interview transcript.
7. Edited and adapted from interview transcript.
8. Edited and adapted from interview transcript.
9. The article earlier discusses the targeting of the Muslims in Azamgarh by security services.
10. The visiting of the holy sites of Mecca, which, unlike hajj, can be performed at any time of year. The *umrah* is seen as increasing one's religious standing and closeness to Allah. However, it does not carry the weight of hajj.
11. Edited and adapted from interview transcript.

10
Marginalisation and connectedness: a conclusion

Figure 10.1   Children peer through a rooftop rail onto the gully below.
Source: author.

This book has traced processes of marginalisation and connectedness across time and space, as well as through networks of production, sociality, affect and migration. Above all else, it has provided a detailed ethnographic account of lives, livelihoods, imaginaries and subjectivities in Saharanpur's woodworking *mohallas*. In the foreground are the narratives and experiences of informants and friends, along with my own descriptions of becoming embroiled (albeit from the privileged position of the anthropologist) in networks of sociality, work and migration. Labour regimes, migration regimes, capitalist development, neoliberal reforms, state interventions, movements of corporate capital and the intensifying marginalisation of Indian Muslims have all acted as structuring forces upon Saharanpur's long-duration woodworking cluster. Spatially configured and enabled through dynamics of class, gender and religion, the niches that constitute the city's wood supply chain (cf. Tsing 2009) are at the core of mediations between the embedded local and global flows of commodities, capital and people. Localised power structures are, to a degree, transformed by demands for cheap production and a flexible, mobile labour force. At the same time continuities and localised sets of relations (both hierarchical ones and those that appear more egalitarian) are put to work and incorporated into globalised modalities of wealth extraction.

Much of this, of course, is not new. Scholars since Marx have concerned themselves with international divisions of labour, and anthropologists have long shown the culturally embedded specificities of global production networks and supply chains. What this book has tried to offer, however, is a particularised and historicised empirical contribution to the array of ethnographies that remind us of the importance of relating world system to local context. It is this attention to the particular that allows a more specific contribution to be drawn out. Concerning Indian Muslims and Muslim artisans in India, the use of marginalisation and connectedness within a dialectical framework has challenged many representations of Muslims in regions of the country where some of the most potent processes of marginalisation have been experienced. An exploration of connections offers a more vivid portrayal of everyday life constituted through variegated networks that provided resources, support, care and moments of empowerment, but also acted, to a degree, to subjugate, control and discipline those within in complex ways.

Throughout these explorations of the political economy of craftwork, and during engagements with circuits of migration, intimacy has been a constant feature. Intimacy, production and migration are, I contend, inseparable, and it is ethnography that provides us with the most powerful tool for understanding the role of intimacy within broader political economies. Dualities of mutuality and exploitation have been a constant presence within these circuits and the latter stages of the book have illustrated that a desire for familiar forms of sociality can act as an enclaving force, a habituated realm that is carried across spaces and places and inscribed through class, ethnicity, religion, gender and status. Within this latter material there is, of course, a nod to Pierre Bourdieu (1977) and, more specifically, to a body of work that utilises his ideas to explore the relationship between the imagination and migration (e.g. Smith 2006; Hage 2005; S. Mishra 2017; Wallinder 2019). Often, this has drawn the eye to change – change in embodied practices, dress, consumption habits, mien, etc. Yet, as Bourdieu (1977: 89) himself points out, the relationship between the body and the world is a dialectical one in which the ability of bodies to act upon the world is mediated by the 'em-bodying of the structures of the world'. Hence, continuities as well as transformative processes have been empirically detailed and given prominence in the analysis presented in this book.

The interrelation between structures, materialities and subjectivities has drawn particular attention to 'space'. Ethno-spatial enclavement, be it along religious lines (as was the case for Muslim artisans in India) or along ethnic lines (as in the Gulf) – as well as the gendered considerations of the *mohallas* themselves – has formed a central mediating factor across this monograph. Marginalisation and spatial enclavement act to intensify levels of embeddedness, rendering the son an employee, the daughter a subcontractor, the friend a *thēkēdār*, the neighbour a forewoman, etc. These are relations that are further mediated through a variety of structural factors and by flows (or non-flows) of capital and power. Thus, forms of neo-bondage, 'inverted bondage', debt and authority have often intermingled with relations of intimacy and care but have also been violently imposed at both the structural and interpersonal levels. Yet, the crafting, or 'work', involved in cultivating the largely informal networks of sociality detailed in this book cannot be seen as merely subjugated to broader, global projects. Like Bourdieu's (1977) dialectic of the body and the world, Ingold's (2013) acknowledgement of interplays between the 'material' and the 'imagined', and Marx's (1990 [1867]) conceptualisation of the artisan as architect, these networks hold their own degrees of agency – a structuring quality.

We have seen this in the lives of woodworking women as they negotiate highly constrained spaces of labour and employment. We have also seen it in patterns of male sociality, in which groups of workers and artisans may forge collective operations around narratives of friendship in order to navigate the precarious fluctuations of the woodworking economy. Affective and informal networks have been shown to extend into the structuring of patterns of migration, where workers move not only for economic gain but also in search of comfort, familiarity and friendship. Within these networks, an enclaved or marginalised subjectivity, I have argued, is mobile. It is something that is carried, tacitly felt and embodied; it is a sensation, a presence, as much as it is a quantifiable and measurable socio-economic reality. Thus the opportunity to attend a religious programme in Kamareddy was declined, or the sense of 'look but don't touch' that underpinned the experiences of workers when outside the labour camps in the Gulf became embodied within forms of self-discipline. Tracing the effects of enclavement across space reveals a prolonged preparation of workers' bodies and subjectivities, stretching from the socialisation of the gullies and the bodily crafting of apprenticeship, to labouring within the 'global factory' and work in the confinements of the Gulf's *kafala* system.

Finally, it is important to make clear that I do not situate the forces producing a physical and subjective sense of marginalisation and enclavement – sometimes immaterial and at others writ large upon the urban landscape or contained within moments of violence – as an exceptional condition. Partha Chatterjee (2004) has made clear, and convincingly (if somewhat homogeneously) so, that marginalisation is the pre-eminent experience of the majority of those in the global south. The intersections and processes that facilitate this are not, however, universalised in the same ways. Saharanpur and its woodworking gullies are full of particularities that make the experiences of Noor, Rizwan, Farhana, Islam, Yousef, Naseer, Gulshan and others specific to this place and these people. Elsewhere, forms of marginalisation and connectedness may be configured differently, but a continuing exploration of the potentialities and constraints that lie in the space between material contexts and imagined worlds offers tantalising possibilities for understanding not just forms of oppression and control but also resistance and transformation.

Figure 10.2 Kites flying in the evening sky over the *mohallas*.
Source: author.

Glossary of Hindi, Urdu and Arabic terms

Ajlaf	Muslims descended from converts from mid-ranking Hindu castes
akelāpan	loneliness
al-haya	Arabic; shyness, modesty
aloo paratha	fried bread (*paratha*) stuffed with potato (*aloo*)
Ansari	Muslim *biradari* or caste (originally weavers)
apna kām	own work
āra	bandsaw
ārī	small fretsaw
Arzal	Muslims descended from converts from the Hindu Dalit caste
ashraf	Muslim elites claiming lineage from the disciples of the Prophet
Azad	used in the Gulf region; sometimes called a 'free visa'. It involves a *kafal* sponsoring a visa for fictive employment
bastī	slum area
beedie	cheap cigarette rolled in a tobacco leaf and tied with thread
bhai	brother (used colloquially as an informal form of address for male friends)
bhut	ghost, spirit
biradari	Muslim 'caste' grouping
Brahmin	member of Hindu high or priest caste
Brahmic	identifiable with high caste or priestly status

burka	head-to-toe garment worn by women in some Islamic traditions (usually black)
chacha	paternal uncle
chai	sweet milky tea
chāl-chalan	a person's behaviour, persona or demeanour
Chamār	Hindu leather-working caste
chaukidār	gatekeeper, watchman
chikan	needle embroidery
chilai	carving
Dalit	low-caste Hindu caste (formerly called 'untouchables')
da'wa	Islamic missionary work, teaching
dhow	lateen-rigged ship common in the Middle East and the Indian Ocean
dilai	metal forge
durgha	Sufi shrine or tomb
Eid al Adha	half or little Eid. It commemorates Abraham's willingness to sacrifice his son for Allah. Often called *bakri Eid* (goat Eid) because of the common practice of slaughtering and consuming a goat reared for the occasion
Eid al Fitr	the largest Islamic festival of the year. The time at which fast is broken after Ramadan.
faltu	useless
gandā	dirty
ghūmnāi	roaming, travelling, sightseeing
gilli-danda	game played with a stick and a small oval of wood (the *gilli*)
gully	narrow lane or street
gundā	thug, criminal
Hadith	reports of the words and deeds of the Prophet Muhammad and other early Muslims
hajj	the Islamic pilgrimage to Mecca and Medina. Ideally undertaken once in the lifetime of every Muslim, it covers a period of six days.

haram	forbidden by Islamic law
hauz	pond
hawala	informal system of transferring money in the Middle East and South Asia. Money is paid to an agent, then the agent contacts another broker elsewhere to pay the final recipient.
humzulf	wife's sister's husband
iddah	a period of mourning undertaken by a Muslim woman after her husband's death (usually four lunar months and ten days)
jajmani	a system of sub-castes which connects groups to a particular type of labour
jamaat	Islamic religious tour or gathering. It usually involves preaching, prayer and discussion. Sometimes used of *khuruj*.
kafal	a sponsor under the *kafala* system. Sponsors a migrant worker's visa and residence and usually acts as their employer throughout the worker's stay. Can be an individual or a company.
kafala system	a regulatory system applied in many Gulf countries which restricts foreign workers' periods of stay, requires a *kafal* (sponsor) and excludes the possibility of citizenship
kārīgar	artisan
kārkhānadar	factory owner
karz	informal interest-free loan
khatra	danger, risk
khurūj	Islamic proselytising tour
kirāya	rent
kismet	fate, destiny
kurta	light cotton clothing/shirt, usually white (sometimes called *kurta pyjama*)
lakh	one hundred thousand
lakri	wood
lassi	yoghurt-based drink. Usually served sweet or salty.
malding	decorative wooden strip, edging
malik	boss, employer, factory owner

mamu	maternal uncle
mandee	recession, period of little work
mandi	market
markaz	mosque acting as a centre for Tabligh work. It is from such centres that *khurūjs* are despatched.
masjid	mosque
mazdoor	labour(er)
mehman	guest
mistrī	tradesperson (e.g. mechanic, builder or carpenter)
mudha	cane stool
murti	small shrine (usually wooden) kept in Hindu households
namāz	Islamic prayer, prostration (salat in Arabic). One of the five pillars of Islam
namkeen	savoury spiced snack or nibble
nazriya	vision, how one sees the world
neta	leader, politician
paisa	one hundredth of a rupee
pān	betel-nut-based stimulant. It is chewed, which produces a red saliva that is usually spat out
purdah	women's seclusion from unrelated men, veiling, curtain partition
pyar	love, affection
Qur'ān Sharif	honoured Holy Quran
Ramadan	a lunar month of fasting (from dawn to dusk), which leads up to Eid
rehal	a folding wooden stand for holding the Holy Quran
rehri	a four-wheeled handcart (often used by street vendors)
rigmal	sandpaper
roti	bread, chapati
saali	wife's sister
sahn	the enclosed courtyard of a house or mosque
sanskritisation	a process by which a lower caste attempts to rise in the social hierarchy by imitating the practices of a higher caste

shāgird	apprentice
shakti	power, strength
sharīf	noble, high-born, honourable
sharīf aadmi	a respectable, gentle or pious man
sifarish	favour, leaning on someone to get something done, nepotism
Tablighi Jamaat	a globally active Islamic reformist movement
tanga	horse-drawn taxi
tankhwa	salary, fixed rate of pay
Teli	the oil-pressing caste (comprising both Muslims and Hindus)
thawb	an ankle-length gown commonly worn by men in the Arabian areas of the Gulf
thēkēdār	middleman, broker, labour contractor
tiffin	lunch box
tikai	fine-grained carving
tikka	piece (from Hindi; used colloquially to express piece-rate payments)
topi	hat (often used for the skullcap worn by Muslim men)
ulama	scholars of Islam and Islamic law
umrah	a pilgrimage made to Mecca and Medina outside the Hajj period
ustād	teacher, master
vasta	procedure for washing before prayers in Islam
wakf board	Muslim charitable trust
wallah	a person associated with a particular activity, place or characteristic (e.g. taxi wallah, Mumbai wallah, small wallah)
waqt	time
wasta	beneficial relationship, nepotism, 'who you know'
zamīndār	landowner class, those leasing to tenant farmers
zardozi	fine, beaded embroidery work

References

Abbas, Rameez. 2016. 'Internal migration and citizenship in India.' *Journal of Ethnic and Migration Studies* 42(1): 150–68.

Abdalla, Mohamad, Dylan Chown and Muhammad Abdullah, eds. 2018. *Islamic Schooling in the West: Pathways to Renewal.* New York: Springer.

Abraham, Vinoj. 2013. 'Missing labour or consistent "de-feminisation"?' *Economic and Political Weekly* 48(31): 99–108.

Abu-Lughod, Lila. 2002. 'Do Muslim women really need saving? Anthropological reflections on cultural relativism and its others.' *American Anthropologist* 104(3): 783–90.

Addleton, Jonathan S. 1992. *Undermining the Centre: The Gulf Migration and Pakistan.* Karachi: Oxford University Press.

Adhikari, J. and M. Hobley. 2015. '"Everyone is leaving. Who will sow our fields?" The livelihood effects on women of male migration from Khotang and Udaypur districts of Nepal, to the Gulf countries and Malaysia.' *Himalaya* 35(1): 11–23.

Afridi, Farzana, Taryn Dinkelman and Kanika Mahajan. 2016. 'Why are fewer married women joining the work force in India? A decomposition analysis over two decades.' IZA Discussion Paper no. 9722. https://papers.ssrn.com/sol3/papers.cfm?abstract_id=2731985 (accessed 5 April 2018).

Afsar, Rita. 2009. *Unravelling the Vicious Cycle of Recruitment: Labour Migration from Bangladesh to the Gulf States.* Geneva: ILO.

Agamben, Giorgio. 2005. *State of Exception,* trans. Kevin Attell. Chicago and London: University of Chicago Press.

Agarwala, Rina. 2013. *Informal Labor, Formal Politics, and Dignified Discontent in India.* Cambridge: Cambridge University Press.

Aggarwal, Ravina. 2004. *Beyond Lines of Control: Performance and Politics on the Disputed Borders of Ladakh, India.* Durham, NC: Duke University Press.

Ahmad, Attiya. 2017. *Everyday Conversions: Islam, Domestic Work, and South Asian Migrant Women in Kuwait.* Durham, NC: Duke University Press.

Ahmad, Imtiaz, ed. 1978. *Caste and Social Stratification among Muslims in India.* New Delhi: Manohar Book Service.

Ahmad, Irfan. 2003. 'A different jihad: Dalit Muslims' challenge to ashraf hegemony.' *Economic and Political Weekly* 38(46): 4886–91.

Ahmad, Mumtaz. 1991. 'Islamic fundamentalism in South Asia: the Jamaat-i-Islami and the Tablighi Jamaat of South Asia.' In *Fundamentalisms Observed,* edited by Martin E. Marty and R. Scott Appleby, 457–530. Chicago: University of Chicago Press.

Akhtar, Aasim Sajjad. 2011. 'Patronage and class in urban Pakistan: modes of labor control in the contractor economy.' *Critical Asian Studies* 43(2): 159–84.

Alam, Arshad. 2008. 'The enemy within: madrasa and Muslim identity in North India.' *Modern Asian Studies* 42(2–3): 605–27.

Alam, Tosib and Surinder Kumar. 2019. 'Social and economic status of backward Muslims in Uttar Pradesh: need for an inclusive policy?' *Social Change* 49(1): 78–96.

Al-Attas, Syed Muhammad Naquib. 1977. 'The concept of education in Islam: a framework for an Islamic philosophy of education.' Keynote address delivered at the First World Conference on Muslim Education, Makkah (Mecca), March.

Alavi, Seema. 2015. *Muslim Cosmopolitanism in the Age of Empire.* Cambridge, MA: Harvard University Press.

Ali, Jan. 2003. 'Islamic revivalism: the case of the Tablighi Jamaat.' *Journal of Muslim Minority Affairs* 23(1): 173–81.

Ali, Jan Ashik. 2006. 'Islamic revivalism: a Study of the Tablighi Jamaat in Sydney.' PhD thesis, University of New South Wales.

Ali, Syed. 2007. '"Go west young man": the culture of migration among Muslims in Hyderabad, India.' *Journal of Ethnic and Migration Studies* 33(1): 37–58.

Aljunied, Khairudin. 2016. *Muslim Cosmopolitanism: Southeast Asian Islam in Comparative Perspective*. Edinburgh: Edinburgh University Press.

Appadurai, Arjun. 1996. *Modernity at Large: Cultural Dimensions of Globalization*. Minneapolis: University of Minnesota Press.

Aryal, Nirmal, Pramod R. Regmi, Edwin van Teijlingen, Padam Simkhada, Pratik Adhikary, Yadav Kumar Deo Bhatta and Stewart Mann. 2016. 'Injury and mortality in young Nepalese migrant workers: a call for public health action.' *Asia Pacific Journal of Public Health* 28(8): 703–5.

Auyero, Javier. 2011. 'Patients of the state: an ethnographic account of poor people's waiting.' *Latin American Research Review* 46(1): 5–29.

Auyero, Javier. 2012. *Patients of the State: The Politics of Waiting in Argentina*. Durham, NC: Duke University Press.

Azeez, Abdul and Mustiary Begum. 2009. 'Gulf migration, remittances and economic impact.' *Journal of Social Sciences* 20(1): 55–60.

Baden, Sally. 1992. *The Position of Women in Islamic Countries: Possibilities, Constraints and Strategies for Change*. Brighton: Institute of Development Studies, University of Sussex.

Bagchi, Amiya Kumar. 1976. 'De-industrialization in India in the nineteenth century: some theoretical implications.' *Journal of Development Studies* 12(2): 135–64.

Bajić Brković, Milica and Mira Milaković. 2011. 'Planning and designing urban places in response to climate and local culture: a case study of Mussafah District in Abu Dhabi.' *Spatium* 25: 14–22.

Balakrishnan, Radhika, ed. 2002. *The Hidden Assembly Line: Gender Dynamics of Subcontracted Work in a Global Economy*. Bloomfield, CT: Kumarian Press.

Banaji, Jairus. 2003. 'The fictions of free labour: contract, coercion, and so-called unfree labour.' *Historical Materialism* 11(3): 69–95.

Barnes, Jessica R. 2018. 'Handmaking your way out of poverty?' In *Craft Economies*, edited by Susan Luckman and Nicola Thomas. London: Bloomsbury Academic, 129–37.

Barrientos, Stephanie. 2008. 'Contract labour: the "Achilles heel" of corporate codes in commercial value chains.' *Development and Change* 39(6): 977–90.

Bashir, Kamran, and Margot Wilson. 2017. 'Unequal among equals: lessons from discourses on "Dalit Muslims" in modern India.' *Social Identities* 23(5): 631–46.

Basu, Ellen Oxfeld. 1991. 'Profit, loss, and fate: the entrepreneurial ethic and the practice of gambling in an overseas Chinese community.' *Modern China* 17(2): 227–59.

Batool, Munazza. 2018. 'Conversion to Islam in the Indian milieu: a reconsideration of Da'wah and conversion process during the pre-Mughal period.' *Journal of the Pakistan Historical Society* 66(1–2): 157–74.

Bauman, Zygmunt. 1999. *In Search of Politics*. Stanford, CA: Stanford University Press.

Bear, Laura. 2014. 'Doubt, conflict, mediation: the anthropology of modern time.' *Journal of the Royal Anthropological Institute* (n.s.) 20(S1): 3–30.

Beck, Ulrich. 2007. 'The cosmopolitan condition: why methodological nationalism fails.' *Theory, Culture & Society* 24(7–8): 286–90.

Beinin, Joel. 2001. *Workers and Peasants in the Modern Middle East*. Cambridge: Cambridge University Press.

Bhagat, Ram B. 2010. 'Internal migration in India: are the underprivileged migrating more?' *Asia-Pacific Population Journal* 25(1): 27–45.

Bhattacharyya, Asmita and Sudeep Basu. 2018. *Marginalities in India: Themes and Perspectives*. Singapore: Springer.

Bhatty, Zarina. 1987. 'Economic contribution of women to the household budget: a case study of the Beedi industry.' In *Invisible Hands: Women in Home-Based Production*, edited by Andrea Menefee Singh and Anita Kelles-Viitanen, 35–50. New Delhi: SAGE Publications.

Bielenin-Lenczowska, Karolina. 2018. 'Spaghetti with ajvar: an ethnography of migration, gender, learning and change.' In *Food Parcels in International Migration: Intimate Connections*, edited by Diana Mata-Codesal and Maria Abranches, 117–39. Cham: Palgrave Macmillan.

Bloch, Maurice. 1991. 'Language, anthropology and cognitive science.' *Man* (n.s.) 26(2): 183–98.

Boeri, Natascia. 2018. 'Challenging the gendered entrepreneurial subject: gender, development, and the informal economy in India.' *Gender & Society* 32(2): 157–79.

Bohannan, Paul and Laura Bohannan. 1968. *Tiv Economy*. Evanston, IL: Northwestern University Press.

Boltanski, Luc and Eve Chiapello. 2005. 'The new spirit of capitalism', trans. Gregory Elliott. *International Journal of Politics, Culture, and Society* 18(3–4): 161–88.

Bourdieu, Pierre. 1963. 'The attitude of the Algerian peasant toward time.' In *Mediterranean Countrymen: Essays in the Social Anthropology of the Mediterranean*, edited by Julian Pitt-Rivers, 55–72. Paris: Mouton.

Bourdieu, Pierre. 1977. *Outline of a Theory of Practice*. Cambridge: Cambridge University Press.

Bourdieu, Pierre. 1990. *The Logic of Practice*. Stanford, CA: Stanford University Press.

Brass, Tom. 1990. 'Class struggle and the deproletarianisation of agricultural labour in Haryana (India).' *Journal of Peasant Studies* 18(1): 36–67.

Brass, Tom. 2003. 'Why unfree labour is not "so-called": the fictions of Jairus Banaji.' *Journal of Peasant Studies* 31(1): 101–36.

Braverman, Harry. 1998. *Labor and Monopoly Capital: The Degradation of Work in the Twentieth Century*. New York: Monthly Review Press.

Breman, Jan. 1996. *Footloose Labour: Working in India's Informal Economy*. Cambridge: Cambridge University Press.

Breman, Jan. 1999. 'Industrial labour in post-colonial India. II: employment in the informal-sector economy.' *International Review of Social History* 44(3): 451–83.

Breman, Jan. 2002. 'Communal upheaval as resurgence of social Darwinism.' *Economic and Political Weekly* 37(16): 1485–88.

Breman, Jan. 2004. *The Making and Unmaking of an Industrial Working Class: Sliding Down to the Bottom of the Labour Hierarchy in Ahmedabad, India*. Amsterdam: Amsterdam University Press.

Brenner, Neil, and Nik Theodore. 2002. 'Cities and the geographies of "actually existing neoliberalism".' *Antipode* 34(3): 349–79.

Bristol-Rhys, Jane, and Caroline Osella. 2016. 'Neutralized bachelors, infantilized Arabs: between migrant and host – gendered and sexual stereotypes in Abu Dhabi.' In *Masculinities under Neoliberalism*, edited by Andrea Cornwall, Frank G. Karioris and Nancy Lindisfarne, 111–24. London: Zed Books.

Buckley, Michelle. 2012. 'From Kerala to Dubai and back again: construction migrants and the global economic crisis.' *Geoforum* 43(2): 250–9.

Buckley, Michelle. 2014. 'On the work of urbanization: migration, construction labor, and the commodity moment.' *Annals of the American Association of Geographers* 104(2): 338–47.

Burawoy, M. 1979. 'The anthropology of industrial work.' *Annual Review of Anthropology* 8: 231–66.

Burki, Abid Aman. 1989. 'Urban informal sector in Pakistan: some selected issues', with comments by Sabur Ghayur. *Pakistan Development Review* 28(4): 911–24.

Campbell, Ben. 2018. 'Moral ecologies of subsistence and labour in a migration-affected community of Nepal.' *Journal of the Royal Anthropological Institute* 24(S1): 151–65.

Cant, Alanna. 2018. '"Making" labour in Mexican artisanal workshops.' *Journal of the Royal Anthropological Institute* 24(S1): 61–74.

Carrier, James G. 1992. 'Emerging alienation in production: A Maussian history.' *Man* 27(3): 539–58.

Carrier, James G. 1999. 'People who can be friends: selves and social relationships.' In *The Anthropology of Friendship*, edited by Sandra Bell and Simon Coleman, 21–38. Oxford: Berg.

Carswell, Grace, Thomas Chambers and Geert De Neve. 2019. 'Waiting for the state: gender, citizenship and everyday encounters with bureaucracy in India.' *Environment and Planning C: Politics and Space* 37(4): 597–616.

Carswell, Grace, and Geert De Neve. 2013a. 'From field to factory: tracing transformations in bonded labour in the Tiruppur region, Tamil Nadu.' *Economy and Society* 42(3): 430–54.

Carswell, Grace, and Geert De Neve. 2013b. 'Labouring for global markets: conceptualising labour agency in global production networks.' *Geoforum* 44(264): 62–70.

Castaldo, Adriana, Priya Deshingkar and Andy McKay. 2012. 'Internal migration, remittances and poverty: evidence from Ghana and India.' Migrating out of Poverty Working Paper 7, University of Sussex.

Castles, Stephen. 2011. 'Migration, crisis, and the global labour market.' *Globalizations* 8(3): 311–24.

Castles, Stephen. 2012. 'Cosmopolitanism and freedom? Lessons of the global economic crisis.' *Ethnic and Racial Studies* 35(11): 1843–52.

Chakrabarty, Dipesh. 1988. 'Class consciousness and the Indian working class: dilemmas of Marxist historiography.' *Journal of Asian and African Studies* 23(1–2): 21–31.

Chakrabarty, Dipesh. 2000. *Rethinking Working-Class History: Bengal, 1890–1940*. Princeton, NJ: Princeton University Press.

Chakraborty, Kabita. 2012. 'Virtual mate-seeking in the urban slums of Kolkata, India.' *South Asian Popular Culture* 10(2): 197–216.

Chakraborty, Kabita. 2016. *Young Muslim Women in India: Bollywood, Identity and Changing Youth Culture*. Abingdon: Routledge.

Chambers, Thomas. 2018. 'Continuity in mind: imagination and migration in India and the Gulf.' *Modern Asian Studies* 52(4): 1420–56.

Chambers, Thomas. 2019. '"Performed conviviality": space, bordering, and silence in the city.' *Modern Asian Studies* 53(3): 776–99.

Chambers, Thomas. Forthcoming. '"Lean on me": sifarish, mediation and the digitisation of state bureaucracies in India.' *Ethnography*.

Chambers, Thomas, and Ayesha Ansari. 2018. 'Ghar mein kām hai (There is work in the house): when female factory workers become "coopted domestic labour".' *Journal of South Asian Development* 13(2): 141–63.

Chandavarkar, Rajnarayan. 1994. *The Origins of Industrial Capitalism in India: Business Strategies and the Working Classes in Bombay, 1900–1940*. Cambridge: Cambridge University Press.

Chandavarkar, Rajnarayan. 2003. *The Origins of Industrial Capitalism in India: Business Strategies and the Working Classes in Bombay, 1900–1940*. Cambridge: Cambridge University Press.

Chandavarkar, Rajnayaran. 2009. *History, Culture and the Indian City*. Cambridge: Cambridge University Press.

Chandavarkar, Raj, Ian Kerr, Dilip Simeon, Janaki Nair, Chitra Joshi and Sumit Sarkar. 2004. 'The return of labour to South-Asian history.' *Historical Materialism* 12(3): 285–313.

Chari, Sharad. 2004. *Fraternal Capital: Peasant-Workers, Self-Made Men, and Globalization in Provincial India*. Delhi: Permanent Black.

Chatterjee, Anasua. 2017. *Margins of Citizenship: Muslim Experiences in Urban India*. Abingdon: Routledge.

Chatterjee, Ipsita. 2009. 'Social conflict and the neoliberal city: a case of Hindu–Muslim violence in India.' *Transactions of the Institute of British Geographers* (n.s.) 34(2): 143–60.

Chatterjee, Ipsita. 2012. 'How are they othered? Globalisation, identity and violence in an Indian city.' *Geographical Journal* 178(2): 134–46.

Chatterjee, Partha. 2004. *The Politics of the Governed: Reflections on Popular Politics in Most of the World*. New York: Columbia University Press.

Chatterjee, Partha. 2011. 'Democracy and economic transformation in India.' In *Understanding India's New Political Economy*, edited by Sanjay Ruparelia, Sanjay Reddy, John Harriss and Stuart Corbridge, 17–34. Abingdon: Routledge.

Chen, Martha. 1995. 'A matter of survival: women's right to employment in India and Bangladesh.' In *Women, Culture, and Development: A Study of Human Capabilities*, edited by Martha C. Nussbaum and Jonathan Glover, 37–59. Oxford: Clarendon Press.

Chen, Martha Alter, ed. 1998. *Widows in India: Social Neglect and Public Action*. London: Sage.

Chigateri, Shraddha. 2008. '"Glory to the cow": cultural difference and social justice in the food hierarchy in India.' *South Asia: Journal of South Asian Studies* 31(1): 10–35.

Chua, Jocelyn Lim. 2011. 'Making time for the children: self-temporalization and the cultivation of the antisuicidal subject in South India.' *Cultural Anthropology* 26(1): 112–37.

Ciotti, Manuela. 2006. 'At the margins of feminist politics? A comparative analysis of women in Dalit politics and Hindu Right organisations in northern India.' *Contemporary South Asia* 15(4): 437–52.

Ciotti, Manuela. 2007. 'Ethnohistories behind local and global bazaars: chronicle of a Chamar weaving community in the Banaras region.' *Contributions to Indian Sociology* 41(3): 321–54.

Clifford, Ruth. 2018. 'Balancing local tradition and global influences: design and business education for traditional artisans in Kachchh, India.' In *The Social Fabric: Deep Local to Pan Global; Proceedings of the Textile Society of America 16th Biennial Symposium*. Presented in Vancouver, BC, 19–23 September 2018. https://digitalcommons.unl.edu/tsaconf/ (accessed 22 August 2019).

Coles, Anne, and Katie Walsh. 2010. 'From "trucial state" to "postcolonial" city? The imaginative geographies of British expatriates in Dubai.' *Journal of Ethnic and Migration Studies* 36(8): 1317–33.

Comaroff, John L. and Jean Comaroff. 1992. *Ethnography and the Historical Imagination*. Boulder, CO: Westview Press.

Conlon, Deirdre. 2011. 'Waiting: feminist perspectives on the spacings/timings of migrant (im)mobility.' *Gender, Place & Culture* 18(3): 353–60.

Cons, Jason. 2013. 'Narrating boundaries: framing and contesting suffering, community, and belonging in enclaves along the India–Bangladesh border.' *Political Geography* 35: 37–46.

Contractor, Qudsiya. 2012. '"Unwanted in my city": the making of a "Muslim slum" in Mumbai.' In *Muslims in Indian Cities: Trajectories of Marginalisation*, edited by Laurent Gayer and Christophe Jaffrelot, 23–42. London: Hurst.

Cross, Jamie. 2010. 'Neoliberalism as unexceptional: economic zones and the everyday precariousness of working life in South India.' *Critique of Anthropology* 30(4): 355–73.

Cross, Jamie. 2014. *Dream Zones: Anticipating Capitalism and Development in India*. London: Pluto Press.

Crossick, Geoffrey, ed. 2016. *The Artisan and the European Town, 1500–1900*. Abingdon: Routledge.

Cunningham, Anthony, Bruce Campbell and Brian Belcher, eds. 2005. *Carving Out a Future: Forests, Livelihoods and the International Woodcarving Trade*. London: Earthscan.

Cwerner, Saulo B. 2001. 'The times of migration.' *Journal of Ethnic and Migration Studies* 27(1): 7–36.

Daehnhardt, Madleina. 2019. *Migration, Development and Social Change in the Himalayas: An Ethnographic Village Study*. Abingdon: Routledge.

Das, Maitreyi Bordia. 2005. 'Self-employed or unemployed: Muslim women's low labor-force participation in India.' In *The Diversity of Muslim Women's Lives in India*, edited by Zoya Hasan and Ritu Menon, 170–203. New Brunswick, NJ: Rutgers University Press.

Das, Runa. 2006. 'Encountering Hindutva, interrogating religious nationalism and (en)gendering a Hindu patriarchy in India's nuclear policies: ordering, bordering and othering.' *International Feminist Journal of Politics* 8(3): 370–93.

Das, Veena, and Deborah Poole. 2004. 'State and its margins: comparative ethnographies.' In *Anthropology in the Margins of the State*, edited by Veena Das and Deborah Poole, 3–33. Santa Fe, NM: School of American Research Press.

Das Gupta, Monica. 1995. 'Life course perspectives on women's autonomy and health outcomes.' *American Anthropologist* (n.s.) 97(3): 481–91.

Das Gupta, Ranajit. 1992. 'Plantation labour in colonial India.' *Journal of Peasant Studies* 19(3–4): 173–98.

Davis, Mike. 2006. *Planet of Slums*. London: Verso.

De Haan, Arjan and Ben Rogaly. 2002. 'Introduction: migrant workers and their role in rural change.' *Journal of Development Studies* 38(5): 1–14.

De Haas, Hein. 2010. 'Migration and development: a theoretical perspective 1.' *International Migration Review* 44(1): 227–64.

Demetriou, Olga. 2013. *Capricious Borders: Minority, Population, and Counter-Conduct between Greece and Turkey*. New York: Berghahn Books.

De Neve, Geert. 1999. 'Asking for and giving baki: neo-bondage, or the interplay of bondage and resistance in the Tamilnadu power-loom industry.' *Contributions to Indian Sociology* 33(1–2): 379–406.

De Neve, Geert. 2005. *The Everyday Politics of Labour: Working Lives in India's Informal Economy*. Delhi: Social Science Press.

De Neve, Geert. 2008. '"We are all *sondukarar* (relatives)!": kinship and its morality in an urban industry of Tamilnadu, South India.' *Modern Asian Studies* 42(1): 211–46.

De Neve, Geert. 2014a. 'Entrapped entrepreneurship: labour contractors in the South Indian garment industry.' *Modern Asian Studies* 48(5): 1302–33.

De Neve, Geert. 2014b. 'Fordism, flexible specialization and CSR: how Indian garment workers critique neoliberal labour regimes.' *Ethnography* 15(2): 184–207.

De Neve, Geert, and Henrike Donner, eds. 2007. *The Meaning of the Local: Politics of Place in Urban India*. Abingdon: Routledge.

DeNicola, Lane. 2016. 'Forging source: considering the craft of computer programming.' In *Critical Craft: Technology, Globalization, and Capitalism*, edited by Clare M. Wilkinson-Weber and Alicia Ory DeNicola, 35–56. London: Bloomsbury Academic.

Desai, Amit. 2012. 'A matter of affection: ritual friendship in central India.' In *The Ways of Friendship: Anthropological Perspectives*, edited by Amit Desai and Evan Killick, 114–32. New York: Berghahn Books.

Desai, Amit, and Evan Killick, eds. 2010. *The Ways of Friendship: Anthropological Perspectives*. New York: Berghahn Books.

De Soto, Hernando. 1989. *The Other Path: The Invisible Revolution in the Third World*. New York: Harper & Row.

Dilley, Roy. 1999. 'Ways of knowing, forms of power: aspects of apprenticeship among Tukulor Mabube weavers.' *Cultural Dynamics* 11(1): 33–55.

Dolan, Catherine, and Dinah Rajak. 2016. 'Remaking Africa's informal economies: youth, entrepreneurship and the promise of inclusion at the bottom of the pyramid.' *Journal of Development Studies* 52(4): 514–29.

Donini, Antonio. 2019. 'Social suffering and structural violence: Nepali workers in Qatar.' *International Development Policy/Revue international de politique de développement* 11: 178–99. http://journals.openedition.org/poldev/3077 (accessed 3 December 2019).

Donnan, Hastings, and Dieter Haller. 2000. 'Liminal no more: the relevance of borderland studies.' *Ethnologia Europaea* 30(2): 7–22.

Donner, Henrike. 2008. *Domestic Goddesses: Maternity, Globalization and Middle-class Identity in Contemporary India*. Aldershot: Ashgate.

Donner, Henrike, and Geert De Neve. 2011. 'Introduction.' In *Being Middle-Class in India: A Way of Life*, edited by Henrike Donner, 1–22. Abingdon: Routledge.

Dorsey, James M. 2014. 'The 2022 World Cup: a potential monkey wrench for change.' *International Journal of the History of Sport* 31(14): 1739–54.

Drori, Israel. 2000. *The Seam Line: Arab Workers and Israeli Managers in the Israeli Textile Industry*. Stanford, CA: Stanford University Press.

Dubey, Amaresh, Wendy Olsen and Kunal Sen. 2017. 'The decline in the labour force participation of rural women in India: taking a long-run view.' *Indian Journal of Labour Economics* 60(4): 589–612.

Dumont, Louis. 1980. *Homo Hierarchicus: The Caste System and Its Implications*. Chicago: University of Chicago Press.

Dyson, Jane. 2010. 'Friendship in practice: girls' work in the Indian Himalayas.' *American Ethnologist* 37(3): 482–98.

Eickelman, Dale F., and James Piscatori, eds. 1990. *Muslim Travellers: Pilgrimage, Migration and the Religious Imagination*. London: Routledge.

Elias, Ana Sofia, Rosalind Gill and Christina Scharff. 2017. 'Aesthetic labour: beauty politics in neoliberalism.' In *Aesthetic Labour: Rethinking Beauty Politics in Neoliberalism*, edited by Ana Sofia Elias, Rosalind Gill and Christina Scharff, 3–49. London: Palgrave Macmillan.

El-Said, Hamed, and Jane Harrigan. 2009. '"You reap what you plant": social networks in the Arab world – the Hashemite Kingdom of Jordan.' *World Development* 37(7): 1235–49.

Elson, Diane, and Ruth Pearson. 1981. '"Nimble fingers make cheap workers": an analysis of women's employment in third world export manufacturing.' *Feminist Review* 7(1): 87–107.

Elyachar, Julia. 2003. 'Mappings of power: the state, NGOs, and international organizations in the informal economy of Cairo.' *Comparative Studies in Society and History* 45(3): 571–605.

Elyachar, Julia. 2005. *Markets of Dispossession: NGOs, Economic Development, and the State in Cairo*. Durham, NC: Duke University Press.

Elyachar, Julia. 2010. 'Phatic labor, infrastructure, and the question of empowerment in Cairo.' *American Ethnologist* 37(3): 452–64.

Engels, Friedrich. 2007 [1845]. *The Condition of the Working-Class in England in 1844*. Gloucester: Dodo Press.

Engineer, Asghar Ali. 1995. 'Communalism and communal violence in 1995.' *Economic and Political Weekly* 30(51): 3267–69.

Engineer, Irfan. 2018. 'Indian Muslims: political leadership, mobilisation and violence.' In *Lives of Muslims in India: Politics, Exclusions and Violence*, edited by Abdul Shaban, 107–30. Delhi: Routledge India.

Epstein, Stephan R. 2008. 'Craft guilds in the pre-modern economy: a discussion.' *Economic History Review* 61(1): 155–74.

Fazal, Shahab. 2000. 'Urban expansion and loss of agricultural land: a GIS based study of Saharanpur City, India.' *Environment and Urbanization* 12(2): 133–49.

Fechter, Anne-Meike, and Katie Walsh. 2010. 'Examining "expatriate" continuities: postcolonial approaches to mobile professionals.' *Journal of Ethnic and Migration Studies* 36(8): 1197–1210.

Feener, R. Michael, and Terenjit Sevea, eds. 2009. *Islamic Connections: Muslim Societies in South and Southeast Asia*. Singapore: Institute of Southeast Asian Studies.

Ferguson, James. 1999. *Expectations of Modernity: Myths and Meanings of Urban Life on the Zambian Copperbelt*. Berkeley: University of California Press.

Ferguson, James, and Akhil Gupta. 2002. 'Spatializing states: toward an ethnography of neoliberal governmentality.' *American Ethnologist* 29(4): 981–1002.

Fernandez, Bina. 2014. 'Degrees of (un)freedom: the exercise of agency by Ethiopian migrant domestic workers in Kuwait and Lebanon.' In *Migrant Domestic Workers in the Middle East: The Home and the World*, edited by Bina Fernandez and Marina de Regt, 51–74. New York: Palgrave Macmillan.

Fernandez, James W. 1982. *Bwiti: An Ethnography of the Religious Imagination in Africa*. Princeton, NJ: Princeton University Press.

Foucault, M. 2008. *The Birth of Biopolitics: Lectures at the Collège de France, 1978–1979*, edited by Michel Senellart, translated by Graham Burchell. Basingstoke: Palgrave Macmillan.

Frantz, Elizabeth. 2013. 'Jordan's unfree workforce: state-sponsored bonded labour in the Arab region.' *Journal of Development Studies* 49(8): 1072–87.

Freeman, Carla. 2014. *Entrepreneurial Selves: Neoliberal Respectability and the Making of a Caribbean Middle Class*. Durham, NC: Duke University Press.

Fumanti, Mattia. 2016. *The Politics of Distinction: African Elites from Colonialism to Liberation in a Namibian Frontier Town*. Canon Pyon: Sean Kingston Publishing.

Gadgil, Dhanannjaya Ramchandra. 2013 [1929]. *The Industrial Evolution of India in Recent Times*. Oxford: Oxford University Press (reprinted by Nabu Press, Charleston, SC).

Gadihoke, Sabeena. 2011. 'Sensational love scandals and their after-lives: the epic tale of Nanavati.' *BioScope: South Asian Screen Studies* 2(2): 103–218.

Gallo, Ester. 2016. 'In the right place at the right time? Reflections on multi-sited ethnography in the age of migration.' In *Multi-Sited Ethnography: Theory, Praxis and Locality in Contemporary Research*, edited by Mark-Anthony Falzon, 87–102. Abingdon: Routledge.

Galonnier, Juliette. 2012. 'Aligarh: Sir Syed Nagar and Shah Jamal, contrasted tales of a "Muslim" city.' In *Muslims in Indian Cities: Trajectories of Marginalisation*, edited by Laurent Gayer and Christophe Jaffrelot, 129–58. London: Hurst.

Gamburd, Michele Ruth. 2000. *The Kitchen Spoon's Handle: Transnationalism and Sri Lanka's Migrant Housemaids*. Ithaca, NY: Cornell University Press.

Gandhi, Ajay. 2011. 'Crowds, congestion, conviviality: the enduring life of the old city.' In *A Companion to the Anthropology of India*, edited by Isabelle Clark-Decès, 202–222. Oxford: Wiley-Blackwell.

Gaonkar, Dilip Parameshwar. 2002. 'Toward new imaginaries: an introduction.' *Public Culture* 14(1): 1–19.

Gardner, Andrew. 2010. *City of Strangers: Gulf Migration and the Indian Community in Bahrain*. Ithaca, NY: ILR Press.

Gardner, Andrew. 2018. 'Reflections on the role of law in the Gulf migration system.' *Journal of Legal Studies* 47(S1): S129–S147.

Gardner, Andrew, Silvia Pessoa, Abdoulaye Diop, Kaltham Al-Ghanim, Kien Le Trung and Laura Harkness. 2013. 'A portrait of low-income migrants in contemporary Qatar.' *Journal of Arabian Studies* 3(1): 1–17.

Gardner, Katy. 2002. *Age, Narrative and Migration: The Life Course and Life Histories of Bengali Elders in London*. Oxford: Berg.

Gardner, Katy. 2018. 'We demand work! "Dispossession", patronage and village labour in Bibiyana, Bangladesh.' *Journal of Peasant Studies* 45(7): 1484–1500.

Gardner, Katy, and Filippo Osella. 2003. 'Migration, modernity and social transformation in South Asia: an overview.' *Contributions to Indian Sociology* (n.s.) 37(1–2): v–xxviii.

Gayer, Laurent, and Christophe Jaffrelot, eds. 2012. *Muslims in Indian Cities: Trajectories of Marginalisation*. London: Hurst.

Geertz, Clifford. 1978. 'The bazaar economy: information and search in peasant marketing.' *American Economic Review* 68(2): 28–32.

Genc, Ismail H., and George Naufal. 2018. 'Outward remittances from the Gulf.' In *South Asian Migration in the Gulf: Causes and Consequences*, edited by Mehdi Chowdhury and S. Irudaya Rajan, 143–64. Basingstoke: Palgrave Macmillan.

Gibson, Chris. 2016. 'Material inheritances: how place, materiality, and labor process underpin the path-dependent evolution of contemporary craft production.' *Economic Geography* 92(1): 61–86.

Gidwani, Vinay, and Kalyanakrishnan Sivaramakrishnan. 2003. 'Circular migration and rural cosmopolitanism in India.' *Contributions to Indian Sociology* 37(1–2): 339–67.

Gieser, Thorsten. 2008. 'Embodiment, emotion and empathy: a phenomenological approach to apprenticeship learning.' *Anthropological Theory* 8(3): 299–318.

Gill, Rosalind, and Andy Pratt. 2008. 'In the social factory? Immaterial labour, precariousness and cultural work.' *Theory, Culture & Society* 25(7–8): 1–30.

Glover, Judith, and Yvonne Guerrier. 2010. 'Women in hybrid roles in IT employment: a return to "nimble fingers"?' *Journal of Technology Management & Innovation* 5(1): 85–94.

Goitein, Shelomo D. 1971. 'Formal friendship in the medieval Near East.' *Proceedings of the American Philosophical Society* 115(6): 484–9.

Goodfriend, Douglas E. 1983. 'Changing concepts of caste and status among Old Delhi Muslims.' In *Modernization and Change among Muslims in India*, edited by Imtiaz Ahmad, 119–52. Delhi: Manohar.

Gooptu, Nandini. 2001. *The Politics of the Urban Poor in Early Twentieth-Century India*. Cambridge: Cambridge University Press.

Gooptu, Nandini. 2013. 'Introduction'. In *Enterprise Culture in Neoliberal India: Studies in Youth, Class, Work and Media*, edited by Nandini Gooptu, 1–24. Abingdon: Routledge.

Gooptu, Nandini. 2018. 'JSAD special issue on skill development in India: introduction.' *Journal of South Asian Development* 13(3): 241–8. https://journals.sagepub.com/doi/abs/10.1177/0973174118822391 (accessed 3 December 2019).

Gordon, Eleanor. 1987. 'Women, work and collective action: Dundee jute workers 1870–1906.' *Journal of Social History* 21(1): 27–47.

Gottschalk, Peter. 2005. *Beyond Hindu and Muslim: Multiple Identity in Narratives from Village India*. Oxford: Oxford University Press.

Govinda, Radhika. 2017. 'Different Dalit women speak differently: unravelling, through an intersectional lens, narratives of agency and activism from everyday life in rural Uttar Pradesh.' In *Dalit Women: Vanguard of an Alternative Politics in India*, edited by Shanmugasundaram Anandhi and Karin Kapadia, 218–244. Abingdon: Routledge.

Gowlland, Geoffrey. 2012. 'Learning craft skills in China: apprenticeship and social capital in an artisan community of practice.' *Anthropology & Education Quarterly* 43(4): 358–71.

Gowlland, Geoffrey. 2019. 'The sociality of enskilment.' *Ethnos* 84(3): 508–24.

Graeber, David. 2011. 'Consumption.' *Current Anthropology* 52(4): 489–511.

Granovetter, Mark. 1985. 'Economic action and social structure: the problem of embeddedness.' *American Journal of Sociology* 91(3): 481–510.

Green, Nile. 2011. *Bombay Islam: The Religious Economy of the West Indian Ocean, 1840–1915*. Cambridge: Cambridge University Press.

Griffiths, Melanie, Ali Rogers and Bridget Anderson. 2013. 'Migration, time and temporalities: review and prospect.' COMPAS Research Resources Paper (March).

Grover, Shalini. 2018. *Marriage, Love, Caste and Kinship Support: Lived Experiences of the Urban Poor in India*. Abingdon: Routledge.

Guérin, Isabelle. 2013. 'Bonded labour, agrarian changes and capitalism: emerging patterns in South India.' *Journal of Agrarian Change* 13(3): 405–23.

Guérin, Isabelle, G. Venkatasubramanian and S. Kumar. 2015. 'Debt bondage and the tricks of capital.' *Economic and Political Weekly* 50(26): 26–7.

Gupta, Akhil. 1995. 'Blurred boundaries: the discourse of corruption, the culture of politics, and the imagined state.' *American Ethnologist* 22(2): 375–402.

Gupta, Akhil. 2012. *Red Tape: Bureaucracy, Structural Violence, and Poverty in India*. Durham, NC: Duke University Press.

Gupta, Natalie. 2011. 'A story of (foretold) decline: artisan labour in India.' BWPI Working Paper no. 156. http://hummedia.manchester.ac.uk/institutes/gdi/publications/workingpapers/bwpi/bwpi-wp-15611.pdf (accessed 2 July 2019).

Haakestad, Hedda, and Jon Horgen Friberg. 2017. 'Deskilling revisited: labour migration, neo-Taylorism and the degradation of craft work in the Norwegian construction industry.' *Economic and Industrial Democracy*, December. DOI: 0143831X17735671.

Hadjimichalis, Costis. 2006. 'The end of Third Italy as we know it?' *Antipode* 38(1): 82–106.

Hage, Ghassan. 2005. 'A not so multi-sited ethnography of a not so imagined community.' *Anthropological Theory* 5(4): 463–75.

Hage, Ghassan. 2010. 'Migration, food, memory, and home-building.' In *Memory: Histories, Theories, Debates*, edited by Susannah Radstone and Bill Schwarz, 416–27. New York: Fordham University Press.

Halfacree, Keith. 2004. 'A utopian imagination in migration's terra incognita? Acknowledging the non-economic worlds of migration decision-making.' *Population, Space and Place* 10(3): 239–53.

Hāṇḍā, Omacanda, and Madhu Jain. 2000. *Wood Handicraft: A Study of Its Origin and Development in Saharanpur*. New Delhi: Indus Publishing

Hansen, Thomas Blom. 1996. 'Recuperating masculinity: Hindu nationalism, violence and the exorcism of the Muslim "other."' *Critique of Anthropology* 16(2): 137–72.

Hansen, Thomas Blom. 2014. 'Migration, religion and post-imperial formations.' *Global Networks* 14(3): 273–90.

Hanson, Kobena. 2005. 'Vulnerability, partnerships and the pursuit of survival: urban livelihoods and apprenticeship contracts in a West African city.' *GeoJournal* 62(1–2): 163–79.

Hardt, Michael, and Antonio Negri. 2000. *Empire*. Cambridge, MA: Harvard University Press.

Harman, Sally. 1977. *Plight of Muslims in India*, 2nd edn. London: DL Publications.

Harris, John R., and Michael P. Todaro. 1970. 'Migration, unemployment and development: a two-sector analysis.' *American Economic Review* 60(1): 126–42.

Harriss-White, Barbara. 2001. 'Development and productive deprivation: male patriarchal relations in business families and their implications for women in S. India.' Queen Elizabeth House Working Paper no. 65, Oxford University.

Harriss-White, Barbara. 2002. 'India's religious pluralism and its implications for the economy.' Queen Elizabeth House Working Paper no. 82, Oxford University.

Harriss-White, Barbara. 2003. *India Working: Essays on Society and Economy*. Cambridge: Cambridge University Press.

Harriss-White, B. 2005. 'Commercialisation, commodification and gender relations in post-harvest systems for rice in South Asia.' *Economic and Political Weekly* 40(25): 2530–42.

Harriss-White, Barbara, and Nandini Gooptu. 2009. 'Mapping India's world of unorganized labour.' In *Working Classes, Global Realities. Socialist Register 2001*, edited by Leo Panitch and Colin Leys, 89–118. London: Merlin.

Hart, Keith. 1973. 'Informal income opportunities and urban employment in Ghana.' *Journal of Modern African Studies* 11(1): 61–89.

Harvey, David. 2000. 'Cosmopolitanism and the banality of geographical evils.' *Public Culture* 12(2): 529–64.

Harvey, Penny, Casper Bruun Jensen and Atsuro Morita. 2017. 'Introduction: infrastructural complications.' In *Infrastructures and Social Complexity: A Companion*, edited by Penny Harvey, Casper Bruun Jensen and Atsuro Morita, 1–22. Abingdon: Routledge.

Harvey, Penny, and Christian Krohn-Hansen. 2018. 'Introduction. Dislocating labour: anthropological reconfigurations.' *Journal of the Royal Anthropological Institute* 24(S1): 10–28.

Hasan, Mushirul. 2008. *Moderate or Militant: Images of India's Muslims*. Oxford: Oxford University Press.

Hasan, Mushirul. 2018. *Legacy of a Divided Nation: India's Muslims from Independence to Ayodhya*. Abingdon: Routledge.

Hasan, Zoya, and Ritu Menon, eds. 2005. *The Diversity of Muslim Women's Lives in India*. New Brunswick, NJ: Rutgers University Press.

Haynes, Douglas E. 2001. 'Artisan cloth-producers and the emergence of powerloom manufacture in Western India 1920–1950.' *Past & Present* 172(1): 170–98.

Haynes, Douglas E. 2012. *Small Town Capitalism in Western India: Artisans, Merchants and the Making of the Informal Economy, 1870–1960*. Cambridge: Cambridge University Press.

Haynes, Douglas E., and Tirthankar Roy. 1999. 'Conceiving mobility: weavers' migrations in pre-colonial and colonial India.' *Indian Economic & Social History Review* 36(1): 35–67.

Headlines Today. 2009. 'Ghost of black cat spreads terror.' 2 September. http://origin-headlinestoday.intoday.in/programme/Ghost%20of%20black%20cat%20spreads%20terror/1/59761.html (accessed 3 April 2013).

Heitmeyer, Carolyn M. 2009a. 'Identity and difference in a Muslim community in central Gujarat, India following the 2002 communal violence.' PhD thesis, London School of Economics and Political Science.

Heitmeyer, Carolyn. 2009b. '"There is peace here": managing communal relations in a town in central Gujarat.' *Journal of South Asian Development* 4(1): 103–20.

Heller, Monica, Sari Pietikäinen and Emanuel da Silva. 2017. 'Body, nature, language: artisans to artists in the commodification of authenticity.' *Anthropologica* 59(1): 114–29.

Herzfeld, Michael. 2004. *The Body Impolitic: Artisans and Artifice in the Global Hierarchy of Value*. Chicago: University of Chicago Press.

Herzfeld, Michael. 2005. 'Political optics and the occlusion of intimate knowledge.' *American Anthropologist* 107(3): 369–76.

Herzfeld, M. 2007. 'Deskilling, "dumbing down" and the auditing of knowledge in the practical mastery of artisans and academics: an ethnographer's response to a global problem.' In *Ways of Knowing: Anthropological Approaches to Crafting Experience and Knowledge*, edited by Mark Harris, 91–110. Oxford: Berghahn Books.

Ho, Karen. 2009. *Liquidated: An Ethnography of Wall Street*. Durham, NC: Duke University Press.

Hochschild, Arlie Russell. 2012. *The Managed Heart: Commercialization of Human Feeling*. Berkeley: University of California Press.

Holmes, Helen. 2015. 'Transient craft: reclaiming the contemporary craft worker.' *Work, Employment and Society* 29(3): 479–95.

Holmström, Mark. 1999. 'A new map of Indian industrial society: the cartographer all at sea.' *Oxford Development Studies* 27(2): 165–86.

Horner, Rory, and James T. Murphy. 2018. 'South–North and South–South production networks: diverging socio-spatial practices of Indian pharmaceutical firms.' *Global Networks* 18(2): 326–51.

Horstmann, Alexander. 2007. 'The inculturation of a transnational Islamic missionary movement: Tablighi Jamaat al-Dawa and Muslim society in Southern Thailand.' *Sojourn: Journal of Social Issues in Southeast Asia* 22(1): 107–30.

Hussain, Aamir. 2016. 'Protection and promotion of traditional crafts and occupations in globalising India: a case study of weavers of Mau (Uttar Pradesh).' *International Journal of Research in Social Sciences* 6(9): 323–38.

India Today. 2015. 'Rags to riches: 7 Indian personalities who never gave up', 21 September. http://indiatoday.intoday.in/education/story/rags-to-riches/1/476147.html (accessed 3 January 2017).

Ingold, Tim. 2000. *The Perception of the Environment: Essays on Livelihood, Dwelling and Skill*. London: Routledge.

Ingold, Tim. 2013. 'Dreaming of dragons: on the imagination of real life.' *Journal of the Royal Anthropological Institute* 19(4): 734–52.

Ismail, Salwa. 2013. 'Piety, profit and the market in Cairo: a political economy of Islamisation.' *Contemporary Islam* 7(1): 107–28.

Jaffrelot, Christophe, and Charlotte Thomas. 2012. 'Facing ghettoisation in "Riot-city": old Ahmedabad and Juhapura between victimisation and self-help.' In *Muslims in Indian Cities: Trajectories of Marginalisation*, edited by Laurent Gayer and Christophe Jaffrelot, 43–80. London: Hurst.

Jain, Prakash C. 2016. 'In search of El Dorado: Indian labour migration to Gulf countries.' In *South Asian Migration to Gulf Countries: History, Policies, Development*, edited by Prakash C. Jain and Ginu Zacharia Oommen, 123–40. Abingdon: Routledge.

Jain, Prakash C., and Ginu Zacharia Oommen, eds. 2016. *South Asian Migration to Gulf Countries: History, Policies, Development*. Abingdon: Routledge.

Jamil, Ghazala. 2017. *Accumulation by Segregation: Muslim Localities in Delhi*. New Delhi: Oxford University Press.

Janson, Marloes. 2006. 'The Prophet's path: Tablighi Jamaat in The Gambia.' *ISIM Review* 17(1): 44–5.

Janson, Marloes. 2014. *Islam, Youth, and Modernity in the Gambia: The Tablighi Jama'at*. New York: Cambridge University Press.

Jasani, Rubina. 2008. 'Violence, reconstruction and Islamic reform: stories from the Muslim "ghetto".' *Modern Asian Studies* 42(2–3): 431–56.

Jeffery, Patricia. 1979. *Frogs in a Well: Indian Women in Purdah*. London: Zed Press.

Jeffery, Patricia, Roger Jeffery and Craig Jeffrey. 2005. 'The mother's lap and the civilizing mission: madrasa education and rural Muslim girls in western Uttar Pradesh.' In *The Diversity of Muslim Women's Lives in India*, edited by Zoya Hasan and Ritu Menon, 91–134. New Brunswick, NJ: Rutgers University Press.

Jeffrey, Craig. 2010. *Timepass: Youth, Class, and the Politics of Waiting in India*. Stanford, CA: Stanford University Press.

Jeffrey, Craig and Jane Dyson. 2016. 'Now: prefigurative politics through a north Indian lens.' *Economy and Society* 45(1): 77–100.

Jeffrey, Craig, Patricia Jeffery and Roger Jeffery. 2004. '"A useless thing!" or "nectar of the gods?" The cultural production of education and young men's struggles for respect in liberalizing north India.' *Annals of the Association of American Geographers* 94(4): 961–81.

Johnson, Mark, and Johan Lindquist. 2019. 'Care and control in Asian migrations.' *Ethnos*. Online. DOI: 10.1080/00141844.2018.1543342.

Johnson, Mark, and Pnina Werbner. 2010. 'Diasporic encounters, sacred journeys: ritual, normativity and the religious imagination among international Asian migrant women.' *Asia Pacific Journal of Anthropology* 11(3–4): 205–18.

Joshi, Chitra. 1999. 'Hope and despair: textile workers in Kanpur in 1937–38 and the 1990s.' *Contributions to Indian Sociology* 33(1–2): 171–203.

Jureidini, Ray. 2010. 'Trafficking and contract migrant workers in the Middle East.' *International Migration* 48(4): 142–63.

Kabeer, Naila. 2000. *The Power to Choose: Bangladeshi Women and Labour Market Decisions in London and Dhaka*. New York: Verso.

Kabir, Nahid Afrose. 2010. *Young British Muslims: Identity, Culture, Politics and the Media: Identity, Culture, Politics and the Media*. Edinburgh: Edinburgh University Press.

Kanna, Ahmed. 2011. *Dubai, the City as Corporation*. Minneapolis: University of Minnesota Press.

Kantor, Paula. 2002. 'Female mobility in India: the influence of seclusion norms on economic outcomes.' *International Development Planning Review* 24(2): 145–59.

Kathiravelu, Laavanya, and Tim Bunnell. 2018. 'Introduction: Urban friendship networks: affective negotiations and potentialities of care.' *Urban Studies* 55(3): 491–504.

Kerr, Ian J. 2006. 'On the move: circulating labor in pre-colonial, colonial, and post-colonial India.' *International Review of Social History* 51(S14): 85–109.

Kelly, Saul. 2013. '"Crazy in the extreme"? The silk letters conspiracy.' *Middle Eastern Studies* 49(2): 162–78.

Khan, Sameera. 2007. 'Negotiating the mohalla: exclusion, identity and Muslim women in Mumbai.' *Economic and Political Weekly* 42(17): 1527–33.

Khan, Yasmin. 2003. 'The arrival impact of Partition refugees in Uttar Pradesh, 1947–52.' *Contemporary South Asia* 12(4): 511–22.

Killick, Evan. 2010. '*Ayompari, compadre, amigo*: forms of fellowship in Peruvian Amazonia.' In *The Ways of Friendship: Anthropological Perspectives*, edited by Amit Desai and Evan Killick, 46–68. New York: Berghahn Books.

Kirsch, Stuart. 2016. 'Virtuous language in industry and the academy.' In *The Anthropology of Corporate Social Responsibility*, edited by Catherine Dolan and Dinah Rajak, 48–66. Oxford: Berghahn Books.

Klasen, Stephan, and Janneke Pieters. 2015. 'What explains the stagnation of female labor force participation in urban India?' World Bank Policy Research Paper no. 7222.

Knorringa, Peter. 1999. 'Agra: an old cluster facing the new competition.' *World Development* 27(9): 1587–1604.

Kodoth, Praveena, and Vekkal J. Varghese. 2012. 'Protecting women or endangering the emigration process: emigrant women domestic workers, gender and state policy.' *Economic and Political Weekly* 47(43): 56–66.

Kollmair, Michael, Siddhi Manandhar, Bhim Subedi and Susan Thieme. 2006. 'New figures for old stories: migration and remittances in Nepal.' *Migration Letters* 3(2): 151–60.

Kudaisya, Gyanesh. 2006. *Region, Nation, 'Heartland': Uttar Pradesh in India's Body Politic*. New Delhi: SAGE Publications.

Kudva, Neema. 2009. 'The everyday and the episodic: the spatial and political impacts of urban informality.' *Environment and Planning A* 41(7): 1614–28.

Kumar, Nita. 2017. *The Artisans of Banaras: Popular Culture and Identity, 1880–1986*. Princeton, NJ: Princeton University Press.

Kundu, Amitabh. 2018. 'Mobility in India: recent trends and issues concerning database.' *Social Change* 48(4): 634–44.

Kuran, Timur. 2004. *Islam and Mammon: The Economic Predicaments of Islamism*. Princeton, NJ: Princeton University Press.

Latour, Bruno. 2012. *We Have Never Been Modern*, translated by Catherine Porter. Cambridge, MA: Harvard University Press.

Lefebvre, Henri. 1991. *The Production of Space*, translated by Donald Nicholson-Smith. Oxford: Blackwell.

Lerche, Jens. 2007. 'A global alliance against forced labour? Unfree labour, neo-liberal globalization and the International Labour Organization.' *Journal of Agrarian Change* 7(4): 425–52.

Lerche, Jens, Alessandra Mezzadri, Dae-Oup Chang, Pun Ngai, Huilin Lu, Aiyu Liu and Ravi Srivastava. 2017. 'The triple absence of labour rights: triangular labour relations and informalisation in the construction and garment sectors in Delhi and Shanghai.' Working Paper no. 32/17, Centre for Development Policy and Research, SOAS, University of London. https://www.soas.ac.uk/cdpr/publications/workingpoor/file118684.pdf (accessed 4 December 2019).

Levitt, Peggy, Josh DeWind and Steven Vertovec. 2003. 'International perspectives on transnational migration: an introduction.' *International Migration Review* 37(3): 565–75.

Levitt, Peggy, and B. Nadya Jaworsky. 2007. 'Transnational migration studies: past developments and future trends.' *Annual Revew of Sociology* 33(1): 129–56.

Lindell, Ilda. 2010. 'Informality and collective organising: identities, alliances and transnational activism in Africa.' *Third World Quarterly* 31(2): 207–22.

Lindquist, Johan. 2012. 'The elementary school teacher, the thug and his grandmother: informal brokers and transnational migration from Indonesia.' *Pacific Affairs* 85(1): 69–89.

Lindquist, Johan. 2017. 'Brokers, channels, infrastructure: moving migrant labor in the Indonesian-Malaysian oil palm complex.' *Mobilities* 12(2): 213–26.

Lindquist, Johan. 2018. 'Infrastructures of escort: transnational migration and economies of connection in Indonesia.' *Indonesia* 105: 77–95.

Longva, Anh Nga. 2019. *Walls Built on Sand: Migration, Exclusion, and Society in Kuwait*. London: Routledge.

Low, Setha M. 1996. 'The anthropology of cities: imagining and theorizing the city.' *Annual Review of Anthropology* 25: 383–409.

Lowrie, Ian. 2018. 'Algorithms and automation: an introduction.' *Cultural Anthropology* 33(3): 349–59.

Madnī, Sayyid Ḥusain Aḥmad. 2005 [1938]. *Composite Nationalism and Islam* (Muttahidah qaumiyat aur Islam), translated [from the Urdu] by Mohammad Anwer Hussain. New Delhi: Manohar.

Mahdavi, Pardis. 2016. *Crossing the Gulf: Love and Family in Migrant Lives*. Stanford, CA: Stanford University Press.

Mahmood, Saba. 2012. *Politics of Piety: The Islamic Revival and the Feminist Subject*. Princeton, NJ: Princeton University Press.

Majumdar, Shruti. 2017. 'In "juridical limbo": urban governance and subaltern legalities among squatters in Calcutta, India.' *Hague Journal on the Rule of Law* 9(1): 83–108.

Malhotra, Neena, and Pushpa Devi. 2016. 'Analysis of factors affecting internal migration in India.' *Amity Journal of Economics* 1(2): 34–51.

Malinowski, Bronislaw. 1920. 'Kula: the circulating exchange of valuables in the archipelagoes of Eastern New Guinea.' *Man* 20: 97–105.

Malit, Froilan T., Mouawiya Al Awad and George Naufal. 2017. 'More than a criminal tool: the Hawala system's role as a critical remittance channel for low-income Pakistani migrants in Dubai.' *Remittances Review* 2(2): 63–88.

Mankekar, Purnima. 2015. *Unsettling India: Affect, Temporality, Transnationality*. Durham, NC: Duke University Press.

Mann, Elizabeth A. 1992. *Boundaries and Identities: Muslims, Work and Status in Aligarh*. Newbury Park, CA: SAGE Publications.

Manseau, Gwenann S. 2007. 'Contractual solutions for migrant labourers: the case of domestic workers in the Middle East.' *Human Rights Law Commentary* 3: 25–47.

Marchand, Trevor H. J. 2008. 'Muscles, morals and mind: craft apprenticeship and the formation of person.' *British Journal of Educational Studies* 56(3): 245–71.

Marchand, Trevor H. J. 2010. 'Making knowledge: explorations of the indissoluble relation between minds, bodies, and environment.' *Journal of the Royal Anthropological Institute* 16 (S1): S1–S21.

Marchand, Trevor H. J. 2013. *Minaret Building and Apprenticeship in Yemen*. London: Routledge.

Marchand, Trevor H. J. 2015. 'Review of *African Children at Work: working and learning in growing up for life* by Gerd Spittler, Michael Bourdillon.' *Zeitschrift für Ethnologie* 140(2): 275–6.

Marcus, Alan P. 2009. 'Brazilian immigration to the United States and the geographical imagination.' *Geographical Review* 99(4): 481–98.

Marcus, George E. 1995. 'Ethnography in/of the world system: The emergence of multi-sited ethnography'. *Annual Review of Anthropology* 24(1): 95–117.

Marcus, George E. 2009. 'Multi-sited ethnography: notes and queries.' In *Multi-Sited Ethnography: Theory, Praxis, and Locality in Contemporary Research*, edited by Mark-Anthony Falzon, 181–96. Farnham: Ashgate.

Marsden, Magnus. 2005. *Living Islam: Muslim Religious Experience in Pakistan's North-West Frontier*. Cambridge: Cambridge University Press.

Marsden, Magnus. 2008. 'Muslim cosmopolitans? Transnational life in northern Pakistan.' *Journal of Asian Studies* 67(1): 213–47.

Marsden, Magnus, and Konstantinos Retsikas, eds. 2013. *Articulating Islam: Anthropological Approaches to Muslim Worlds*. London: Springer.

Marx, Karl. 1990 [1867]. *Capital: A Critique of Political Economy*, vol. 1, translated by Ben Fowkes. London: Penguin Classics.

Massey, Doreen. 1994. *Space, Place and Gender*. Cambridge: Polity Press.

Massey, Doreen. 2005. *For Space*. London: SAGE Publications.

Mathew, Leya. 2018. 'Aspiring and aspiration shaming: primary schooling, English, and enduring inequalities in liberalizing Kerala (India).' *Anthropology & Education Quarterly* 49(1): 72–88.

Mauss, Marcel. 2002. *The Gift: The Form and Reason for Exchange in Archaic Societies*. Abingdon: Routledge.

McLaughlin, Meredith. 2017. 'The politics of inclusivity: civic conduct among Hyderabadi Muslims.' *Contributions to Indian Sociology* 51(1): 25–51.

Meagher, Kate. 2006. 'Social capital, social liabilities, and political capital: social networks and informal manufacturing in Nigeria.' *African Affairs* 105(421): 553–82.

Mehta, Deepak. 1997. *Work, Ritual, Biography: A Muslim Community in North India*. Delhi: Oxford University Press.

Mellström, Ulf. 2017. *Masculinity, Power and Technology: A Malaysian Ethnography*. London: Routledge.

Metcalf, Barbara. 1978. 'The madrasa at Deoband: a model for religious education in modern India.' *Modern Asian Studies* 12(1): 111–34.

Metcalf, Barbara. 1984. 'Islamic reform and Islamic women: Maulānā Thānawī's *Jewelry of Paradise*.' In *Moral Conduct and Authority: The Place of Adab in South Asian Islam*, edited by Barbara Daly Metcalf, 184–95. Berkeley, Los Angeles, London: University of California Press.

Metcalf, Barbara Daly, ed. 1996. *Making Muslim Space in North America and Europe*. Berkeley and Los Angeles: University of California Press.

Metcalf, Barbara D. 1999. 'Nationalism, modernity, and Muslim identity in India before 1947.' In *Nation and Religion: Perspectives on Europe and Asia*, edited by Peter van der Veer and Hartmut Lehmann, 129–43. Princeton, NJ: Princeton University Press.

Metcalf, Barbara. 2003. 'Travelers' tales in the Tablighi Jamaat.' *Annals of the American Academy of Political and Social Science* 588(1): 136–48.

Metcalf, Barbara. 2007. 'Madrasas and minorities in secular India.' In *Schooling Islam: The Culture and Politics of Modern Muslim Education*, edited by Robert Hefner and Muhammad Qasim Zaman, 87–106. Princeton, NJ: Princeton University Press.

Metcalf, Barbara D. 2014. *Islamic Revival in British India: Deoband, 1860–1900*. Princeton, NJ: Princeton University Press.

Mezzadri, Alessandra. 2008. 'The rise of neo-liberal globalisation and the "new old" social regulation of labour: the case of Delhi garment sector.' *Indian Journal of Labour Economics* 51(4): 603–18.

Mezzadri, Alessandra. 2012. 'Reflections on globalisation and labour standards in the Indian garment industry: codes of conduct versus "codes of practice" imposed by the firm.' *Global Labour Journal* 3(1): 40–62.

Mezzadri, Alessandra. 2016. *The Sweatshop Regime: Labouring Bodies, Exploitation, and Garments Made in India*. New York: Cambridge University Press.

Miller, Daniel. 2005. *Materiality*. Durham, NC: Duke University Press.

Mills, Mary Beth. 1997. 'Contesting the margins of modernity: women, migration, and consumption in Thailand.' *American Ethnologist* 24(1): 37–61.

Mills, Mary Beth. 2017. 'Gendered morality tales: discourses of gender, labour, and value in globalising Asia.' *Journal of Development Studies* 53(3): 316–30.

Millward, Peter. 2017. 'World Cup 2022 and Qatar's construction projects: relational power in networks and relational responsibilities to migrant workers.' *Current Sociology* 65(5): 756–76.

Mines, Mattison. 1972. 'Muslim social stratification in India: the basis for variation.' *Southwestern Journal of Anthropology* 28(4): 333–49.

Ministry of External Affairs. [2019]. Annual Report 2018–19. http://www.mea.gov.in/Uploads/PublicationDocs/31719_MEA_AR18_19.pdf (accessed 28 December 2019).

Ministry of Overseas Indian Affairs. [2007]. Annual Report 2006–07. https://www.mea.gov.in/images/pdf/annual-report-2006–07.pdf (accessed 5 May 2018).

Ministry of Overseas Indian Affairs. [2015]. Annual Report 2014–15. https://www.mea.gov.in/images/pdf/annual-report-2014–15.pdf (accessed 5 May 2018).

Mishra, Deepak K., ed. 2016. *Internal Migration in Contemporary India*. New Delhi: SAGE Publications India.

Mishra, Swati. 2017. 'Recasting respectability: imagination, desire and modernity among call-center workers in India.' *Asian Journal of Women's Studies* 23(2): 203–23.

Misra, Bankey Bihari. 1961. *The Indian Middle Classes: Their Growth in Modern Times*. London: Oxford University Press.

Mittermaier, Amira. 2010. *Dreams that Matter: Egyptian Landscapes of the Imagination*. Berkeley: University of California Press.

Mohsini, Mira. 2010. 'Becoming an "Asli Karigar": the production of authenticity among old Delhi's Muslim artisans.' PhD thesis, School of Oriental and African Studies, University of London.

Mohsini, Mira. 2016. 'Crafting Muslim artisans: agency and exclusion in India's urban crafts communities.' In *Critical Craft: Technology, Globalization, and Capitalism*, edited by Clare M. Wilkinson-Weber and Alicia Ory DeNicola, 239–58. London: Bloomsbury Academic.

Mollona, Massimiliano. 2005. 'Gifts of labour: steel production and technological imagination in an area of urban deprivation, Sheffield, UK.' *Critique of Anthropology* 25(2): 177–98.

Mollona, Massimiliano. 2009. *Made in Sheffield: An Ethnography of Industrial Work and Politics*. Oxford: Berghahn Books.

Monsutti, Alessandro. 2007. 'Migration as a rite of passage: young Afghans building masculinity and adulthood in Iran.' *Iranian Studies* 40(2): 167–85.

Mookherjee, Nayanika. 2008. 'Culinary boundaries and the making of place in Bangladesh.' *South Asia: Journal of South Asian Studies* 31(1): 56–75.

Moreland, William Harrison. [1929] 2011. *The Agrarian System of Moslem India: A Historical Essay with Appendices*. Cambridge: Cambridge University Press.

Moreton, Bethany. 2009. *To Serve God and Wal-Mart: The Making of Christian Free Enterprise*. London: Harvard University Press.

Mosse, David, Sanjeev Gupta, Mona Mehta, Vidya Shah, Julia Rees and KRIBP Project Team. 2002. 'Brokered livelihoods: debt, labour migration and development in tribal western India.' *Journal of Development Studies* 38(5): 59–88.

Muhammad, Shan. 2002. *Education and Politics: From Sir Syed to the Present Day: The Aligarh School*. New Delhi: APH Publishing.

Mukherjee, Nandini, and Jhilam Ray. 2014. 'Are female headed households in distress? Recent evidence from Indian labour market.' Munich Personal RePEc Archive. https://mpra.ub.uni-muenchen.de/64490/ (accessed 21 March 2018).

Mukundan, Monisha. 1999. *The Carpenter's Apprentice: From Stories Published in Target Magazine, Selected by Vijaya Ghose*, edited by Rosalind Wilson. New Delhi: Katha.

Murphy, Rachel. 2000. 'Return migration, entrepreneurship and local state corporatism in rural China: the experience of two counties in south Jiangxi.' *Journal of Contemporary China* 9(24): 231–47.

Naidu, Sirisha C. 2016. 'Domestic labour and female labour force participation: adding a piece to the puzzle.' *Economic and Political Weekly* 51(44–5): 101–8.

Nakassis, Constantine V. 2013. 'Youth masculinity, "style" and the peer group in Tamil Nadu, India.' *Contributions to Indian Sociology* 47(2): 245–69.

Nandy, S. N. 2019. 'Development disparities in India: an inter-state and intra-state comparison.' *Journal of Land and Rural Studies* 7(2): 99–120.

Naqvi, Saeed. 2016. *Being the Other: The Muslim in India*. New Delhi: Aleph.

Narayana, M. R. 2006. 'Formal and informal enterprises: concept, definition, and measurement issues in India.' In *Linking the Formal and Informal Economy: Concepts and Policies*, edited by Basudeb Guha-Khasnobis, Ravi Kanbur and Elinor Ostrom, 93–118. Oxford: Oxford University Press.

Nash, June C., ed. 1993a. *Crafts in the World Market: The Impact of Global Exchange on Middle American Artisans*. Albany, NY: State University of New York Press.

Nash, June C. 1993b. *We Eat the Mines and the Mines Eat Us: Dependency and Exploitation in Bolivian Tin Mines*. New York: Columbia University Press.

Nasir, Sadaf. 2011. 'Social exclusion among Muslims: A case study of Aligarh lock industry.' *Journal of Exclusion Studies* 1(2): 94–100.

Nasr, Seyyed Hossein. 1990. *Islamic Art and Spirituality*. Oxford: Oxford University Press.

Naudé, Wim, Melissa Siegel and Katrin Marchand. 2015. 'Migration, entrepreneurship and development: a critical review.' IZA Discussion Paper no. 9284. https://ssrn.com/abstract=2655324 (accessed 14 March 2016).

Navaro-Yashin, Yael. 2012. *The Make-Believe Space: Affective Geography in a Postwar Polity*. Durham, NC: Duke University Press.

Nevill, H. R., ed. 1909. *Saharanpur: A Gazetteer, Being Volume II of the District Gazetteers of the United Provinces of Agra and Oudh*. Allahabad: Printed by F. Lukar, Supdt., Govt. Press, United Provinces. British Colonial Administration for the British Crown.

Nisbett, Nicholas. 2007. 'Friendship, consumption, morality: practising identity, negotiating hierarchy in middle-class Bangalore.' *Journal of the Royal Anthropological Institute* 13(4): 935–50.

Nowicka, Magdalena, and Steven Vertovec. 2014. 'Comparing convivialities: dreams and realities of living-with-difference.' *European Journal of Cultural Studies* 17(4): 341–56.

Office of the Registrar General & Census Commissioner, India. 2011. 2011 Census data. http://censusindia.gov.in/2011-Common/Archive.html (accessed 2 December 2019).

Ong, Aihwa. 1988. 'The production of possession: Spirits and the multinational corporation in Malaysia.' *American Ethnologist* 15(1): 28–42.

Ong, Aihwa. 1991. 'The gender and labor politics of postmodernity.' *Annual Review of Anthropology* 20: 279–309.

Ong, Aihwa. 2006. *Neoliberalism as Exception: Mutations in Citizenship and Sovereignty*. Durham, NC: Duke University Press.

Ong, Aihwa. 2010. *Spirits of Resistance and Capitalist Discipline: Factory Women in Malaysia*, 2nd edn. Albany, NY: State University of New York Press.

Ortner, Sherry B. 2005. 'Subjectivity and cultural critique.' *Anthropological Theory* 5(1): 31–52.

Osella, Caroline, and Filippo Osella. 1998. 'Friendship and flirting: micro-politics in Kerala, South India.' *Journal of the Royal Anthropological Institute* 4(2): 189–206.

Osella, Caroline, and Filippo Osella. 2008. 'Food, memory, community: Kerala as both "Indian Ocean" zone and as agricultural homeland.' *South Asia: Journal of South Asian Studies* 31(1): 170–98.

Osella, Caroline, and Filippo Osella. 2011. 'Migration, networks, and connectedness across the Indian Ocean.' In 'Migrant Labor in the Gulf', Summary Report. Center for International and Regional Studies, Georgetown University School of Foreign Service in Qatar, 10–11. https://eprints.soas.ac.uk/12410/1/eprints_osella_georgetown_qatar.pdf (accessed 25 February 2017).

Osella, Filippo. 2012. 'Malabar secrets: South Indian Muslim men's (homo)sociality across the Indian Ocean.' *Asian Studies Review* 36(4): 531–49.

Osella, Filippo. 2014. 'The (im)morality of mediation and patronage in south India and the Gulf.' In *Patronage as Politics in South Asia*, edited by Anastasia Piliavsky, 365–94. Cambridge: Cambridge University Press.

Osella, Filippo, and Caroline Osella. 2000. 'Migration, money and masculinity in Kerala.' *Journal of the Royal Anthropological Institute* 6(1): 117–33.

Osella, Filippo, and Caroline Osella. 2007. '"I am Gulf": the production of cosmopolitanism in Kozhikode, Kerala, India.' In *Struggling with History: Islam and Cosmopolitanism in the Western Indian Ocean*, edited by Edward Simpson and Kai Kresse, 323–355. London: Hurst.

Osella, Filippo, and Caroline Osella. 2008. 'Introduction: Islamic reformism in South Asia.' *Modern Asian Studies* 42(2–3): 247–57.

Osella, Filippo, and Caroline Osella. 2009. 'Muslim entrepreneurs in public life between India and the Gulf: making good and doing good.' *Journal of the Royal Anthropological Institute* 15(S1): S202–S221.

Osella, Filippo, and Caroline Osella. 2011. 'Migration, neoliberal capitalism, and Islamic reform in Kozhikode (Calicut), South India.' *International Labor and Working-Class History* 79(1): 140–60.

Osella, Filippo, and Caroline Osella, eds. 2013. *Islamic Reform in South Asia*. Cambridge: Cambridge University Press.

Ouellette, Laurie. 2017. 'Dream jobs? The glamourisation of beauty service work in media culture.' In *Aesthetic Labour: Rethinking Beauty Politics in Neoliberalism*, edited by Ana Sofia Elias, Rosalind Gill and Christina Scharff, 183–98. London: Palgrave Macmillan.

Oza, Rupal. 2012. *The Making of Neoliberal India: Nationalism, Gender, and the Paradoxes of Globalization*. London: Routledge.

Pahl, Ray. 2000. *On Friendship*. Cambridge: Polity.

Parker, Andrew. 2006. 'Lifelong learning to labour: apprenticeship, masculinity and communities of practice.' *British Educational Research Journal* 32(5): 687–701.

Parnell, Susan, and Edgar Pieterse. 2014. *Africa's Urban Revolution*. London: Zed Books.

Parreñas, Rhacel Salazar. 2005. *Children of Global Migration: Transnational Families and Gendered Woes*. Stanford, CA: Stanford University Press.

Parry, Jonathan P. 1999. 'Two cheers for reservation: the Satnamis and the steel plant.' In *Institutions and Inequalities: Essays in Honour of André Béteille*, edited by Ramachandra Guha and Jonathan P. Parry, 128–69. New Delhi: Oxford University Press.

Parry, Jonathan P. 2001. 'Ankalu's errant wife: sex, marriage and industry in contemporary Chhattisgarh.' *Modern Asian Studies* 35(4): 783–820.

Parry, Jonathan P. 2003. 'Nehru's dream and the village "waiting room": long-distance labour migrants to a central Indian steel town.' *Contributions to Indian Sociology* 37(1–2): 217–49.

Parry, Jonathan. 2008. 'Cosmopolitan values in a central Indian steel town.' In *Anthropology and the New Cosmopolitanism: Rooted, Feminist and Vernacular Perspectives*, edited by Pnina Werbner, 325–43. Oxford: Berg.

Parry, Jonathan. 2013. 'Company and contract labour in a central Indian steel plant.' *Economy and Society* 42(3): 348–74.

Pattisson, Pete. 2013. 'Revealed: Qatar's World Cup 'slaves'', *Guardian*, 25 September. https://www.theguardian.com/world/2013/sep/25/revealed-qatars-world-cup-slaves (accessed 6 December 2019).

Percot, Marie. 2006. 'Indian nurses in the Gulf: two generations of female migration.' *South Asia Research* 26(1): 41–62.

Perlin, Frank. 1983. 'Proto-industrialization and pre-colonial South Asia.' *Past & Present* 98: 30–95.

Pernau, Margrit. 2017. 'Love and compassion for the community: emotions and practices among North Indian Muslims, c. 1870–1930.' *Indian Economic & Social History Review* 54(1): 21–42.

Pessoa, Silvia, Laura Harkness and Andrew M. Gardner. 2014. 'Ethiopian labor migrants and the "free visa" system in Qatar.' *Human Organization* 73(3): 205–13.

Phillips, Nicola. 2013. 'Unfree labour and adverse incorporation in the global economy: comparative perspectives on Brazil and India.' *Economy and Society* 42(2): 171–96.

Phillips, Nicola, Resmi Bhaskaran, Dev Nathan and C. Upendranadh. 2011. 'Child labour in global production networks: poverty, vulnerability and "adverse incorporation" in the Delhi garments sector.' Chronic Poverty Research Centre Working Paper no. 177. http://www.chronicpoverty.org/uploads/publication_files/WP177%20Phillips%20et%20al.pdf (accessed 11 January 2020).

Picherit, David. 2012. 'Migrant labourers' struggles between village and urban migration sites: labour standards, rural development and politics in South India.' *Global Labour Journal* 3(1): 143–62.

Picherit, David. 2018. 'Rural youth and circulating labour in South India: the tortuous paths towards respect for Madigas.' *Journal of Agrarian Change* 18(1): 178–95.

Pigg, Stacy Leigh. 1995. 'The social symbolism of healing in Nepal.' *Ethnology* 34(1): 17–36.

Pitt-Rivers, Julian. 1973. 'The kith and the kin.' In *The Character of Kinship*, edited by Jack Goody, 89–105. Cambridge: Cambridge University Press.

Pitt-Rivers, Julian. 2016. 'The paradox of friendship.' *HAU: Journal of Ethnographic Theory* 6(3): 443–52.

Platt, Maria, Grace Baey, Brenda S. A. Yeoh, Choon Yen Khoo and Theodora Lam. 2017. 'Debt, precarity and gender: male and female temporary labour migrants in Singapore.' *Journal of Ethnic and Migration Studies* 43(1): 119–36.

Polanyi, Karl. 1968. *Primitive, Archaic, and Modern Economies: Essays of Karl Polanyi*, edited by George Dalton. Garden City, NY: Anchor Books.

Pollock, Sheldon, Homi K. Bhabha, Carol A. Breckenridge and Dipesh Chakrabarty. 2002. 'Cosmopolitanisms.' In *Cosmopolitanism*, edited by Carol A. Breckenridge, Sheldon Pollock, Homi K. Bhabha and Dipesh Chakrabarty, 1–14. Durham, NC: Duke University Press.

Portisch, Anna Odland. 2010. 'The craft of skilful learning: Kazakh women's everyday craft practices in western Mongolia.' *Journal of the Royal Anthropological Institute* (n.s.) 16: S62–S79.

Prahalad, Coimbatore K. 2009. *The Fortune at the Bottom of the Pyramid: Eradicating Poverty through Profits*, revised and updated 5th anniversary edn. Upper Saddle River, NJ: Pearson Education.

Prakash, B. A. 1998. 'Gulf migration and its economic impact: the Kerala experience.' *Economic and Political Weekly*, 12 December, 3209–13.

Prasad, Kunwar Jagdish. 1907. *Monograph on Carpet Making in the United Provinces*. Allahabad: Superintendent, Government Press, United Provinces.

Prentice, Rebecca. 2017. 'Microenterprise development, industrial labour, and the seductions of precarity.' *Critique of Anthropology* 37(2): 201–22.

Pritchett, James Anthony. 2007. *Friends for Life, Friends for Death: Cohort and Consciousness among the Lunda-Ndembu*. Charlottesville: University of Virginia Press.

Punathil, Salah. 2013. 'Kerala Muslims and shifting notions of religion in the public sphere.' *South Asia Research* 33(1): 1–20.

Qureshi, Ayaz. 2013. 'Structural violence and the state: HIV and labour migration from Pakistan to the Persian Gulf.' *Anthropology & Medicine* 20(3): 209–20.

Qureshi, M. A. 1990. 'Social linkages of artisans with technology: upgradation of village pottery craft.' *Economic and Political Weekly* 25(13): 683–8.

Rabikowska, Marta. 2010. 'The ritualisation of food, home and national identity among Polish migrants in London.' *Social Identities* 16(3): 377–98.

Radhakrishnan, Ratheesh. 2009. 'The Gulf in the imagination: migration, Malayalam cinema and regional identity.' *Contributions to Indian Sociology* 43(2): 217–45.

Rafique Wassan, M., Zubair Hussain, Muhbat Ali Shah and Sara N. Amin. 2017. 'International labor migration and social change in rural Sindh, Pakistan.' *Asian and Pacific Migration Journal* 26(3): 381–402.

Rai, Pronoy. 2018. 'The labor of social change: seasonal labor migration and social change in rural western India.' *Geoforum* 92: 171–80.

Rai, Santosh Kumar. 2013. 'The fuzzy boundaries: *Julaha* weavers' identity formation in early twentieth century United Provinces.' *Indian Historical Review* 40(1): 117–43.

Rajan, S. Irudaya, ed. 2016. *South Asia Migration Report 2017: Recruitment, Remittances and Reintegration.* London: Routledge.

Ramanamma, A., and Usha Bambawale. 1987. *Women in Indian Industry.* Delhi: Mittal Publications.

Ramaswamy, Vijaya, ed. 2017. *Migrations in Medieval and Early Colonial India.* London: Routledge.

Ramnarain, Smita. 2015. 'Universalized categories, dissonant realities: gendering postconflict reconstruction in Nepal.' *Gender, Place & Culture* 22(9): 1305–22.

Rao, J. Mohan. 1999. 'Agrarian power and unfree labour.' *Journal of Peasant Studies* 26(2–3): 242–62.

Ratnam, Charishma. 2018. 'Creating home: intersections of memory and identity.' *Geography Compass* 12(4).

Ray, Raka, and Seemin Qayum. 2009. *Cultures of Servitude: Modernity, Domesticity, and Class in India.* Stanford, CA: Stanford University Press.

Richard, Analiese, and Daromir Rudnyckyj. 2009. 'Economies of affect.' *Journal of the Royal Anthropological Institute* 15(1): 57–77.

Rizzo, Matteo. 2017. *Taken for a Ride: Grounding Neoliberalism, Precarious Labour, and Public Transport in an African Metropolis.* Oxford: Oxford University Press.

Robinson, Francis. 1999. 'Religious change and the self in Muslim South Asia since 1800.' *South Asia: Journal of South Asian Studies* 22(supp. 1): 13–27.

Robinson, Rowena. 2007. 'Indian Muslims: the varied dimensions of marginality.' *Economic and Political Weekly* 42(10): 839–43.

Rodrigues, Louiza. 2019. 'Gujarat ornamental furniture: artisans, techniques, skills and global markets during the nineteenth century.' In *Knowledge and the Indian Ocean: Intangible Networks of Western India and Beyond*, edited by Sara Keller, pp. 113–36. Cham: Palgrave Macmillan.

Rogaly, Ben. 2008. 'Migrant workers in the ILO's *Global Alliance Against Forced Labour* report: a critical appraisal.' *Third World Quarterly* 29(7): 1431–47.

Rogaly, Ben, Daniel Coppard, Kumar Rana, Abdur Rafique, Amrita Sengupta and Jhuma Biswas. 2003. 'Seasonal migration, employer–worker interactions, and shifting ethnic identities in contemporary West Bengal.' *Contributions to Indian Sociology* 37(1–2): 281–310.

Ross, Andrew. 2004. 'Made in Italy: the trouble with craft capitalism.' *Antipode* 36(2): 209–16.

Routray, Sailen. 2017. *Everyday State and Politics in India: Government in the Backyard in Kalahandi.* London: Routledge.

Roy, Abhik. 2004. 'The construction and scapegoating of Muslims as the "other" in Hindu nationalist rhetoric.' *Southern Journal of Communication* 69(4): 320–32.

Roy, Ananya. 2011. 'Slumdog cities: rethinking subaltern urbanism.' *International Journal of Urban and Regional Research* 35(2): 223–38.

Roy, Tirthankar. 1993. *Artisans and Industrialization: Indian Weaving in the Twentieth Century.* Oxford: Oxford University Press.

Roy, Tirthankar. 1999. *Traditional Industry in the Economy of Colonial India.* Cambridge: Cambridge University Press.

Roy, Tirthankar. 2007. 'Out of tradition: master artisans and economic change in colonial India.' *Journal of Asian Studies* 66(4): 963–91.

Roy, Tirthankar. 2008. 'Sardars, jobbers, kanganies: the labour contractor and Indian economic history.' *Modern Asian Studies* 42(5): 971–98.

Roy, Tirthankar. 2010. 'Consumption and craftsmanship in India, 1870–1940.' In *Towards a History of Consumption in South Asia*, edited by Douglas Haynes, Abigail McGowan, Tirthankar Roy and Haruka Yanagisawa, 268–98. Delhi: Oxford University Press.

Roy, Tirthankar. 2013. 'Apprenticeship and industrialization in India, 1600–1930.' In *Technology, Skills and the Pre-Modern Economy in the East and the West*, edited by Maarten Prak and Jan Luiten van Zanden, 69–92. Leiden: Brill.

Rudnyckyj, Daromir. 2009. 'Spiritual economies: Islam and neoliberalism in contemporary Indonesia.' *Cultural Anthropology* 24(1): 104–41.

Ruthven, Orlanda. 2008. 'Metal and morals in Moradabad: perspectives on ethics in the workplace across a global supply chain.' DPhil thesis, University of Oxford.

Ruthven, Orlanda. 2010. 'Government inspectors and "ethical" buyers: regulating labour in Moradabad's metalware industry.' *International Review of Sociology* 20(3): 473–90.

Saberwal, S. 2010. 'On the making of Muslims in India historically.' In *The Handbook of Muslims in India: Empirical and Policy Perspectives*, edited by Rakesh Basant and Abusaleh Shariff, 37–67. Oxford: Oxford University Press.

Sabri, Bushra, Shrutika Sabarwal, Michele R. Decker, Abina Shrestha, Kunda Sharma, Lily Thapa and Pamela J. Surkan. 2016. 'Violence against widows in Nepal: experiences, coping behaviors, and barriers in seeking help.' *Journal of Interpersonal Violence* 31(9): 1744–66.

Sachar, Rajindar. 2006. *Social, Economic and Educational Status of the Muslim Community of India: A Report* (the Sachar Committee Report). New Delhi: Prime Minister's High Level Committee, Cabinet Secretariat, Government of India.

Sahlins, Marshall. 2011.'What kinship is (part one).' *Journal of the Royal Anthropological Institute* 17(1): 2–19.

Salem, Hajer Ben Hadj. 2016. 'American Orientalism: how the media define what average Americans know about Islam and Muslims in the USA.' *International Journal of Humanities and Cultural Studies* 2(3), 156–72.

Sanchez, Andrew. 2012. 'Deadwood and paternalism: rationalizing casual labour in an Indian company town.' *Journal of the Royal Anthropological Institute* 18(4): 808–27.

Sancho, David. 2015. '"Keeping up with the time": rebranding education and class formation in globalising India.' *Globalisation, Societies and Education* 14(4): 477–91.

Sanyal, Kalyan. 2014. *Rethinking Capitalist Development: Primitive Accumulation, Governmentality and Post-Colonial Capitalism*. New Delhi: Routledge India.

Sasikumar, S. K., and Rakkee Thimothy. 2015. *From India to the Gulf Region: Exploring Links between Labour Markets and the Migration Cycle*. Geneva: International Labour Organization. https://www.ilo.org/wcmsp5/groups/public/–asia/–ro-bangkok/–sro-new_delhi/documents/publication/wcms_397363.pdf (accessed 30 December 2019).

Sassen, Saskia. 2005. 'The embeddedness of electronic markets: the case of global capital markets.' In *The Sociology of Financial Markets*, edited by Karin Knorr and Alex Preda, 17–37. Oxford: Oxford University Press.

Saxena, Shobhan. 2011. 'Escape from Azamgarh.' *The Times of India*, 24 July, 8. https://timesofindia.indiatimes.com/home/sunday-times/deep-focus/Escape-from-Azamgarh/articleshow/9340855.cms (accessed 21 December 2019).

Schmidt, Suzanne C. 2018. 'Precarious craft: a feminist commodity chain analysis.' *Migration and Development*: 1–18.

Schmoller, Jesko. 2017. 'Embodying moral superiority: the master–apprentice relationship and national cultural heritage in Uzbekistan.' *Problems of Post-Communism* 64(6): 370–81.

Schulten, Susan. 2001. *The Geographical Imagination in America, 1880–1950*. Chicago: University of Chicago Press.

Scott, James C. 1990. *Domination and the Arts of Resistance: Hidden Transcripts*. New Haven, CT: Yale University Press.

Scott, James C. 2009. *The Art of Not Being Governed: An Anarchist History of Upland Southeast Asia*. New Haven, CT: Yale University Press.

Scrase, Timothy J. 2003. 'Precarious production: globalisation and artisan labour in the Third World.' *Third World Quarterly* 24(3): 449–61.

Seabrook, Jeremy, and Imran Ahmed Siddiqui. 2011. *People without History: India's Muslim Ghettos*. London: Pluto Press.

Sen, Arup Kumar. 2002. 'Mode of labour control in colonial India.' *Economic and Political Weekly* 37(38): 3956–66.

Sen, Atreyee. 2012. '"Exist, endure, erase the city" (*Sheher mein jiye, is ko sahe, ya ise mitaye?*): child vigilantes and micro-cultures of urban violence in a riot-affected Hyderabad slum.' *Ethnography* 13(1): 71–86.

Sen, Samita. 1999. *Women and Labour in Late Colonial India: The Bengal Jute Industry*. Cambridge: Cambridge University Press.

Sennett, Richard. 2008. *The Craftsman*. London: Yale University Press.

Sethi, Aman. 2015. 'Love Jihad.' *Granta* 130. https://granta.com/love-jihad/ (accessed 22 March 2019).

Shaban, Abdul, ed. 2018. *Lives of Muslims in India: Politics, Exclusion and Violence*. New Delhi: Routledge.

Shah, Alpa. 2006. 'The labour of love: seasonal migration from Jharkhand to the brick kilns of other states in India.' *Contributions to Indian Sociology* 40(1): 91–118.

Shah, Nasra M., and Indu Menon. 1999. 'Chain migration through the social network: experience of labour migrants in Kuwait.' *International Migration* 37(2): 361–82.

Shaheen, Jack G. 2003. 'Reel bad Arabs: how Hollywood vilifies a people.' *Annals of the American Academy of Political and Social Science* 588(1): 171–93.

Sharma, Kaamya. 2019. 'The orientalisation of the sari: sartorial praxis and womanhood in colonial and post-colonial India.' *South Asia: Journal of South Asian Studies* 42(2): 219–36.

Shaw, Rosalind. 2002. *Memories of the Slave Trade: Ritual and the Historical Imagination in Sierra Leone*. Chicago: University of Chicago Press.

Shever, Elana. 2008. 'Neoliberal associations: property, company, and family in the Argentine oil fields.' *American Ethnologist* 35(4): 701–16.

Shever, Elana. 2012. *Resources for Reform: Oil and Neoliberalism in Argentina*. Stanford, CA: Stanford University Press.

Siddiqi, Bulbul. 2012. 'Reconfiguring the gender relation: the case of the Tablighi Jamaat in Bangladesh.' *Culture and Religion* 13(2): 177–92.

Siddiqui, Kalim. 2017. 'Hindutva, neoliberalism and the reinventing of India.' *Journal of Economic and Social Thought* 4(2): 142–86.

Simmel, Georg. 2013. 'The metropolis and mental life.' In *The Urban Sociology Reader*, edited by Jan Lin and Christopher Mele, 23–31. Abingdon: Routledge.

Simone, AbdouMaliq. 2004. 'People as infrastructure: intersecting fragments in Johannesburg.' *Public Culture* 16(3): 407–29.

Simpson, Edward. 2006a. 'Apprenticeship in western India.' *Journal of the Royal Anthropological Institute* 12(1): 151–71.

Simpson, Edward. 2006b. *Muslim Society and the Western Indian Ocean: The Seafarers of Kachchh*. Abingdon: Routledge.

Siriwardane, R. 2014. 'War, migration and modernity: the micro-politics of the Hijab in Northeastern Sri Lanka.' ZEF Working Paper Series no. 127. Zentrum für Entwicklungsforschung/ Centre for Development Research (ZEF), University of Bonn.

Sivramkrishna, Sashi. 2009. 'Production cycles and decline in traditional iron smelting in the Maidan, Southern India, c. 1750–1950: an environmental history perspective.' *Environment and History* 15(2): 163–97.

Sloane, Patricia. 1999. *Islam, Modernity and Entrepreneurship among the Malays*. Basingstoke: Palgrave Macmillan in association with St Antony's College, Oxford.

Smith, Andrew. 2006. '"If I have no money for travel, I have no need": migration and imagination.' *European Journal of Cultural Studies* 9(1): 47–62.

Solomon, Harris. 2015. 'Unreliable eating: patterns of food adulteration in urban India.' *BioSocieties* 10(2): 177–93.

Srivastava, Ravi S. 2005. 'Bonded labor in India: its incidence and pattern.' *Digital Commons*, 4 January. https://digitalcommons.ilr.cornell.edu/forcedlabor/18/ (accessed 5 August 2018).

Stensrud, Astrid B. 2017. 'Precarious entrepreneurship: mobile phones, work and kinship in neoliberal Peru.' *Social Anthropology* 25(2): 159–73.

Stoller, Paul. 2008. 'African/Asian/uptown/downtown.' In *The Blackwell Cultural Economy Reader*, edited by Ash Amin and Nigel Thrift, 193–209. Chichester: John Wiley & Sons.

Stoller, Paul, and Cheryl Olkes. 1987. *In Sorcery's Shadow: A Memoir of Apprenticeship among the Songhay of Niger*. Chicago: University of Chicago Press.

Stratford, Charles. 2006. 'Cramped in a room with poor wages and diseases to boot.' *Gulf News*, 9 April. http://gulfnews.com/news/gulf/uae/employment/cramped-in-a-room-with-poor-wages-and-diseases-to-boot-1.232227 (accessed 30 September 2013).

Streefkerk, Hein. 1985. *Industrial Transition in Rural India: Artisans, Traders, and Tribals in South Gujarat*. Bombay: Popular Prakashan.

Street, Alice. 2009. 'Failed recipients: extracting blood in a Papua New Guinean hospital.' *Body & Society* 15(2): 193–215.

Sukarieh, Mayssoun, and Stuart Tannock. 2014. *Youth Rising? The Politics of Youth in the Global Economy*. London: Routledge.

Susewind, Raphael. 2017. 'Muslims in Indian cities: degrees of segregation and the elusive ghetto.' *Environment and Planning A: Economy and Space* 49(6): 1286–1307.

Taussig, Michael T. 2010 [1980]. *The Devil and Commodity Fetishism in South America*. 30th anniversary edn. Chapel Hill: University of North Carolina Press.

Thapan, Meenakshi, Anshu Singh and Nidhitha Sreekumar. 2016. 'Women's mobility and migration: an exploratory study of Muslim women migrants in Jamia Nagar, Delhi.' In *Internal Migration in Contemporary India*, edited by Deepak K. Mishra, 47–70. New Delhi: Sage Publications India.

Thompson, Edward P. 1967. 'Time, work-discipline, and industrial capitalism.' *Past & Present* 38: 56–97.

Thorner, Daniel, and Alice Thorner. 1962. '"De-industrialization" in India, 1881–1931.' In *Land and Labour in India*. Bombay: Asia Publishing House.

Tice, Karin E. 1995. *Kuna Crafts, Gender, and the Global Economy*. Austin: University of Texas Press.

Tripp, Charles. 2006. *Islam and the Moral Economy: The Challenge of Capitalism*. Cambridge: Cambridge University Press.

Tsing, Anna. 2009. 'Supply chains and the human condition.' *Rethinking Marxism* 21(2): 148–76.

Tsing, Anna Lowenhaupt. 2012. 'Empire's salvage heart: why diversity matters in the global political economy.' *Focaal* (64): 36–50.

Tsing, Anna. 2016. 'What is emerging? Supply chains and the remaking of Asia.' *Professional Geographer* 68(2): 330–7.

Turna, Nalan. 2019. 'Ottoman apprentices and their experiences.' *Middle Eastern Studies* 55(5): 683–700.

Tweedie, Dale. 2017. 'The normativity of work: retrieving a critical craft norm.' *Critical Horizons* 18(1): 66–84.

Ugargol, Allen Prabhaker, and Ajay Bailey. 2018. 'Family caregiving for older adults: gendered roles and caregiver burden in emigrant households of Kerala, India.' *Asian Population Studies* 14(2): 194–210.

Unni, Jeemol, and Suma Scaria. 2009. 'Governance, structure and labour market outcomes in garment embellishment chains.' *Indian Journal of Labour Economics* 52(4): 631–50.

Upadhya, Carol. 2009. 'India's "new middle class" and the globalising city: software professionals in Bangalore, India.' In *The New Middle Classes: Globalizing Lifestyles, Consumerism and Environmental Concern*, edited by Hellmuth Lange and Lars Meier, 253–68. Dordrecht: Springer.

Ussher, Jane M., Janette Perz and Chloe Parton. 2015. 'Menopause and sexuality: resisting representations of the abject asexual woman.' In *The Wrong Prescription for Women: How Medicine and Media Create a 'Need' for Treatments, Drugs, and Surgery*, edited by Maureen C. McHugh and Joan C. Chrisler, 123–46. Santa Barbara, CA: Praeger.

Vanina, Eugenia. 2004. *Urban Crafts and Craftsmen in Medieval India: Thirteenth–Eighteenth Centuries*. New Delhi: Munshiram Manoharlal.

Van Schendel, Willem. 2002. 'Geographies of knowing, geographies of ignorance: jumping scale in Southeast Asia.' *Environment and Planning D: Society and Space* 20(6): 647–68.

Varrel, Aurélie. 2012. 'NRIs in the city: identifying international migrants' investments in the Indian urban fabric.' *South Asia Multidisciplinary Academic Journal* 6.

Venkatesan, Soumhya. 2009. 'Rethinking agency: persons and things in the heterotopia of "traditional Indian craft".' *Journal of the Royal Anthropological Institute* 15(1): 78–95.

Venkatesan, Soumhya. 2010. 'Learning to weave: weaving to learn … what?' *Journal of the Royal Anthropological Institute* 16(s1): S158–S175.

Verma, Aayushi, and Ila Gupta. 2017. 'A study on geometrical motifs with special reference to old *Havelis* of Saharanpur.' In *Understanding Built Environment: Proceedings of the National Conference on Sustainable Built Environment 2015*, edited by Fumihiko Seta, Arindam Biswas, Ajay Khare and Joy Sen, 201–17. Singapore: Springer.

Verstappen, Sanderien. 2017. 'Mobility and the region: pathways of travel within and beyond Central Gujarat.' *Journal of South Asian Development* 12(2): 112–35.

Vertovec, Steven. 2009. *Transnationalism*. London: Routledge.

Vora, Neha. 2013. *Impossible Citizens: Dubai's Indian Diaspora*. Durham, NC: Duke University Press.

Wacquant, Loïc. 2009. 'The body, the ghetto and the penal state.' *Qualitative Sociology* 32(1): 101–29.

Wadhawan, Neha. 2018. 'India labour migration update 2018.' Working Paper RAS/16/10/JPN-[ILO_REF], International Labour Organization. https://www.ilo.org/newdelhi/whatwedo/publications/WCMS_631532/lang–en/index.htm (accessed 28 November 2019).

Wahba, Jackline, and Yves Zenou. 2012. 'Out of sight, out of mind: migration, entrepreneurship and social capital.' *Regional Science and Urban Economics* 42(5): 890–903.

Waheed, Abdul, ed. 2006. *Muslim Artisans, Craftsmen, and Traders: Issues in Entrepreneurship*. New Delhi: Icon Publications.

Wallinder, Ylva. 2019. 'Imagined independence among highly skilled Swedish labour migrants.' *Sociologisk Forskning* 56(1): 27–51.

Walsh, Katie. 2018. *Transnational Geographies of the Heart: Intimate Subjectivities in a Globalising City*. Hoboken, NJ: John Wiley & Sons.

Watt, George. 1903. *Indian Art at Delhi, 1903: Being the Official Catalogue of the Delhi Exhibition, 1902–1903*. Delhi: Motil District Gal Banarsidass.

Weber, Max. 1968. *On Charisma and Institution Building: Selected Papers*. Chicago: University of Chicago Press.

Werbner, Pnina, ed. 2008. *Anthropology and the New Cosmopolitanism: Rooted, Feminist and Vernacular Perspectives*. Oxford: Berg.

Werbner, Pnina. 2018. 'Commentary: urban friendship: towards an alternative anthropological genealogy.' *Urban Studies* 55(3): 662–74.

White, Jenny B. 2004. *Money Makes Us Relatives: Women's Labor in Urban Turkey*. 2nd edn. New York: Routledge.

Wilkinson, Steven I. 2006. *Votes and Violence: Electoral Competition and Ethnic Riots in India*. Cambridge: Cambridge University Press.

Wilkinson-Weber, Clare M. 1999. *Embroidering Lives: Women's Work and Skill in the Lucknow Embroidery Industry*. Albany, NY: State University of New York Press.

Wilkinson-Weber, Clare M., and Alicia Ory DeNicola, eds. 2016. *Critical Craft: Technology, Globalization, and Capitalism*. London: Bloomsbury Academic.

Williams, Philippa. 2011. 'An absent presence: experiences of the "welfare state" in an Indian Muslim mohallā.' *Contemporary South Asia* 19(3): 263–80.

Williams, Philippa. 2012. 'India's Muslims, lived secularism and realising citizenship.' *Citizenship Studies* 16(8): 979–95.

Williams, Philippa, Al James, Fiona McConnell and Bhaskar Vira. 2017. 'Working at the margins? Muslim middle class professionals in India and the limits of "labour agency".' *Environment and Planning A: Economy and Space* 49(6): 1266–85.

Willis, Paul. 2017. *Learning to Labour: How Working Class Kids Get Working Class Jobs*. London: Routledge.

Wimmer, Andreas, and Nina Glick Schiller. 2002. 'Methodological nationalism and beyond: nation-state building, migration and the social sciences.' *Global Networks* 2(4): 301–34.

Wise, Amanda, and Selvaraj Velayutham. 2014. 'Conviviality in everyday multiculturalism: some brief comparisons between Singapore and Sydney.' *European Journal of Cultural Studies* 17(4): 406–30.

Witsoe, Jeffrey. 2016. 'The politics of caste and the deepening of India's democracy: the case of the backward caste movement in Bihar.' In *Social Movements and the State in India: Deepening Democracy?*, edited by Kenneth Bo Nielsen and Alf Gunvald Nilsen, 53–74. London: Palgrave Macmillan.

Wolf, Diane L. 1992. *Factory Daughters: Gender, Household Dynamics, and Rural Industrialization in Java*. Berkeley: University of California Press.

Yang, Jie. 2010. 'The crisis of masculinity: class, gender, and kindly power in post-Mao China.' *American Ethnologist* 37(3): 550–62.

Yang, Jie. 2014. 'The happiness of the marginalized: affect, counseling and self-reflexivity in China.' In *The Political Economy of Affect and Emotion in East Asia*, edited by Jie Yang, 45–61. Abingdon: Routledge.

Zachariah, Kunniparampil Curien, Elangikal Thomas Mathew and S. Irudaya Rajan. 2001. 'Social, economic and demographic consequences of migration on Kerala.' *International Migration* 39(2): 43–71.

Zaloom, Caitlin. 2003. 'Ambiguous numbers: trading technologies and interpretation in financial markets.' *American Ethnologist* 30(2): 258–72.

Zubaida, Sami. 2002. 'Middle Eastern experiences of cosmopolitanism.' In *Conceiving Cosmopolitanism: Theory, Context, and Practice*, edited by Simon Learmount, Steven Vertovec and Robin Cohen, 32–41. Oxford: Oxford University Press.

Index

accumulation: of capital 9, 11–12, 26, 51–2, 65, 99, 143; primitive 11
aesthetic labour 138, 143
aesthetics 53, 138, 140, 166, 206, 207
affect: and communal relations 46; entrepreneurialism 140–5; Islam 136, 151, 157, 167; labour 140–5, 163; media 102, 136; migration 188, 200, 202, 205, 207, 209, 222, 253, 237–8, 242; neoliberalism 136–40; networks 7, 200, 212; supply chains 94; theoretical approaches 137–40
Agamben, Giorgio 14–15
apprenticeship 107–34; and commodification 127; conflict 126–31; family 118–19, 121–6; formal education 120, 126; Islam 113–15; theoretical approaches 110–16; women 89–91; youth 129–31; *see also* education
art 11, 114
artisans: anthropology of 12–13; class 26–8, 36, 75; decline 25–7; history 23–7, 44–5; marginalisation 11–13, 25–7; theoretical approaches 11–13; *see also* craftwork
authenticity 27, 53

biradari 19, 34, 38, 40–3, 163, 167, 175–6
bonded labour 53, 55–6, 67, 91, 156, 164, 212, 218, 221–2; 231, 247; inverted bondage 61–3, 67, 155, 247; neo-bondage 55–8, 61–2, 75, 222, 247
borders 13–18, 93, 95, 111, 163, 172–3, 193, 223–4, 242
Bourdieu, Pierre 112, 178, 246–7

capitalism 6, 10–12, 24–7, 36, 47, 50–1, 56, 59, 65–7, 84, 111–13, 130, 137–8, 143, 164, 178, 181, 193, 246
care 7, 67–8, 74, 103, 111, 221, 246–7
caste 9, 20, 25, 32, 34, 37, 40–3, 52, 54, 83, 93, 101–2, 116, 121, 128, 163, 165–7, 193, 218
charity 52, 73, 144, 156, 179
Citizenship Amendment Act (CAA) 20, 46
class 9, 11, 13, 19, 26–30, 34, 50, 59, 65, 75, 80–3, 85, 103, 120–1, 163–4, 170, 189, 193, 210, 212, 218–20; consciousness 9, 56; middle class 120–1, 140, 168, 241, 246; Muslim middle class in India 29–30, 34
colonialism/post-colonialism: and Indian artisans 20, 23–7, 35–6, 40, 53, 65, 112,

115; and Indian Muslims 23, 25, 28–9, 40; and migration 219, 224, 226; outside India 140, 178, 191, 219; 224; and urban space 8, 23, 59; and women 83
coming of age 131, 173, 197, 209, 212
commodification 70, 127
communalism 4–5, 7, 9, 17, 30, 44–6, 101, 147, 171–2, 189, 206
composite nationalism 33
consumption: of craft goods 24, 36, 59, 198; and self-making/identity 8, 131, 143, 206, 227–8, 233, 247
conviviality 21, 33, 46, 70, 163–4
Corporate Social Responsibility (CSR) 53–4
cosmopolitanism: limits of 164, 193, 209, 237, 241; and migration 193, 209, 217, 237, 239, 241; Muslim, 7, 151; subaltern 192–3, 217, 241
craftwork: and agricultural/agrarian connections 37–8, 40; 65–7, 82, 125, 199; capitalist transformations 26–8, 39; definitions 6, 20, 75; and gender 18–19; informality 26, 38, 164; marginalisation 5, 10–13, 50; and migration/mobility 6, 19, 25, 190, 193, 195–213, 222, 228, 246; neoliberalism 45, 138, 144; political economy 11–13, 48, 50–1, 75, 111–12, 157, 168, 184, 246; precarity 39, 195; temporalities of 168, 177–82, 204; women *see* women craftworkers; *see also* artisans

Dalits 20, 48; Chamārs 54, 93, 96, 101–2, 121; Dalit Muslims 41, 102
Darul Uloom Deoband Madrassa 7, 21, 28–9, 31, 33, 119, 146, 150
debt/credit 53, 55, 57–9, 61–2, 67, 85, 92, 94, 140, 143–4, 155, 180–1, 247; *see also* bonded labour
de-industrialisation 25, 40
Deobandi Muslims 7, 150
deskilling 12, 113, 229

education: access to/cost 89–90, 118, 121, 164, 218, 220; 233–4; and aspirations 16–17, 120–1, 126, 131, 233–4; Islamic 114–15, 119, 152, 166; non-formal 112, 114; views on 121–3, 126; *see also* apprenticeship
embeddedness 45, 47–8, 50–5, 67, 71, 138, 140–1, 247

emotions: and craft production 68, 70–1, 111; history of 167; in fieldwork 160–2, 184, 194; in friendships 71, 167–8; migration 188, 195, 208–9, 212, 238; neoliberalism 137–8; performances of 94, religiosity 138, 151, 167

entrepreneurialism 136, 138–40, 142–5, 154, 157, 181, 204, 220, 235

ethnographic fieldwork: descriptions of 2–4, 19, 49–50, 79–80; 107–10, 136, 160–2, 184, 187, 216–17; gender 50, 81, 91, 105

export markets/exporters 26–7, 30, 35–8, 42, 45, 48, 50, 52–3, 59, 61, 63, 72, 81, 117–18, 174, 195–6, 198

fashion/style 8, 31, 122, 131, 142–3, 148, 153, 158, 196, 200, 226, 228, 235, 242

fate (kismet) 73, 93–4, 204

flirting 168–72

Fordism/post-Fordism 35, 58, 138–9, 141, 143, 178

friendship: and class, caste and religion 163–4, 167–8; and fieldwork 109–10, 160–3, 184; in Islam 147, 151, 166–7; and precarious labour 163–82; as a subaltern resource 182–5; in supply chains/craft production 18, 52–3, 64, 67–71, 116, 151; theoretical approaches 163–8; urban space 163–4, 168–73

garment/textile production 27, 35, 55, 61, 67, 81–2, 84, 131, 153

gender: and apprenticeship 89–91, 112, 127; and craft production 18–19, 54, 57–8, 71–2, 74, 80, 88, 99–100, 104, 165, 167; and migration/mobility 6, 221–2; temporalities 181–2; and urban space 8, 71, 74, 80–2, 84, 87–8, 105, 121, 163–6, 168–70, 247

ghettoisation 6, 9, 148, 157, 233–4

Global Production Networks see supply chains

globalisation 3, 11, 82, 112, 193, 226

Gulf Cooperation Council (GCC) 217–23, 226, 227, 229, 231, 242–4

Herzfeld, Michael 11–13, 112, 116

Hindu nationalism 5, 20–1, 43–4

imagination: and artisans 11; materiality 10, 191, 194; 237, 240; and migration 188, 190–4, 196–7, 208–9, 212, 217, 226, 234–8, 241–2, 247; theoretical approaches 10, 13, 137, 188, 190–4

Indian Muslims: history of 20, 23, 25–35, 40, 43, 167; marginalisation 5–10, 19–20, 45–8; 246; middle class 29, 30; migration 189, 212, 219; and stratification 41–3; representations of 6; in Saharanpur 5

informal economy see informality

informality: definitions 14, 50, 184; economic 3, 26, 35, 50, 52–5, 59; 64–5, 70, 88–9, 94, 118, 125, 131, 137, 139; and migration 188, 199, 217, 221–3, 226, 231, 238, 240, 247; social 7, 59, 88–9, 109, 119, 125, 157, 163, 166–8, 177, 247; urban 5, 7, 18

intimacy 7, 18–19, 51, 58, 64, 68–70, 75, 102, 111, 164, 184, 188, 194, 208–9, 212, 221, 238, 240, 246–7

Islamic economies/business practices 57, 59, 145, 155, 183, 204

labour: artisanal 35, 130; disciplining of 9, 31, 45, 51–2, 54–5, 80, 82, 98–9, 103, 111, 113, 115–16, 123, 125, 129, 163, 178–81, 219–20, 242, 246; feminisation 81–3, 138; health issues 60, 79–80, 94, 134, 191, 218; hierarchies 9–10, 75, 80, 85–6, 94, 104, 137, 139, 182; learning to 89–90, 105, 111–12; migration see migration; regimes 6, 51, 54, 138, 141, 246; reproduction 52, 80, 88, 111–12, 115, 119, 130, 168, 242; resistance by see resistance

labour contractors/thēkēdārs/brokers 52, 55, 63–71, 74, 98, 100–11, 119, 127, 141, 173–4, 198

liberalisation 44–5, 65, 125, 137, 139, 145

marginalisation: artisans/craftworkers 5, 10–13, 25–7, 50; Indian Muslims 5–10, 19–20, 45–8; 246; in migration 187–9, 200, 212, 217; subjectivities 8–10, 13–18; theoretical approaches to 6, 9–10, 15, 18, 246–8

marriage 16–17, 42, 57, 89; 90–2, 170, 173, 206; and migration 233; as recruitment 90

Marx, Karl 11, 53, 67, 181, 246–7

masculinities 71, 112, 131, 166, 169, 171

Massey, Doreen 8, 34, 43, 164, 192

Maulana Hussain Ahmad Madani 31–3

Maulana Muhammad Ilyas 146, 159

migration 2–3, 6, 14, 18–19, 133, 157, 163, 186–244; and agency of workers 55, 58, 221–2, 247; artisan histories 24; brokerage 67, 221–4, 226, 231; continuity 184, 222, 240–2; and citizenship 217, 219–20, 234; and class 218, 220, 241; and colonialism 191, 219, 224, 226; and coming of age 131, 197, 209, 212, 242; and cosmopolitanism 193, 209, 217, 237, 239, 241; and dietary practices 201, 205–7, 210, 227, 230, 239, 241; and disjuncture 188, 190, 193–4; and dormitory blocks in the Gulf 194, 212, 216–17, 238–41, 243; and entrepreneurialism 204, 220, 235; and friendship 177, 188, 194, 198, 208–9, 223, 247; and gender 220–2, 246–247; Gulf migration 214–44; health and safety 218; and imagination 6–7, 188, 190–4, 196–7, 208–9, 212, 217, 226, 234–8, 241–2, 247; Indian Muslims 189, 212, 219; informality of 188, 199, 217, 221–3, 226, 231, 238, 240, 247; internal 186–214; and Islam 211, 222, 228, 236; and loneliness 208, 226, 232, 247; and marginalisation 187–9, 200, 212, 217; and partition 29–30; precarity 197, 200, 204, 212, 218, 226, 231; and race/ethnicity 219, 220, 233, 241; regimes 6–7, 219–21, 223,

231, 246; remittances 218, 221, 233; and subjectivities 163, 188, 191–2, 194, 217, 220, 234, 242; visas and 'free visas' 216, 221, 223, 230, 232

modernity 12, 28, 120, 193, 241

morality 31, 70, 80, 84–5, 98–100, 110–12, 114, 146, 156, 166, 226–7, 235

National Register of Citizens (NRC) 20, 46

neoliberalism 6, 18, 45, 50, 58, 99, 112, 130, 136, 135–40, 143–4, 157, 181, 196, 220, 246

partition 16, 29–35, 42, 60, 121–2, 195–7

piece rate work 55, 68, 87, 93, 119, 175, 209, 211

Polanyi, Karl 50–1, 53

resistance (by labour) 9–10, 12, 24, 26, 52, 56, 75, 80, 103–4, 113, 126, 137–8, 163, 174, 177–9, 184, 192–3, 221–2, 242, 248

self-employment (apna kām) 55, 135, 140–2, 144, 154, 156–7, 179, 200, 202–4, 208, 225, 231

skill: and apprenticeship 108, 110–16, 119–21, 123, 129–30, 132–3; craftwork 3, 12, 20, 25, 30; 35, 41, 60, 75, 118, 179, 196, 198, 207, 210; decline of 129–30; and labour contractors/employers 67, 69, 143; and migration 143, 219–21, 228–9; women 72, 75, 81–2, 88–90, 105; see also deskilling

state, the 5–6, 9, 12, 14–16, 20, 24, 33, 39, 41, 46, 53, 119, 172–3, 192, 224, 246; claim-making from 128, 182; documents 160–2; role in migration 189, 221; state-run sector 52–3, 61, 137, 139, 205, 233

subjectivities: and affect 136–8; and apprenticeship 111, 115–16, 127, 129; and gender 80–1, 84, 93, 103; and Islam 136, 145; and late capitalism/

neoliberalism 5, 127, 136, 145, 181; and marginalisation 8–10, 13–18; and migration 163, 188, 191–2, 194, 217, 220, 234, 242; precarity 93, 127, 144, 181; and urban space 9–10, 93, 145, 164

supply chains 7, 30, 49–77, 83, 89, 94, 104, 111–12, 115, 123, 127, 129, 141, 151, 164, 178, 182, 246

Tablighi Jamaat 110, 136, 145–57, 159, 174, 211, 235

temporality 112, 138, 163, 177–82, 192, 219

thēkēdārs see labour contractors/thēkēdārs/brokers

Thompson, E.P. 178

unionisation, lack of 26, 82, 87, 102

urban space 8–10, 40, 47, 96; and communalism 9, 189; and community formation 7; contestations of 13, 47 168–73; and cosmologies 4–5, 8, 16, 216, 233, 239; and marginalisation 5, 9, 189, 239; sociality 163–4, 168–73; and subjectivities 9–10, 93, 145, 164

Uttar Pradesh: and Gulf migration 219–20, 230, 233, 237, 244; history of 19–20, 29, 45, 48; industries 30, 41, 61, 113; internal migration from 189, 207; politics of 19–20, 102, 128; representations of 5, 220

women craftworkers 18–19, 72–106; and agency 84, 103–4; and factory work 95–102; as homeworkers 72–5, 83, 85–6, 92–3, 100–1; labour force participation 80–3; learning to labour 89–90; networks among 91–5; purdah/piety/chāl-chalan 74, 80–5, 100, 102, 203, 221; and sexual harassment 86, 99; skill 72, 75, 81–2, 88–90, 105; and subcontracting 87–9; wages 85; widows and divorcees 85–7, 98, 101, 106